INDIGENEITY ON THE MOVE

INDIGENEITY ON THE MOVE

Varying Manifestations of a Contested Concept

Edited by
Eva Gerharz
Nasir Uddin
Pradeep Chakkarath

berghahn
NEW YORK·OXFORD
www.berghahnbooks.com

First published in 2018 by
Berghahn Books
www.berghahnbooks.com

© 2018, 2020 Eva Gerharz, Nasir Uddin, and Pradeep Chakkarath
First paperback edition published in 2020

All rights reserved. Except for the quotation of short passages
for the purposes of criticism and review, no part of this book
may be reproduced in any form or by any means, electronic or
mechanical, including photocopying, recording, or any information
storage and retrieval system now known or to be invented,
without written permission of the publisher.

Library of Congress Cataloging-in-Publication Data

A C.I.P. cataloging record is available from the Library of Congress

British Library Cataloguing in Publication Data

A catalogue record for this book is available from the British Library

ISBN 978-1-78533-722-2 hardback
ISBN 978-1-78920-828-3 paperback
ISBN 978-1-78533-723-9 ebook

Contents

List of Illustrations		vii
Preface *Adam Kuper*		viii
Acknowledgments		xiii
List of Abbreviations		xv
Introduction	Exploring Indigeneity: Introductory Remarks on a Contested Concept *Nasir Uddin, Eva Gerharz, and Pradeep Chakkarath*	1

Part I. Struggles over Land and Resources

Chapter 1	On the Nature of Indigenous Land: Ownership, Access, and Farming in Upland Northeast India *Erik de Maaker*	29
Chapter 2	Considering the Implications of the Concept of Indigeneity for Land and Natural Resource Management in Cambodia, Thailand, and Laos *Ian G. Baird*	49

Part II. Becoming Indigenous

Chapter 3	Processes of Modernization, Processes of Indigenization: An Amazonian Case (Yanomami, Southern Venezuela) *Gabriele Herzog-Schröder*	71
Chapter 4	Indigenous Activism beyond Ethnic Groups: Shifting Boundaries and Constellations of Belonging *Eva Gerharz*	92

Chapter 5	In Search of Self: Identity, Indigeneity, and Cultural Politics in Bangladesh *Nasir Uddin*	119

Part III. Indigeneity as a Political Resource

Chapter 6	Different Trajectories of Indigenous Rights Movements in Africa: Insights from Cameroon and Tanzania *Michaela Pelican*	143
Chapter 7	Politics of Indigeneity in the Andean Highlands: Indigenous Social Movements and the State in Ecuador, Bolivia, and Peru (1940–2015) *Olaf Kaltmeier*	172
Chapter 8	Conflicting Dimensions of Indigeneity as a Contested Political Resource in Contemporary Mexico *Gilberto Rescher*	199

Part IV. Indigeneity and the State

Chapter 9	Intimate Antagonisms: Adivasis and the State in Contemporary India *Uday Chandra*	221
Chapter 10	Indigeneity, Culture, and the State: Social Change and Legal Reforms in Latin America *Wolfgang Gabbert*	240
Chapter 11	Fluid Indigeneities in the Indian Ocean: A Small History of the State and Its Other *Philipp Zehmisch*	270
Postscriptum	The Futures of Indigenous Medicine: Networks, Contexts, Freedom *William S. Sax*	294
Index		315

Illustrations

Figures

Figure 3.1. This shed hosts the school in Caño Bocón, where the people who formerly called themselves Hapokashitha settled in the late 1990s. The humble shelter is covered with aluminum, which was obtained from the mission post. 79

Figure 3.2. The school in Sheroana is located within the circle of the *shapono* in a small hut thatched with palm leaves under a tree. Next to the school is the lean-to roof where communal shamanic sessions take place nearly every day. 80

Tables

Table 6.1. Illustration of parallel and partly conflicting categories. 151

Table 6.2. Perspectives on primary entitlement to land on the basis of the categorizations in Table 6.1. 152

Maps

Map 3.1. The map shows the central part of the area inhabited by the Yanomami in 2012. It outlines the territory of the Yanomamï or the "central Yanomami" and depicts the locations of the selected Yanomami communities and the mission posts discussed in the text. There are many more Yanomami villages or *shaponos* in this region which are not shown here. 74

Preface
Adam Kuper

Towards the end of the first United Nations "Decade of Indigenous Peoples," I published a critical review of the "indigenous peoples" discourse, arguing that the very idea of "indigenous peoples" was conceptually incoherent; that it relied on obsolete and completely discredited notions about "primitive peoples"; that it romanticized the past; and that its political uses were by no means self-evidently generous and harmless (Kuper 2003).

Heated debate followed. Few anthropologists mounted a defense of the "indigenous peoples" discourse, but some insisted that, whatever its intellectual deficiencies, it was politically useful. Alcida Rita Ramos even advocated strategic self-censorship. She warned that academic critics might provide ammunition to sinister forces, including "some oppressive governments that, in disclaiming the political agency of indigenous peoples, attribute their actions to the manipulative powers of non-Indian agitators" (Ramos 2003: 397).

Other anthropologists protested that academic reservations are neither here nor there. The key imperative is action. The indigenist rhetoric may come across as essentialist and romantic, Steven Robins admitted, and yet "such rhetorical strategies often make for effective activism" (Robins 2003: 398.). Alan Barnard added that if there was an element of romanticism, that was not necessarily to be deplored. "In fact the romantic imagery at the root of the indigenous peoples movement is part of anthropology too, and I don't think any of us who work with former hunter-gatherers are immune to it" (Barnard 2004: 19).

Yet the romanticism is not innocent, or free from troubling implications. James Suzman pointed out that the indigenist discourse promotes stereotypes of so-called primitive folk and "may well reinforce the very structures of discrimination that disadvantage these peoples in the first place." Indeed, many of the peoples identified as "indigenous" are precisely those who featured most prominently as "primitive" in Victorian anthropology. Suzman added that San people in Southern Africa "are frustrated not because they cannot pursue their 'traditional culture' but because they are impoverished, marginalized, and exploited by the dominant population" (Suzman 2003: 400).

Nor is Robins' "effective activism" always to be uncritically applauded. Where "indigenous peoples' movements" book local successes, this may be at a cost to others—often themselves poor and disadvantaged. Surely a more defensible politics would seek to help the unfortunate whoever they are, without discriminating on the basis of descent.[1]

Perhaps the knottiest questions have to do with the very definition of "indigenous peoples." International organizations that have engaged with the indigenous peoples' movement struggle to define just whom they are supposed to represent. The term "indigenous" cannot be taken to refer simply to the presumptive descendants of the first inhabitants of a country, because the indigenous peoples' movement has nothing to do with (for example) European nativist movements. Nor can it just mean former hunter-gatherers, since we are all descended from hunter-gatherers. At what stage, after how many centuries, is the status of "former hunter-gatherer" lost? In any case, some of the most assertive members of the indigenous peoples' movement represent Maori or Inuit, or descendants of the Aztecs and Incas, who ceased to be hunter-gatherers hundreds or even thousands of years ago.

Some authorities, such as the International Labour Organization (ILO), suggest that "indigenous" peoples should be defined rather with reference to political identity. They are minority groups, marked out by cultural difference and subjected to discrimination. Their status is "regulated wholly or partially by their own customs or traditions or by special laws or regulations" (ILO 1989). Obviously, these criteria would apply equally to Roma in Eastern Europe, members of scheduled castes in India, or Christians in Saudi Arabia, none of whom are classed as "indigenous" peoples. Nor can it be a blanket term for peoples whose lands had been colonized by European states, since most African countries are home to populations with a variety of cultural traditions, who came there at different times, some as rulers, others as refugees, and who have intermingled and intermarried for centuries. (Significantly, no African country signed up to the UN draft treaty on indigenous peoples.)

Even if there is some agreement as to what constitutes an indigenous grouping in a particular country today, there are problems about who can claim membership of it, and in particular whether the crucial criterion should be "cultural" or "racial." This has proved a difficult problem for some indigenous movements, in North America in particular. In practice, the general rule is that descent—a specified number of grandparents—trumps "culture," language, or way of life.

The UN Permanent Forum on Indigenous Issues simply sidestepped the whole question of definition. "In the case of the concept of 'indigenous peoples,' the prevailing view today is that no formal definition of the term is necessary" (United Nations 2004: 4). But it *is* necessary. If the goal is to do something to help "indigenous peoples," one has to know what—and whom—one is talking about.

In 2003, Richard Horton, Editor in Chief of *The Lancet*, one of the world's most influential medical journals, proclaimed that there was "an overwhelming need for action" to better the health of the world's indigenous peoples, and he published a series of six papers to document the crisis. In 2005, *The Lancet* reported that there were between 257 and 350 million indigenous people (Stephens et al. 2005: 11). The following year, Horton wrote that there were 370 million indigenous people spread through seventy countries, accounting for 6 percent of the world's population (Horton 2006). Three years later, also in *The Lancet*, Professor Michael Gracey and Professor Malcolm King reported that "the world's almost 400 million indigenous people have low standards of health" (Gracey and King 2009: 65). Had the population expanded so very rapidly within a year or two, or are the criteria for inclusion so vague that the numbers make little sense? It is hard to say, since none of *The Lancet*'s authors ventures a clear definition of who counts as "indigenous," although several do note that there is a definitional problem—and then briskly move on.

And what health problems are these hard-to-define peoples supposed to have in common? In an overview of six papers published in *The Lancet*, Horton reported that, when compared to non-indigenous populations, life expectancy is lower, and afflictions such as respiratory disease and diabetes occur more frequently. He cited three examples of special risks faced by indigenous populations: "Maori (heart disease), Canadian First Nation peoples (intentional self-harm), and Native American and Alaskan Natives (assault)." Obviously, these are not problems that go hand in hand with being indigenous. And there is no evidence that any of these particular afflictions are shared by all, or even many of the populations lumped together as indigenous by the contributors to *The Lancet*. Nor is it apparent that the health problems of so-called indigenous peoples in any country are worse than, or even different from, those of other disadvantaged minorities. The real causes of many public health problems are social factors such as poverty and discrimination, which are hardly unique to "indigenous peoples."

Many anthropologists have been recruited by NGOs working in the "indigenous peoples" field, or given evidence in support of land claims in the courts, or engaged in advocacy. Yet there are obviously dangers if anthropology becomes, as Plaice remarks, "the academic wing of the indigenous rights movement" (Plaice 2003: 397). If ethnographers report only what is politically convenient and refrain from analyzing intellectual confusions, then our ethnographies will lose their credibility and authority. And, fortunately, a number of ethnographers—activists among them—have contributed insightful analyses of particular movements. The present volume is packed with valuable case studies of local land struggles, the travails of traditional medical practitioners, and the often unintended effects of state policies.

But while local case studies are often illuminating, various indigenist movements across the world do share an ideology, if little else. In part, this is obviously because international agencies and NGOs have fostered a common doctrine. Several anthropologists have also related the emergence of the indigenous peoples' movement to an even more widespread fashion for movements of ethnic assertion (see, e.g., Friedman 1994; Hannerz 1996). The example of racial and ethnic movements in the USA, the end of the Cold War, and the rise of NGOs are all relevant. The internet has become the indispensable medium of internationalization. Some of the most interesting recent studies address the global discourse of indigeneity, and the interplay between international agencies, local activists, and the people they target. This volume is distinguished not only by the quality of its regional case studies, but also by the attention given to the whole machinery of the global indigenous peoples' movements. And it moves the discussion on, posing the important and difficult question of the future of indigeneity.

Adam Kuper (PhD, Cambridge) is a visiting professor at both the London School of Economics and Political Science and at Boston University, and he is a Fellow of the British Academy. Among his books are *The Chosen Primate: Human Nature and Cultural Diversity* (Harvard University Press, 1994), *'Culture': The Anthropologists' Account* (Harvard University Press, 1999), *The Reinvention of Primitive Society* (Routledge, 2005), *Incest and Influence: The Private Life of Bourgeois England* (Harvard University Press, 2009), and *Anthropology and Anthropologists: The British School in the Twentieth Century* (4th edition, Routledge, 2016).

Note

1. On the sorts of issues that recur where activists do engage, see, for instance, Dombrowski (2002), or an interesting ethnographic report by Robins (2001) himself, and also several illuminating case studies in the present volume.

Bibliography

Barnard, Alan. 2004. "Indigenous Peoples: A Response to Justin Kenrick and Jerome Lewis." *Anthropology Today* 20(2): 19.
Dombrowski, Kirk. 2002. "The Practice of Indigenism and Alaska Native Timber Politics." *American Anthropologist* 104(4): 1,062–73.
Friedman, Jonathan. 1994. *Cultural Identity and Global Process*. London: Sage.
Gracey, Michael and Malcolm King. 2009. "Indigenous Health Part 1: Determinants and Disease Patterns." *The Lancet* 374(9,683): 65–75.
Hannerz, Ulf. 1996. *Transnational Connections: Culture, People, Places*. London and New York: Routledge.
Horton, Richard. 2006. "Indigenous Peoples: Time to Act Now for Equity and Health." *The Lancet* 367(9,524): 1,705–7.
ILO (International Labour Organization). 1989. *Indigenous and Tribal Peoples Convention (No. C169)*. Retrieved 28 July 2017 from http://www.ilo.org/dyn/normlex/en/f?p=NORMLEXPUB:12100:0::NO:12100:P12100_ILO_CODE:C169.
Kuper, Adam. 2003. "The Return of the Native." *Current Anthropology* 44(3): 389–402.
Plaice, Evie. 2003. "Comment on 'The Return of the Native'." *Current Anthropology* 44(3): 397–98.
Ramos, Alcida Rita. 2003. "Comment on 'The Return of the Native'." *Current Anthropology* 44(3): 397–98.
Robins, Steven. 2001. "NGOs, 'Bushmen' and Double Vision: The ≠ Khomani San Land Claim and the Cultural Politics of 'Community' and 'Development' in the Kalahari." *Journal of Southern African Studies* 27(4): 833–53.
———. 2003. "Comment on 'The Return of the Native'." *Current Anthropology* 44(3): 398–99.
Stephens, Carolyn, et al. 2005. "Indigenous Peoples' Health—Why Are They Behind Everyone, Everywhere?" *The Lancet* 366(9,479): 10–13.
Suzman, James. 2003. "Comment on 'The Return of the Native'." *Current Anthropology* 44(3): 399–400.
United Nations. 2004. "The Concept of Indigenous Peoples." Background paper prepared by the Secretariat of the Permanent Forum on Indigenous Issues for the *Workshop on Data Collection and Disaggregation for Indigenous Peoples*. New York: Department of Economic and Social Affairs.

Acknowledgments

This book is the outcome of our joint efforts to explore how indigeneity has been reinvented, adopted, and reinterpreted in various local contexts, in light of recent initiatives taken by global civil society and international institutions. Although we share a common interest in South Asia, we seek to move beyond this regional focus and take a deeper look into the manifestations of indigeneity on a more global scale. In order to bring together scholars working on indigeneity in different parts of the world, we organized an informal workshop entitled "Futures of Indigeneity: Spatiality, Identity and Politics" at Ruhr-University Bochum in autumn 2013. This event turned out to be an extraordinary space for thought-provoking and productive exchanges, not only across world regions but also across disciplines. For us, the opportunity to continue this joint effort in the form of a book project became the option that would also enable us to extend this space of constructive engagement towards the wider community, particularly those who are interested in the various issues surrounding indigeneity as an academically and politically challenging concept, and as a project in (trans-)local identity politics. We sincerely hope that as many readers as possible share our interest.

During the past five years, we have received constant support, suggestions, and assistance in various forms from individuals and institutions. Without their commitment, this book would never have reached this point. First of all, we are grateful to our colleagues who have contributed their pieces and thereby turned this project into the book you are now reading. Their high level of commitment, anecdotic patience, and responses to all sorts of editorial queries have been invaluable. We sincerely mean it when we say that this book is the result of a truly collective effort.

This book would not have seen the light of day if not for the commitment, support, and encouragement extended to us by a number of individuals. In particular, we are indebted to Jürgen Straub, Ellen Bal, and Cora Bender for their significant contributions, and also to William

Sax and Willem van Schendel for their suggestions. With their relentless support, they have made this project academically enlightening. We also thank Berlin-based filmmaker Shaheen Dill-Riaz for showing his award-winning documentary *Sand and Water* at the workshop and for sharing his perspectives and invaluable insights with us. Last but not least, we are grateful to Adam Kuper, who wrote the preface to this volume.

We are particularly thankful to the Alexander-von-Humboldt Foundation for its generous support, which allowed Nasir to work in Bochum as a Fellow under the Georg-Forster-Programme. Having the chance to collaborate so closely for more than a year has been decisive in turning our project into something lasting. We also wish to express our thanks to the Hans Kilian and Lotte Köhler Center (KKC) for Cultural Psychology and Historical Anthropology and the Center for Mediterranean Studies for their generous support. The Faculty of Social Science at Ruhr-University Bochum provided us with logistical support.

We are thankful to Bernadette Möhlen, Corinna Land, Katrin Renschler, and Arne Oster, who have provided valuable support in organizing our meetings and preparing the manuscript. We also thank Charlotte Thornton and Tom Triglone for proofreading previous versions of the chapters and the final draft of the volume. This project has also greatly benefitted from the comments and suggestions made by two anonymous reviewers. We would also like to thank Sasha Puchalski, Amanda Horn and Burke Gerstenschlager for their support throughout the process.

Eva Gerharz
Nasir Uddin
Pradeep Chakkarath

Abbreviations

AAJVS	Andaman Primitive Tribal Welfare Association
ACHPR	African Commission on Human and Peoples' Rights
ADB	Asian Development Bank
AIPP	Asia Indigenous Peoples Pact
AL	Awami League
ANPATR	Andaman Nicobar Protection of Aboriginal Tribes Regulation
ANTRI	Andaman Nicobar Tribal Research and Training Institute
ASI	Anthropological Survey of India
ATR	Andaman Trunk Road
BAF	Bangladesh Adivasi Forum
BJP	Bharatiya Janata Party
BNP	Bangladesh Nationalist Party
CAM	complementary and alternative medicine
CCM	Chama Cha Mapiduzi
CHT	Chittagong Hill Tracts
CIA	Central Intelligence Agency
CMLN	Co-Management Learning Network
CONAIE	Confederation of Indigenous Nationalities of Ecuador
CONFENIAE	Confederation of Indigenous Nationalities of the Ecuadorian Amazon
CSH	Supreme Hñähñu Council
CSO	civil society organizations
CSUTCB	Unified Syndicalist Confederation of Rural Workers of Bolivia
DINEIB	National Board of Intercultural and Bilingual Education

FEI	Ecuadorian Federation of Indios
FPIC	Free Prior and Informed Consent
FPP	Forest Peoples Programme
GAPE	Global Association for People and the Environment
GOB	Government of Bangladesh
GoC	Government of Cambodia
GOL	Government of Laos
IAITPTF	International Alliance of Indigenous and Tribal Peoples of the Tropical Forests
III	Inter-American Indigenist Institute
IIP	National Indigenist Institute
IKAP	Indigenous Knowledge and Peoples Network
ILO	International Labour Organization
INDEPA	Instituto Nacional de los Pueblos Andinos, Amazónicos y Afroperuanos
IO	international organizations
IWGIA	International Work Group for Indigenous Affairs
JLT	Jharkhand Liberation Tigers
KIPOC	Korongoro Integrated People Oriented to Conservation
LFNC	Lao Front for National Construction
MAS	Movimiento al Socialismo
MBOSCUDA	Mbororo Social and Cultural Development Association
MIP	Movimiento Indígena Pachakuti
MNR	Movimiento Nacionalista Revolucionario
MRTA	Movimiento Revolucionario Tupac Amaru
MRTKL	Movimiento Revolucionario Tupaj Katari de Liberación
MUPP-NP	Movimiento de Unidad Plurinacional Pachakutik-Nuevo País
NGO	non-government organizations
NPA	non-profit association
OAS	Organization of American States
PCJSS or JSS	Parbatya Chattagram Jana Samhati Samiti
PDR	People's Democratic Republic
PINGO	Pastoralists Indigenous Non-Governmental Organization

PLFI	People's Liberation Front of India
PRD	Partido de la Revolución Democrática
PRI	Partido Revolucionario Institucional
PRODEPINE	Pilot Project for Indigenous Peoples
PTG	Primitive Tribal Group
ST	Scheduled Tribes
SUYAO	Shaponos Unidos de los Yanomami del Alto Orinoco
TAN	transnational activist networks
TAPHGO	Tanzania Pastoralist Hunter & Gatherers Organization
TCM	traditional Chinese medicine
UN	United Nations
UNDP	United Nations Development Programme
UNDRIP	United Nations Declaration on the Rights of Indigenous Peoples
UNESCO	United Nations Educational, Scientific and Cultural Organization
UNFPII	United Nations for Indigenous Peoples
UN-REDD	United Nations Reduced Emissions from Deforestation and Degradation
USA	United States of America
USAID	Inter-American Development Bank
WHO	World Health Organization

Introduction

EXPLORING INDIGENEITY
Introductory Remarks on a Contested Concept
Nasir Uddin, Eva Gerharz, and Pradeep Chakkarath

While popular images tend to depict indigenous people as having lived a "simple" and unspoiled lifestyle before they became threatened by the "evils" of modernity and (neo)colonial exploitation, there is evidence for the argument that, in many parts of the world, indigenous people were neither "locally locked" in the deep forest or remote hills, nor socioculturally "isolated," dissociated from others and the outside world. Historians, political scientists, and anthropologists have shown that trade networks reached not only over great distances but also to remote places, and that, even though they may have been able to elude the power of state societies (Scott 2009), people living in those places were never completely isolated. This makes it even more astonishing that the notion of indigeneity has become a universalist concept that has gained global recognition for representing exactly this: a population that is economically "backward," due to a lack of modern technology, and politically "independent," due to the freedom from external forces and global capitalism, and therefore in need of protection. Such images tend to ignore the fact that it was colonialism itself that produced the well-known image of the noble or dangerous savage: simple, innocent, even childish, yet untamed and therefore threatening people, who lived in harmony with nature. But while colonial and postcolonial imaginations rested upon the idea that human progress is inevitably connected with a clearly defined path towards modernization, today's discourse on indigeneity considers the indigenous "way of life" as being endangered by the latter, and therefore as requiring protection. Both approaches disregard the fact that their universalist claims do not necessarily match the self-images of the populations usually labeled "indigenous." They also tend to ignore that, like other people all over the world, these populations are extensively connected to, and deeply influenced by, transformative global socioeconomic and political rhetoric and realities (for more detail, see Cadena and Starn 2007; Clifford 2013). Mobility is a feature of the modern world as people, goods, and ideas move rapidly from one place to another. This fosters the emergence of new visions and aspirations for development that are embedded in the dynamics of local and global statecraft. While one should refrain from constructing indigenous people as clearly demarcated "groups" who exist "out there," and even when one accepts that in general the world's population struggles with the impact of neoliberal notions of economic formation and governmentality, it is also important to recognize that the label "indigenous" has recently become a powerful category that continues to inspire identity politics, emancipatory projects, and protectionist measures worldwide.

Even today, indigenous activists across the world to some extent tend to reproduce images of locally locked, culturally confined, socially egalitarian, economically self-sufficient, and politically independent "peoples" in international forums and indigenous peoples' rights discourses in order to pursue particular claims. These images are particularly plausible and illustrative because they constitute a counter-narrative to modernization—a discourse frequently pursued by activists' main opponent, the nation-state. Modernization, globalization, industrialization, and other forms of what we call "neoliberalism" are not projects "out there" that hang over people's heads like a phantom, but strategies that are being pursued, and quite often actively protected and promoted, by the nation-state. Accordingly, indigenous activism mostly addresses state actors who are regarded as complicit in "selling out" indigenous rights to lands and natural resources without recognizing their way of life as being different to that of the majority population. This explanation, however, does not tell the entire story. It ignores the fact that the national imagination of many postcolonial states rests upon the ideal of a culturally homogenous society, for which minorities constitute a potential threat (Appadurai 2006). It also ignores the fact that within nation-states it is not only the so-called indigenous people who have been marginalized, but also often other segments of society who have not been able to gain recognition and influence. In contrast to explanations that tend to ignore the complexity of historical processes—that is, those acted out by a variety of protagonists at various global and local scales—this volume addresses the question of how indigeneity has manifested itself as a global discourse, feeding into very concrete policies and politics at different moments in time. It highlights that the concept itself is not a new invention, with a clearly defined meaning and scope, and related to a well-crafted set of rights, but rather that it has been used in many different ways by various actors. Accordingly, it has been used as an ascriptive and self-ascriptive category, as it is strategically employed by activists in order to pursue a particular set of claims, and by governments to defeat said claims or to make strategic concessions. Indigeneity has been appropriated by states and organizations exactly because it carries a particular meaning that is loaded with essentialist sentiments. However, it is not the validity of these sentiments over which activists continue to fight, but rather access to resources, rights, and dignity. This volume presents empirically grounded case studies from different parts of the world, which show that indigeneity is a contested concept and manifests itself in various ways.

Being concerned with "indigeneity on the move" indicates a keen interest in the question of how far, and under what conditions, the concept of indigeneity, which can be considered one of the key concepts of current social sciences, has the potential to change, alongside the rapidly changing lives and lifestyles of indigenous peoples across the world. And by extension, how these changes might reshape or at least modify our perspectives on established theories about social, economic, and political dynamics and their underlying factors. The concept of "indigeneity" and the various understandings of its meaning have had an impact not only on how social scientists think about the interconnections of identity, space, language, history, and culture, but also on how they describe the increasingly complex interplay of diverse players and agents within dynamic global socioeconomic, and political realities, and the rhetoric that accompanies it.

Indigeneity has become a resource in identity politics, a matter of "deep belonging," desired more than discouraged, and proclaimed more than hidden as one's attachment to a particular place, culture, and nation. It is woven together in an intricate web of concepts such as ethnicity, identity, hybridity, authenticity, autochthony, diaspora, nation, and homeland, and the ways in which these ideas are formed, developed, and "owned." In so far as territoriality and ancestral rights over land are inscribed into the notion of indigeneity, the imagination of place, space, and time are central analytical dimensions that are highly relevant, particularly with regard to questions concerning the redistributive power of states and political (e.g., democratic) processes. Although indigeneity is primarily expressed as an attachment to land, locale, and nation, the relationship between indigeneity and belonging is reworked and modified in translocal and transnational communicative and interactive processes. Consequently, these concepts intersect with local, national, and global sociopolitical debates and are confronted with the challenges posed to indigenous aspirations by the neoliberal agenda of nation-states and their concerns with sovereignty. Therefore, apart from being of academic interest, the politics of indigeneity are significant in the context of nation-building, the accommodation of minority rights, neoliberal policy reforms, and political debates in growing rights activism at a global scale. Given these contexts, how should we address indigeneity on the move in its various manifestations at different levels? What are the challenges that indigenous peoples across the world face in the interface between local, nationalist rhetoric and global, political dynamics? How are these challenges crucial for indigenous people living in different regions across the globe? These are the leading questions, in relation to national and transnational indigenous activism, that this book seeks to address, with the aim of shaping a potential framework to better understand the various manifestations of indigeneity.

Apart from some very good ethnographies on indigenous issues published across the world, there exist various edited volumes on indigeneity, on the indigenous dynamics of translocal politics, and on indigenous cosmopolitanism (see, e.g., Cadena and Starn 2007; Dev, Kelkar, and Walter 2004; Forte 2010; Karlsson and Subba 2006; Rycroft and Dasgupta 2011; Venkateswar and Hughes 2011), which focus mainly on the present discourse on indigeneity and the struggles of indigenous people with the diverse issues they experience, in the context of a recurrent and rapidly transforming socioeconomic and political reality. These collections portray the present situation as a consequence of the past, where indigenous people were thought of as a "backward human race," this category being produced in colonial scholarship on civilization in the mid nineteenth century. However, the situation has now considerably—though not completely—changed; indigenous peoples receive global attention, and their rights are acknowledged in different international forums. Indigenous people represent themselves at every level of society—locally, nationally, regionally, and globally—which gives birth to potentially new, as well as problematic, dimensions of the concept of both indigeneity itself and concurrent identity politics. This book focuses on "indigeneity on the move" with a critical assessment of local, translocal, and transnational figurations, and their relevance to the notions of indigeneity and indigenous activism, based on empirically informed analyses of past experiences and present challenges.

Indigeneity, Identity Politics, and Nation-States

The idea of indigeneity as a political resource in identity politics, referring to individual and collective attachment to a particular place, culture, and nation, is not a new phenomenon. It intersects with local, national, and global sociopolitical debates following the framework of "us" versus "them" in various contexts. The politics of nationalism, and that of naming and categorizing in postcolonial states, along with developmental interventions and displacements and, more recently, certain states' neoliberal agendas, have seen indigenous activists and those sympathetic to indigenous claims fight for legal and constitutional recognition within the political space of particular nation-states. Such recognition is usually framed in the language of rights (Cowan 2001; Gellner 2011) and relates to ideals of justice, equity, development, and democracy.

Ethnographies from all over the world have shown that the negotiations between indigenous activists and governments are framed within very different discourses, which differ from region to region and from one country to another. For instance, in the Americas, the discourse has been determined by images of indigenous people as the victims of settler colonialism, while in postcolonial states in South and Southeast Asia it involves cultural politics and the exclusionary policies of nation-building and state formation. In many countries, development programs directed towards economic growth at the cost of indigenous people and their habitats have given activists grounds to criticize development both as a discourse and as a set of practices (Escobar 1995; Ferguson 1994; Ziai 2013). Economic, political, and social marginalization have fostered the emergence of new, pioneering indigenous movements, which have been (partly) successful in introducing policy reforms and formulating alternative visions of society (e.g., Esteva and Prakash 1998; Laurie, Andolina, and Radcliffe 2005). Taking up a notion of indigeneity that is strongly linked with environmentalism and that line of activism, some movements have produced new visions for development, and new concrete versions thereof, such as the Buen Vivir initiative (see Ruttenberg 2013; Villalba 2013). Some of these activist movements have become particularly successful in claiming access to state resources, as the cases of Bolivia and Ecuador show (see Molyneux and Thomson 2011).

Whereas definitions of indigenous people in the Americas have been largely undisputed, activists in many parts of Africa and Asia, in contrast, have faced more difficulties because of different historical backgrounds or ethnic settings. Many Asian and African states refrain from acknowledging indigenous people as a category of citizens who are eligible for special rights and benefits on the basis of being oppressed (Gerharz 2014; Hodgson 2011; Pelican 2009). The arguments employed by these governments often rely on an interpretation of the notion of indigenous people that relates to specifics of the American populations—for example, the exposure to a colonialist force and its repercussions. At the same time, activists draw upon globalized notions of indigeneity to legitimize their claims. Paradoxically, both of these strategies can be interpreted as being directly related to globalization, in the sense of deterritorialization, which has opened up new avenues for denationalization and the permeability of boundaries, and therefore paves the way for universalist claims, such as human rights or collective rights pertaining to the specific conditions assigned to the indigenous "way of life." In this sense, the emergence of indigenous activism can be regarded as a challenge to the modernization efforts of nation-states (Clifford 2013). However, the rising number of incidents of collective violence can also be traced back to growing pressure from globalizing forces, which threatens nationalist ideals of cultural purity within nation-states and leads to the reassertion of us/them constructions in ethnic terms (Appadurai 2006). Minorities with cultural differences thus become a problem because they challenge, from the statist perspective, the national narratives of social cohesion, solidarity, and homogeneity. In stark contrast to the universalist claims that unfold in transnational social spaces, we witness the recurrence of nationalist claims to social and cultural homogeneity.

Indigeneity as a Subject of Global Policy

Whereas indigeneity remains a highly contested concept in many countries with respect to the ideas of modern nation-states, a global discourse with more or less transnationally standardized meanings and connotations has emerged, especially following the support of international organizations with measures such as the International Labour Organization (ILO) conventions, the definition by the World Bank, and the United Nations Declaration on the Rights of Indigenous Peoples (UNDRIP). These imply the right to self-identification and self-definition, for example, but also offer guarantees such as freedom from oppression, as well as enshrining a special relationship between indigenous people and their land, and seeing mobility as a way of life. Debates on indigeneity and indigenous activism have shown a remarkable continuity throughout recent decades and have led to "place-making" at the level of the United Nations (Muehlebach 2001). In the early 1980s, the United

Nations had already started to respond to the claims of indigenous activists, who highlighted the marginalization of so-called indigenous peoples. With the formation of the UN Working Group on Indigenous Populations (WGIP), in 1982, struggles for equality that had been taking place in several nation-states around the world gained global recognition, and regular meetings within the UN also encouraged local civil society groups and rights organizations to expand their networks beyond the national space by building connections with transnational indigenous activism. These alternate, global institutionalizations were accompanied by an increasing interest from the ILO, which adopted the first international legal mechanism for the protection of indigenous peoples in 1989, in the form of the ILO Convention 169.

Due to the continuous efforts of the WGIP to raise the concerns of indigenous people, the UN Human Rights Council proposed to the General Assembly that 1993 should be named as the "International Year of the World's Indigenous People."[1] This was followed by the first "International Decade of the World's Indigenous People" (1995–2004). Indigenous activists made use of these ten years to initiate a variety of activities, including resolving problems related to the rights to lands, the preservation of nature and protection of habitats, health and education issues, and the constitutional recognition of identity—in all parts of the world. The Permanent Forum on Indigenous Issues was formed in 2000, and a UN Special Rapporteur on the Rights and Fundamental Freedoms of Indigenous People was appointed in 2001, although the impact of these measures on UN policies was limited.[2] Consequently, the UN declared 2005–14 as a second International Decade of the World's Indigenous People, making the "integrity and dignity" of indigenous peoples across the world a goal, which was in turn crucial for growing indigenous activism at both the global and local level, refueling as it did the rights movement of indigenous peoples working for cooperation, dignity, and integrity. Amidst this mounting indigenous activism, indigeneity became "a global ethnoscape" (Appadurai 1996), which now serves as a powerful tool for political negotiations because the international recognition of indigeneity has created a political space for indigenous people across the world to press their claims and demands (see Gerharz 2012; Ghosh 2006).

These international developments in creating and developing legal instruments were supplemented by the rights-based and promotional activities of transnationally organized initiatives such as the Environmental Defense Fund, the Forest People's Movement, Survival International, Cultural Survival, and Rainforest Action Network, among others.[3] Much of this transnational activism relates to global debates on environmentalism, both in the 1980s when the Green Movement gained momentum and, more recently, in relation to the climate change discourse. At the same time, the relative success of indigenous activists in lobbying for their goals by relating them to environmental issues has convinced other activists that it is a strategy worth following (Baviskar 2006). Such a strategy therefore holds enormous potential for claims articulated in various political domains. While some scholars are skeptical about an essential affinity between the environment and indigenous people (e.g., Linkenbach 2004), others strongly favor the idea that indigenous people are the best caretakers of environmental and natural resources (see Laungaramsri 2002). Moreover, Shalini Randeria (2003) demonstrates that the focus on environmentalism might lead to new strategic alliances with other civil society actors.

Indigeneity as an Academic Concept

Among activists, indigeneity is commonly defined by referring to collectives of people who believe that they share specific historical roots and experiences that are closely tied to certain territories, specific ethnic traits and linguistic autonomy, as well as specific customs, institutions, worldviews, and a characteristic way of life. Researchers seeking to document the project of indigenous identity politics have supported these activist claims with their academic analyses. With a tendency to embark on ethnographic naturalism, however, these perspectives have dismissed the essentialist connotations entailed in the notion of "indigenous peoples." Adam Kuper's much-cited article "The Return of the Native" (2003) strongly criticizes the entire idea of indigeneity as a postcolonial reproduction of what Andre Béteille calls "the re-emergence of primitivity" (see also Béteille 1998). These critical voices have reminded us that research on indigenous peoples entails several ethical and analytical dilemmas that need to be explicitly addressed. According to Linda Tuhiwai Smith (2012: 1), "The word itself, 'research,' is probably one of the dirtiest words in the indigenous world's vocabulary. When mentioned in many indigenous contexts, it stirs up silence, it conjures up bad memories, it raises a smile that is knowing and distrustful." However, ethnographers undertaking intensive research on indigenous peoples during the last couple of decades have been more sensitive to the colonial past in dealing with indigeneity and formerly colonized peoples, and also more politically conscious about the politics of representation (see Bal 2007; Hodgson 2011; Shah 2010).

A different path out of the impasse has been chosen by Kay Warren and Jean Jackson (2003). Based on their observation that, in order to represent indigeneity to make their claims, activists have adopted the notion of culture as a concept to depict commonality among particular groups and thus embarked on strategic essentialism, Warren and Jackson draw a sharp distinction between the culture concept applied by activists and the perspective of the researcher. Their task is not to reproduce the essentializing view of culture by isolating cultural practices that are used as markers of identity, but to examine "the ways essences are constructed in practice and disputed in political rhetoric" (ibid.: 9). Acknowledging that indigeneity has become a powerful tool in identity politics thus opens an analytical perspective academics have from the very beginning been trying to find a "middle point" between the perspectives of activists and an essentialist framework of categorical approaches in understanding the concept of indigeneity (see Barnard 2006; Merlan 2009).

One should, however, also be aware that for some decades now, "indigeneity" has been discussed in various academic disciplines, under varying perspectives, and sometimes detached from identity politics and the sociopolitical framework that has come to dominate the social scientific discussions of the concept in many research fields. In the field of psychology, for example, so-called "indigenous psychology" has taken the form of a sub-discipline with a growing number of representative and influential scholars worldwide. Although this academic movement's beginnings and goals can quite easily be traced back to the beginnings of postcolonial studies, psychological research is less interested in the potential political nature of the sub-discipline's origins; rather, its interest focuses on the question of whether there are psychological traits, pathologies, intervention strategies, therapies, and other psychologically relevant phenomena, including theories and methods, that—for good reasons—can be understood as indigenous features of very specific groups with very specific histories and their very own ways of experiencing, thinking, feeling, and behaving (Chakkarath 2012, 2013). Similar questions have been raised and investigated in other fields, such as the educational sciences (Snively and Corsiglia 2001; Verran 2001), sociology (Khoury and Khoury 2013; Morgan 1997), within the discourse on postcolonialism (Baber 2002), or archaeology (Bruchac, Hart, and Wobst 2010), to name just a few. One of the main queries that resonates from all of these concerns with the human psyche and so-called indigenous science approaches is the crucial academic question of whether our scientific theories can claim universal validity unless they have successfully met the challenges embedded in and conveyed by the concept of indigeneity.

Since questions like these are fundamental questions within the general philosophy of science, we should be cautious when merely treating these issues as simple offshoots of the postcolonial discourse, identity politics, and their sociohistorical background. This is another important reason why the contributions to this book attempt to understand indigeneity as an academic perspective beyond political and cultural binaries, while paying particular attention to the context that has been shaped in relation to manifold discourses and their various manifestations.

From Rights to Dignity

The last four decades of indigenous activism can be summarized as the era of movements, struggles for international recognition of identity, and campaigns for rights to lands, forest, natural resources, and habitats—on both local and global scales. Following the two International Decades of the World's Indigenous People (1995–2004 and 2005–14), and the continuing annual International Day of the World's Indigenous Peoples (9 August), indigenous peoples have gained the support of the international community and human rights bodies, as well as national-level civil society organizations. In this process, the rights of indigenous peoples have been established by international legal protections; however, at the country level, many indigenous peoples are still waiting for official recognition. Currently, the futures of indigenous people lie with the state of dignity they look to gain at both local and global levels. In contrast to those who have made attempts to minimize the existing diversities of indigenous people, by formulating standard frames to ensure the rights and dignity of all indigenous people, Kuper (2003) concludes that there is no global solution for this diversity worldwide. One of the main focuses of this book is to present how indigenous peoples in various parts of the world are simultaneously involved with movements for indigenous peoples' rights, as well as the struggle to improve their socioeconomic and political positioning in the national space, in order to gain dignity. Identity politics also feature in the indigenous movements in some nation-states, precisely because they are categorically excluded from the process of homogenous nation-building and the majoritarian policies of state formation. Therefore, indigenous peoples try to build relationships with the state that involve a dialectical engagement, in the tradition of Justin Kenrick and Jerome Lewis (2004), who present indigeneity as a sort of relationship—to culture, to land, and to ethnic historiography, or to put it another way, "indigeneity as a cultural concept." Joanna Pfaff-Czarnecka and Gérard Toffin (2011) have taken a similar view in favor of culturalist groups, explaining that indigeneity involves multiple attachments and senses of belonging, which constitute their social and cultural bases. However, many scholars, like Dipesh Chakrabarty (2002), argue that the idea of indigeneity is broadly a political concept, and has nothing to do with culture. Putting aside these debates over whether the idea of indigeneity is a political concept or a cultural one, it becomes important to determine the particular rights for indigenous peoples that ensure a certain level of dignity both as human beings and indigenous people on global and local scales.

Indigeneity, Land, and Resources

Struggles for land resources are one of the major challenges indigenous people face in all parts of the world. This has to do with the common view that land constitutes a core issue of indigeneity. In Chapter 1, Erik de Maaker explores the relationship between modes of land ownership, conceptualizations of land and nature, and notions of indigeneity. He states that the portrayal of upland communities of Northeast India as "indigenous" depends to a large extent on a presumably inextricable relationship between people and land (Karlsson 2011; Li 2010). Upland people are believed to "belong" to their land, and its forests, in the sense that it is considered sacred to them. One way in which this essential bond to the land is expressed is in joint land ownership. In the Garo Hills of Meghalaya, collective ownership was legally secured in the colonial period. Although its original aim was to avoid villagers losing their land, it has been unable to counteract the disparities in power and wealth that have always been prevalent within village communities. Moreover, in much of the Garo Hills there is a tendency towards the privatization of land use, as well as ownership. This commodification of land is unavoidable for the modernization of agriculture, and yet it challenges Garo notions of indigeneity, as well as related perceptions of land and nature. De Maaker, in this chapter, analyzes the transformation of land relationships, the legalities in which these are founded, and the consequences they have for Garo notions of indigeneity.

In another case from Southeast Asia, Ian Baird in Chapter 2 discusses how indigeneity functions as a strong political resource, using the case of land management in Cambodia, Thailand, and Laos. He brings out the political rhetoric of indigenous people, explaining that over the last couple of decades the concept of "indigenous peoples" has gained increasing traction in Asia, with some countries—such as the Philippines, Japan, Taiwan, and Cambodia—having adopted legislation that recognizes indigenous peoples. Still, other national governments in Asia continue to resist, with many following the "saltwater theory," which specifies that the concept of indigenous peoples is only applicable in places where there has been considerable European settler colonization (such as the Americas, Australia, and New Zealand). Elsewhere, the concept is seen as irrelevant, since everyone is considered to be indigenous. Still, even in these countries the movement has made some inroads, albeit unevenly, due to varying political and historical circumstances. Much of the increased attention on the concept of indigenous peoples is linked to advocacy associated with attempts to gain increased access and control over land and other natural resources. In this chapter, Baird considers the links between the indigenous peoples' movement and land and resource tenure issues in three countries in mainland Southeast Asia where the concept of indigeneity is variously recognized.

Becoming 'Indigenous'

Indigeneity is also challenged by various local, regional, and international political dynamics of identity and locally embedded public and political discourse. Therefore, a deeper understanding of the dynamics of indigeneity depends on how local political rhetoric negotiates with international indigenous activism. In Chapter 3, Gabriele Herzog-Schröder draws our attention to the Yanomami of Venezuela and Brazil, who are often represented as an "isolated," indigenous, ethnic group of the South American lowlands, prototypically as Amerindian societies of Amazonia. In the Brazilian part of their territory they have, over the last three decades, been invaded and abused as part of a disgraceful gold rush. However, anthropologists, too, became notorious for inappropriate projections of the Yanomami in Venezuela. Due to this history of invasion and worldwide media attention, the Yanomami have been subject to representation as the stereotypical "exotic" within both anthropological academia and beyond. This widespread publicity has obscured the fact that presently, growing contact with the "outside" world is taking place in quite heterogeneous ways among the Yanomami. While some Yanomami personalities are well informed about city life and symptoms of globalization—for example, the famous Davi Kopenawa from Brazil—the majority of Yanomami have not yet traveled outside their traditional territories. The misrepresentation of indigeneity, and the processes of approximation of an isolated area in southern Venezuela, demonstrate how a gradual understanding of the "outside world" goes hand in hand with the Yanomami's own understanding of being "indigenous." At the same time, this new indigenous identity situates the actors as members of a nation, and makes them appear as belonging to a particular indigenous group within a choir of other indigenous people within these newly conceived national complexes. These freshly acquainted forms of identity—being "Yanomami" (as an indigenous group), being indigenous, and being Venezuelan or Brazilian—are contested by a traditional cosmological worldview, in short by being determined as "shamanic." New forms of "knowledge," as well as spatial imaginaries—novel to the traditional worldview—are discussed in this chapter, focusing particularly on schooling as an interface between indigeneity and modernity.

The increasing pace of connectivity and networking is helping indigenous activism reach translocal and transnational spaces, which in turn provide transnational incentives to local and national activism. In Chapter 4, Eva Gerharz argues that indigeneity is made use of by activists as a crucial category, one that signifies belonging in various ways, and more or less successfully. Using the case of Bangladesh's indigenous activist movement and its demands for the recognition of diversity as an example, the article identifies three different domains in which indigenous activism is at work, and locates these within translocal space. In particular, Gerharz shows how international claims to indigenous rights are translated into the national legal framework and how these attempts are being negotiated between actors who draw on globalized concepts and discourses in different ways. A second domain is development, one of the classical fields of international and transnational interaction in Bangladesh, in which indigenous issues have been taken up only recently. These initiatives, however, have provoked quite controversial debates, especially from those actors who seek to preserve indigeneity as a distinct way of life. The third dimension is concerned with the ambiguities emerging from the representation of indigenous people, their culture, and way of life in the public space of the Bengali-dominated national society. These three dimensions, Gerharz argues, rest upon activist configurations that are marked by dynamic boundary-making processes, which are enacted in multiethnic settings and not only allow the inclusion of non-indigenous activists but also foster the exclusion of indigenous people who do not support the political claims and demands of the movement. Gerharz argues that understanding the constellations of belonging from a translocal perspective helps us to move beyond essentializing concepts of indigeneity that run the risk of reproducing stereotypical images.

In Chapter 5, Nasir Uddin also focuses on indigenous people in Bangladesh, but from a different angle. His interest is in the various forms of identity politics, cultural politics, and the politics of nationalism that are produced locally, but that also compete with global notions of indigeneity, and which therefore also deserve attention, critical discussion, and analysis from academics. He particularly focuses on the complex networks of the politics of indigeneity, in which the identity of a particular group of people becomes a conflict between local articulations of selfhood, national politics of "otherness," and transnational discourses of indigeneity. His discussion critically engages with recurrent debates on indigeneity, identity politics, and the politics of nationalism in local, national, and transnational spheres, using the case of the Khumi people who live in the Chittagong Hill Tracts (CHT), in southeastern Bangladesh. The Khumi, culturally different from the majority Bengali population and from other ethnic minorities in Bangladesh, confront multiple identities—Khumi, Pahari, *upajatee* (sub-nation), tribe, *jumma* (shifting cultivators), *adivasi* or indigenous people, *khudra-nrigoshti* (ethnic minority), and so on—amid the local and global politics of indigeneity. The state's politics of nationalism, transnational politics of indigeneity, and postcolonial practice of colonial discourse in the South Asian subcontinent place the Khumi in an identity crisis, and demonstrates the problems with subscribing to the idea of indigeneity as an international category. Consequently, the Khumi are now in the position of losing their "self" in "others" who themselves claim to be indigenous people. With the case of the Khumi, Uddin examines the idea of indigeneity, politics of identity, and belonging, as well as the notions of nationalism in Bangladesh, against the wider background of the relation of the CHT to the state, which has been shaped over time and through regimes, from the colonial (British), through the semi-colonial (Pakistan), to the post/neocolonial (Bangladesh) era.

Indigeneity as a Political Resource

The emergence of the idea of indigeneity was strongly motivated by indigenous activism across the world, which resulted in the international endorsement of various legal frameworks for the rights of indigenous people. Since then, indigeneity has become a political resource.

In Africa, "indigeneity" has been a highly contested concept. Michaela Pelican explains in Chapter 6 that during the past twenty years, many ethnic and minority groups in Africa have laid claim to "indigeneity," in their country or region of residence, on the basis of their political marginalization and cultural difference. They have drawn inspiration from the UN definition of "indigenous peoples" as a legal category with collective entitlements, and have linked up with the global indigenous rights movement. Concurrently, there has been an extensive debate within Africanist anthropology on the concept's analytical usefulness. Moreover, several African governments have questioned its applicability to the African continent, arguing that all population groups may count as "indigenous." However, with the adoption of the Declaration on the Rights of Indigenous Peoples in 2007, conceptual criticism has abated, and many African governments have made attempts to integrate the indigenous rights discourse in their policies and development programs—with varied outcomes. Pelican outlines the different trajectories of the indigenous rights movement in Africa and discusses the factors that may contribute to its success or decline. In particular, she compares two case studies. The first is the Mbororo of Cameroon, a pastoralist group that in 2005 became internationally recognized as an indigenous people, and whose socioeconomic and political trajectory she has followed since the 1990s. The second is the Maasai of Tanzania, whose involvement in the indigenous rights movement dates back to the late 1980s.

Apart from Asia and Africa, Latin America is also an important geographical region with its own ethno-historical background where indigeneity has taken a very significant position in the political sphere. In Chapter 7, Olaf Kaltmeier argues that the Indian question lies at the heart of the political-cultural definition of the Americas, in the process of colonization. The identitarian concept of "Indian" is a colonial intervention and an exercise of epistemological power, subsuming different peoples and empires under a single signifier. Thereby, this classification has been used since colonial times to design ethnic policies of domination. Nevertheless, in order to frame their protests, subaltern actors have frequently made use of this concept, which finds its ultimate expression in the politicization of the indigenous question in the 1990s. Kaltmeier analyzes the different conjunctures of the political use of indigeneity in modern Latin America, from the beginning of the twentieth century to the present. Relying on Latin American postcolonial and cultural studies, the chapter unravels the conjunctures of state-driven inter-American *indigenismo, indianismo,* and indigenous autonomy and pluri-nationality. Finally, Kaltmeier discusses whether the pluri-national redefinition of Andean societies marks a turning point towards the end of coloniality, or whether we face a new conjuncture of colonization based on the closure of the Indian mobilization cycle and the emergence of a regime of accumulation based on appropriation.

In Chapter 8, Gilberto Rescher shows that self-representation is also an important means of indigenous representation that can be considered an alternative approach to the politics of representation adopted by the unitary nation-state. Based on his empirical investigation into public discourses on indigenous people in Mexico, he shows that these frequently emphasize their supposed backwardness, and consequently conceptualize indigenous groups as marginalized and trapped in clientelist relations. However, indigenous villages are localities where local and translocal processes intersect, facilitating social, economic, and political transformations. In Mexico, Rescher argues, indigenous villages normally present themselves as indigenous communities, and these can be seen as an important basis of the political system, because they are conceived as a unit of potential political mobilization in favor of specific political actors. This allegiance was classically thought to be secured in the manner of a clientelist exchange of (state) resources for political loyalty. Though local political actors seldom employ the term indigenous, the communities' representatives allude to relevant imaginaries and views, strategically employing suitable representations in political negotiations through a variety of means. The underlying relative unity of the communities is achieved by social cohesion based as much on several forms of pressure as on a belonging resulting from inter alia day-to-day interactions. The (often prejudiced) views of indigenous communities are embodied by their members and the affiliation is both internally and externally displayed. Indigeneity and representation as consolidated communities are important political resources, even though these groups, far from being homogeneous, are often affected by internal conflicts and power relations. Thus, the social positioning of these indigenous groups initially stays the same. Nevertheless, indigenous communities may use this (self-)representation to promote a transformation of (local) political relations. Party affine organizations that seek to transnationally re-establish networks of political co-optation are also frequently ethnically framed, employing discourses that emphasize a pretended shared ethnic identity. Thus, indigeneity can be both part of practices that enhance political transformations, and a discursive instrument to revive clientelist modes of political interaction.

Indigeneity and the State

Around the world, states always constitute a major stakeholder in the realm of indigeneity, either as promoters of indigenous people or as forces against them. In fact, people who claim (or are claimed) to be indigenous continuously negotiate their local identity with translocal politics, and their cultural identity with political entanglement. Recognition of indigeneity is therefore said to have challenged the idea of a unitary nation-state that upholds the notions of nation through the minority-exclusionary politics of majority inclusion, which excludes cultural "others" through the spheres of rights and entitlements (see Uddin 2014). Uday Chandra in Chapter 9 discusses the case of Maoists in Jharkhand, India, to illustrate relations between indigeneity and the state. He argues that the Communist Party of India (Maoist), in both its own words and those of its critics, is fighting a revolutionary guerrilla war to overthrow the bourgeois state in India. Yet everyday local realities in their tribal bases show Maoist cadres making claims on the state to raise minimum wages, implement new forest laws, and ensure the timely payment of rural employment guarantee funds. Since 2009, Maoist factions and splinter groups have also routinely campaigned for *adivasi* political parties, such as the Jharkhand Mukti Morcha (JMM), and have even begun contesting state and panchayat elections in scheduled tribe constituencies. By participating in the electoral arena, are Maoist rebels abandoning their radical political project in favor of indigenous politics? Or does the agenda for radical social change spill over into "revisionist" avenues such as elections? To explain this apparently anomalous state of affairs, Chandra proposes the notion of "radical revisionism," encompassing political practices that work within existing democratic structures but push them to the hilt and seek to transform them from below, in the hope of radical democratic futures. He draws on extensive ethnographic fieldwork in central and southern Jharkhand to shed light on the everyday tactics and maneuvers of *adivasi* youth, who, as radical revisionists in Khunti and West Singhbhum districts, abandon the party line and, paradoxically, accentuate the modern state-making process in the tribal margins of modern India. In particular, Chandra focuses on how new political subjectivities, as well as new notions of democratic citizenship, community, and leadership, emerge on the ground.

Within the framework of state–indigeneity relations, Wolfgang Gabbert discusses in Chapter 10 how, since the 1980s, constitutions in several Latin American countries have been reformed to acknowledge the multicultural and ethnically diverse character of the nations and to recognize existing indigenous legal and political practices. Thus, a first step in creating a more accessible and more adequate legal system has been taken. However, these legal reforms touch on a number of practical and theoretical issues related to such fundamentals of social anthropology as the reification of culture and tradition. Gabbert discusses four of these topics: the political fragmentation of the indigenous populations; their cultural heterogeneity; the relationship between law and social structure; and the incidence of power relations in customary law. He argues that much of the current debate on the recognition of so-called indigenous customary law applies to an earlier model of the nation-state, thereby running the risk of fostering new forms of cultural homogenization and sustaining the current domination by the state over indigenous groups.

Philipp Zehmisch discusses the issue of state and non-state relations in Chapter 11 in relation to the idea of indigeneity, by arguing that discourses, definitions, and practices relating to indigeneity have shifted across time, spaces, and contexts. He understands the term as contingent upon the relationship between the state and non-state actors. Zehmisch captures indigeneity as a dialectical process between essentialist classifications of indigenous groups by authorities, and creative appropriations of such categories by indigenous people themselves. His ethnographic example, the Andaman Islands, serves to demonstrate the trajectory of the notion of indigeneity. Here, popular definitions, representations, and discourses of the British Empire, the Indian nation-state, and the global sphere intersect. The shifting notions are scrutinized by looking at state policies and indigenous–settler dynamics. He highlights how specific spatial arrangements and contact scenarios were interpreted, explained, and described through references to indigeneity. In the Andamans, colonial notions of "savagery" were indicative of indigenous warfare and co-optation at the frontier; they justified the taming and civilizing of "primitive" islanders and their forests through the settling of convicts and "criminal tribes" from the Indian subcontinent. The transformation of ecological "wilderness" into ordered settler colony spaces was executed by "aboriginal" forest laborers: *adivasi* migrants from Chota Nagpur, the Ranchis, and the Karen, a Burmese "hill tribe." After independence, anthropologically informed "tribal" governance led to protection acts, reserve zones, and welfare policies. Parallel to that, forestry, infrastructure development, and migrations degraded indigenous resources and led to violence. More recently, transnational, national, and local civil society actors have appropriated the notion of indigeneity. Conservationists and indigenous activists have promoted their own "ecologically noble savage" agenda when involved in conflicts with the government about the isolation of indigenous peoples; in contrast, local politicians advocate the "mainstreaming" of backward *"junglees."* Beyond that, Ranchi elites are fighting for official recognition of their indigenous status, while the majority of *adivasi* peoples are threatened by eviction due to environmental governance. Such conflicting and fluid characteristics appear to be essential elements of indigenous futures.

Indigenous Knowledge and Its Futures

The idea of indigeneity is quite often discussed within the paradigm of indigenous knowledge, as indigenous peoples have for generations been effectively practicing a particular type of knowledge system that is now recognized as eco-friendlier, more sustainable, and more productive than the modern Westernized developmentalist paradigm (see Sillitoe 1998). Therefore, a deeper understanding of the significance of indigenous knowledge is important to comprehend indigeneity on the move. As part of this debate, the ideas and roles of indigenous medicines have appeared as substitutes for biomedicine because of their effective, lasting, and significant capacity for healing diseases. Therefore, the futures of indigeneity demand a serious discussion on the futures of indigenous medicine, which William Sax addresses with empirically based information and analysis in the postscriptum. It has been argued that although biomedicine (also called "modern medicine," "cosmopolitan medicine," or "allopathy") began as a form of indigenous or local knowledge in Europe, it then transcended its origins and became universal or "cosmopolitan." It is therefore often regarded as a timeless and culture-free form of universal (as opposed to indigenous) knowledge that can be transplanted from place to place without undergoing fundamental change, much like chemistry, physics, or mathematics. Sax argues that, on the contrary, although there may be some heuristic value in describing it as an abstract system divorced from its context, knowledge is in fact always "done": acquired, owned, disputed, implemented, or, as the positivists would have it, "discovered." Knowledge has no ontological status outside the human practices that produce and reproduce it, and such practices are always historical and contextual. Thus, argues Sax, all medicine, including modern cosmopolitan medicine, is "indigenous" at the point of application. Although it is true that in our times, biomedicine is epistemologically, institutionally, and politically dominant, this has to do less with universal and context-free truths than with the circumstances of its dissemination. When we compare what are called "indigenous medicines" (e.g., tribal medicines, traditional healing) with modern biomedicine, we are not comparing a context-bound with a context-free system, because there are no forms of knowledge that are free of context. Rather, we are dealing with what Bruno Latour would call "networks" of different sizes. Sax discusses and compares several of these networks, focusing on various forms of "traditional" and "religious" healing from Asia, in an attempt to show that their growth in recent decades has much to do with their context dependency.

Conclusion

The book brings together the findings of empirically grounded research from different parts of the world, particularly in the "Global South." Based on various transdisciplinary contexts—anthropology, sociology, political science, psychology, geography, and history—it critically engages with debates on indigeneity and its historical and ideological trajectory, in order to determine its theoretical and political destination. The scholars who have contributed to this book examine the current state of indigeneity as an active force, the potential space of identity in a deterritorialized world, and highlight the scalar and temporal dimensions of indigeneity's sources, contents, and connectedness with related concepts and ideas. When taken together, the book explores the ways in which indigeneity becomes relevant with regard to knowledge, representation, and individually and collectively negotiated "ways of being." With a focus on the politics of identity and belonging, it attempts to offer new frames through which one may understand the relationships of such politics with many contemporary nation-states, and seeks to provide a critical overview of current research on indigeneity. It also identifies the issues that must be addressed in future research and discussions, in order to investigate indigeneity and its role within changing political and economic environments with greater refinement. For this purpose, the contributors to this book reflect upon their research to engage critically in debates on indigeneity, and thus provide solid theoretical and empirical examinations into indigeneity in the globalized world. Much of this revolves around the observation that the recurrent indigenous activism occurring around the world could lend an honorable dignity to struggles to establish rights. This diverse collection attempts to help readers to acquire comprehensive knowledge about contemporary research that has shaped scholarship on indigeneity and indigenous mobility, and to show promising directions for future research.

Nasir Uddin (PhD, Kyoto) is a cultural anthropologist based in Bangladesh, and Professor of Anthropology at Chittagong University. He studied and carried out research at the University of Dhaka, the University of Chittagong, Kyoto University, the University of Hull, Delhi School of Economics, Ruhr-University Bochum, VU University Amsterdam, Heidelberg University, and the London School of Economics (LSE). His research interests include indigeneity and identity politics; dialectics between colonialism and postcolonialism; refugee, statelessness, and citizenship; notions of power and the state in everyday life; the Chittagong Hill Tracts; and South Asia. His latest book is *Life in Peace and Conflict: Indigeneity and State in the Chittagong Hill Tracts* (Orient BlackSwan, 2017).

Eva Gerharz (Dr.phil., Bielefeld) is Professor of Sociology with a special focus on globalization at Fulda University of Applied Sciences, Germany. She previously held the position of Junior Professor for Sociology of Development and Internationalization at Ruhr-University Bochum, and Interim Professor of Development Sociology at Bayreuth University from 2017 to 2018. Until 2010, she was a researcher in the Department of Social Anthropology, Faculty of Sociology at Bielefeld University, Germany, and also Associate Scientist at the International Centre for Integrated Mountain Development (ICIMOD), Kathmandu. With a major focus on South Asia (Bangladesh and Sri Lanka), her research deals with indigeneity, ethnicity and conflict, development and reconstruction, political activism, and transnationalism. Eva has published in several academic journals, including *Mobilities, Conflict and Society, Asian Ethnicity*, and *Indigenous Policy Journal*. As well as her monograph, *The Politics of Reconstruction and Development in Sri Lanka* (Routledge, 2014), she has co-edited *Governance, Development and Conflict in South Asia* (Sage, 2015, with Siri Hettige) and *Land, Development and Security in South Asia* (SAMAJ, 2016, with Katy Gardner).

Pradeep Chakkarath (Dr.phil., Konstanz) is a cultural psychologist at Ruhr-University Bochum, Germany, and (together with Jürgen Straub) co-director of the Hans Kilian and Lotte Köhler Centre (KKC) for Cultural Psychology and Historical Anthropology. He is a lecturer at universities in Germany, Austria, and Switzerland, Editor in Chief of the German journal *psychosozial,* and a fellow alumnus of the Center of Excellence at the University of Konstanz, Germany. He was a visiting professor at the Université Evangélique du Cameroun. After having completed his Master's degree in philosophy and history and his PhD in psychology, he conducted cross-cultural research on children's development and parent–child relationships with an emphasis on Asian–European comparisons. Currently, his main interests are in human development from an interdisciplinary perspective, the history and methodology of the social sciences, and the indigenous psychology approach.

Notes

1. See http://www.refworld.org/docid/3b00f04e10.html (accessed 16 March 2017).
2. See http://www.culturalsurvival.org/news/none/un-tracks-progress-second-international-decade-world-s-indigenous-people (accessed 16 March 2017).
3. Beth Conklin and Laura Graham explain that continuous media reporting on global warming, declining biodiversity, and deforestation brought, for example, the plight of local Amazon Indians and their conflict over natural resources to the attention of a broader international audience (see Conklin and Graham 1995).

Bibliography

Appadurai, Arjun. 1996. *Modernity at Large: Cultural Dimensions of Globalization.* Minneapolis, MN and London: Minnesota University Press.

———. 2006. *Fear of Small Numbers: An Essay on the Geography of Anger.* Durham, NC and London: Duke University Press.

Baber, Zaheer. 2002. "Orientalism, Occidentalism, Nativism: The Culturalist Quest for Indigenous Science and Knowledge." *The European Legacy* 7: 747–58.

Bal, Ellen. 2007. *They Ask if We Eat Frog: Garo Ethnicity in Bangladesh.* Leiden: International Institute for Asian Studies.

Barnard, Alan. 2006. "Kalahari Revisionism, Vienna and the Indigenous Peoples Debate." *Social Anthropology* 14(1): 1–16.

Baviskar, Amita. 2006. "The Politics of Being 'Indigenous'." In *Indigeneity in India*, ed. Bengt G. Karlsson and Tanka B. Subba, 33–50. London: Kegan Paul.

Béteille, André. 1998. "The Idea of Indigenous People." *Current Anthropology* 39(2): 187–92.

Boyer, Dominic. 2009. "Making (Sense of) News in the Era of Digital Information." In *The Anthropology of News and Journalism: Global Perspectives*, ed. S. Elizabeth Bird, 241–256. Bloomington, IN: Indiana University Press.

Boyer, Dominic. 2012. "From Media Anthropology to the Anthropology of Mediation." In *The SAGE Handbook of Social Anthropology*, ed. Richard Fardon, Oliva Harris, Trevor Marchand, Cris Shore, Veronica Strang, Richard Wilson, Mark Nuttall, 383–392. London et al.: Sage.

Bruchac, Margaret, Siobhan Hart, and H. Martin Wobst (eds). 2010. *Indigenous Archaeologies: A Reader on Decolonization.* Walnut Creek, CA: Left Coast.

Cadena, Marisol de la, and Orin Starn (eds). 2007. *Indigenous Experience Today.* New York: Berg.

Chakkarath, Pradeep. 2012. "The Role of Indigenous Psychologies in the Building of Basic Cultural Psychology." In *The Oxford Handbook of Culture and Psychology*, ed. J. Valsiner, 71–95. New York: Oxford University Press.

Chakkarath, Pradeep. 2013. "Indian Thoughts on Psychological Human Development." In *Psychology and Psychoanalysis* (Vol. XIII, Part 3, of *History of Sci-*

ence, Philosophy and Culture in Indian Civilization), ed. G. Misra, 167–190. New Delhi: Munshiram Manoharlal Publishers.

Chakrabarty, Dipesh. 2002. *Habitations of Modernity: Essays in the Wake of Subaltern Studies*. Chicago, IL: University of Chicago Press.

Clifford, James. 2013. *Returns: Becoming Indigenous in the Twenty-First Century*. Cambridge, MA: Harvard University Press.

Conklin, Beth A., and Laura A. Graham. 1995. "The Shifting Middle Ground: Amazonian Indians and Eco-Politics." *American Anthropologist* 97(4): 695–710.

Cowan, Jane K. 2001. "Ambiguities of an Emancipatory Discourse: The Making of a Macedonian Minority in Greece." In *Culture and Rights: Anthropological Perspectives*, ed. Jane K. Cowan, Marie-Bénédicte Dembour, and Richard Wilson, 172–176. Cambridge and New York: Cambridge University Press.

Dev, Nathan, Govind Kelkar, and Pierre Walter (eds). 2004. *Globalization and Indigenous People in Asia: Changing the Local-Global Interface*. Thousand Oaks, CA and London: Sage.

Escobar, Arturo. 1995. *Encountering Development: The Making and Unmaking of the Third World*. Princeton, NJ: Princeton University Press.

Esteva, Gustavo and Prakash, Madhu. 1998. *Grassroots Post-modernism: Remaking the Soil of Cultures*. London and New York: Zed Books.

Ferguson, James. 1994. *The Anti-Politics Machine: "Development" Depoliticization, and Bureaucratic Power in Lesotho*. Minneapolis, MN and London: University of Minnesota Press.

Forte, Maximilian C. 2010. *Indigenous Cosmopolitans: Transnational and Transcultural Indigeneity in the Twenty-First Century*. New York: Peter Lang Publishing.

Gellner, David. 2011. "Belonging, Indigeneity, Rites, and Rights: The Newar Case." In *The Politics of Belonging in the Himalayas*, ed. Joanna Pfaff-Czarnecka and Gérard Toffin, 45–76. Delhi: Sage.

Gerharz, Eva. 2012. "Approaching Indigenous Activism from the Ground Up: Experiences from Bangladesh." In *Beyond Methodological Nationalism: Research Methodologies for Cross-Border Studies*, ed. Anna Amelina et al., 129–154. London: Routledge.

Gerharz, Eva. 2014. "Recognising Indigenous People, the Bangladeshi Way: The United Nations Declaration for Indigenous People's Rights, Transnational Activism and the Constitutional Amendment Affair of 2011." *Indigenous Policy Journal* 24(4): 64–79.

Ghosh, Kaushik. 2006. "Between Global Flows and Local Dams: Indigenousness, Locality and the Transnational Sphere in Jharkhand, India." *Cultural Anthropology* 21(4): 501–34.

Hodgson, Dorothy. 2011. *Being Maasai, Becoming Indigenous: Postcolonial Politics in a Neoliberal World*. Bloomington, IN: Indiana University Press.

Karlsson, Bengt. 2011. *Unruly Hills: A Political Ecology of India's Northeast*. New York: Berghahn Books.

Karlsson, Bengt, and Tanka B. Subba (eds). 2006. *Indigeneity in India*. London: Kegan Paul.

Kenrick, Justin, and Jerome Lewis. 2004. "Indigenous Peoples' Rights and the Politics of the Term 'Indigenous'." *Anthropology Today* 20(2): 4–9.

Khoury, Seif Da'Na, and Laura Khoury. 2013. "Geopolitics of Knowledge: Constructing an Indigenous Sociology from the South." *International Review of Modern Sociology* 39: 1–28.

Kuper, Adam. 2003. "The Return of the Native." *Current Anthropology* 44(3): 389–402.

Laungaramsri, Pinkaew. 2002. *Redefining Nature: Karen Ecological Knowledge and the Challenge to the Modern Conservation Paradigm*. Chennai: Earthworm Books.

Laurie, Nina, Robert Andolina, and Sarah Radcliffe. 2005. "Ethnodevelopment: Social Movements, Creating Experts and Professionalising Indigenous Knowledge in Ecuador." *Antipode* 37(3): 470–96.

Li, Tania Murray. 2010. "Indigeneity, Capitalism, and the Management of Dispossession." *Current Anthropology* 51(3): 385–414.

Linkenbach, Antje. 2004. "Lokales Wissen im Entwicklungsdiskurs: Abwertung, Aneignung oder Anerkennung des Anderen?" In *Lokales Wissen: Sozialwissenschaftliche Perspektiven*, ed. Nikolaus Schareika and Thomas Bierschenk, 233–57. Münster: Lit.

Merlan, Francesca. 2009. "Indigeneity: Global and Local." *Current Anthropology* 50(3): 303–33.

Miller, Daniel. 2011. *Tales from Facebook*. Cambridge and Malden: Polity Press.

Molyneux, Maxine, and Marilyn Thomson. 2011. "Cash Transfers, Gender Equity and Women's Empowerment in Peru, Ecuador and Bolivia." *Gender & Development* 19(2): 195–212.

Morgan, Gordon. 1997. *Toward an American Sociology: Questioning the European Construct*. Westport, CT: Praeger Publishers.

Muehlebach, Andrea. 2001. "'Making Place' at the United Nations: Indigenous Cultural Politics at the UN Working Group on Indigenous Populations." *Cultural Anthropology* 16(3): 415–48.

Pelican, Michaela. 2009. "Complexities of Indigeneity and Autochthony: An African Example." *American Ethnologist* 36(1): 149–62.

Pfaff-Czarnecka, Joanna, and Gérard Toffin. 2011. "Introduction: Belonging and Multiple Attachments in Contemporary Himalayan Societies." In *The Politics of Belonging in the Himalayas: Local Attachments and Boundary Dynamics*, ed. Joanna Pfaff-Czarnecka and Gérard Toffin, xi–xxxviii. New Delhi: Sage.

Randeria, Shalini. 2003. "Cunning States and Unaccountable International Institutions: Legal Plurality, Social Movements and Rights of Local Communities to Common Property Resources." *European Journal of Sociology* 44(1): 27–60.

Ruttenberg, Tara. 2013. "Wellbeing Economics and Buen Vivir: Development Alternatives for Inclusive Human Security." *PRAXIS: The Fletcher Journal of Human Security* 68(28): 68–92.

Rycroft, Daniel J., and Sangeeta Dasgupta (eds). 2011. *The Politics of Belonging in India: Becoming Adivasi*. Abingdon: Routledge.

Schüttpelz, Erhard. 2007. "Ein absoluter Begriff. Zur Genealogie und Karriere des Netzwerkbegriffs." In *Vernetzte Steuerung: Soziale Prozesse im Zeitalter technischer Netzwerke*, ed. Stefan Kaufmann, 25–46. Zürich: Chronos.

Scott, James. 2009. *The Art of Not Being Governed: An Anarchist History of Upland Southeast Asia*. New Haven, CT: Yale University Press.

Shah, Alpa. 2010. *In the Shadows of the State: Indigenous Politics, Environmentalism, and Insurgency in Jharkhand, India.* Durham, NC: Duke University Press.
Sillitoe, Paul. 1998. "The Development of Indigenous Knowledge: A New Applied Anthropology." *Current Anthropology* 39(2): 223–52.
Smith, Linda Tuhiwai. 2012. *Decolonizing Methodologies: Research and Indigenous Peoples,* 2nd ed. London and New York: Zed Books.
Snively, Gloria, and John Corsiglia. 2001. "Discovering Indigenous Science: Implications for Science Education." *Science Education* 85: 6–34.
Uddin, Nasir. 2014. "Paradigm of 'Better Life': 'Development' among the Khumi in the Chittagong Hill Tracts." *Asian Ethnicity* 15(1): 62–77.
Venkateswar, Sita, and Emma Hughes. 2011. *The Politics of Indigeneity: Dialogues and Reflections on Indigenous Activism.* London and New York: Zed Books.
Verran, Helen. 2001. *Science and an African Logic.* Chicago, IL: University of Chicago Press.
Villalba, Unai. 2013. "Buen Vivir vs. Development: A Paradigm Shift in the Andes?" *Third World Quarterly* 34(8): 1,427–42.
Warren, Kay B., and Jean E. Jackson. 2003. *Indigenous Movements, Self-Representation, and the State in Latin America.* Austin, TX: University of Texas Press.
Ziai, Aram. 2013. "The Discourse of 'Development' and Why the Concept Should Be Abandoned." *Development in Practice* 23(1): 123–36.

PART I

STRUGGLES OVER LAND AND RESOURCES

 1

On the Nature of Indigenous Land
Ownership, Access, and Farming in Upland Northeast India
Erik de Maaker

Indigeneity and Nature

In January 2014 it became clear that the UK-based Vedanta Mining Corporation would lose its concession to mine for bauxite in the Niyamgiri hills of Odisha (India). A campaign by representatives of the Dongria Khond "tribe," actively supported by Survival International, had been successful. The campaign stated that the hills are "sacred" to the Dongria Khond. "To be a Dongria Khond is to farm the hills' fertile slopes, harvest their produce, and worship the mountain god Niyam Raja and the hills he presides over…." In short, "Niyamgiri is our soul," as stated on the webpages about the Dongria land struggle (Survival International 2014). At the core of the campaign was a compelling short documentary film, *Mine, Story of a Sacred Mountain,* narrated by UK celebrity Joanna Lumley, which emphasized the cultural and economic dependence of the Dongria Khond on the Niyamgiri hills.[1] This film helped to convey the struggle of the Dongria Khond for their land to a broad international audience. The campaign by Survival International contributed significantly to rallying support for this cause both internationally and in India, as was evident from the eventual ruling of the New Delhi Supreme Court in their favor. Supporting and explaining that decision, the editorial of the prominent Indian national daily *The Hindu* concluded: "It is beyond doubt that there is an organic connection between tribals and the land … That bond must be respected" (*The Hindu* 2013). Attributing an "indigenous" community, such as the Dongria Khond, a privileged relationship to land and nature is common practice. Claims to such relationships tend to be compelling, and are not easily disputed by either policy makers or the general public on the Indian subcontinent. Alpa Shah has shown, in a study on indigenous politics, environmentalism, and insurgency in the central Indian state of Jharkhand, how indigenous activists' portrayal of the Munda community as "nature loving" played an important role in advocacy for the creation of that state. The creation of Jharkhand by subdividing the state of Bihar, in the year 2000, was generally regarded as a triumph for its "tribal" majority (Shah 2010; see also Chandra 2013).

The two cases mentioned above reveal the leverage that claims based on the assumed privileged relationships of indigenous people to nature can yield. Internationally, the communities which are referred to within India as "tribes," tend to be equated with "indigenous people." Globally, policy makers, journalists, and the general public are open and sympathetic to the idea that the "sacrality" of nature is central to the worldview of indigenous people. This allows perceptions of nature, which such communities supposedly collectively hold, to play a central role in legitimizing claims that extend well beyond vegetation and animals to soil, and thus the "place" at which such groups are or want to be located. These kinds of claims are rooted in oral histories, myths, and religious rituals that state that the people concerned (or better, their predecessors) were the "first" to arrive, and that its members are consequently the oldest settlers on their land (Kuper 2003: 390). Such a claim necessarily denies "firstness" to other inhabitants of the same area, whom it consequently positions as later settlers.

From the 1970s onwards, demands made in the name of indigenous people have increasingly gained international credibility. Indigenous people have come to be perceived as "nations": communities with a shared ethnicity, language, history, and culture. Often, they tend to be cast as victims of "internal colonialism," that is, colonized by the states within which they are located. Consequently, international public opinion is increasingly in favor of indigenous communities maintaining, gaining, or regaining control of the resources they depend on. In several cases, indigenous communities' claims to "firstness" have translated into legal rights, granted (or perhaps better, acknowledged) by the "modern" states in which they are included. Examples include the granting of forest rights by the Brazilian government to the Amazonian Kayapo (Conklin and Graham 1995), the Canadian government's acknowledgment of Inuit land claims in the creation of Nunavut, as well as Australian Aborigines' continuing, and in certain respects successful, struggle for control of ancestral territory (Havemann 1999).

For indigenous communities, nature is often the prime resource upon which people depend for their livelihood. This dependence, coupled with omnipresent "noble savage"-like imaginations, which position indigenous people as almost part of nature, lends credence to the common idea that their connectedness to land is characterized by "deep ecological knowledge" (Karlsson 2006: 187–88). In popular perception, such knowledge assumes a harmonious engagement with nature. Or, as the United Nations Permanent Forum on Indigenous Issues states, "Indigenous people … possess invaluable knowledge of practices for the sustainable management of natural resources" (United Nations Permanent Forum on Indigenous Issues n.d.: 2). Such resource use, which is "traditional" in the sense that it was supposedly also practiced by prior generations, entails techniques of cultivation and extraction that are deemed sustainable, given that they have been supported by the natural environment over many, perhaps innumerable, generations. Because indigenous extractive practices tend to be regarded as far less exploitative than those of their more "modern" competitors (who mine, log, or create large-scale plantations), indigenous demands for land rights are frequently phrased in terms of environmental struggle (Dove 2006). In short, in popular perception, a lot of credibility is granted to what Baviskar (2006: 38) has called the "organic linkage" between indigenous culture and ecology. This also suggests that indigenous land claims are in line with more general conservationists' concerns. To sum up, this positions people such as the Dongria Khond as archetypical conservationists, driven by the "sacrality" which they locate in nature.

For any community to fit in with what Karlsson (2003) has called the "indigenous slot," it is compulsory that they meet the kind of expectations outlined above. This particularly holds for people's perception of nature, and their relatedness to land. More problematically still, it presumes that indigenous communities are internally homogeneous when it comes to perspectives on land and nature, and the kind of engagement this translates into. This is not at all self-evident, as it disregards the often substantial disparities between the interests of urban, educated activists who have the connections and the communicative skills to advocate an indigenous cause at a national and international level, and the (often) rural people on whose behalf they claim to speak (Shah 2010). Romantic and reified interpretations of the cultural practices of the latter then provide the arguments that indigenous activists draw upon.

Referring to these disparate interpretations of culture, Adam Kuper (2003: 395) has argued that "indigenous movements" base themselves on "obsolete anthropological notions and a romantic and false ethnographic vision," thus "fostering essentialist ideologies of culture and identity." Accordingly, claims made with reference to "being indigenous" are then primarily politically motivated, which creates doubts about their authenticity and legitimacy. But rather than playing down the social relevance of indigenous claim making, which would not do justice to the complexity of the political realities in which a term like this figures, I want to follow Barnard (2006). Barnard argues that even though, from the perspective of anthropological theory, indigeneity is an essentialist concept, "the legitimate claims of 'indigenous peoples' appeal not to objective elements of anthropological theory, but to common identities objectified by participants … [and] … who are we to deny the ethnic identity, or the 'indigenous' identity, of others, however unscientific such a claim may seem to us?" (Barnard 2006: 13).

Indigeneity, "Tribe," and Indigenous Activism in India

In India, the formal position of the state is that all Indians are indigenous to the country. Consequently, no citizen is by birth entitled to rights that surpass those of others (Xaxa 2008). Yet the Indian state has instituted policies of preferential discrimination that aim at improving the position of (among others) the communities it categorizes as "tribes." The erstwhile colonial administration coined "tribe" as an administrative category, which has however proven difficult to apply. For instance, going by sociological indicators, it is often impossible to distinguish between "tribes" and castes. Inclusion in the category of "tribe," notably, can be advantageous, given the benefits bestowed by policies of preferential discrimination. There have been quite a few cases where communities earlier categorized as "caste" have managed to be reclassified as "tribe" after a prolonged political struggle.

So what, according to the Indian state, characterizes a "tribe"? According to the Draft National Tribal Policy (a Policy for the Scheduled Tribes of India), "tribes" are "known to dwell in compact areas, follow a community way of living, in harmony with nature, and have a uniqueness of culture, distinctive customs, traditions and beliefs which are simple, direct and non-acquisitive by nature" (Ministry of Tribal Affairs 2006: 2). This suggests that "tribes" are isolated, if not excluded, vis-à-vis encompassing structures such as markets and the state. At the same time, this definition has evolutionist connotations, since "simplicity" of "traditions and beliefs" relegates a "tribal" community to a presumably lower scale on the civilizational ladder. Scholars have severely criticized this usage of the category "tribe" as archaic and deterministic (Bates 1995; Béteille 1998; Rycroft and Dasgupta 2011). Yet many people to whom the concept applies—that is, "tribals"—indicate that they do not necessarily experience it as discriminatory. Quite apart from the question of self-identification, one explanation might be that the Indian state's preferential discrimination policies are on the whole much appreciated.

Beyond the more immediate interests associated with the categorization of communities as "tribal," indigenous claim making is more generally of great political significance in South Asia. One region in which this is particularly evident is Northeast India. In Northeast India, activist groups and political parties playing the indigenous card have dominated the political sphere for decades, and the struggle for political power and state-associated resources has mainly been fought along ethnic lines (Vandekerckhove 2009). The region has gained a reputation over the last four to five decades as one of the most troubled parts of the South Asian subcontinent. Ever since India gained independence from colonial dominance, Northeast Indian insurgent groups have disputed the authority of the Indian state. Apart from electoral contests and civil protests, this has resulted in violent confrontations and draconian counter-insurgency measures (Baruah 2005). Geographically, Northeast India is almost entirely surrounded by international borders. This has allowed militants to seek shelter abroad, outside the reach of the Indian security forces. The insurgent groups tend to phrase their cause in ethno-nationalist terms, positioning themselves as representatives of "communities" or "people" who seek a certain degree of self-rule and self-administration to control natural and other resources, vis-à-vis people who are "outsiders" to their homeland (Bhaumik 2009). The most important resource by far is land, and disputes in relation to it are central to all of the insurgencies of the North Eastern region (Barbora 2002; Fernandes 2005).

One area in which ethno-nationalist insurgent groups have, over the last decade, gained increasing prominence is the Garo Hills. Encompassing the western third of the state of Meghalaya, the Garo Hills have seen an ever-increasing number of militants, who battle the Indian security forces.[2] More so, these insurgent groups challenge the presence of non-Garo people residing in the area. The prime political demand of these militant groups is the creation of Garoland, a separate Garo state that would continue to be part of the Indian union. The influential student unions of the Garo region, as well as some of the regionally important political parties, support this demand. Contrary to the militant groups the latter operate within the confines of Indian democracy. These political groups are primarily composed of urban-based (or at least urban-educated) activists.

All these various indigenous activists claim, for the Garo, an intrinsic relatedness to land, which they locate almost exclusively within the cultural sphere of the rural "traditional" Garo, located in a "rural" environment. Rather than unquestioningly accepting that the Garo, as a "tribal" community, have an "organic linkage" to nature and land, in this chapter I explore Garo villagers' perspectives on their environment. The Garo Hills have been subject to major transformations in terms of the utilization of land as a resource. I argue that these contribute to increasingly objectified and utilitarian perspectives on land.

Statements through Calendar Art

Garo urban, indigenous activists refer in their publicity materials to a traditional Garo culture that is inevitably rural. This is evident, for instance, in the calendars that are distributed by local student associations. The calendars are sold in support of these organizations to private persons and shop owners. They are written in the Garo language, and are primarily of relevance to readers (and speakers) of Garo. A calendar distributed by the A'chik [Garo] Youth and Cultural Organisation (AYCO) for the year 2006 emphasized the closeness to nature of the Garo people in its imagery. The top half of the calendar had pictures of Garo Wangala dancing, which is regarded as emblematic of the Garo community (de Maaker 2013a). The lower half was dedicated to shifting cultivation, or swiddening. Swidden cultivation is generally considered the cornerstone of the "traditional" Garo lifestyle, since it is seen as a technology that has been sustained over centuries, and distinguishes the hill-farming Garo from the communities of the plains.

The AYCO calendar had several smaller picture-inserts, one of which shows a group of Garo youths posing as "real tribesmen" in a swidden. Going by the caption of this inserted picture, the men are positioned in the field to guard it against other people, "enemies," who pose a threat to the control of "Garo soil." The men are dressed in loincloths, which used to be the dress of Garo villagers but is rarely seen nowadays. The youths also wear turbans on top of their long, uncut hair. The headgear, and the uncut hair, are markers of the Garo community religion, although in reality, men belonging to that religion (Songsareks) never untie their hair in public. Moreover, Songsareks tie their turbans tight, and not loose, as is shown in the picture. It is highly unlikely that the Garo youth shown in the calendar are Songsareks, since without exception all urban Garo are Christians. To anonymize their scarcely clothed bodies, and perhaps to reduce the shame Christians are likely to experience due to being pictured in loincloths, the pictured youths have their backs turned to the camera.

Swidden cultivation continues to be important in the Garo Hills, though it is practiced much less now than it was a couple of decades ago. However, swidden cultivation is primarily, if not only, practiced by villagers. Urban youth do not engage in it. They not only consider it tedious to do such work, but also render it a primitive and ineffective agricultural technique, even though it is "truly" Garo. Then, significantly, the bodies of the men shown in the calendar insert mentioned above are relaxed, even though they are keeping guard, suggesting that they are in an environment that is benevolent, a view in line with the globally increasingly dominant "urban" perspective on nature as beautiful, benevolent, and essentially bereft of danger (Ingold 2011). In this chapter, I attempt to explore the Garo relationship to land and nature. The chapter is based on extensive ethnographic fieldwork that I have conducted in the Garo Hills region over the last fifteen years, starting with an intensive two-year fieldwork period, during which I researched changing religious practices in the context of my PhD.

Founding Myths and the Inheritance of Collective Claims

In the following sections I will discuss how Garo villagers perceive and use land, and the swidden cultivation that is traditionally practiced on it. Garo only practice swidden cultivation in hill areas. There, "village heads" (*nokma*s) hold title to what are generally contiguous areas of land (*a'king*). This encompasses the land that people live on, the fields they cultivate, and jungle areas that may or may not in a subsequent year be transformed into swidden. The people who live on the land, most of whom can, in one way or another, trace kin ties to the village head, have the right to use it for hunting, and collecting fruits, wood, and bamboo. In addition, jungle can be cleared to make fields for swidden cultivation. For a couple of decades now, hill land has also been increasingly used for small orchards, as well as for the mining of coal.[3] Land ownership is collective, in that the rights of the village head extend to each of his relatives in the village.[4] The village head (a man) and his wife are categorized as "kin seniors" to many of the villagers, and theirs is a hereditary position that carries over from one village head to the next.[5]

The village head-couple are regarded as the lawful owners, in the sense that they hold legally recognized and recorded property rights. Their title also derives its legitimacy from being rooted in stories of origin. Regarding the village where I conducted most of my fieldwork, people stated that it had been founded "hundreds of years ago," by a couple who had earlier lived in a village about four miles to the north. When the founding couple died, people said, their place was taken by their daughter and her husband, who became the subsequent village heads. This succession continued for at least "a hundred generations."

According to the story of origin, the founding couple brought some heavy boulders from a nearby river and planted these in what would become the center of the new village. The planting of the main boulder required the sacrifice of a human to the *Guira*, a god and ancestor. The head of this victim (it had to be a man) had been buried under the main boulder, I was told. People said that whenever the boulders were replanted, this ritual was repeated, although nowadays the sacrifice of a dog (rather than a human) would do. Quite a few older inhabitants of the village told me that in their youth they had witnessed many of these sacrifices, but since by now the vast majority of the Garo have converted to Christianity, their performance has become very rare.

Conducting sacrifices to the boulder (or rather to *Guira*) was said to be entirely the responsibility of the village head, his wife's close matrilineal relatives, and the spouses of the latter. "Anyone else would become blind or lame," an old man told me. The position of the village head-couple, as heirs to the founders of the village, is thus legitimized by particular ritual capabilities, such as the care of the "seat" of *Guira*. The village head is also in charge of core elements of some of the rituals of the annual cycle (where these are still conducted). From a religious perspective, this vests the village head with major responsibilities regarding the existence of the village, and claims to the land surrounding it that its inhabitants utilize. The boulder, with its capacity to "protect" people, thus also represents part of the claim that people make to the land. Nowadays, due to the omnipresence of Christianity, few people continue to acknowledge deities like *Guira*. Nevertheless, throughout the Garo Hills, the boulders continue to be identified as claims to territory, which in the early twentieth century have translated into legally registered land titles.[6]

A Non-Benevolent Environment?

According to the Garo community religion, the environment in which people live is not necessarily benevolent. Humans and animals did not settle in an "empty" land. Rather, people came to live amidst a variety of entities, generally referred to as *mitdes* (deities), who are mostly of a malevolent nature. The existence of these deities precedes the creation of the world and the humans who inhabit it. The deities are believed to live on blood, or "life fluid," which they suck from people as well as from animals and plants (such as rice). The deities are normally invisible, but people at times encounter them in their dreams. Some of the fiercest deities are located in patches of forest land that, due to the presence of these deities, are regarded as "austere land" (*a'a raka*) that should not be cultivated. A woman who had dreamed of these deities told me that they are "large, muscular people," whose bodies are covered with hair from top to toe. A son of hers, who had also encountered them in his dreams, said: "They tried to tie me up, to beat me to death." People's identification of certain patches of jungle as "austere land" derives from experiential knowledge that has been carried over from preceding generations. But, with regards to most of the deities, they lack any such knowledge, which renders them a "presence" that is both unpredictable and uncontrollable.

Quite apart from these predatory deities, Garo people do not normally experience nature as friendly. Most notably during the wet season, every inch of greenery can harbor unpleasant surprises in the form of leeches, centipedes, poisonous spiders, and snakes. The land around houses is kept clear of any greenery, to reduce the chances of encountering these kinds of creatures. For the same reason, and especially in the rainy season, people will avoid walking through shrubs and grass. This does not mean they are afraid of the environment they live in, but a perception of nature as peaceful and harmonious, as suggested by the Garo indigenous activists' calendar pictures, is certainly unusual to most rural Garo.

Competition, Cooperation, and Exclusion in Swidden-Making

The "organic linkage" to nature that is attributed to indigenous communities is thought to align with an egalitarian social structure (Scott 2009: 18). Throughout much of upland Asia, in which swidden cultivation was (and to a certain degree still is) the dominant mode of production, "hill polities are, almost invariably, redistributive, competitive feasting systems held together by the benefits they are able to disburse" (ibid.: 22). This implies a shared management of resources that make specific demands on the organization of social relationships, and influences the ways in which people engage with land. This also implies, at least according to the community religion of the Garo, making fields in an environment in which humans are but one of many presences.

Each year, in Garo Hills, swidden cultivators open up new fields, which they create in the jungle that covers the hills. Depending on the number of years that it has had to recuperate between cultivations, this vegetation consists either of shrubs or relatively mature trees. Following cultivation, a swidden field should ideally be left fallow for several years. The longer the jungle has had to grow back, the better the soil is able to recuperate and the larger the expected yields. Therefore, in each new year, ideally the oldest jungle should be used to make new swiddens. In preparation for swidden farming, all shrubs are cut and all but the largest trees are chopped down. For several weeks, the cut shrubs and trees are left to dry. Larger tree trunks are sold as firewood; the rest is burned so that the ashes can fertilize the soil.

In November, when the dry season is well underway, male representatives of all the families who would like to cultivate a swidden meet. This meeting, which is chaired by the village head, requires people to agree on the patch, or patches, of forest that will be cleared. As part of my ethnographic fieldwork, I attended three of these meetings, and each time it was difficult for the men to agree. Increasingly, people have started planting orchards on land that was previously used for swidden cultivation, which now renders it almost impossible to clear contiguous stretches of forest. The meetings about new fields are not only meant to decide which stretches of forest will be cleared, but more specifically which family will cultivate which field. Even when covered by trees and shrubs, people can identify the boundaries of fields that have previously been cultivated by small streams, ridges, large trees, and the remnants of paths. These boundaries are known to those who have been involved in previous cycles of cultivation. Having cultivated a field in a prior cycle of cultivation grants a family a certain precedence to claim it again, but whether or not such a right can be effectuated also depends on the relations with the other families that are involved in the claiming of land. In these land "claims," the most important factor is no doubt the hierarchical order in which families choose the fields they desire to work. The family of the title holder to a patch of land and his closest relatives have the right to choose first. Men representing other families who are more distantly related to the title holder can then opt for a field after the others have chosen. Families who are not close kin of the village head but are still residents of the village also have a right to claim a swidden and cultivate it. This pattern of claims is comparable to that of swidden cultivators in neighboring hill areas, and it is also found in other areas of Southeast Asia (Murray Li 2010).

It is advantageous to be able to choose a field first, since field characteristics differ depending on the composition of the soil and its placement on a hilltop, a slope, or in a valley. Swidden cultivation is entirely rain-dependent, and in the Garo Hills, a couple of weeks into the growth season, the rains stop. This leaves fields that are located at the top of a hill relatively dry, which is good for the cultivation of cotton, but less favorable when it comes to vegetables or rice. At the foot of a hill the soil retains moisture, which is more suitable for the latter crops.

Even though families have some sort of rights to earlier worked fields and are aware of its boundaries, the occupation of new swidden is unlikely to be the same as that of a previous cycle of cultivation. Families may want a field that is larger, or smaller, than the one they cultivated previously. From one cycle of cultivation to another, some families may have lost members, or families may even have ceased to exist, while other families have newly come into being. Moreover, over the last century the rural population of the Garo Hills has multiplied at least four-, if not six-fold, and the demand for land has gradually increased. It could also be that people may simply want to work a different field from the one they worked before, to see if it results in better yields. Or they may want to work roughly the same field as before but change its boundaries, making it either bigger or smaller to suit their needs.

Ideally, no family should claim more land than it can work. People speak with disdain of such families, whose fields end up being overgrown with weeds. All this means that negotiations about who will work which field are complicated, demanding, and prone to create conflicts. Conflicting interests are ideally negotiated through long discussions mediated by the most senior men. It is the responsibility of the village head to guarantee that all resident families get access to land, but he can only accomplish this with the support of his wife's close relatives and their in-laws. The collective usage rights of swiddens are thus realized with the consent of the most important families, who in turn support the village head.

Once a meeting in which the men decide about the new fields has ended (and they have in principle reached an agreement), they go to the forest to physically "claim" (*kanga*) their new swidden. This involves a quick survey of the forest, followed by a short ritual that serves to demand an omen from the deities. The man who imposes the claim makes a small clearing, in which he plants a stick that is split at the top. In the split, some folded leaves are placed. The omen is said to come to the one who requested it, in a dream, during the following night. The dream informs the person who claimed the land of its future yield, and thus also, more implicitly, of the judgment of the deities about its cultivation. Although the "claiming" ritual is primarily justified in religious terms, it is of great social significance as well, since it visually displays the entitlement of a certain man to a specific field-to-be vis-à-vis the other men of his village. In this sense, it underscores that the fields that people claim belong to their family only. The claim translates into what is perhaps best termed a private usage right. All the labor required is provided by the family who makes the claim, and the eventual harvest will be its exclusive property.

The Garo community religion, while now seriously marginalized due to the growing number of people who are converting to Christianity, continues to be closely tied to swidden cultivation. It encompasses a variety of mediatory rituals, aimed at negotiating the cultivation of swidden with the omnipresent deities. As significantly, these practices result in the expression of social relationships among villagers that warrant, balance, and "normalize" the use of swidden among the people who, in belonging to a particular village, share its ownership (de Maaker 2013b). Ritual practices that are attributed great significance tend to be primarily the responsibility of the village head, and their conduct emphasizes the importance of the village head-couple for the entire village. At the same time, the village head depends on the support of families that consider themselves closely related to him for the conduct of these rituals. They extend support in terms of supplying cooked rice and meat, as well as by participating in the celebrations. In this sense, the position of the village head depends on the families who "produce" him as a central religious figure. Land distribution practices thus prioritize access to swidden for families who are close to the village head. Moreover, it restricts access to only the inhabitants of the village (but this includes non-Garo who have married into Garo families). This link of rights to occupation and village residence works towards the exclusion of people who do not belong to a given village. Among Garo, the management of land used for swidden cultivation thus foregrounds ties traced among matrilineal kin. Such ties primarily involve Garo, and unless a marital relationship is traced exclude people of different communities.

Inclusion of the Garo Hills into State and Market Structures

The "community way of living," as mentioned in the Indian Draft National Tribal Policy, which is projected onto communities such as the Garo, suggests that people are only partially integrated in the overarching structures of market and state. For the Garo, this may have been true in precolonial times, but currently, they are gradually becoming more and more encapsulated by market and state. In precolonial times, the Garo Hills seem to have consisted of semi-autonomous villages.

Landlords based in the plains and foothills levied tribute at weekly or monthly markets (*hats*), but this did not imply territorial-political or administrative control (Misra 2011). When the colonial state expanded from Bengal to Assam in the early nineteenth century, the Garo Hills were initially omitted, since the area had few resources that were of importance to the colonial economy, and deadly strains of malaria discouraged early colonial administrators and clergymen and -women. When the region was eventually colonized, it became a "lightly" administered district, which allowed for a certain degree of exclusion from colonial control. This state of exclusion was instituted after independence under the sixth schedule of the Indian constitution.

Garo upland farmers have a long history of producing for markets. Over time, the importance of these markets for the sale of their produce, and the acquisition of other goods, has increased. This has led to a change in agricultural practices. Experimentation with the cultivation of permanent crops on the hill slopes has a long history, extending to the early days of colonial expansion in the region. In the village where I did most of my research, older people remembered that when they were young, none of the hill slopes had been permanently cultivated. But over the last two to three decades, there has been a rapid increase in the amount of hill land that is used for orchards. The most popular orchard crops are areca and cashew. Most significantly, villagers themselves have been searching for alternatives to make the cultivation of their fields more profitable. This has been especially notable since the 1980s, when due to reduced rainfall, and the subsequent shortening of the crop cycle, swidden yields began to drop.

The occupational pattern of the swiddens is facilitating a changeover to the cultivation of permanent crops. Rather than abandoning a swidden after two years of cultivation, which was the standard practice until a couple of decades ago, people simply continue to occupy it. Soon after they sow their first swidden crops, those who intend to keep their swidden as an orchard will plant saplings on it. After one or two years, when the field is no longer used as a swidden, they continue to care for the saplings so that these can grow into trees that bear fruit. Even in those locations where land is abundant, this gradual increase of permanent cultivation eventually creates shortages of land that is available for swidden cultivation.

This permanent occupation of land does not translate into ownership rights, but it does create a right to permanent usage that is so "solid" that it can be sold between villagers. The regional body in charge of land management, the Garo Hills District Council, officially supports the continuation of communal land ownership. But contrary to official policy, many officers involved with agriculture in the region are convinced that a change from swidden agriculture to permanent crops is part of an inevitable, and in a way desirable, modernization of agriculture, which necessarily includes the "individualization" of the landholdings that accompany it. Permanent crops are generally considered more profitable, and the resulting cash income is believed to allow families to accumulate surplus more easily than from the subsistence crops that are central to swidden agriculture. However, the price of some of these cash crops, such as areca nuts, has declined for many years in a row. And the prices of cash crops do not necessarily keep pace with inflation, which reveals some of the vulnerabilities of market-oriented agricultural production.

Transforming swiddens into orchards also only makes sense to families who can mobilize the labor to maintain them. Even though areca and cashew trees are relatively low maintenance, people do need to keep them free from weeds and creepers in order for them to thrive. Young saplings, such as those of areca nut trees, also need to be protected from wild and domestic animals, and demand fencing. Since people need to stay close to their orchards, this limits them in maintaining their swiddens, because of the distances between them. Consequently, once orchards gain importance, people end up living dispersed across the land that belongs to their village, abandoning the village nuclei that until recently were considered characteristic of the Garo. This lends further support to the common idea that traditional Garo culture is closely tied to swidden cultivation, and the former loses meaning once the latter ceases to be practiced.

One major consequence of the increasing importance of permanent cultivation is that it "fixes" the access that families have to land. The more families depend on orchards to which they maintain a permanent claim, the less they depend on the village head and the families who are close to him, to obtain access to land. This means that villagers become less dependent on one another, in an economic sense, than they previously were. The communal resource management, which is so much at the center of popular imaginations of indigenous people's connectedness to nature, is increasingly challenged.

Christianity and the Pacification of the Environment

As previously mentioned, according to Garo community religion, the village head not only positions himself as an experienced leader, but also facilitates and hosts some of the most important ceremonial interactions with the deities. Remarkably, it is in villages where most of the land has become permanently cultivated that the majority of people have converted to Christianity. This implies the abandonment of most, if not all, of the earlier religious responsibilities of the village head. Most people are aware of the close link between swidden agriculture and the community religion, and in the cases where swidden agriculture has declined, the practicing of community religion has followed, and vice versa. In addition to ascribing the ownership of the land and the crops it yields to the deities, these celebrations epitomize people's mutual dependencies. In order to make and cultivate swidden, people need to cooperate, and thus overcome any conflicts of interest that they may face.

The conversion to Christianity in the Garo Hills has not so much meant an "erasing" of the traditional cosmology, but rather the imposition of Christian religious tenets onto the existing pantheon (de Maaker 2013b). Christianity projects an omnipotent God, who thus encapsulates the deities and other entities identified within the community religion. The Christian clergy have subsequently emerged, with regards to agriculture, as the negotiators to the divine. People who have become Christians no longer take part in the collective celebrations that are so central to the community religion. The seasonal Christian celebrations that have replaced them no longer emphasize relationships between families, the way those linked to the community religion do, and do not underscore the position of the village head as a senior kinsman to the entire village.

The "privatization" of land use, in combination with the conversion to Christianity, also reduces the mutual dependence between villagers. Previously, economic success would translate into prestige, under a broad array of socioreligious mechanisms. In the course of that translation process, much of the wealth (e.g., animals for meat, and heirlooms or valuables) that people collected would be redistributed in potlatch-like feasting. The conversion to Christianity sharply reduced the need for this redistributive feasting, thereby placing those who are Christians in a better position to accumulate wealth. Nowadays, such wealth typically takes the form of a brick house, or consumer goods such as furniture, a television, a bicycle, or a motorbike—which in turn imbue social status. The weakening of the earlier redistributive mechanisms makes way for an increase in income disparities among villagers. Owning houses and consumer goods is an increasingly important "modern" ideal, in which villagers identify with an "outside" world, in line with their incorporation into global Christianity.

The abandoning of swidden cultivation, combined with the conversion to Christianity, also changes the ways in which people interact with the environment. Since Christianization in a way "numbs" the entities who, according to the community religion, are present in the land, it changes the way in which people perceive the nature amidst which they live. This gradually creates room for a less complicated exploitation of the land, as well as for more objectified notions of nature as "beautiful" and "sound" in its own right. With the predatory entities being granted less of a presence, people are free to use, exploit, and control their environment, without facing the threat of (supernatural) retaliation. Likewise, that same nature can serve as décor for the aspirations of ethno-nationalist groups, who consider themselves the ultimate owners of nature vis-à-vis non-Garo outsiders, against whom they agitate.

Conclusion: Ownership, Access, and Belonging

In this chapter, I have explored Garo perceptions of land and nature, and how these are changing over time. I have shown how these perceptions are inspired by religious ideas, and rooted in agricultural practices. I started out by showing that the "sacrality" of land for indigenous people provides a powerful argument against its alienation by capitalist forces. In the struggle for land fought by the Dongria Khond, it seems likely that this argument proved convincing, and helped them to win the case against the Vedanta mining company. Ethnic activists who campaign for the creation of a Garo homeland, such as the Garo student unions, appeal to a similar sentiment when they call for the defense of Garo soil against outsiders. However, referring to this special relationship in the Garo case seems to neglect the fact that, at least traditionally, Garo did not primarily consider nature as beneficial. According to Garo practitioners of the community religion, the land in which they live is inhabited by primordial entities with whom they need to negotiate its occupation. This negotiation, which involves acknowledgment of the deities as well as extensive sacrifices, creates a privileged relationship, which in turn produces the exclusion of outsiders.

The conversion of many Garo to Christianity has implied gaining control of, if not the numbing of, the deities of the community religion by Christian divinity. People therefore no longer need to justify and negotiate their usage of the land with its primordial owners. Even in the cases where people have not converted to Christianity, and continue to practice the community religion, the growing Christian presence has resulted in a gradual decline of their fear of the primordial entities.

Consequently, these conversions have facilitated more "possessive" and permanent forms of cultivation, for example the creation of orchards. Religious conversions have also weakened the position of the village head, since it has taken away some of the responsibilities of his office. Instead, the authority of the village head has come to depend largely on legal entities created by the Indian state. This shift in terms of legality has contributed significantly to the emergence of conditions that have rendered privatization viable over collective ownership.

In the Garo Hills, indigenous claims tend to be formulated by urban Christian activists, who themselves have little or no involvement with agriculture, or rural life for that matter. Privatized agriculture does not fit with their projections of Garo indigeneity. Rather, they consistently link the latter to swidden cultivation. As I have shown, this emphasis fits in with national expectations of "tribe" and global ideas about indigenous people, but does not necessarily do justice to Garo villagers' much more complex and engaged understandings of the environment in which they live.

Erik de Maaker (PhD, Leiden) is a researcher and lecturer at the Institute of Cultural Anthropology and Development Sociology of Leiden University in the Netherlands. He studied anthropology in Amsterdam and Leiden and wrote a PhD dissertation that takes mortuary rituals as a starting point for an analysis of social and economic transformation in upland Northeast India. His current research focuses on the redefinition of land as a resource, as well as its changing importance in processes of "place" making in the extended eastern Himalayas. Erik has published several articles in academic journals and edited volumes, and is preparing a monograph on economic and religious transformations of society in upland Northeast India. For more details regarding his research and publications, see https://leidenuniv.academia.edu/ErikdeMaaker.

Notes

1. The film was produced by Survival International, and can be viewed on their website at http://www.survivalinternational.org/films/mine (accessed 11 December 2014).
2. In January 2014, Garo Hills had approximately sixteen militant groups. Although no one could give exact numbers, the general impression was that some of these were very small, almost non-existent. Others supposedly counted several dozen, if not several hundred, men and women. Some of the better-known "underground" groups are the Garo National Liberation

Army (GNLA), the A'chik National Liberation Army (ANLA), the Garo Liberation Tigers (GLT), and the A'chik (Garo) Tiger Force (ATF). In 2004 the A'chik National Volunteers Council (ANVC) signed a ceasefire agreement, and is transforming itself into a regular political group. Sections of it have contested local elections as the ANVC-D (Democratic).
3. Coal mining was an important economic activity until early 2014, when the National Green Tribunal (a national Indian Legislative Council) imposed a ban on small-scale unlicensed mining. The ban has been largely successful, and coal mining in the state has mostly come to a halt.
4. Garo social models emphasize kin ties, but it is important to note that kinship is always defined in a broad sense, and thus not limited to relationships defined by "blood." Rather, kinship provides an encompassing social "grid" that allows people to frame all the relationships that they trace among each other. For instance, Garo traditionally value cross-cousin marriages. Given that kinship is classificatory, who exactly qualifies as cross-cousins is open to interpretation.
5. Garo trace matrilineal descent, and village headmanship is carried over from mother to daughter. The headman title thus rests with the husbands of these successive women. This male entitlement through marriage explains why marriage alliances, that are carried over from various generations, tend to be a central cultural concern (de Maaker 2012).
6. This explains why the boulder principle has also been appropriated to substantiate ethno-nationalist claims. In 1997 in Tura, the largest town of the Garo Hills, a *kusi*-boulder was erected by its "citizens" (according to the plaquette placed on it). Its planting, in the central area of Ringre, emphasizes that Tura is above all a "Garo" town. Yet historically, Tura has had a largely non-Garo population, created as it was by the former colonial administration, who brought in a lot of Bengali and Assamese, and lately their numbers have been on the rise. As a reaction to this, it seems, Garo indigenous activists want to claim the city as exclusively Garo.

Bibliography

A'chik Youth and Cultural Organisation. 2006. Jachang (Calendar). Tura: AYCO.
Barbora, Sanjay. 2002. "Ethnic Politics and Land Use: Genesis of Conflicts in India's North-East." *Economic and Political Weekly* 37(13): 1285–92.
Barnard, Alan. 2006. "Kalahari Revisionism, Vienna and the 'Indigenous Peoples' Debate." *Social Anthropology* 14(1): 1–16.
Baruah, Sanjib. 2005. *Durable Disorder: Understanding the Politics of Northeast India*. Delhi and Oxford: Oxford University Press.
Bates, Crispin. 1995. "Lost Innocents and the Lost of Innocence: Interpreting Adivasi Movements in South Asia." In *Indigenous Peoples of Asia*, eds. R.H. Barnes, Andrew Gray, and Benedict Kingsbury, 103–119. Ann Arbour, MI: Association of Asian Studies.
Baviskar, Amita. 2006. "The Politics of Being 'Indigenous'." In *Indigeneity in India*, ed. Bengt G. Karlsson and Tanka B. Subba, 33–50. London: Kegan Paul.

Béteille, André. 1998. "The Idea of Indigenous People." *Current Anthropology* 39(2): 187–92.
Bhaumik, Subir. 2009. *Troubled Periphery: The Crisis of India's North East*. New Delhi: Sage Publications.
Chandra, Uday. 2013. "Beyond Subalternity: Land, Community, and the State in Contemporary Jharkhand." *Contemporary South Asia* 21(1): 52–61.
Conklin, B.A. and L.R. Graham. 1995. "The Shifting Middle Ground: Amazonian Indians and Eco-Politics." *American Anthropologist* 97(4): 695–710.
de Maaker, Erik. 2012. "Negotiations at Death: Assessing Gifts, Mothers and Marriages." In *Negotiating Rites*, ed. Ute Hüsken and Frank Neubert, 43–55. Oxford: Oxford University Press.
———. 2013a. "Performing the Garo Nation? Garo Wangala Dancing between Faith and Folklore." *Asian Ethnology* 72(2): 221–39.
———. 2013b. "Have the Mitdes Gone Silent? Conversion, Rhetoric, and the Continuing Importance of the Lower Deities in Northeast India." In *Asia in the Making of Christianity: Conversion, Agency, and Indigeneity, 1600s to the Present*, eds. Richard F. Young and Jonathan A. Seitz, 135–162. Leiden: Brill.
Dove, Michael R. 2006. "Indigenous People and Environmental Politics." *Annual Review of Anthropology* 35: 191–208.
Fernandes, Walter. 2005. "North Eastern India: Land, Identity and Conflicts." Paper presented at the *Silver Jubilee Lecture, 26 August 2004*. Allahabad: GB Pant Institute of Social Sciences.
Havemann, P. 1999. *Indigenous Peoples' Rights in Australia, Canada, and New Zealand*. Oxford: Oxford University Press.
The Hindu. 2013. "The Significance of Niyamgiri." Retrieved 7 January 2015 from http://www.thehindu.com/opinion/editorial/the-significance-of-niyamgiri/article4677438.ece.
Ingold, Tim. 2011. *The Perception of the Environment: Essays on Livelihood, Dwelling and Skill*. Abingdon: Routledge.
Karlsson, Bengt. 2003. "Anthropology and the 'Indigenous Slot': Claims to and Debates about Indigenous Peoples' Status in India." *Critique of Anthropology* 23(4): 403–23.
———. 2006. "Indigenous Natures: Forest and Community Dynamics in Meghalaya, North-East India." In *Ecological Nationalisms: Nature, Livelihoods, And Identities in South Asia*, ed. Gunnel Cederlöf and K. Sivaramakrishnan, 170–198. Seattle, WA: University of Washington Press.
———. 2011. *Unruly Hills: A Political Ecology of India's Northeast*. New York: Berghahn Books.
Kuper, Adam. 2003. "The Return of the Native." *Current Anthropology* 44(3): 389–402.
Ministry of Tribal Affairs (ed.). 2006. *National Tribal Policy* (draft). New Delhi: Ministry of Tribal Affairs.
Misra, Sanghamitra. 2011. *Becoming a Borderland: The Politics of Space and Identity in Colonial Northeastern India*. New Delhi: Routledge.
Murray Li, Tania. 2010. "Indigeneity, Capitalism, and the Management of Dispossession." *Current Anthropology* 51(3): 385–414.
Rycroft, Daniel J. and Sangeeta Dasgupta (eds). 2011. *The Politics of Belonging in India: Becoming Adivasi*. Abingdon: Routledge.

Sangma, Balsa B. 2008. "The Alienation of Land among the Garos." In *Land, People and Politics: Contest Over Tribal Land in Northeast India*, ed. Walter Fernandes and Sanjay Barbora (eds), *Land, People and Politics: Contest over Tribal Land in Northeast India*, 53–57. Guwahati: North Eastern Social Research Centre.

Scott, J. 2009. *The Art of Not Being Governed: An Anarchist History of Upland Southeast Asia*. New Haven, CT: Yale University Press.

Shah, A. 2010. *In the Shadows of the State: Indigenous Politics, Environmentalism, and Insurgency in Jharkhand, India*. Durham, NC and London: Duke University Press.

Survival International (ed.). 2014. *We'll Lose Our Soul. Niyamgiri Is Our Soul*. Retrieved 11 December 2014 from http://www.survivalinternational.org/tribes/dongria.

United Nations Permanent Forum on Indigenous Issues. n.d. "Factsheet: Indigenous Peoples, Indigenous Voices." Retrieved 7 January 2015 from http://www.un.org/esa/socdev/unpfii/documents/5session_factsheet1.pdf.

Vandekerckhove, N. 2009. "We are Sons of this Soil: The Dangers of Homeland Politics in India's Northeast." *Critical Asian Studies* 41(4): 523–548.

Xaxa, Virginius. 2008. *State, Society, and Tribes: Issues in Post-colonial India*. New Delhi: Dorling Kindersley.

 2

Considering the Implications of the Concept of Indigeneity for Land and Natural Resource Management in Cambodia, Thailand, and Laos

Ian G. Baird

The concept of "indigenous peoples"—which is today often linked to emancipatory support for ethnic minorities—is relatively new to Asia. Of course, the word "indigenous" has been used in Asia by Europeans since at least the nineteenth-century European colonial period, but during that time it was used to distinguish between colonial Europeans and colonized "natives," regardless of ethnic background. In other words, it was an Othering tool of European colonialism, deployed in the defense of colonial power. For example, the British in Burma used the term "indigenous" to distinguish the British from Britain from colonial subjects (Keyes 2002). In French Indochina, the Garde Indigène (Indigenous Guard), a military unit made up of people of Asian descent, was specifically employed to help protect colonial power (Baird 2015). The United States government similarly applied the concept of "indigenous" during the postcolonial period, and in 1975—as the communists were taking over Laos, Cambodia, and Vietnam—Americans working for the Central Intelligence Agency (CIA) were ordered to assist with the evacuation of "Key Indigenous Personnel."[1] The CIA in Cambodia also referred to all Cambodians as "indigenous" during the same period (Conboy 2013). In both of these examples it was citizenship, rather than ethnicity, that was the focus. But since the 1980s and 1990s, some Asians have begun to adopt a new concept of indigeneity, one previously largely restricted to the Americas, Australia, and New Zealand. This new concept is fundamentally different to those previously used.

First, it recognizes and identifies groups based on ethnic difference, not on their country of origin. Second, it is based on self-determination (at least at the United Nations Permanent Forum on Indigenous Issues),[2] something that was not previously the case (see ILO 1989). Third, in Asia it is now frequently associated with those who have historically been "colonized people" (Baird 2008, 2011b; Erni 2008; Gray 1995). It is also a term that is becoming globalized (Dirlik 2003); thus, the concept of indigenous peoples is being exported to various parts of the world, including Southeast Asia. It is becoming increasingly translocal, with intensely global and local elements, hybridized in particular ways depending on the context (Baird 2015). These new meanings of indigenous peoples make it possible for even relatively recent migrants to cross present-day national borders and claim to be indigenous, especially if they were historically dominated or oppressed by those in neighboring countries. It allows for "indigeneity without borders." For example, the Hmong in Thailand and Laos, even though they migrated from China one to two hundred years ago and were not the "first" or the "original" peoples in either country, are now considered by some to be "indigenous peoples" (Baird 2015; Morton and Baird forthcoming). Indeed, "indigenous" is often associated—among both Asians and non-Asians—with the concept of "original" or "first" peoples (Dirlik 2003). But what constitutes arriving first, or being indigenous, remains contested throughout much of the region. Looking at the issue on a scale of continents, or nation-states, some argue that all Asians, or members of particular countries in Asia, are indigenous. The Congress of World Hmong People, a group of Hmong in St. Paul, Minnesota, opposed to the Lao People's Democratic Republic (Lao PDR) government, regularly sends delegations to the United Nations Permanent Forum on Indigenous Issues' annual sessions in New York. Even though they are based in the United States of America and not Laos, they still identify as indigenous peoples (Baird 2015).[3]

Indeed, throughout much of Asia it is not always easy to identify who is indigenous and who is not. As Charles Keyes pointed out in his 2002 Presidential Address to the Annual Meeting of the Association of Asian Studies, "The efforts by others to classify peoples of Asia by race all have failed because of the fact that all humans can interbreed, and physical characteristics do not remain unchanged among the same people from one generation to the next" (Keyes 2002: 1,166). Nevertheless, most governments in Asia have adopted variations of what has become known in scholarly circles as the "saltwater theory," which involves recognizing the concept of indigenous peoples in places where European settler colonization has occurred, but not in Asia where it happened to a much lesser extent. Thus, for many governments in the region, the designation of indigenous peoples is relevant globally, yet not in their own particular circumstances. It was with this understanding that many governments in Asia agreed to sign the United Nations Declaration on the Rights of Indigenous Peoples (UNDRIP) in September 2007 (Baird 2011b, 2015). The debate regarding who should be considered indigenous and who should not has been coined by Benedict Kingsbury as the "Asian controversy" (Kingsbury 1998, 1999).

Nevertheless, over the last couple of decades, the concept of indigenous peoples has become increasingly accepted in parts of Asia, with some governments recently legally recognizing the existence of indigenous peoples in their countries, including the Philippines, Taiwan (Republic of China), Japan, and Cambodia (IWGIA 2009, 2010). In each of these countries, the legal recognition of indigeneity has been relevant in relation to cultural protection and language-use rights issues, but it has also been particularly significant for gaining access to, or excluding others from, land and other natural resources (Hall 2013; Hall, Hirsch, and Murray Li 2011). That is, the recognition of indigeneity has had important implications in relation to nature–society relations, including land and resource tenure. For example, in the Philippines the designation of "ancestral domain" for indigenous peoples has given them significant rights over land and resources (Bertrand 2011; Bryant 2000; Theriault 2011, 2013), and in Taiwan increased rights over particular lands and resources have been granted to indigenous peoples since their indigenous status was recognized (IWGIA 2009).

In this chapter, however, I focus on just three countries in mainland Southeast Asia—Cambodia, Thailand, and Laos—and the role that the newly developing concept of indigenous peoples has had, and is having, on land and resource access and tenure issues over the last couple of decades. Indeed, despite the governments of all three countries having signed the UNDRIP, the concept of indigenous peoples has been accepted to varying degrees, with differing impacts in each country. In Cambodia, the legal designation of indigenous peoples was first established in the 2001 Land Law and 2002 Forestry Law, which have had significant impacts on land and resource tenure issues (see Baird 2011b, 2013; Keating 2013; Milne 2013; Padwe 2013; Swift 2013). In Thailand, however, "indigeneity" has not been officially recognized by the government, but is nevertheless becoming increasingly utilized among academics, non-government organizations (NGOs), and some government officials and rural peoples (Morton and Baird forthcoming). Due to a lack of official recognition, though, the concept has so far had limited influence on natural resource management, although it has been evoked during some contentious debates and claims regarding land and natural resources over the last couple of decades. There have been attempts to employ the concept of indigeneity to protect land and resource rights of indigenous peoples, albeit sometimes with limited impact (Baird 2015, 2016; Milne 2013). Still, indigenous leaders are increasingly conceptualizing and articulating their concerns within an indigenous peoples framework (Morton and Baird forthcoming). In Laos, the government has recently shown increased resistance to the idea of indigeneity, despite earlier efforts by NGOs, multilateral banks, and the United Nations to introduce the concept, often in the context of natural resource management (Baird 2015). Here we examine in further depth the varying ways that the concept of indigeneity is impacting land and natural resource management in these three countries.

Cambodia

When the present constitution of Cambodia was adopted in 1993, there was no mention of indigenous peoples, "ethnic minorities," or even more generally "ethnic nationalities." It referred only to "Khmer people" and the "Khmer nation." However, by the end of the 1990s, international NGOs working in Cambodia were able to effectively introduce the concept of "indigenous peoples" (*chunchiet doeum pheak tech* in Khmer) to the country, and through advocacy efforts which I have described in detail elsewhere (Baird 2011b) successfully had the concept inserted into Land Law in 2001 and Forestry Law in 2002.[4]

The most significant aspect of the 2001 Land Law for Indigenous Peoples was the establishment of precedent for recognizing indigeneity at the community level. Indeed, Article 23 of the law explicitly defined the term "indigenous community," a first for Cambodia, as "a group of people that resides in the territory of the Kingdom of Cambodia whose members manifest ethnic, social, cultural and economic unity and who practice a traditional lifestyle, and who cultivate the lands in their possession according to customary rules of collective use." The spatiality of the term and its link to customary forms of land and natural resource use is clearly evident.

The most important practical aspect of the 2001 Land Law has been the provision of the right for those defined as indigenous peoples to obtain communal land titles.[5] Article 25 states: "The lands of indigenous communities are those lands where the said communities have established their residences and where they carry out traditional agriculture … The lands of indigenous communities include not only lands actually cultivated but also includes reserved land necessary for the shifting of cultivation..." Critically, the law does not allow ethnic Khmer people to obtain communal land titles. This distinction has been crucial in legally separating people in Cambodia based on ethnic background, and providing these different groups with different rights by law. At the time the 2001 Land Law was enacted, there were no standards for how to legally distinguish between indigenous and non-indigenous peoples. Thus, in 2009, the Government of Cambodia (GoC) adopted a sub-decree regarding communal land titling for indigenous peoples that includes steps for registering communities as indigenous, making them eligible to receive communal land titles (Baird 2013).

Since the adoption of the 2009 sub-decree, various communities have made efforts to navigate the sometimes frustrating multi-step process for registering indigenous communities. Because of the complex and expensive nature of the process, communities engaged in this registration process receive support from NGOs and international donor agencies. While few communal land titles have been granted so far, as of January 2012 there were 153 villages at various stages of either being registered as an indigenous entity or receiving a communal land title as a registered indigenous community (Baird 2013).

It might actually be more advantageous to allow all Cambodians—not just the 1–1.4 percent of the population who are classed as "indigenous"—to obtain communal land titles, as this could lead to greater societal support for communal land titles in the country (Baird 2013). In Laos, for example, communal land titling has also been introduced, but is permitted for all citizens regardless of ethnicity (Bounmany, Phommasane, and Greijmans 2012). In addition, while in Cambodia communal land titles cover only agricultural lands and land being reserved for agriculture, and not areas of forest, in Laos communal land titles can encompass significant areas of forest as well, an option that would appear to fit the actual needs and desires of local people much better (Baird 2013).

While only a small number of communities (villages) in Cambodia have so far been granted communal land titles, many are expected to receive them in the near future (Baird 2013). Still, the process has been frustratingly slow, and heavily dependent on foreign donor support to pay for the implementation of the legal process. Thus, one could say that the biggest impact of the introduction of communal land titling for indigenous peoples in Cambodia has not been any great practical gains in the ensuring of land security, but rather the adoption of the concept of indigenous peoples. This concept has been ontologically significant by creating a legally recognized boundary between indigenous and non-indigenous peoples, a designation with the potential to benefit the population of Cambodia believed to be indigenous, but also to create divisions and incite conflict between indigenous and non-indigenous peoples, through the granting of different legal rights (see Baird 2016). Moreover, in the minds of many Khmers, the concept of indigenous peoples serves to reify them as "primitive relics of the past," who due to racialized differences require particular attention and support from the majority Khmer population. Illustrative of this sort of Khmer mindset, Prime Minister Hun Sen stated that those designated as indigenous peoples would lose their "indigenous" status once they had become "developed" up to the level of the majority Khmer population (see Baird 2011b). In another more recent case in 2012, the prime minister visited the indigenous peoples'-dominated northeastern province of Ratanakiri to hand out land titles. During his visit, four indigenous ethnic Jarai people from the Bokeo District tried to present him with a petition related to a land dispute they were having with an outside Cambodian company, on which he commented: "I was so angry. Do you want to have development or do you want to have the indigenous people collecting stuff in the forest?" (Ratha 2012). He later contradictorily qualified that he would protect the land and natural resources of indigenous peoples (Ratha 2012). These comments indicate that for Prime Minister Hun Sen (and presumably many other Khmers), the concept of indigeneity is fundamentally linked to being primitive and undeveloped, and remains contested and confusing to most. Kuper (2003), in a similar vein, criticized the use of the concept of indigeneity in North America because it supported a similar idea of "the return of the native."

The 2002 Forestry Law in Cambodia also provides particular rights to indigenous peoples, stating in Article 15 that anyone with a logging concession must ensure "that the operation does not interfere with ... [c]ustomary user rights taking place on land property of indigenous community [sic] that is registered with the state consistent with the Land law." In addition, Article 37 of the same law stipulates that "local communities that traditionally practice shifting cultivation may conduct such practices on land property of indigenous community [sic] which registered with the state." The demonstrated impact of this law so far has, however, been less than hoped for by indigenous peoples and their supporters.

In conclusion, it is evident that although the current circumstances of indigenous peoples in Cambodia remain far from ideal, at the same time advances in the legal recognition and support for the rights of indigenous peoples to access land and natural areas have surpassed those in Thailand and Laos, the other two countries that are the focus of this chapter. I now turn my attention to those countries, beginning with Thailand.

Thailand

Approximately 2.3 percent of Thailand's population consists of ethnic minorities or indigenous peoples (Clarke 2001). Unlike in Cambodia, however, the concept of "indigenous peoples" (*chon phao pheun muang* in Thai) has not yet been legally recognized, and those considered to be indigenous are frequently treated by Thai officials and society as inferior or even as if they were not Thai citizens (Clarke 2001; Kampe 1997; Keyes 2002; Morton and Baird forthcoming). Illustrative of the official position, the government of Thailand informed the United Nations in 1992 that hill tribes in Thailand are *"ethnic groups"* but *"are not considered to be minorities nor indigenous peoples* but as *Thais who are able to enjoy fundamental rights ... as any other Thai citizen"* (Kingsbury 1999: 357; emphasis in original). They also reiterated this claim in the early 2000s (Morton and Baird forthcoming). Thailand is unique to mainland Southeast Asia in that large numbers of ethnic minorities living in upland areas in northern Thailand have either only recently been granted citizenship, or are still awaiting citizenship, even in cases where they were born on Thai soil (Kampe 1997; Keyes 2002; Leepreecha, McCaskill, and Buadaeng 2008; Morton and Baird forthcoming), although recently there have been some improvements. The Thai government has tended to distinguish upland peoples both discursively and legally as "non-Thai"; that is, they are typically referred to racially as *"chao khao"* or "hill tribes," without explicitly linking them to the Thai nation (Keyes 2002), something that separates Thai policy from that of many other Asian countries since the end of the European colonial era (Baird 2011b, 2015; LFNC 2005). Although more recently they have been referred to as *"chao thai phu khao"* or "mountain Thais," a policy to encourage minorities to feel "Thai" has been relatively slow to develop, this term is rarely used in common discussion. Still, the indigenous peoples' movement in the country has grown significantly over the last couple of decades (Leepreecha, McCaskill, and Buadaeng 2008; Morton and Baird forthcoming), and there is now a strong network of indigenous advocacy organizations, academics, and individuals supporting this movement. This network is concentrated in the northern Thai city of Chiang Mai and surrounding areas. While many in this network recognize peoples to be *"chon phao pheun muang"* (indigenous peoples), there has been considerable debate regarding whether this term is appropriate, or whether another relatively recently coined Thai term, "*chattiphan,*" which refers to different ethnic groups (Keyes 2002), is preferable (Baird et al. 2017; Morton and Baird forthcoming). To elaborate on this debate would, however, exceed the scope of this chapter.

While advocacy efforts by NGOs in the mid to late 1990s, related to establishing community forestry legislation, did not explicitly draw on the concept of indigeneity, land and forest rights have nonetheless been a key priority for the indigenous movement in Thailand since its emergence in the early 1990s (Morton and Baird forthcoming. For example, Prasert Trakansuphakon (1996: 176) wrote: "Tribal/indigenous organizations were established in 1993 as a result of a number of traditional villages realizing the need to organize themselves in response to the pressures of government [agriculture and forestry] policy and its relocation plans." Chayan Vaddhanaputhi (1996: 83) also reported on villager demonstrations in northern Thailand in 1995:

> In May 1995, there was a large demonstration by ethnic minorities, mostly Karen, protesting against the Royal Forest Department's policy of relocation and implementation of watershed conservation programmes which will not allow people to continue to live there. The hill-tribe peoples' demonstration is the first such event in modern Thai history and indicates the frustration of the minority peoples who have not been treated justly. This clearly reflects the problematic of the relationship between the state and the ethnic minorities.

The indigenous peoples' movement maintains a vested interest in linking indigeneity with land and natural resource management issues, in cases where they affect community livelihoods. In fact, some involved in the movement have advocated using the term *chon phao pheun muang* instead of *chattiphan* because they believe that indigenous peoples have particular problems distinct from those of other ethnic minority groups, such as securing full legal citizenship and land rights, and that the framework of indigeneity is the most appropriate for addressing these problems (Morton and Baird forthcoming). Indeed, the natural resource management issues linked to particular government policies and practices are key arguments for many activists in justifying further advocacy of indigenous rights in Thailand.

In the early 1990s, indigenous NGOs, including the Thai NGO IMPECT and the regional NGO based in Thailand, the Asia Indigenous Peoples Pact (AIPP), began to work closely with international NGOs from Europe and North America to support efforts to prevent deforestation and degradation of tropical and subtropical forests in Southeast Asia. These indigenous NGOs partnered with such international groups as the Forest Peoples Programme (FPP), the International Alliance of Indigenous and Tribal Peoples of the Tropical Forests (IAITPTF), and other European groups such as the Dutch organization Novib, thus elevating struggles over land rights and protection of forests by the indigenous movement in Thailand to international levels.

One important example of the use of narratives relating to indigenous peoples' rights to land and natural resources in Thailand involved attempts by an activist for Akha rights, the American Matthew McDaniel, to raise concerns about the extensive loss of agricultural and forest lands by a number of Akha communities beginning around the year 2000. The situation became particularly tense in 2003 when Akha communities from the Yooh Hoh area in the Mae Fah Luang District in the Chiang Rai Province lost most of their land to a Royal Project supported by the Queen of Thailand. In response, McDaniel organized an international campaign that linked the Akha he was defending with the concept of indigeneity. Although McDaniel was expelled from Thailand over the issue in April 2004, he continued to campaign from abroad for the return of the land taken by the project to the Akha. In 2007, McDaniel was able to enlist the support of Rudolfo Stavenhagen, the United Nations special rapporteur on indigenous issues, who investigated and took action on behalf of the Akha. Thus, on 8 October 2007, Mr Stavenhagen, along with the UN special rapporteur on food, officially brought the issue to the attention of the government of Thailand. In April 2008, the government responded to the allegations as follows:

> The Royal Thai Government ... does not recognize the existence of indigenous peoples in Thailand ... Hill Tribes peoples in Thailand are migrants to the country, who by nature and historical background are not indigenous to the country. The Government noted that, since there are no indigenous peoples in Thailand, it is under no obligation to make clarifications pertaining to indigenous issues, but since the allegations presented, according to the Government, defame and tarnish the reputation and noble image of the royally-sponsored Project, which has been recognized worldwide as a model for sustainable alternative development and community empowerment, the Government considered it necessary to respond.[6]

The campaign certainly succeeded in garnering attention from the government of Thailand, and made them realize that even a Royal Project could be drawn into such a fray. It also resulted in only a partial confiscation of lands from the Akha villages, instead of a complete confiscation, the most likely outcome had McDaniel not organized the campaign. In the end, however, McDaniel can be seen as being only partially successful, as he was unable to pressure the Royal Project to return all the land that it had taken from the Akha villages.[7]

Indigenous activists in Thailand have recently unsuccessfully tried to gain Thai government support for draft legislation associated with the recognition of indigenous peoples in Thailand. Thailand's Office of Ethnic Affairs prefers the term *chattiphan* to the more political concept of *chon phao pheun muang*, or indigenous peoples (see Baird et al. 2017).

This notwithstanding, there have been some promising developments in recent years. In particular, in 2010 the Thai government agreed, in two separate cabinet resolutions, to establish "special cultural zones" (*khet wattanatham phiset* in Thai) for the seafaring Moken or "Chao Lay" people in southern Thailand and the ethnic Karen in western and northern Thailand.[8] The first resolution, issued on 2 June, was titled "Revitalizing the Sea People's Way of Life." The second, adopted on 3 August, was titled "Revitalizing the Karen Way of Life." These resolutions fall short of recognizing the concept of indigeneity, but they are significant developments, as they at least provide government recognition and support for protecting the particular lifestyles and livelihoods of two groups of people based on ethnicity—a first for Thailand. It is not surprising, for various reasons, that the Karen were among the first to be connected to this sort of designation, as their agricultural and natural resource management practices have been romanticized to some extent among activists and scholars (see Forsyth and Walker 2008; Walker 2001). Many Karen also have closer ties and a longer history with Thai lowlanders and Buddhism than other ethnic groups such as the Hmong, Iu-Mien, Akha, Lisa, and Lahu, thus making them potentially more acceptable and familiar to Thai government officials.

While the practical value of these resolutions remains to be seen, and while they have been criticized by some Thai academics for not going far enough, they have so far resulted in the establishment of provincial committees in each of the provinces where substantial numbers of people from these two groups are found. These committees are tasked with developing plans for successfully protecting the cultures of these groups, including considering ways in which aspects of local cultures linked to natural resource management can be protected. The proposed measures have important potential to provide these indigenous communities with more rights in relation to their self-management of natural resources, although the extent to which they can be effectively implemented remains uncertain. Other indigenous groups in Thailand have also expressed interest in having similar "special cultural zones" designated for them, but it remains unclear whether these groups will receive the same considerations.

The following excerpt from an August 2011 statement made by indigenous representatives on behalf of the Network of Indigenous Peoples and Ethnic Groups in Thailand, on the occasion of the Fifth Festival of Indigenous Peoples in Thailand, at Thapae Gate in Chiang Mai, illustrates the link between the indigenous peoples' movement and land and resource issues:

> Our cultures are closely attached to our land, water and forest resources, especially with respect to the rotational farming which has been part of our identity and traditions for generations. This right is enshrined in the Thai constitution of 2007 under Articles 66 and 67, as well as many international laws including the International Convention on Bio-diversity (Articles 8[j] and 10[c]).
>
> We ask the responsible government agencies to work for the revision of laws and policies on natural resources conservation and management which conflict with the constitution and international agreements and obligations. Moreover, we call for the cessation of actions which diminish and abuse these rights of community use of natural resources in a sustainable manner and institution of measures promoting community rights and authority in environmental resource management. Mechanisms must be in place which ensure joint and genuine community-state participation, as well as state policies and laws which clearly specify local and community rights in these matters.[9]

Interestingly, indigenous activists are linking their narratives to the Thai constitution (see Baird et al. 2017) and international agreements such as the Convention on Biodiversity. Even if indigenous peoples are not yet legally recognized in Thailand, their movement has certainly become more sophisticated than it was just a few decades ago.

Lao People's Democratic Republic

The Lao People's Democratic Republic (Lao PDR or Laos) has the greatest ethnic diversity of the three countries under consideration here, and it is generally acknowledged that over half of the population of the country is made up of people outside of the dominant Lao ethnic group and that at least one-third of the population speak first languages other than those in the Tai-Lao language family (IWGIA 2009). The Government of Laos (GoL) recognizes forty-nine distinct ethnic groups, and over 160 ethnic subgroups (IWGIA 2013; LFNC 2005). Although the GoL has not recognized the concept of "indigenous peoples" (*xon phao pheun muang* in Lao), they have nevertheless recognized people from all ethnic groups within their territorial confines as lawful citizens (Baird 2015). For example, Article 22 of the 1991 constitution of Lao PDR states: "Ethnic groups are all equal before the law." In line with this, the GoL has long been firmly against discrimination based on ethnicity. For example, in 2009 the vice-president of the Lao Front for National Construction (LFNC) was quoted by the *Vientiane Times* (2009) as stating, "any acts creating division and discrimination among ethnic groups were prohibited." However, the GoL abides by a version of the saltwater theory, which fits with their longstanding policy that all citizens, whether they belong to an ethnic group or not, have equal rights (Baird 2015; LFNC 2005; *Vientiane Times* 2009). This is essentially a policy that recognizes ethnic diversity, but is ultimately founded on equality between ethnic groups rather than differences. Multicultural equality is the officially stated goal, even when the reality often falls short of official rhetoric, as reflected in the examples of restrictions associated with swidden or shifting cultivation, and the resettlement of minorities from villages in the uplands to settlements along major roads and in the lowlands (Baird and Shoemaker 2007).

There were reasons to believe that the GoL was becoming more accepting of the concept of indigenous peoples in the mid to late 2000s. In 2007, for example, they signed onto the UNDRIP, as did all other countries in Asia, and in 2008 and 2009 the United National Development Programme (UNDP) collaborated with the Ministry of Foreign Affairs and the LFNC to recognize "Indigenous Peoples' Day" in Vientiane, the capital city (IWGIA 2010; Phongkhao 2008; *Vientiane Times* 2009). Since then, however, no further government-endorsed celebrations have been permitted. Moreover, over the last few years, the GoL has increasingly objected to the use of the term "indigenous peoples" in project documents prepared by NGOs, international organizations, and donors, typically insisting on its replacement with the term "ethnic peoples." Furthermore, whereas at least two local organizations linked to particular ethnic groups were registered in around 2009 (IWGIA 2011), the GoL is not presently allowing any new civil society organizations, or non-profit associations (NPAs) as they are known in Laos, to register if they have links to ethnic groups. Illustrative of this trend, on 27 April 2012 the Interior Division of Champasak Province, in southern Laos, denied the request made by a group of indigenous peoples to establish an NPA linked to "ethnic groups" in the province. The reason given for this denial was that the NPA would not be related to vocational training, and was therefore prohibited due to local interpretation of the Lao law. In addition, written correspondence stated that the LFNC and other GoL officials were sufficiently positioned to work with the different ethnic groups, thus making such an NPA unnecessary (Saisopha 2012).

The main organizations that have been at the forefront of promoting an indigenous agenda in Laos have been NGOs, multilateral banks, and organizations within the United Nations system (Baird 2015). NGOs have introduced and repeatedly used the concept of indigenous peoples through various interactions with indigenous peoples and their ethnic Lao and international supporters, and have provided funding and other forms of assistance for particular natural resource management initiatives, where indigenous peoples' rights are the main focus. In recent years, this has included providing support for local chapters of regional initiatives such as the Indigenous Knowledge and Peoples Network (IKAP) and the Co-Management Learning Network (CMLN).[10] Both IKAP and CMLN in Laos have collaborated with the Global Association for People and the Environment (GAPE), a Canadian NGO. IKAP has also partnered with local organizations interested in indigenous knowledge issues. With regard to CMLN, GAPE has been working with local governments and indigenous peoples, located within and adjacent to the Xe Pian National Protected Area in the southernmost part of the country, in order to improve relations between indigenous peoples and government, and to provide indigenous peoples with more of a voice in managing the National Protected Area (Baird 2015).

Both the Asia Indigenous Peoples Pact (AIPP) and the International Work Group for Indigenous Affairs (IWGIA), the main NGOs supporting the indigenous movement in Asia at regional levels, have taken a strong interest in natural resource management issues of various types, including those in recent years related to dramatic increases in large-scale land concessions to private corporations and other forms of land grabbing (NGO Forum on Cambodia 2006; see also Baird 2010, 2011a, 2013; Keating 2013; Neef, Touch, and Chiengthong 2013; Swift 2013), conflicts associated with protected area management (Colchester and Erni 1999; Howitt, Connell, and Hirsch 1996), and climate change mitigation measures related to land and forest management (AIPP et al. 2010). Indicative of this, the IWGIA has given GAPE funding to provide indigenous peoples facing critical land alienation with basic legal training, so as to support their efforts to both resist attempted land concessions and negotiate better deals when resistance is not viable. Thus, much of the NGO support for the concept of indigenous peoples in Laos has been linked to natural resource management issues of various types.

Multilateral banks, such as the World Bank and the Asian Development Bank (ADB), have also played important but quite different roles in introducing the concept of indigenous peoples to Laos and other countries in Asia (ADB 1998, 2002; World Bank 2005). The World Bank and ADB have both adopted operational directives on indigenous peoples that have been significant in promoting a global concept of indigeneity in Asia. These policies stipulate that if development projects supported by the banks have the potential to negatively impact on indigenous peoples, the proponents of the projects are required to develop "Indigenous Peoples' Plans" in order to ensure that indigenous issues are being adequately considered and mitigated. As the ADB states on its website:

> ADB's indigenous peoples safeguards aim to ensure that the design and implementation of projects foster full respect for indigenous peoples' identity, dignity, human rights, livelihood systems, and cultural uniqueness as defined by the indigenous peoples themselves so that they receive culturally appropriate social and economic benefits, are not harmed by the projects, and can participate actively in projects that affect them.[11]

Despite these policies, the insistence on Indigenous Peoples' Plans has not had a great deal of measurable impact in Laos, due to the fact that the banks have done little to promote the concept of indigenous peoples in the public realm, leaving the concept as one that exists internally in the implementation of their own operational project policies. Moreover, some of the projects they have supported have not appropriately recognized groups of indigenous peoples (Manorom, Baird, and Shoemaker 2017).

The third organizational group that has had an influence on the indigenous movement in Laos is the United Nations. They have supported the development of the concept of indigeneity in Laos through the ILO Convention 169 (ILO 1989), the UNDRIP, and most recently through the United Nations Reduced Emissions from Deforestation and Degradation (UN-REDD) program. In particular, UN-REDD, together with various international donors and NGOs, has attempted to introduce "Free Prior and Informed Consent" (FPIC) to Laos, a concept initially intended to ensure that indigenous peoples are fully informed and consulted about, and that they are in favor of, pertinent REDD+ projects before they proceed. Indeed, Article 19 of the UNDRIP requires governments to "consult and cooperate in good faith with the indigenous peoples concerned through their own representative institutions in order to obtain their free, prior and informed consent before adopting and implementing legislative or administrative measures that may affect them." However, since 2009, FPIC has not only been applied (in Laos and other countries) in cases of indigenous peoples affected by REDD+ projects, but also for other forest-dependent people regardless of their ethnicity or status in terms of indigeneity (GIZ 2011). In any case, the GoL would not have allowed FPIC if it had only been applicable to indigenous peoples. However, the GoL has approved guidelines for consulting with people from ethnic groups who have been negatively impacted by development projects (Vongsack 2013), so there does appear to be some development in the ability to differentiate between ethnic groups, provided that the concept of indigenous peoples is not applied.

Conclusions

The key conclusion when it comes to considering the impacts of the concept of indigenous peoples in Cambodia, Thailand, and Laos is that it is a concept strongly associated with nature–society relations. These include land and natural resource management issues, albeit in different ways, and with varying levels of impact in the three countries. It is also clear that, in general, the impact of the newly introduced concept of indigeneity has been uneven, not only between the countries discussed in this chapter, but within each of the countries as well, based on a number of political, geographical, economic, and historical factors. This certainly has a lot to do with the fact that the government of Cambodia recognizes the concept of indigenous peoples, while the governments of Thailand and Laos do not. However, the policies of Laos and Thailand with regards to indigenous peoples also differ significantly. Thailand has designated special cultural protection zones based on ethnic differentiation, while Laos, despite its refusal to develop policies that differentiate based on ethnicity and instead strongly advocating for equality between peoples from all ethnic groups, has nevertheless introduced special guidelines for consulting "ethnic groups" about the impacts of development projects.

Essentially, the present concept of indigenous peoples, one that is linked to the global indigenous peoples' movement and emancipatory efforts to support groups seen to be disadvantaged and historically colonized, is being introduced to different places in mainland Southeast Asia with varying effects, depending on the circumstances. This leads to the development of hybrid policies and practices, and sometimes confused and contradictory positions, thus opening up a fascinating field for study. While the concept of indigenous peoples is increasingly gaining recognition in Asia, it is also certainly true that it remains a highly contested idea, one that is likely to develop and transform in different and potentially surprising ways in the coming years.

Ian G. Baird (PhD, British Columbia) is Associate Professor of Geography and Southeast Asian Studies at the University of Wisconsin-Madison. Before coming to UW-Madison in 2010, he spent most of the previous twenty-five years living in Southeast Asia and working for

NGOs. He has considerable experience conducting research in both lowland and upland mainland Southeast Asia, especially Laos, Thailand, and northeastern Cambodia. He works in particular with ethnic Lao, Thai, Hmong, and Brao peoples. He has been conducting research regarding indigeneity in Cambodia, Laos, and Thailand for many years. He edited special sections for peer-reviewed journals focused on "Indigeneity and Natural Resources in Cambodia" for *Asia Pacific Viewpoint* in 2013, and on "Indigeneity in Southeast Asia" for *Asian Ethnicity* in 2016.

Notes

An earlier version of this chapter was presented at "Futures in Indigeneity: Spatiality, Identity Politics and Belonging," a workshop at the Ruhr University in Bochum, Germany, 6–8 November 2013. I would like to thank Dr Nasir Uddin for allowing me to participate, and the Graduate School of the University of Wisconsin-Madison for supporting part of the travel costs to attend the workshop. Micah Morton, Matthew McDaniel, Richard Hackman, and various others in Cambodia, Thailand, and Laos assisted in providing data.

1. Interview with an anonymous Central Intelligence Agency officer who worked in Laos in 1975, 20 August 2013.
2. For the last twelve years, in May, the United Nations Permanent Forum on Indigenous Issues has organized ten-day sessions in New York, where members of many self-declaring indigenous peoples, including those not necessarily recognized by national governments, address indigenous issues.
3. See http://www.cwhp.net/Indigenous.html (accessed 24 January 2015).
4. Government of Cambodia 2001. *Land Law.* NS/RKM/0801/14. Phnom Penh; Government of Cambodia 2002. *Law on Forestry.* NS/RKM/0802/016. Phnom Penh.
5. There has been considerable interest among the indigenous movement in Asia to develop communal land rights for indigenous peoples (see, e.g., Colchester 2004).
6. See http://www.akha.org/upload/documents/2008thaigovresponsehoohyoh.pdf (accessed 24 January 2015).
7. Matthew McDaniel, personal communication, 30 October 2013.
8. The so-called "Chao Lay" have other names for themselves in their own languages, for example Moken.
9. Fifth Annual "Festival of Indigenous Peoples in Thailand," 7–9 August 2011 [2554], Chiang Mai.
10. The IKAP network includes partners in Laos, Burma, Thailand, Vietnam, Cambodia, and southwestern China. CMLN originally involved partners in Laos, Cambodia, Vietnam, Thailand, Malaysia, Indonesia, and the Philippines.

11. See http://www.adb.org/site/safeguards/indigenous-peoples (accessed 24 January 2015).

Bibliography

ADB (Asian Development Bank). 1998. *Policy on Indigenous Peoples.* Manila: ADB.

——— (ed.). 2002. *Indigenous Peoples, Ethnic Minorities and Poverty Reduction, Cambodia.* Manila: ADB.

AIPP (Asia Indigenous Peoples Pact), FPP (Forest Peoples Programme), IWGIA (International Work Group for Indigenous Affairs), and Tebtebba (eds). 2010. *What to Do with REDD? A Manual for Indigenous Trainers.* Chiang Mai: St. Film and Plate.

Baird, Ian G. 2008. "Colonialism, Indigeneity and the Brao." In *The Concept of Indigenous Peoples in Asia: A Resource Book,* ed. Christian Erni, 201–221. IWGIA Document No. 123. Copenhagen and Chiang Mai: IWGIA and AIPP.

———. 2010. "Land, Rubber and People: Rapid Agrarian Change and Responses in Southern Laos." *Journal of Lao Studies* 1(1): 1–47.

———. 2011a. "Turning Land into Capital, Turning People into Labour: Primitive Accumulation and the Arrival of Large-Scale Economic Land Concessions in Laos." *New Proposals: Journal of Marxism and Interdisciplinary Inquiry* 5(1): 10–26.

———. 2011b. "The Construction of 'Indigenous Peoples' in Cambodia." In *Alterities in Asia: Reflections on Identity and Regionalism,* ed. Leong Yew, 155–176. London: Routledge.

———. 2013. "'Indigenous Peoples' and Land: Comparing Communal Land Titling and Its Implications in Cambodia and Laos." *Asia Pacific Viewpoint* 54(3): 269–81.

———. 2015. "Translocal Assemblages and the Circulation of the Concept of 'Indigenous Peoples' in Laos." *Political Geography* 46: 54–64.

———. 2016. "Should Ethnic Lao People Be Considered Indigenous to Cambodia? Ethnicity, Classification and the Politics of Indigeneity." *Asian Ethnicity* 17(4): 506–26.

Baird, Ian G., Prasit Leepreecha, and Urai Yangcheepsujarit. 2017. "Who Should Be Considered 'Indigenous'? A Survey of Ethnic Groups in Northern Thailand." *Asian Ethnicity* 18(4): 543–562.

Baird, Ian G. and Bruce P. Shoemaker. 2007. "Unsettling Experiences: Internal Resettlement and International Aid Agencies in the Lao PDR." *Development and Change* 38(5): 865–88.

Bertrand, Jacques. 2011. "'Indigenous Peoples' Rights' as a Strategy of Ethnic Accommodation: Contrasting Experiences of Cordillerans and Papuans in the Philippines and Indonesia." *Ethnic and Racial Studies* 34(5): 850–69.

Bounmany, Lounthong, Souvanhpheng Phommasane, and Martin Greijmans. 2012. *Communal Land Titles for 5 Bamboo Producing Communities in Sangthong District, Vientiane Capital, Lao PDR.* Vientiane: District Land Management Authority and SNV.

Bryant, Raymond L. 2000. "Politicized Moral Geographies: Debating Biodiversity Conservation and Ancestral Domain in the Philippines." *Political Geography* 19: 673–95.
Clarke, Gerald. 2001. "From Ethnocide to Ethnodevelopment? Ethnic Minorities and Indigenous Peoples in Southeast Asia." *Third World Quarterly* 22(3): 413–36.
Colchester, Marcus. 2004. "Indigenous Peoples and Communal Tenures in Asia." In *Land Reform, Land Settlement and Cooperatives, 2004/1*. Rome: Food and Agriculture Organization of the United Nations, available at http://www.fao.org/docrep/007/y5407t/y5407t07.htm.
Colchester, Marcus and Christian Erni (eds). 1999. *Indigenous Peoples and Protected Areas in South and Southeast Asia: From Principles to Practice*. Copenhagen: IWGIA.
Conboy, Kenneth. 2013. *The Cambodian Wars: Clashing Armies and CIA Covert Operations*. Lawrence, KS: University Press of Kansas.
Dirlik, Arif. 2003. "Globalization, Indigenism, and the Politics of Place." *Ariel* 34(1): 15–29.
Erni, Christian (ed.). 2008. *The Concept of Indigenous Peoples in Asia: A Resource Book*. IWGIA Document No. 123. Copenhagen and Chiang Mai: IWGIA and AIPP.
Forsyth, Tim and Andrew Walker. 2008. *Forest Guardians, Forest Destroyers: The Politics of Environmental Knowledge in Northern Thailand*. Seattle, WA: University of Washington Press.
GIZ (Deutsche Gesellschaft für Internationale Zusammenarbeit) (ed.). 2011. *Proposed Drafting of FPIC Guidelines and Piloting a Free, Prior, and Informed Consent Process in CliPAD Project Communities in Cooperation with Lao Biodiversity Association*. Vientiane: GIZ.
Gray, Andrew. 1995. "The Indigenous Movement in Asia." In *Indigenous Peoples in Asia*, ed. Robert H. Barnes, Andrew Gray, and Ben Kingsbury, 35–58. Ann Arbor, MI: Association of Asian Studies.
Hall, Derek. 2013. *Land*. Cambridge: Polity Press.
Hall, Derek, Philip Hirsch, and Tania Murray Li. 2011. *Powers of Exclusion: Land Dilemmas in Southeast Asia*. Honolulu, HI: University of Hawai'i Press.
Howitt, Richie, John Connell, and Philip Hirsch (eds). 1996. *Resources, Nations and Indigenous Peoples in Australasia, Melanesia and Southeast Asia*. Melbourne: Oxford University Press.
ILO (International Labor Organization). 1989. *Convention 169: Indigenous and Tribal Peoples Convention, 1989 (No. 169). Convention Concerning Indigenous and Tribal Peoples in Independent Countries*. Geneva: ILO.
IWGIA (International Work Group on Indigenous Affairs). 2009. *The Indigenous World 2009*. Copenhagen: IWGIA.
———. 2010. *The Indigenous World 2010*. Copenhagen: IWGIA.
———. 2011. *The Indigenous World 2011*. Copenhagen: IWGIA.
———. 2013. *The Indigenous World 2013*. Copenhagen: IWGIA.
Kampe, Ken. 1997. "What Does Foreign Aid for Education Contribute to the Maintenance of Indigenous Knowledge in Laos, Thailand and Vietnam?" *Asia Pacific Viewpoint* 38(2): 155–60.

Keating, Neil B. 2013. "Kuy Alterities: The Struggle to Conceptualize and Claim Indigenous Land Rights in Neoliberal Cambodia." *Asia Pacific Viewpoint* 54(3): 309–22.

Keyes, Charles F. 2002. "Presidential Address: 'The Peoples of Asia'—Science and Politics in the Classification of Ethnic Groups in Thailand, China and Vietnam." *Journal of Asian Studies* 61(4): 1,163–203.

Kingsbury, Benedict. 1998. "Indigenous Peoples in International Law: A Constructivist Approach to the Asian Controversy." *American Journal of International Law* 92(3): 414–57.

———. 1999. "The Applicability of the International Legal Concept of 'Indigenous Peoples' in Asia." In *The East Asian Challenge for Human Rights*, ed. Joanne R. Bauer and Daniel A. Bell, 336–378. London: Cambridge University Press.

Kuper, Adam 2003. "The Return of the Native." *Current Anthropology* 44(3): 389–402.

Leepreecha, Prasit, Don McCaskill, and Kwanchewan Buadaeng (eds). 2008. *Challenging the Limits: Indigenous Peoples of the Mekong Region.* Chiang Mai: Mekong Press.

LFNC (Lao Front for National Construction). 2005. *The Ethnic Groups of Lao PDR.* Vientiane: Ethnic Department.

Manorom, Kanokwan, Ian G. Baird, and Bruce Shoemaker. 2017. "The World Bank, Hydropower-Based Poverty Alleviation and Indigenous Peoples: On-the-Ground Realities in the Xe Bang Fai River Basin of Laos." *Forum for Development Studies* 44(2): 275–300.

Milne, Sarah. 2013. "Under the Leopard's Skin: Land Commodification and the Dilemmas of Indigenous Communal Title in Upland Cambodia." *Asian Pacific Viewpoint* 54(3): 323–39.

Morton, Micah, and Ian G. Baird. Forthcoming. "From Hill Tribes to Indigenous Peoples: The Localization of a Global Movement in Thailand." *Journal of Southeast Asian Studies.*

Neef, Andreas, Siphat Touch, and Jamaree Chiengthong. 2013. "The Politics and Ethics of Land Concessions in Rural Cambodia." *Journal of Agricultural and Environmental Ethics* 26(6): 1,085–103.

NGO Forum on Cambodia. 2006. *Land Alienation in Indigenous Minority Communities—Ratanakiri Province, Cambodia.* Phnom Penh: NGO Forum on Cambodia.

Padwe, Jonathan. 2013. "Highlands of History: Indigenous Identity and its Antecedents in Cambodia." *Asia Pacific Viewpoint* 54(3): 282–95.

Phongkhao, Somsack. 2008. "Laos Marks Indigenous People's Day." *Vientiane Times.*

Ratha, Sok. 2012. "Hun Sen Mocks Land Dispute." *Radio Free Asia,* 7 December.

Saisopha, Sathian. 2012. *Cheng kan leuang kho sang tang samakhom banda phao houam chai phattana you muang Pakse, khveng Champasak* [Announcement Regarding the Request to Establish an Association for Jointly Developing the Various Ethnic Groups, in Pakse District, Champasak Province, Interior Division, Champasak Province]. Document 104, 27 April, Pakse: Interior Division.

Swift, Peter. 2013. "Changing Ethnic Identities among the Kuy in Cambodia: Assimilation, Reassertion, and the Making of Indigenous Identity." *Asia Pacific Viewpoint* 54(3): 296–308.

Theriault, Noah. 2011. "The Micropolitics of Indigenous Environmental Movements in the Philippines." *Development and Change* 42(6): 1,417–40.

———. 2013. "Agencies of the Environmental State: Difference and Regulation on the Philippines' 'Last Frontier'." PhD dissertation. University of Wisconsin-Madison.

Trakansuphakon, Prasert. 1996. "The History and Contemporary Situation of Karen and other Indigenous Tribal Peoples' Movements in Thailand." In *"...Vines that Won't Bind...": Indigenous Peoples in Asia*, ed. Christian Erni, 173–177. Proceedings of a Conference held in Chiang Mai, Thailand, 1995. Copenhagen: IWGIA.

Vaddhanaphuti, Chayan. 1996. "The Present Situation of Indigenous Peoples in Thailand." In *"...Vines that Won't Bind...": Indigenous Peoples in Asia*, ed. Christian Erni, 79–88.

Vientiane Times. 2009. "Laos Celebrates International Indigenous Day." 11 August.

Vongsack, Sayamang. 2013. *Bot ne nam va douay kan pheuksa ha leu bep mi souan houam kap xon phao thi dai hap phon katop chak khong kan* [Recommendations Regarding Participatory Consultations with Ethnic Groups that Are Impacted by Projects] [Lao language]. 17 May. Vientiane: Lao Front for National Construction Committee.

Walker, Andrew. 2001. "The 'Karen Consensus', Ethnic Politics and Resource-Use Legitimacy in Northern Thailand." *Asian Ethnicity* 2(2): 145–62.

World Bank. 2005. *Operational Policy/Borrower Policy 4.10 Indigenous Peoples*. Updated in 2013. Washington, DC: World Bank.

PART II

BECOMING INDIGENOUS

3

Processes of Modernization, Processes of Indigenization
An Amazonian Case (Yanomami, Southern Venezuela)

Gabriele Herzog-Schröder

"Hiramamotima kua—We Now Have a School!"

Hiramamotima kua[1] was one of the first pieces of information I was confronted with when revisiting the people I had not seen for ten years. Exactly thirty years after I had first visited the Yanomami community of Patanowëtheri in the remote hinterlands of the Upper Orinoco, I was astonished to see a small frugal hut: the village school, with a single teacher in charge. It is the first non-indigenous institution in this isolated region. In my investigations, I learned that this school was one of only a very few that had recently been established at the request of the inhabitants of small settlements in the tropical forest. In earlier times, schools in the Venezuelan Yanomami territory had—if they existed at all—been rather a component of the Catholic mission posts located at the river.

Along with rudimentary schools of this kind within the dense rainforest setting of the broader Upper Orinoco area, the relativity of indigeneity will be discussed here in relation to spatial distance from local centers alongside the Orinoco River. One aim of this chapter is to show that different factors influence indigeneity, other than the obvious spatial factor—the closer a community moves towards more advanced areas, the more it is transformed in line with "modernization." Modernization is used here in the sense that the population in the remote hinterland gradually departs from former lifestyles and everyday practices in which they possessed a limited number of belongings, which in turn enabled them to maintain the traditional semi-sedentary existence.

In addition to the expected influence of distance on indigeneity, there are further relevant factors that relate to inherent attitudes: to enact the "traditional" can be seen as a step towards voluntarily "being indigenous." The implementation and practice of "indigeneity," as one lifestyle option among others, can—paradoxically—itself be described as a local form of "modernization."

Another instance that aptly illustrates the inverted opposition between indigenization and modernization touches on traditional cosmological perceptions that have been challenged since the appearance of non-indigenous people at the Orinoco River in the middle of the twentieth century—missionaries, extractivists like miners and loggers, as well as military personnel (see also Caballero Arias 2005, 2014). Traditional views, however, rather than being abandoned, continue to exist and even flourish, in parallel with an increasing orientation towards the non-indigenous world. In the context of knowledge or wisdom acquisition, attending school and simultaneously striving to become a shaman are shown not to be competing aims, but analogous processes on a local scale. Shamanic visions are realized in a "modern" world and non-indigenous or *napë* knowledge is indigenized.[2]

This chapter is structured as follows. First, the ethnographic setting of the studied communities will be outlined. The difference between the river communities and the communities of the hinterland will be specifically handled before the settings of the schools are described. Schools—not education—prove to be objects or places for the transportation of modernity. These institutions bind imaginations; at the same time, they reveal local discrepancies and embrace local attitudes towards cultural change, whereby these attitudes are influenced by conflicting ideals. In the final section, another view of modernity versus indigeneity is presented in the context of knowledge or wisdom as taught in schools, as opposed to the acquired expertise of shamanic practice.

Ethnographic Setting

I am particularly acquainted with two villages in the middle of the Venezuelan rainforest—Sheroana and Hapokashitha—and it is these villages that I report on here. In the early 1980s, when I first visited the region, the people of these settlements formed one large local community: the Patanowëtheri or people of Patanowë.[3] The communities of the Patanowë group that shifted their semi-permanent settlements in the hinterlands of the Upper Orinoco far beyond the mission post in El Platanal/Mahekoto will be the focus of this chapter. They can be seen as exemplary of the traditional people of lowland South America, an image of the prototypical indigenous that has been widely represented in the anthropological literature. As such, the Yanomami are well known in the anthropological community and beyond, yet at the same time, their settlements themselves remain remote and virtually isolated in extended zones.

The two settlements—or *shaponos* as they are called here—of Sheroana and Hapokashitha, whose history I have documented over time (Herzog 1990; Herzog-Schröder 2000), will be the center of my specific perspectives on indigeneity and modernity with respect to inner-Yanomami relations. I would like to point out that my view is confined to Venezuelan state territory and excludes lands inhabited by the Yanomami in Brazil. It must be made clear that the situation of the Yanomami in Brazil is, in many aspects, very different, due to the historical catastrophe of the invasion by gold prospectors in the 1970s, continuing through to the 1990s (Albert 1992; Kopenawa and Albert 2013; Ramos 1995).

The territory of the entire ethnic group of the Yanomami people comprises the southeast of the federal state of Amazonas of the Bolivarian Republic of Venezuela and the state of Roraima in Brazil. The Yanomami region is situated west of the Guiana Shield between latitudes 5°N and the equator and between longitudes 61°W and 67°W. The terrain in its central and southern areas is almost completely covered with tropical humid forest; the entrance into the zone is restricted as it is borderland and at the same time protected as a UNESCO biosphere reservation. Communication is conducted in Yanomami, a language specific to the Yanomami people, which itself has four distinct dialects, one of them being Yanomamï.[4] The specific region detailed here—the villages near the Upper Orinoco—is inhabited by the Yanomami subgroup "Yanomamï" also called the "central Yanomami." The Patanowë groups also belong to the Yanomamï.

The Yanomami are a hunter-gatherer and swidden-horticultural society with a population of about thirty-five thousand people, as suggested by new census data.[5] Each village consists of three to eight extended families, which are united by marital relations. Among the Yanomamï in the far south of Venezuela and some neighboring regions in Brazil, family homes are built close together in a circle. These *shaponos*—large, palm-thatched, circular communal dwellings—have become legendary through promotion by mass media. They and the surrounding garden sites are located in dense rainforest. As one approaches the river, these *shapono*-rounds have been replaced in many cases by a circle of singular huts, mostly thatched in traditional form.

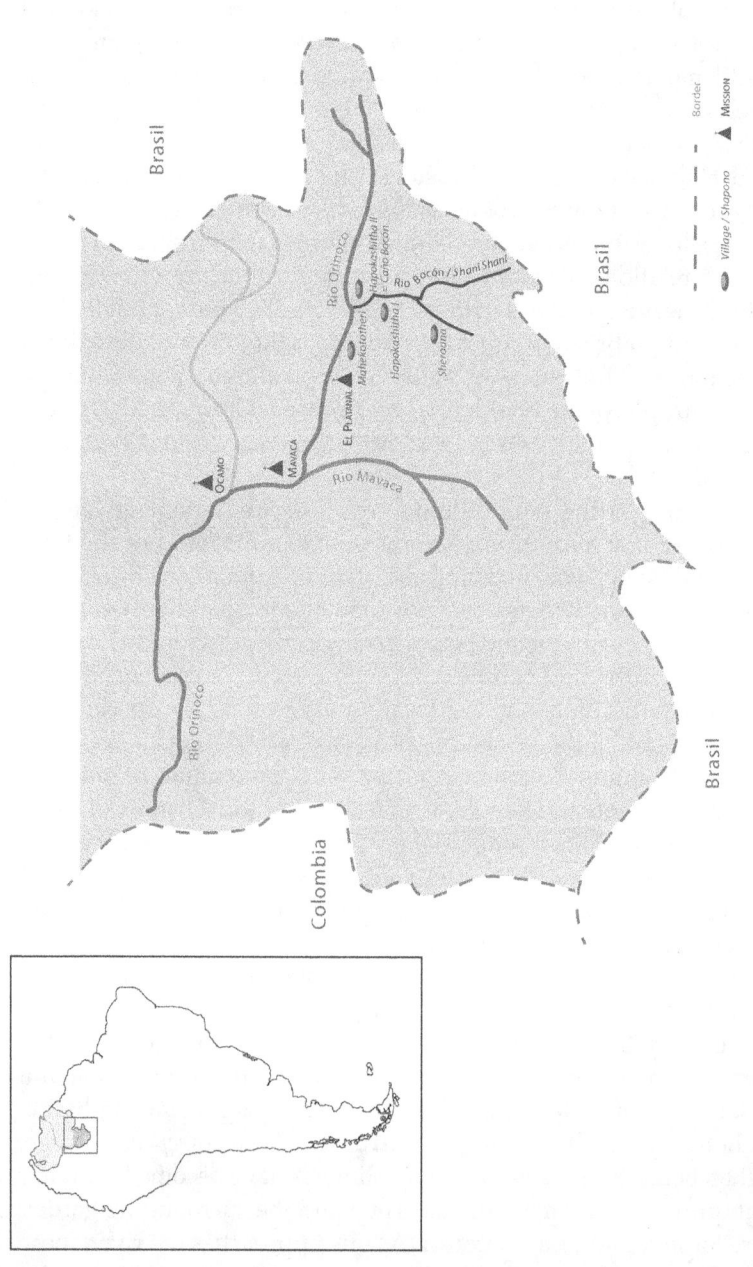

Map 3.1. The map shows the central part of the area inhabited by the Yanomami in 2012. It outlines the territory of the Yanomamï or the "central Yanomami" and depicts the locations of the selected Yanomami communities and the mission posts discussed in the text. There are many more Yanomami villages or *shaponos* in this region which are not shown here. © G. Herzog-Schröder.

The main crop of the Yanomami is plantain, although manioc has become increasingly popular in recent decades. The basic diet is supplemented by corn, sweet potatoes, yams, sugar cane, and other forms of garden produce (Milliken, Albert, and Gomez 1999). Hunting and fishing are important subsistence techniques and they provide a conceptual frame of "predation," which has been widely discussed in the context of lowland South American peoples and beyond (Fausto 1999; Herzog-Schröder 2000; Viveiros de Castro 1992, 1998).

Until the 1960s, the Yanomami were considered to be hunters and incipient horticulturalists who had only recently progressed from fulltime hunting-gathering and taken on basic gardening (Steward and Faron 1959: 434; Wilbert 1963: 187–88). Their more recent classification as foragers and horticulturalists has nonetheless been beyond dispute for several decades. However, gardening itself has become much more effective with increased access to metal tools (Ferguson 1995). This transformation occurred, to a large degree, with the founding of the Catholic Salesian mission posts in Venezuela at the beginning of the 1960s.

Before commenting further on the work of the missions, an important cultural trait of the Yanomamï needs to be mentioned. Several times a year, they leave their stable village constructions to dwell in the forest in small camps. Traditionally, the Yanomamï spent up to five or six months a year in temporary sites in the jungle, often near former garden sites, where hunting for game is easier. This customary routine, called *wayumï*, during which they would complete the garden harvest, is important for their subsistence practices. Nowadays, Yanomami groups that reside near mission posts have almost completely abandoned these trips into the forest, primarily due to the amount of possessions they now own. It is now simply no longer possible for one person to take all of his or her belongings with them on these forest trips. Many Yanomami also hold jobs at the missions or at a state or government post situated near the mission stations. Therefore, many cannot easily afford to move away from the main traffic artery — the river. The people of Sheroana and Hapokashitha, however, still engage in *wayumï* trips, due to their more traditional lifestyle. Regularly visiting traditional sites and former gardens where the yield of game is higher is a much-respected practice among the Yanomami. Therefore, there exists a marked difference in the practice of mobility between the Yanomami near the river and those living away from the Orinoco in the hinterlands.

There are four Salesian mission posts located along the large rivers in the southernmost part of Venezuela. Mavaca and El Platanal are situated on the banks of the Orinoco; the mission post Ocamo a little to the north, at the confluence of the Ocamo River and the Orinoco; and Mavaquita is situated on the Mavaca River, a tributary of the Orinoco to the southwest. One of the principal aims of the Salesian missions—apart from offering medical care and proselytizing, which is a relatively reserved effort—has been to provide education for the children. A school has been established in the compound of each of the mission posts. Here, local indigenous children are not only taught reading, writing, and arithmetic, but courses are also offered in swimming, cooking, and handicrafts. Students in higher grades also learn to speak and read Spanish within a bilingual educational system. In the early years, the clergy, which was comprised of the *padres* and *hermanas*—the Salesian Fathers and Salesian Sisters of Don Bosco—conducted the lessons themselves, but they soon started to train young Yanomami boys and girls to take over some of the teaching duties. Teaching materials, such as schoolbooks, posters, and maps, were developed by the Salesians in accordance with the bilingual state requirements and with the professional help of anthropologists and linguists, such as Jacques Lizot and Marie-Claude Mattéi-Muller.[6] The content of the teaching materials is carefully designed in accordance with the Yanomami culture; foreign images or contexts unfamiliar to their forest lifestyle are avoided. The stories and material used to learn how to read and write, for example, are all taken from Yanomami everyday experiences or from their mythology.

Discourses on the Yanomami

Before discussing the indigenous schools in the Orinoco hinterlands, some brief remarks are necessary about the popular image the Yanomami have acquired due to debates based on questionable publications, such as *Yanomamö: The Fierce People* (Chagnon 1968), *Darkness in Eldorado* (Tierney 2001), and *Secrets of the Tribe* (Padilha 2010). These present a rather general, stereotypical image of the Yanomami. Representations of the abused Yanomami are partly accurate for some Yanomami groups, particularly those who live in close contact with non-Yanomami, that is, those in the villages near the Orinoco. However, the image of the isolated, jungle-dwelling Yanomami is also not adequate for all Yanomami, nor is it true that unethical anthropologists have mistreated all Yanomami. Taking a non-paternalistic position, the Yanomami are very well able to defend themselves against occasional misbehavior by anthropologists. At any rate, the higher visibility of the "River Yanomami," as they are portrayed in the media, should not disguise the fact that there are far more Yanomami villages in the remote hinterlands than in the settlements on the relatively easily accessible riverbanks, which are most often described in the press. Traditional life is maintained in many of the communities near the river, and even more so in the more remote areas: life is orientated around subsistence—a combination of hunting, fishing, and gathering, complemented by garden harvests. Affiliation to a community is based primarily on kin, and institutionalized power positions at the village level are divided between spiritual specialists (there are several shamans in each local group), political leaders, and other personalities who are often characterized by outstanding rhetorical abilities.[7] Capitalism has not yet affected the traditional lifestyle in this remote area, although the significance of money has been recognized and metal tools and aluminum ware have replaced stone axes and old ceramics for some decades. However, as Sahlins (1999) claimed, the appropriation of a number of industrially manufactured objects should not be misinterpreted as the breakdown of a traditional way of life. This is especially true for the most remote regions where there are no roads, no electricity, no water pipelines, and no mobile communications network or internet coverage. It is important to realize, however, that these disparities between different areas within the Yanomami zone have increased only recently and are related to the degree of contact with non-Yanomami, mainly the missionaries and medical and military personnel.

Schools, the State, and the Salesian Missions

Due to the presence of schools at the mission posts, people living closer to the mission stations, and especially their children, are much more "educated" in the sense of Western standards or "global schooling" (Anderson-Levitt 2003), as opposed to the residents of more remote areas. The younger Yanomami know some Spanish and have acquired certain competencies in reading and arithmetic, which enables them to communicate with non-indigenous people who find their way into this restricted area. The area itself is heavily controlled by the military, stationed here to protect the Venezuelan border with Brazil. Foreigners who come into contact with the Yanomami are members of military patrols, national health service teams passing through on vaccination tours, and, occasionally, an anthropologist—not forgetting the presence of the missionaries. It goes without saying that there is more human traffic on the river, and it should be mentioned that since the late president Hugo Chávez came to power, the socialist Venezuelan government has dramatically increased grants for boats, outboard motors, and generators in the area, with the idea of giving everybody in the country an equal share. In many cases, however, this has left the local people with an acute and permanent need for gasoline, batteries, and spare parts. These government grants have either just barely reached the groups in the remote and hilly areas or not reached them at all. Many of these grants are, moreover, not suited to or valuable for the inhabitants of the hinterland communities, as it is simply too exhausting to carry heavy cans of petrol uphill on narrow paths for several hours. This means that life away from the river remains more traditional as opposed to the areas where there is more contact with the outside world. It is important to remember such differences concerning the frequency of contact with outsiders, knowledge about the outside world, and the differing value placed on commodities when we talk about "the Yanomami," rather than speaking of them as a homogeneous group of jungle-dwellers.

To put the small, simple school-huts that I saw in Hapokashitha and Sheroana in 2012 in a regional and national context, it is important to explain the basic system of schooling in this remote area of Venezuela. There are no public schools as there is little infrastructure apart from the missions' facilities and hospital wards located at the mission posts. The Salesians, together with some laypeople from the apostolic community, run the schools at the mission stations in Ocamo, Mavaca, and El Platanal. These schools are legally private schools commissioned by the state. The missionaries do not teach religion in these schools, which follow state guidelines; religious instruction is provided separately.

The basic syllabus is determined by the Ministry of Education and modified by the teachers of the respective schools in accordance with intercultural and bilingual requirements. Specific guidelines for indigenous schooling in the Bolivarian Republic of Venezuela are given in the Ley Orgánica de Pueblos y Comunidades Indígenas (law for native peoples and communities) as part of the Venezuelan constitution, which was passed in 2005. Title IV of the law is concerned with "education and culture"; it guarantees the consideration of sociocultural values, traditions, and needs specific to the given indigenous society (Article 74). The law also requests the recruitment of teaching staff from within the respective indigenous group if possible. This was the case in Hapokashitha, where a young local man was engaged as the teacher. In Sheroana, a young man from Mahekoto taught the pupils.

The constitution also states that schools and schooling should not be imposed upon an indigenous group or village. If, however, an indigenous community requests a school, it should receive state assistance and support in its endeavor to implement it. Naturally, these ideals,

Figure 3.1. This shed hosts the school in Caño Bocón, where the people who formerly called themselves Hapokashitha settled in the late 1990s. The humble shelter is covered with aluminum, which was obtained from the mission post. © G. Herzog-Schröder, 2012.

guaranteed by the constitution, cannot always be so easily implemented due to the remoteness and lack of transport to some communities, but this constitutional right has been invoked by the local groups that are central to this chapter, at least at the time of my visit in 2012. I do not know how the people of Hapokashitha or Sheroana originally found out about their constitutionally granted rights. Sheroana, for example, has always shown a detachment with respect to the non-indigenous institutions, which typically engage with the fast-changing way of life in the communities along the Orinoco River. Further questions about the organizational background will be dealt with later.

The small schools that have been established away from the mission posts are called *escuelas de extensión*, extension schools, as they are outposts of one of the larger main schools on the river. At the time of writing, there have only been four *escuelas de extensión* on the upper part of the Upper Orinoco, and two of them were associated with the Patanowë villages of Hapokashitha and Sheroana. These schools were attached to the mission at El Platanal. The other two extension schools were associated with the school at the mission post in Mavaca. Due to

Figure 3.2. The school in Sheroana is located within the circle of the *shapono* in a small hut thatched with palm leaves under a tree. Next to the school is the lean-to roof where communal shamanic sessions take place nearly every day. © G. Herzog-Schröder, 2012.

their relative remoteness, I have disregarded the *escuelas de extensión* related to the mission post in Ocamo, but I was informed that there are some four or five of these outposts along the Ocamo River.[8]

The young and rather inexperienced teachers in these distant schools are dependent on the main school for the curriculum and structure of the lessons. The teachers in the main schools, who are much more experienced, plan the structure of the next two to three weeks in advance and personally deliver the instructions to the teachers at the remote *escuelas de extensión*. Personnel at the main schools—often Salesian Sisters of Don Bosco—visit the extension schools, and also bring food for the free school lunches, which are guaranteed by the state. The salaries of the teachers at the *escuelas de extensión*, which are paid by the state (as long as the political and economic situation in Venezuela allows for this), are controlled by the mission on the state's behalf. The indigenous teachers—called *promotores*—receive lower salaries than teachers in state-run schools. However, teachers' salaries are very high compared to other forms of income in these remote communities, where commercial transactions are very seldom practiced. In 2012, the teachers at Hapokashitha and Sheroana were the only people in their respective communities with any kind of income at all. The position of these teachers as the sole money earners, and the attraction of free meals for the children attending school, certainly deserve a broader discussion than is possible here. These ideas would necessarily feed into an ecological reasoning regarding the demand for schools within a deeper analysis. I intend, however, to attempt to explain the motivation for the establishment of schools in these remote Yanomami communities from a strictly emic perspective.[9]

This introduction to the ethnographic setting of the mission schools on the rivers, and their relation to the smaller village schools, serves as a basis for the following reflections on "indigenous modernity." It was necessary to clarify the two different levels of contact with the outside world of the Yanomami to provide an understanding of the village schools as remote extensions of the river schools, and appropriate to view this through the perspective "of" the Yanomami themselves, that is, to take an etic approach. I will, however, attempt to invert this perspective in the following sections, adopting the view of the Yanomami in the more remote areas towards the more acculturated river areas, one that might be summarized as from the "traditional" towards the "modern." I begin with a closer look at the two villages that are the focus of this study.

Sheroana and Hapokashitha: Fractions of the Mighty Patanowë

The two local groups of Sheroana and Hapokashitha were formed by members of a formerly larger community—the Patanowë—which split in the early 1980s (Herzog 1990). These two groups, the Sheroana and Hapokashitha, were comprised of fifty-two and fifty-six inhabitants respectively in early 2012. The settlements of Sheroana and Hapokashitha are separated by a five to seven hour walk and maintain regular contact due to close marital ties. They are both allies of the Mahekototheri, whose settlement is located in the immediate vicinity of El Platanal, the southernmost mission post, and both also maintain friendly relations with other settlements neighboring the mission posts of Ocamo. They also enjoy close familiar relations, especially with some families near Mavaca. However, due to the relative closeness of El Platanal, separated only by a two to three hour ride by motorboat or a one to two day walk, the Mahekototheri are, in many respects, first-choice partners.

Until recently, both Patanowë groups were located quite a distance from the main river in the region, the Orinoco. However, the Hapokashitha have made decisive moves towards the Orinoco in the past two decades and are now actually located at the Orinoco's confluence with the River Shani-shani, or Caño Bocón.

When visiting these groups in February and March 2012, I observed a number of changes in comparison with my visit ten years before, many of which could be discussed using such concepts as "indigenous modernity" or "alternative modernity" as presented by various theorists (Canclini 1990; Knauft 2002; Pitarch and Orobitg 2012). Prominent changes concerned settlement architecture, hairstyles, the use of Spanish names for themselves, and the practice of speaking these names out loud (traditional names had customarily been kept secret and kin terms were used to address each other). Other observations, such as the use of mosquito nets, which brought about a considerable decrease in malaria cases, had also resulted in an increased spacing between hammocks in the dwelling areas and, thus, a significant change in the social setting. Finally, new team sports, which had become fashionable in the villages and had brought with them changes to their social life, should at least be mentioned as potential indicators of cultural change.

To examine aspects of modernization juxtaposed with different features of indigenization, I have chosen to study the specific context of schools. However, I will not consider the schools at the mission posts, but rather the extension schools in the remote villages of Sheroana and Hapokashitha. Correspondingly, my reflections do not aim to look at the "educational" aspects of the schools, which might befit our understanding of education as a civil value in a Western-type culture or as might befit the understanding of the World Bank or UNESCO of education as an agent of global schooling culture. Taking an emic approach, I would prefer to examine schools as a symbol of *intended* cultural change or as a mark of "development" or "progress." In the context of development, I prefer to see these schools as expressions of the Yanomami's will to participate in the processes of the wider world of the *criollo,* as the non-indigenous population is called in Venezuela. The key to accepting this perspective is to try to understand what the inhabitants of these villages expect from "having a school of their own."

The schools I saw in Sheroana and Hapokashitha in 2012 could hardly be humbler: a very plain single hut with one simple bench and a table made from wooden beams. In one case, this hut has an aluminum roof, and in the other, a more traditional roof made with palm leaves; each school has only one teacher.

I could not be present when pupils were being taught, since I visited during the school holidays in 2012, but I did have the chance to talk at some length with one of the teachers, a young man from the local Hapokashitha group who knows a little Spanish, and who went to school in Mavaca for two or three years while living with relatives there. The teacher in the Sheroana school was not a native of the village. As was mentioned earlier, he was from Mahekoto and only stayed in Sheroana during term times. At the time of my visit, there was no one in Sheroana who could read or write, and therefore no one who would have been qualified to be a teacher. There was, however, one young man, the son of an important shaman and nephew of the current political leader, who was studying at the schools attached to the mission posts with the objective of working in the village as a teacher in the future.

A Closer Look and Internal Differentiations

The *shapono* of Sheroana is located in the hilly hinterlands, and it is essential to explain the relationship of this remote local group to people who live closer to the river and therefore closer to non-indigenous influences. To explain the ambivalent feeling that the Sheroanatheri, the people of Sheroana, have towards the villages near the river, it is useful to reflect on the term *napë*, which is the Yanomami word for "stranger" or "enemy" but also for "non-indigenous person." In the past, the Sheroanatheri frequently said to me, "we do not want to become *napë*." This signifies that they do not want to change into someone other than Yanomami, as happens to those who live in close contact with the mission posts.

In accordance with the concept of belonging, and also adhering to their shamanic worldview—that a person's identity is not intrinsically stable[10]—the Sheroanatheri see the Yanomami who live near the river more as *criollo* than Yanomami. Due to their intense contact with non-indigenous people, these Yanomami take on *napë*-like characteristics or even become *napë* themselves. In some sense, this belonging to the *napë* world is supported by friends and relatives who provide the Yanomami with goods and information from the outside world. We are confronted here with a paradoxical representation of strangers—even enemies—within a relationship of being allies, all of which is encompassed by the emic term *"napë."*

In contrast to the Sheroanatheri, the people of Hapokashitha have been striving for many years for more contact with the *napë* world. In the 1990s, Hapokashitha wanted to build a *medicatura,* a hospital ward, and joined forces with the autonomous organization SUYAO (Shaponos Unidos de los Yanomami del Alto Orinoco).[11] In the same period, they declared their desire to have a school like the ones near the mission posts on the Orinoco. Such an institution would be worthwhile, I was told repeatedly in the 1990s. At that time, establishing a school there seemed to me simply impossible as they were too far away from the mission facilities. Striving for an institution like a school is an expression of a will to emulate the lifestyle of the *napë* or *criollo*, and, consistent with this, they actually changed the name of their group from Hapokashitha to Caño Bocón—the Spanish name for the river the Yanomami call Shani-shani. The crucial point here is not so much relinquishing the name "Hapokashitha," but the change from a Yanomami name to a Spanish, a *criollo* one.[12]

Let me now draw attention to the disparity between the respective positions of Sheroana and Hapokashitha/Caño Bocón with regard to the river people. Whereas the Hapokashithatheri have drawn closer to a more "modern" way of life, the Sheroanatheri passionately declared in 2002 that they do not want to be influenced too much by those in and around the mission posts who allow themselves to be transformed into *napë* or *criollo*. The Sheroanatheri also stated their desire to remain Yanomami, with their traditional clothing,[13] and their opposition to moving their village towards the river, where there are so many illnesses that would then necessitate a *medicatura*. Considering this historical context, I was quite astonished in 2012 not only to find a school in the community of Hapokashitha, which by then had moved down towards the riverbank, but also to find a school in the more remote settlement of Sheroana, home of the supposed "traditionalists."

The view of the two villages with respect to non-indigenous people, the *napë*, as just described, seemed quite different, and in 2012, this conflicting notion was still quite palpable, despite the fact that the inhabitants of both communities now called a small hut in their respective settlements "our school." My explanation for the difference between these two remote villages is that both communities, Sheroana as well as Hapokashitha, represent a kind of "indigenous modernity," the particular characteristics of which, however, differ in the respective expression of the traditional as opposed to the new or modern. While the Hapokashithatheri, the people of Caño Bocón, orientated themselves both perceivably and physically towards the river, the Sheroanatheri played the "tradition" card. However, the latter also acted in response to changes in other communities situated along the river and effectively secured community partners in the more remote hinterlands and thus gained not only partners from the more "traditional" sphere, but also the possibility to obtain raw materials and handicrafts, which they could then trade further as *artesania* (craftworks) at the river centers (SUYAO). They even operated as facilitators who "traded people"—

laborers to help construct new houses or clear garden sites—from the hinterlands to Mahekoto for example, a village near the El Platanal mission. It should be understood that the Yanomami from very remote areas are not well acquainted with the "river people" and are often anxious about meeting these *napë*-like Yanomami. They would rather rely on their allies from Sheroana to facilitate labor transactions, so that they do not find themselves in uncomfortable situations.

The Sheroanatheri themselves obviously profited from their position as intermediaries, as indicated by their subsequent accumulation of metal tools (Ferguson 1995). Their location and networking strategy resulted in larger gardens, with correspondingly more food and better health. This further enabled them to host allies from the hinterlands on festive occasions. The people from Hapokashitha, by contrast, moved their settlement from the hinterlands closer to the river; here, they come into more intimate contact—but at the same time into competition—with the river groups, who already enjoy more direct relationships with the *napë*, be they non-indigenous, like the missionaries, or indigenous "in transformation." It can be said that the people of Sheroana were no less "modern" in their political movement, as they purposefully played the "traditional" card, yet by savvy negotiating with the river people, they too profited from this contact.

My interpretation of the situation, already true in the early 1990s, differentiates within a theoretical frame of modernity. One might assume that the more remotely people live, the more "untouched" they are by the outside world, and at first glance this assumption might apply to the case of Sheroanatheri. The more "modern" case is obviously represented by the Hapokashithatheri and their move towards the river, its residents, and their lifestyle, symbolically expressed by their adoption of a Spanish name for their group: Caño Bocón.

I have tried to show, however, that the "indigenization" of the Sheroanatheri, their retention of traditional values, and their declared distance from the *napë* world is not simply a sign of the traditional, but rather reflects an "indigenous modern" perspective as these people are quite well informed about the changes brought about by living in the river communities and do not at all indulge themselves uncritically in a pristine ethnic state. The Sheroanatheri have chosen a different approach, perhaps as a reaction to developments in the river regions. These supposed "provincials" in fact employ a variant of "indigenous modernity." They practice a form of self-representation that constitutes a continuation of traditions. Careful analysis reveals their self-representation as traditionalists as a constructed process, one that can certainly be described as "alternatively modern."

Cosmological Traits

In addition to the socio-anthropological ideas of tradition versus modernity that are centered around the schools and were elaborated on in relation to distinct attitudes towards new life forms, I would like to present a further perspective, where communities practice a different kind of self-locating or self-positioning within their geological, and mytho-geological, maps. In Yanomami cosmology, the relationship between the center and the periphery appears inverse to that which has been demonstrated so far: the mountain range, water from which helps feed the Orinoco River to the west, the Branco River to the east, and the Rio Negro to the south, also marks the frontier between Venezuela and Brazil. The Yanomami recognize these mountains—known as the Serra Parima—as their place of origin. The highlands, where the rivers begin—being the historic region of origin—epitomize the *mythical* center, where shamans find direction in their endeavors to understand and interpret the world and its phenomena. The importance of this mythical center, and its orientation in opposition to the physical landscape, becomes evident when one considers the journey of the tutelary spirits, with the help of whom the shamans enact their power, who return to the areas way "upriver" after a shaman's death (Herzog-Schröder 2006; Kopenawa and Albert 2013). These areas are the ones from which the original ancestors of the Yanomami came and from where the shamans still receive their "songs"—these songs being tantamount to shamanic knowledge. In "mythical times" as well as in shamanic topology, the upriver and uphill areas are "central," whereas downriver is more connected to what we could call the "periphery." So, from an emic view, the non-indigenous/*napë* come from "river down," and, while it has brought with it many welcome commodities, this is also where destructive forces are to be found, as illustrated by it being designated as the origin of many illnesses.

When one characterizes the arrival of an institution—a school—as a mark of modernity in remote villages, it might seem surprising that evidence of shamanic activity has not declined as a consequence of this new history but has on the contrary increased. In connection with the two villages in this text, when I visited in 2012 there appeared to be an increase in shamans since my previous visit, and they were evidently serious in their spiritual endeavor. The introduction of schools in the communities did not show the effects that one might associate with a process of modernization, that is, a decrease in traditional shamanic practices. On the contrary, these newly established spaces—the schools—where new practices of knowledge are introduced, seem to coexist with traditional spiritual practices. Before schools were part of these communities, shamanism was the only social or cultural context in which teaching and learning was explicitly practiced. Other forms of knowledge had been passed on in a more tacit way.[14] Now, however, we can observe two settings where the explicit transfer of knowledge is undertaken: in schools and through shamanic teaching.

It seems useful to include this perspective in an exploration of the emic meaning of the schools. They can be interpreted as places or means of a perception of "selfness" and "otherness." An inherent paradox, intrinsic to concepts of alternative or indigenous modernities (Halbmayer 2012), is therefore well illustrated in this example. Arguing within a framework of indigenous cosmology, the self-authorized introduction of schools into the communities of the Hapokashitha and Sheroana could be understood as an attempt to "domesticate" the "strangers." This image fits well with Yanomami cosmology: the shamans offer their body—to be specific, their chests—to the shamanic tutelary spirits, the *hekura*, so that they can take residence within them.[15] This is how the shaman turns into a master of the spirits during an initiation, and receives the spirit's help. In physical accordance with this powerful image, the Yanomami offer a hut in their village-round for the foreign knowledge— the spirits—to take up residence. The formerly wild spirits are tamed by the shaman and used in his practices. This understanding of knowledge is a way to understand the desire to have a school—a strange institution—in order to "tame" the foreignness. In a broader context, this idea has been suggested in other publications such as that of Bruce Albert and Rita Ramos (2002) regarding the indigenous people of the Brazilian lowlands, which is titled *Pacificando o branco*, "pacifying the white man." There is substantial evidence that a similar interpretation fits well for the Yanomami in southern Venezuela in their encounters with modernity.

Gabriele Herzog-Schröder (Dr.phil., Berlin [Free University]) trained in social and cultural anthropology at the Ludwig-Maximilians University of Munich (LMU) and at the Free University in Berlin. She has been doing fieldwork among the Yanomami of southern Venezuela since the early 1980s. Currently she holds a position as senior lecturer at the Institute of Social and Cultural Anthropology at the LMU, Munich. Aside from her academic work, she also holds diverse responsibilities in the context of ethnographic collections and exhibitions mainly related to lowland South America.

Notes

The author is indebted to the Film Archive of Human Ethology of the Senckenberg Gesellschaft für Naturforschung; formerly Film Archive of Human Ethology of the Max-Planck-Society, Andechs, Germany, without whom research for this chapter would not have been possible. I also want to thank the staff of the Institute of Social and Cultural Anthropology at the Ludwig-Maximilian-University, Munich, for their interest and discussions.

1. *Hiramamoremi* = school, a neologism that derives from *hira-aï* = to teach, to instruct; and *kua* = to have, to be.
2. The Yanomami term for foreign is *napë*. *Napë* refers to any kind of stranger or foreigner, be they indigenous or non-indigenous. Bilingual Yanomami often use the term *criollo* for non-Yanomami instead of *napë*. *Criollo* is used in all of Venezuela to apply to non-indigenous people. By using this term, these Yanomami declare themselves somehow alien to their own traditional setting.
3. The Patanowëtheri are also mentioned in early documentation of this region: Chagnon (1968), Zerries and Schuster (1974), as well as Valero, Agagliate and Fuentes (1984), to name but a few. The legendary film documentary *The Ax Fight* by T. Asch and N.A. Chagnon (1975) was actually made in Patanowë.
4. An overview of the division of the different dialects is given in Mattéi-Müller et al. (2007).
5. For detailed information on census data concerning the Yanomami in Brazil and Venezuela, see Scholz and Mansutti (2011).
6. Schooling, medical care, and participation in the political decisions of the respective countries in which they live (Venezuela and Brazil) have become important issues for the Yanomami communities, particularly those near the river. Yanomami groups increasingly speak for themselves about their own issues and, in many regards, are disengaging themselves not only from their dependence on the Christian missions, but also from NGOs who support or in some cases try to dominate them (depending on the individual NGO's perspective). Ever since the late Hugo Chávez came to power in Venezuela 1999, the processes of politicization have been acute and, at times, aggressive, and have even spread into relatively isolated areas. For the Yanomami in Venezuela, particularly those located close to the rivers, this has meant an increased interest and involvement in processes of indigenous self-declaration. Involvement in these processes has only sporadically and slowly reached the hinterland areas.
7. Although important positions are often held by men, women are regularly present at public discussions, and their influence in communal decisions can be described as informal but persuasive. For more detailed information on aspects of gender power, see Herzog-Schröder (2000, 2003, 2013).
8. I am particularly indebted to Monika Mühlthaler, who has lived in Mavaca for many years as a layperson and has taken on much responsibility for managing the schools and curriculum at the mission posts. She has

shared with me particular information about the dependence of the smaller schools upon the larger institutions.
9. In his dissertation, José Antonio Kelly (2011) undertook a similar approach, centering on state healthcare among the Yanomami from the Ocamo area, downriver from the Upper Orinoco region that is dealt with here.
10. This ontological condition is consistent with the constant notion of "transformation" in ritual life, one that also pervades the everyday life of the Yanomami.
11. The SUYAO was a cooperative craftwork trading association that received goods such as metal tools or textiles in return for handicrafts from the village communities; it operated from the late 1980s until the late 1990s. It has now been replaced by HORONAMI, an organization that is more informed about Venezuelan state issues, but also more influenced by Venezuelan political parties.
12. The name Hapokashitha indicates the place where clay (*shi-*) for the manufacturing of pots (*hapoka*) could be found, a practice that was abandoned by the Yanomami more than thirty years ago.
13. By "clothing," the leader of the Sheroana people meant a red loincloth, which was actually only introduced to the Yanomami some thirty to forty years ago but is still conventional in many hinterland communities.
14. I describe elsewhere how the women vehemently insist on not having been *taught* how to weave, cook, or work in the gardens. They always declared in their interviews with me that they had *acquired* this specific knowledge—as their bodies have grown (Herzog-Schröder 2000: 253, 269).
15. The tutelary spirits among the Yanomamï of the Upper Orinoco area are most often called *hekura* or *shapori*. These terms are equivalent to *xipiri* (Kopenawa and Albert 2013), as expressed in the eastern dialect.

Bibliography

Albert, Bruce. 1992. "Indian Lands, Environmental Policy and Military Geopolitics in the Development of the Brazilian Amazon: The Case of the Yanomami." *Development and Change* 23(1): 35–70.

Albert, Bruce and Alcida R. Ramos (eds). 2002. *Pacificando o branco: cosmologias do contato no norte-amazônico*. São Paulo: Unesp.

Anderson-Levitt, Kathryn (ed.). 2003. *Local Meanings, Global Schooling: Anthropology and World Culture Theory*. New York: Palgrave Macmillan.

Asch, Tim and Napoleon A. Chagnon. 1975. *The Ax Fight*. Documentary Educational Resources, Watertown, MA.

Caballero Arias, Hortensia. 2005. "Primeros encuentros: Los Yanomami en las representaciones post-coloniales de la primera mitad del siglo XX." *ANTROPOLOGICA* 104: 5–34.

Caballero Arias, Hortensia. 2014. *Desencuentros y encuentros en el Alto Orinoco: Incursiones en territorio yanomami, siglos XVIII-XIX*. Caracas: Ediciones IVIC.

Canclini, Néstor G. 1990. *Culturas híbridas : Estrategias para entrar y salir de la modernidad*. Mexico: Grijalbo.

Chagnon, Napoleon A. 1968. *Yanomamö: The Fierce People.* New York: Holt, Rinehart and Winston.
Fausto, Carlo. 1999. "Of Enemies and Pets: Warfare and Shamanism in Amazonia." *American Ethnologist* 26(4): 933–56.
Ferguson, R. Brian. 1995. *Yanomami Warfare.* Santa Fe, NM: SAR.
Halbmayer, Ernst. 2012. "Dossier: Debating Animism, Perspectivism and the Construction of Ontologies." *Indiana* 29: 9–24.
Herzog, Gabriele. 1990. *Patanowëtheri: eine Dorfgemeinschaft der Yanomamï im Südlichen Venezuela.* Hohenschäftlarn: Klaus Renner Verlag.
Herzog-Schröder, Gabriele. 2000. *Okoyoma: Die Krebsjägerinnen. Vom Leben der Yanomamï-Frauen in Venezuela.* Münster and Hamburg: LIT-Verlag.
———. 2003. "Yanomami." In *Encyclopedia of Sex and Gender in the World's Cultures Topics and Cultures,* ed. Carol R. Ember and Melvin Ember, 967–975. Vol. 2. New York: Springer.
———. 2006. "Zyklische Zeiten und das Tabu der Erinnerung – ein Fallbeispiel aus Amazonien." In *Memoria y olvido de la historia,* eds. Christiane Kunst and Verónica M. González, 149–162. Castelló de la Plana: Publicaciones de la Universitat Jaume I.
———. 2013. "La menstruación, el cangrejo, el novio y el homicidio: Consideraciones sobre el concepto de la persona y las relaciones familiares a la luz de los rituales de los Yanomami del Alto Orinoco (Venezuela)." In *Wege im Garten der Ethnologie,* ed. Hanna Heinrich and Harald Grauer, 159–187. Sankt Augustin: Academia Verlag.
Kelly, José A. 2011. *State Healthcare and Yanomami Transformations: A Symmetrical Ethnography.* Tucson, AZ: University of Arizona Press.
Knauft, Bruce M. (ed.). 2002. *Critically Modern: Alternatives, Alterities, Anthropologies.* Bloomington, IN: Indiana University Press.
Kopenawa, Davi and Bruce Albert. 2013. *The Falling Sky: Words of a Yanomami Shaman.* Cambridge, MA: Harvard University Press.
Mattéi-Müller, Marie-Claude, et al. 2007. *Lengua y cultura yanomamï: diccionario ilustrado yanomamï-español, español-yanomamï.* Caracas: UNESCO.
Milliken, William, Bruce Albert, and Gale G. Gomez. 1999. *Yanomani: A Forest People.* Kew, London: Royal Botanic Gardens.
Padilha, José. 2010. *Secrets of the Tribe.* Watertown, MA: Documentary Educational Resources.
Pitarch, Pedro and Gemma Orobitg (eds). 2012. *Modernidades indígenas.* Madrid and Frankfurt: Vervuert Iberoamericana.
Ramos, Alcida R. 1995. *Sanumá Memories: Yanomami Ethnography in Times of Crisis.* Madison, WI: University of Wisconsin Press.
Sahlins, Marshall. 1999. "What is Anthropological Enlightenment? Some Lessons of the Twentieth Century." *Annual Review of Anthropology* 28(1): i–xxiii.
Scholz, Andrea and Mansutti Rodríguez, A. 2011. "Situation der indigenen Bevölkerung: Neue Vielfalt im multikulturellen Staat oder Einheitsstaat in multikultureller Verkleidung?" In *Venezuela heute - Politik, Wirtschaft, Kultur,* Vol. 140, ed. A. Boeckh, F. Welsch and N. Werz, 77–104. Berlin: Bibliotheca Ibero-Americana Ibero-Amerikanisches Institut Preußischer Kulturbesitz.
Steward, Julian H. and Louis C. Faron. 1959. *Native Peoples of South America.* New York: McGraw-Hill.

Tierney, Patrick. 2001: *Darkness in El Dorado: How Scientists and Journalists Devastated the Amazon*. New York: W.W. Norton & Company.
Valero, Helena, Renato Agagliate and Emilio Fuentes. 1984. *Yo soy Napëyoma: relato de una mujer raptada por los indígenas yanomami*. Caracas: Fundación La Salle de Ciencias Naturales.
Viveiros de Castro, Eduardo. 1992. *From the Enemy's Point of View: Humanity and Divinity in an Amazonian Society*. Chicago, IL: University of Chicago Press.
———. 1998. "Cosmological Deixis and Amerindian Perspectivism." *Journal of the Royal Anthropological Institute* 4(3): 469–88.
Wilbert, Johannes. 1963. *Indios de la región Orinoco-Ventuari*. Caracas: Fundación La Salle de Ciencias Naturales.
Zerries, Otto and Meinhard Schuster. 1974. *Mahekodotedi: Monographie eines Dorfes der Waika-Indianer (Yanoama) am oberen Orinoco (Venezuela)*. Munich: K. Renner.

# 4

INDIGENOUS ACTIVISM BEYOND ETHNIC GROUPS
Shifting Boundaries and Constellations of Belonging
Eva Gerharz

Since the United Nations (UN) initiated the International Day of the World's Indigenous Peoples in 1995 with the intention to promote and protect the rights of the world's indigenous people,[1] this occasion has been celebrated all over the world. In Bangladesh, so-called indigenous people make up less than 3 percent of the country's total population (AIPP 2009: 15). They live dispersed throughout the country, and are of remarkable linguistic and religious diversity; however, they hold a marginal position amidst the overwhelming majority of Bengali-speaking Muslims in Bangladesh, in economic, cultural, and political terms. For the activists who claim to represent the concerns and demands of those populations who consider themselves indigenous, the International Day of the World's Indigenous Peoples offers an arena in which they not only receive public attention, but "have the floor" to reiterate their demands concerning more equality and recognition. All over the country, but mainly in the capital Dhaka, groups representing "indigenous culture" gather to perform shows in their "traditional" costumes. They hold processions and demonstrations, public speeches are given by indigenous representatives, activists belonging to the Bengali population, and supportive politicians. Quite frequently, activists also ask representatives of international organizations who are stationed in Dhaka to join in and speak on behalf of indigenous people.

Starting from these observations about the International Day of the World's Indigenous Peoples in Dhaka, in which I have repeatedly participated during the last few years, this contribution seeks to investigate the translocalization of the activist movement for the rights of

Bangladesh's indigenous people. Activist movements that campaign to remake the world in line with a consciously articulated program (Gellner 2009), offer particularly interesting ways to investigate how such campaigns relate to political programs that are informed not only by immediate grievances, but by conceptual propositions borrowed from elsewhere. In the case of indigenous activism, the intensification of a global indigenous movement, following the announcement of two consecutive UN Decades of the World's Indigenous People, and the attempt to define who indigenous people are and recommend how they should be protected, has been highly relevant.[2] My interpretations are based on the results of qualitative research, which I conducted between 1999 and 2013 during several field visits in Bangladesh.[3] From 2003 onwards, I have also been involved in lobbying work for human rights and development-related topics in Bangladesh, and Europe, which has offered important insights into the world of transnational activism.[4] The findings elaborated in this chapter are thus based on a threefold methodological approach, which includes genuine ethnographic inquiry, research with a focus on activism, and being an "activist researcher" (Hale 2001). While requiring thorough reflection on my position vis-à-vis the field, this approach enables me to investigate the subject from various angles—which is what I intend to offer in this contribution.

The main concern pursued in this chapter starts with the observation that the increasing attention that indigenous people and indigenous rights have received nationally and globally, within so-called civil society and the United Nations, has become an important resource for activists of the indigenous movement. This has led, firstly, to greater involvement in transnational activist networks (TAN), which operate across national borders as pressure groups (della Porta and Tarrow 2005; Keck and Sikkink 1998; Tarrow 2005). At the center of the activists' endeavors is the desire to overcome marginalization, social stigmatization, and economic discrimination (Chakma 2010; Karim 1998; Uddin 2010). Secondly, Bangladeshi activists have also been involved with various institutions, working groups, and forums within the UN system (Dahl 2012). Activists have particularly drawn on the exchange of knowledge and experiences with colleagues from other Asian countries, such as Nepal, India, Thailand, and the Philippines. However, as I will show in this chapter, the emerging actor constellation and the representations used by the activists to signify the demands of indigenous people are quite diverse. On the one hand, the boundaries of the movement itself, which refers to indigeneity as a category of belonging, may be drawn in open or narrow ways; on the other hand, the activists make use of images that relate indigeneity to essentializing categorical thinking. This leads to an apparently unresolvable dilemma.

Based on my empirical analysis, I develop two arguments that relate to the alteration of actor constellations. The first relates to the intrinsic structuration of the movement. Quite often, indigenous movements are depicted in a homogenizing manner and are treated as groups. This chapter seeks to move beyond this kind of "groupism" (Brubaker 2002). By adopting a perspective that aims at elucidating the structuration of social configurations, in this case an activist movement, this chapter reveals the relationships between individuals and collectives taking part in activism. It thus proposes a perspective on constellations of belonging, in the sense of individual and/or collective positioning. The advantage of the belonging concept is that it emphasizes the relational dimensions of inclusion and exclusion, and avoids the "fixations" that the concept of identity necessarily implies (Anthias 2002; Pfaff-Czarnecka 2010; Yuval Davis 2006). These configurations are not restricted to particular categories of belonging, for example ethnicity, class, gender, or caste, per se. Although ethnicity is considered to be the foundation for what are now called "indigenous groups" in our common understanding, my empirical research shows that processes of inclusion and exclusion take place along different lines. According to the activists' view, some members of so-called ethnic groups are positioned "outside" the movement, and conversely, members of the ethnic "other" may be included for a variety of reasons. As a result, activist collectives are characterized by multiethnic configurations that may evolve in particular situations, or even be institutionalized.

The second argument is based on the assumption that this situativeness rests upon complex spatiality. Activist movements usually do not fit neatly into preconfigured spatial orders: they can be national and transnational, local and global at the same time, and although activists often foster institutionalization at the national level, their work also connects simultaneously with globalized rhetoric and local knowledge. Thus, there is a strong tendency to traverse sociality defined in spatial terms. Case studies from other contexts have highlighted the existence of frictions between activists and the people they seek to represent (Ghosh 2006; Li 2000; Pfaff-Czarnecka 2007). My empirical case confirms this assumption, yet I seek to demonstrate that crossing national borders, which has been the center of attention in the scholarship on transnational activism, is not always what activists desire. Rather, activism may oscillate between different spatial scales while simultaneously relating to them, both in discursive and practical ways. Thus, I propose to conceptualize indigenous activists' movements as constituting translocal spaces (Gerharz 2012; Lachenmann 2008, 2010), as this notion can cope with the complexity of spatial orderings and the social dynamics spanning between them. On this basis, the chapter seeks to offer a new way to reconceptualize the relationship between activist representation and membership.

In the next section, the discourse on indigeneity in Bangladesh and the South Asian context will be assessed in close relation to the emergence of indigenous activism on a global scale. In the main part of this chapter, three dimensions of indigenous activism in Bangladesh, which have been identified on the basis of the empirical material collected, will be developed. This leads to the main argument, which refers, in line with current relational approaches, to the shifting constellations of belonging in indigenous activism. By revealing two processes—the enlargement and the closure of boundaries—it will be shown how these shifts come into being. The conclusions focus on the increasing divergence of representation and configuration in activism.

Indigeneity in Bangladesh

The history of indigeneity in South Asia is varied and complicated. During colonialism, sections of society were labeled as "tribal," a notion that clearly carries with it connotations of backwardness and primitivism (Kuper 2003; Schendel 2011). These "tribes" were considered to be different from the majority populations in religious, linguistic, and cultural terms. Apart from different cultural practices, slash-and-burn farming has been a common mode of agricultural production. Inasmuch as the notion of the "tribal" has become an administrative term in India nowadays, providing an important basis for defining collectives subjected to affirmative action, the pejorative implication remains. In India, the rise of so-called separatist movements has been accompanied by an increasing awareness of identity politics, and the label "tribal" has been seriously questioned (see, e.g., Shah 2007; Vanderkerckhove 2009). In order to avoid the connotations of racial superiority and the (post)colonial policies of exclusion associated with the term "tribal," activists and those they seek to represent prefer the term *"adivasi"* (Bates 1995). These debates have arisen in Bangladesh over the last fifteen years, during which indigenous people have come to incorporate the language of indigeneity. Referring to themselves as "indigenous people," analogous to the Bengali terms *adivasi*,[5] *pahari* (hill people), or *jumma* (slash-and-burn farmer),[6] they use these alternative terms of varying origins as tools to counter their marginalization within the nation-state, which has been dominated by a majoritarian nation-building project since the country's independence in 1971. This process has fostered a tendency towards cultural homogeneity, and has used the Bengali culture and also Islam to construct national identities (Jahangir 1986; Mohsin 1997). The nationalizing trend has been accompanied by a deepening economic and political marginalization, as well as a social exclusion of minorities, including Hindus, but also the indigenous population in almost every part of the country—who had already been exposed to the politics of primitive tribalism and backwardness throughout colonial and Pakistani rule.

The largest concentration of indigenous people in Bangladesh can be found in the southeastern hilly region called the Chittagong Hill Tracts (CHT). In contrast to "plainland *adivasi*" in other parts of the country who look back on a history of enduring marginalization and see limited scope for activist engagement (Bleie 2005), indigenous representatives from the CHT have been more eloquent in raising their voices. Activism explicitly criticizing state policy dates back to the early days of postcolonial state formation, when the Pakistani government[7] decided to construct a reservoir dam in the 1960s. This "development project" displaced and impoverished large parts of the population. Only a few years after the state of Bangladesh was formed in 1971, an armed conflict between militant representatives of the indigenous groups and the military flared up, putting the region into a state of continuous emergency. The government refused to attribute a separate status to the residents of the CHT and maintained colonial protective measures.[8] In lieu of concessions, the government responded to the demands of the indigenous people with massive militarization and an aggressive settlement policy (Arens 1997; Aziz-al Ahsan and Chakma 1989). The resettlement of large numbers of landless Bengalis in this region has significantly altered the demographic composition. Today, the indigenous population, who once formed a majority of approximately 90 percent of the people living in the CHT, are estimated to make up less than half of the total population there.[9] Forced displacement, illegal land grabbing, and the unlawful distribution of land were then fuel for the armed conflict. The war was officially brought to an end with a peace treaty and the disarmament of the guerrilla forces in 1997, but armed conflicts between different local groups, expulsion of populations from their land, and communal conflicts over land still determine everyday life in many parts of the Chittagong Hill Tracts (Adnan and Dastidar 2011). Arable farm land continues to diminish, and "land grabs" have assumed alarming proportions. The marginalization of the indigenous population, therefore, exhibits a certain continuity.

Although these difficulties prevail, the previously militant guise of indigenous activism has transformed into a more civilian one. Activists of the Chittagong Hill Tracts have partnered with plainland *adivasi* representatives and formed a national movement. Nationwide, several organizations, such as the Bangladesh Indigenous People's Forum, fight for the allocation of minority rights, and particularly indigenous rights, from the state. One of their major arguments is that the inclusion of indigenous people into the national Bengali-Muslim-dominated mainstream can only be achieved when collective rights, including those ensuring access to land, are conceded to them. By arguing that inequality, based on culture and ethnic-religious belonging, characterizes nationalism in Bangladesh, the activist demands highlight models of a more democratic, diverse, and pluralistic society (Schendel 2001). It will be shown later that the demands for constitutional recognition symbolize this kind of vision.

The UN Initiative and Bangladeshi Responses

The formation of activist groups for the rights of the indigenous people in Bangladesh coincided with the institutionalization of indigenous people's issues as a policy field at the global level, in particular involving the UN. When the UN proclaimed the First Decade for the World's Indigenous People in 1995, it confirmed the need to develop appropriate mechanisms for the protection of the rights of indigenous people on a global scale. Prior to this, the issue had already been on the agenda of the International Labour Organization (ILO) and the UN Sub-Commission on the Prevention of Discrimination and the Protection of Minorities, which instigated the formation of a Working Group on Indigenous Populations (WGIP) in 1982 (Muehlebach 2001; Pelican 2009: 55). One of the WGIP's tasks was to develop a draft declaration, which was completed in 1993, but it took a further fourteen years until the final version of the Declaration on the Rights of Indigenous Peoples was adopted by the General Assembly in 2007 (Oldham and Frank 2008). Prior to the announcement of the Second UN Decade of the World's Indigenous People, from 2005 to 2014, the Permanent Forum on Indigenous Issues was established in 2000. As a central coordinating body, the Permanent Forum functions in an advisory role to the Economic and Social Council. Since 2011, the Permanent Forum has a Bangladeshi member, Chakma Raja Devasish Roy.[10] In addition, several Bangladeshi activists have had the chance to participate in the UN's activities, such as world conferences and the fellowship program, under which indigenous people can visit the Office of the United Nations High Commissioner for Human Rights in Geneva to learn about UN mechanisms for dealing with human rights and indigenous issues.

In the course of this institutionalization at the global level, "indigenous people" became an established term as part of an attempt at a comprehensive definition of the same (Karlsson 2003; Li 2000; Muehlebach 2003; Tsing 2007). Bangladeshi activists tend to use the notion of "indigenous people" when articulating their claims in international contexts. For them, the advantage of the working definition on which the UN institutions agreed after lengthy debates lies in the fact that it sees indigenous people as "prior inhabitants" rather than "original inhabitants" (Gray 1995: 39), making the right to self-determination central. Self-determination, in this context, is framed in such a way that it is not reduced to claims of statehood but is used in the sense of a "much broader vision of justice and equality" (Muehlebach 2003: 259). Although the UN Declaration on the Rights of Indigenous Peoples offers an understanding that steers away from a clear-cut definition and thus leaves space to accommodate a variety of interpretations (Oldham and Frank 2008), some actors, and governments in particular, stick to a narrower definition of indigeneity. Especially among Asian and African governments, there is a tendency to employ arguments against those who claim to be indigenous people today, and to utilize narrower definitions referring to "original settlers," as is the case in Australia and most American countries (Karlsson 2003: 407; Pelican 2009: 55). As we shall see later, the government of Bangladesh has also decided to follow this trend.

Despite repeated opposition in national identity politics, indigenous demands from Bangladesh are still acknowledged within the UN system, and global civil society and activists continue to make demands for recognition at the national level. It is mainly thanks to the United Nations' initiative and voices from global activists that indigenous matters have also found their way onto the agenda of global development cooperation in Bangladesh. In the programs of some organizations, the protection of indigenous peoples has been handled within the sphere of activity of "assistance for minorities," and is treated with so-called "rights-based approaches." The link between activist involvement and development cooperation is clearly observable in Bangladesh.[11] Several foreign partner organizations, including the UN Development Programme (UNDP), have promoted the development of largely neglected regions, such as the Chittagong Hill Tracts.[12] Indigenous activism also experiences direct support. The European Commission, for example, cooperated with indigenous organizations, and their activities on the International Day of the World's Indigenous Peoples have received financial support from foreign donors.[13] The national indigenous movement in Bangladesh hopes that cooperation at this level will give more credit to their claims.[14] How these claims are articulated in and adapted to particular contexts is shown in the following section, and will provide the basis for a deeper understanding of the translocal constellations emerging from these encounters.

Dimensions of Indigenous Activism

Activists play a key role in transmitting and translating global ideas and concepts to local and national levels. By taking over the position of a "broker" (Bierschenk, Chaveau, and Olivier de Sardan 2001), they mediate between different knowledge systems and transform the "codes" in such a way that they fit into the sociocultural frameworks. Thus, knowledge constitutes a resource that is flexible, situative, and can be adopted in specific ways. It is mediated through various links between the activities and claims of groups organized locally and nationally on the one hand, and globally circulating rhetoric on the other, which is characterized by complex translation processes and the dynamics of adaption. The processes constituting these links can be analytically captured with the concept of vernacularization (Merry 2006). This concept analyzes the ways in which "transnational ideas"—such as human rights or minority rights, labor, social, or environmental standards—are adapted in local social settings. Thus, it can help to illuminate social interaction in the spaces "in between," by looking at how intermediately positioned actors translate between the different levels constituting translocal space. To legitimize their demands, activists (and also politicians) seize on global discourses and adapt them into local concepts. In Bangladesh, at least three dimensions can be distinguished in which national politics and global rhetoric are directly connected. The first relates to the official recognition of indigenous people in Bangladesh's legal framework. The second dimension in which the inclusion of indigenous ideals is pursued concerns development activities, which are subject to negotiations between donors, national developmental actors, and local initiatives. The third dimension deals with the media representation of indigenous people. Based on an analysis within these three social fields, I put forward some thoughts concerning the configurations in translocal activism.

The National Legal Framework and Indigenous Peoples' Claims

According to the Declaration on the Rights of Indigenous Peoples, groups identified as such should be endowed with a special status—as deserving of protection. In 2011, a discussion about an amendment to the Bangladeshi constitution offered a window of opportunity to demand changes, particularly to Article 29, which allocates special provisions for so-called "backward sections of citizens." A parliamentary caucus comprising members belonging to the indigenous groups and their allies from the leftist parties[15] demanded the inclusion of the category "indigenous people" into the constitution, in order to lay the basis for receiving a special status, as promoted by the UN declaration. In addition, activists lobbied for the ratification of ILO Convention 169, which is, apart from the UN declaration, one of the major international treaties safeguarding the rights of indigenous people—which has not been ratified by Bangladesh. During the celebrations for the International Day of the World's Indigenous Peoples on 9 August 2010, the need for the recognition of the notion of "indigenous people" was vigorously propagated. The activists had reworked the lyrics of a "traditional" song in such a way that it contained the line "we want constitutional recognition" as a refrain—a creative engagement with culture that serves as an illustrative example of the particular ways in which global discourse is vernacularized at the local level. At the same time, the refrain was sung in English, and addressed not only Bangladeshi audiences but international visitors and media representatives.

That the committee charged with advising on possible revisions to the constitution ignored the indigenous demands and suggested the use of the term "small ethnic minorities" in March 2011 was strongly criticized by the indigenous activists, political parties belonging to the left, human rights activists, and academics. One of the reasons given by the co-speaker was that the definition given by the United Nations does not apply to the indigenous population of Bangladesh. By referring to the concept in which indigenous people are defined as "original inhabitants," the foreign minister stated in July 2011 that the people living in the CHT were not indigenous, but came as asylum seekers and economic migrants. The Bengali-speaking Muslim majority should be considered the original settlers in the territory today called Bangladesh, whereas those with different religions and languages constituted "small ethnic minorities." This statement, which has become the government's official position, prompted the traditional chief of the Chakma, Raja Devasish Roy, to criticize the foreign minister's statement as flawed. The internationally represented Chittagong Hill Tracts Commission[16] also responded with a letter, in which they referred to a number of comparable cases in South and Southeast Asia, and to the use of the term "indigenous" in a range of policy documents in Bangladesh's history. The justice minister, in turn, reacted by reiterating that its official position was in line with the ILO definition, which refers to "those living in a particular area before a country's independence." Therefore, "American Red Indians and Australian aborigines could be called indigenous," but the situation in Bangladesh was different.[17] A few days later, the foreign minister repeated in a meeting with foreign diplomats and media editors that "indigenous people" was a "misnomer" in the context of Bangladesh.[18] Since then, the government has continuously reiterated its position and has taken a very critical view on indigenous activism.

This dispute illustrates how the debate about competing concepts, which has been fought out in a lengthy process at the UN level, has been translated into the Bangladeshi context. The activists grounded their demands by referencing the version that was finally endorsed by the declaration, which highlights the right to self-determination. The government, on the other hand, reiterated the position promoted in countries where indigenous people are "original settlers" and translated it into Bengali-nationalist language. The government of Bangladesh also follows similar standpoints taken by other governments in African countries and, most importantly, in India.[19] Indigeneity in Bangladesh, then, as a category of group identification and belonging, is negotiated in the translocal space which appears, in the case presented here, as a border-crossing formation spanning different spatial contexts. At the same time, the above example reveals that at the national level, different actors take up and relate to differing conceptual frameworks, which they gain access to by taking part in the constitution of translocal spaces, and combat disputes over the authority of such concepts by incorporating them into the national discursive frame.

Developmental Demands

Another set of demands that has been repeatedly outlined by indigenous activists concerns the explicit consideration of the interests of the indigenous population in national development programs. These demands include the equal treatment of indigenous citizens in relation to land rights (see, e.g., Roy 2000), access to public goods and administrative positions, and improved access to social services and economic opportunities. A large number of the indigenous people living in the plains and the CHT depend on agriculture for their livelihoods, and many of those inhabiting the hilly areas in particular perform slash-

and-burn cultivation, known locally as *jhum*. Although economic activities have diversified since colonial times,[20] more recently land dispossessions have forced a considerable portion of indigenous people, both in the hills and the plains, to seek further income alternatives (Adnan and Dastidar 2011). Especially on the plains, the percentage of indigenous people categorized as poor or very poor exceeds the national average (Barkat et al. 2009: 267). Several international development organizations cooperating with partners in Bangladesh have stressed the particular need to provide assistance to this section of society. During interviews conducted throughout my fieldwork, representatives of international organizations highlighted the need not only to improve the marginal socioeconomic position of the indigenous population, but also to alter their disadvantaged position in terms of health, education, and livelihoods. In the CHT, the formal peace in 1997 coincided with a global initiative to combine development assistance with conflict resolution or peace building (Gerharz 2002). Donors saw this as a window of opportunity, since Bangladesh was considered to be a comparatively uncomplicated partner country. Subsequent to initial wide-ranging attempts to formulate an agenda for development in the CHT, however, the security situation deteriorated and forced many donors to withdraw. Today, the UNDP, with its co-funded CHT Development Facility, constitutes the main international presence in the CHT. In addition, several national NGOs, many of them with a special focus on promoting microcredit schemes, have established themselves in the region, and a couple of local NGOs have entered into developmental partnerships with donors from the Global North.

During my fieldwork experiences, both in 2000 and subsequent to 2008, it emerged that developmental activities, although initially highly appreciated, had turned into what some describe as an "intrusion." During interviews, some activists complained about the predominantly top-down approach, especially adopted by the larger initiatives. They also argued that the organizations were "taking away our brains" and "steal[ing] our ideas" (see also Chittagong Hill Tracts Commission 2009: 20), and feared that developmental hierarchies would lead to an exploitation of the scarce knowledge resources available among the indigenous population. In contrast, international development organizations emphasized that local development NGOs lacked know-how and implementation capacities, complaining of the difficulties in finding qualified personnel. This exemplifies one of the crucial challenges in contexts where development cooperation has just begun. Whereas large parts of the developing world have adapted to the requirements of international agencies—that is, they have developed appropriate structural conditions and a labor force that caters to them—areas that have been isolated, for example through armed conflicts, lack such infrastructure. Consequently, knowledge repertoires of local indigenous representatives do not comply with the needs of international development cooperation but are instead more in line with indigenous discourses, stressing distinctiveness and local knowledge.

Another case relates to the implementation of microcredit schemes, which were first distributed by the Grameen Bank and have evolved into a kind of panacea. Although the benefits of this strategy have been hotly debated in relation to empirical findings from other parts of Bangladesh (Lewis 2011: 119; White 1999), microcredit schemes continue to be offered by Bengali NGOs. When these NGOs started to introduce these schemes in the Chittagong Hill Tracts, where much of the economic activity has traditionally taken place in the subsistence sector, and as a consequence the level of monetarization has remained low, they were met with heavy criticism. Local critics argued that the scheme is an inappropriate tool for accelerating development among farmers who primarily depend on *jhum* cultivation (Gerharz 2002). This argument carries strong traditionalist connotations as it assumes that this intervention would "alienate" people from their traditional culture, of which *jhum* is an integral part. Another criticism is that the ability to make use of micro-loans in productive ways would necessitate a transformation from a subsistence-based economy to a cash economy, and this would force indigenous people into competition with the Bengali settlers, whose access to trade networks and other assets would put them at a competitive advantage. Furthermore, Bengali NGOs implementing microcredit schemes have been harshly criticized for demanding high interest rates, and thereby exploiting and deepening poverty among the local indigenous population. Local NGO representatives highlighted the special needs of the hill population, which then require appropriate development strategies. Although some Bengali-led NGOs have attempted integrative approaches, and partially included the indigenous population in the project region, many indigenous activists insist on the value of cultural differences in development, and that structurally inherent socioeconomic inequalities can only be countered by special measures.

The call for local development strategies was supported by smaller international organizations that mainly cooperated with local NGOs and some individual activists. Labeled as "indigenous peoples' development," this mode of development is clearly demarcated from the national mainstream, as it is geared towards including elements of traditional economic practices, and environmentally friendly and sustainable methods. A Bengali consultant, who supported the local experts in their venture, explained in interviews held in 2009 and 2013 that the group tried to develop a particular vision of what he called *"adivasi* development," for which he received inspiration from experiences of working in Jharkhand, India.

Thus, in the field of development, indigenous activists pursue their demands through developing alternative approaches that fit into what they regard as indigenous culture and traditions. In light of increasing interest and recognition of the need to support indigenous people, which has emerged among both international and national development actors, these demands are particularly pertinent. My respondents voiced the fear that "foreign approaches" do not apply to specific local needs. At the same time, NGO representatives argued that the technocratization that accompanies large-scale programs would lead to the elimination of the scarce human capacities and skills that are available locally.

The translocalization of development, targeting indigenous people in Bangladesh, leads to renegotiations of indigeneity in relation to developmental interventions. The notion of indigeneity as such becomes even more virulent when discussed in the context of development, as it serves as a basis for identifying particular cultural sentiments, which are interpreted in traditionalist terms. This, in turn, contributes to the "fixing" of indigenous cultures by exempting them from social change, which would threaten indigenous people with "losing their traditional values." In addition, developmental hierarchies carry with them the danger of losing the authority over developmental knowledge. But development cooperation also bears the potential to strengthen translocal connections, in which representatives of international organizations and well-minded Bengalis may act as supporters. Some Bengali academics and civil society representatives engage in *adivasi* rights activism, while others relate indigenous demands to their work in either human rights or environmental organizations. Such partnerships are strategically important, especially when it comes to the representation of indigenous demands.

Representing Indigenous People in Public Space

Since the category of indigenous people has become more widespread in Bangladesh, popular images of indigenous people have changed. One reason is the rise of private television channels and the diversification of print media. Since the Peace Accord in the CHT in 1997, the region has been reported on regularly, which has contributed to a better nationwide understanding of the region's specifics. My respondents highlighted that the increased attention would instigate the transformation of previous images of indigenous people as "backward" and "primitive," and that this constituted an important step in the process of attaining an emphasis on equality. To attain this goal, activists use various strategies. They try to put the issue on the agenda of both those domestic and foreign media who inform people about lifestyle and cultural practices. This has happened to a certain extent, with the help of a growing number of journalists with indigenous backgrounds reporting in newspapers on a regular basis. At the same time, Bengali professionals have shown increased interest in indigenous issues. This became evident during my participant observation of the 2008 and 2010 celebrations of the annual International Day of the World's Indigenous Peoples, where I witnessed a large number of journalists with professional camera equipment, eager to shoot revealing pictures, which were included in their stories about the celebrations either on that same evening or the next day. This strategy, however, is laden with complications. Activists complain that representations of indigenous practices in the national media tend to alienate, exoticize, and depreciate indigenous people. As illustrative evidence of this, one need look no further than the film productions and websites of government agencies, such as the Bangladesh Tourism Board, which construct images in line with colonial images of the "noble savage"—girls and boys with distinctive facial features dressed in colorful "tribal costumes," performing traditional rituals, dance, and music.

Some indigenous representatives themselves contribute to this exoticization through the way in which they pursue identity politics. While events such as "cultural shows" enjoy great popularity, they also provoke controversial debates. This was the case during a cultural show in August 2010, when some activists expressed indignation about the "modern" face of the performance, as the performers had chosen contemporary Indian pop music instead of "traditional" instrumental music. But these shows, combining as they do performances designed to appeal with the transmission of political messages, are also instrumental for attracting the attention of the general public, as well as potential non-indigenous Bangladeshis and foreign supporters. Apart from development professionals who were invited to deliver speeches, foreign researchers are expected to act as advocates for the movement as they are asked to "take along" the political demands and bring them to the attention of potential allies in other parts of the world.[21]

Thus, the representation of indigenous claims is a matter involving a variety of individuals and institutions who are not always "indigenous" themselves. Persons belonging to so-called national civil society, as well as representatives of cooperating foreign development organizations, are requested to speak on behalf of the movement in political debates at a national level and to take a stand for their concerns. These representations, however, can be ambivalent or even contradictory. An emphasis of the exotic "tribal" is prevalent, which comes close to the romanticizing images of the "noble savage" of colonial times. These images fit well with the ways in which indigenous people are often described in the current transnational rhetoric and relate to the political project of "protecting them" because they still live in harmony with nature (Shah 2007: 1,817). In the Bangladeshi context, these constructions link with images of indigenous people as backward and premodern, which become meaningful in two ways. First, they constitute a promising resource for tourism and create the opportunity to promote particular areas, especially the CHT, as touristic hotspots. This "commodification" of ethnicity (Comaroff and Comaroff 2009) relates also to development, as the promotion of "tradition" carries with it the potential for income generation by marketing "traditional indigenous culture," in the production of handicrafts and in the tourism sector. Second, the reconstruction of indigenous people's backwardness justifies the nationalist approach, which is based on the superiority of the Muslim Bengali-speaking majority, in the course of which military violence may be employed to protect the indigenous population from itself, and "help them find the road to civilization" (Schendel 2011: 26).

Among the Bangladeshi activists who work for the recognition of indigenous people, these constructions are highly problematic, because they do not relate to people's everyday lives, and contradict their quest for recognition as equal citizens. Although tendencies to exoticize indigenous people prevail, the terminology itself constitutes a powerful communicative resource in activism, on both national and global scales. These representations are employed by actors who are part of particular constellations that may not necessarily embody, and may substantially differentiate from, the promoted images.

Indigeneity and Belonging

Approaches to depicting "indigenous peoples" and their identities have tended to represent the collectives as clearly demarcated groups, bearing particular cultural characteristics. Consequently, indigenous movements have often been understood as relating ethnic affiliation as a central feature of belonging. However, activists converge not just based on ethnic similarities, but also co-opt sympathizers who do not identify with ethnically conceived characteristics. Thus, instead of predefined characteristics, a subjective sense of "wanting to belong" comes to the fore. The belonging approach helps us to "explore the shifting character of borders and frontiers, imagined or real, as well as the possibilities of boundary-crossing, boundary-shifting, and boundary-blurring" (Pfaff-Czarnecka and Toffin 2011: xiv, Wimmer 2008). These authors further remark that with the concept of belonging, and indeed its German equivalents, a distinction can be made between two dimensions. On the one hand, *Zugehörigkeit* denotes an individual belonging to a collective, while on the other hand, *Zusammengehörigkeit* highlights "togetherness" (ibid.: xix). This distinction is central when analyzing the constellations of belonging in contemporary indigenous activism, because it highlights the fact that inclusion is a two-dimensional process.

Adopting a perspective on constellations of belonging refrains from taking for granted belonging to a particular category, contrary to the contemporary readings of indigeneity in Bangladesh, which continue to embark on differentiated categories defined in ethnic terms. Strictly speaking, however, indigeneity is not an ethnic category but an inclusive category, which incorporates a variety of collectives with different cultural characteristics, thus allowing for great ethnic heterogeneity. Cultural, but also racially justified characteristics, commonly conceived in ethnic terms, constitute the frame of reference to which activists primarily refer. This relies upon a concept of group boundaries, which are constituted by linguistic and cultural differences, and which continue to structure everyday life. For the activist movement, however, indigeneity serves as an essential point of reference, and underlies the reciprocal process of identity establishment and reaffirmation. By applying indigeneity as the identifying characteristic of the movement, its significance as a differentiation category is strengthened, and it is turned into an essential political resource in the fight for minority rights in general.

Contrary to the identity categories that are reproduced within the movement itself, the analysis presented in this chapter reveals that the actual actor constellation is composed in very different ways. Belonging, therefore, does not equate with a prescribed identity, but the ethnic boundaries become blurred and produce more or less stable constellations. This can be best explained by two processes: the enlargement and the confinement of the boundaries of social constellations.

Boundary Enlargement

The indigenous movement in Bangladesh today is multiethnic, in a variety of ways. Whereas the existing ethnic heterogeneity in the CHT has been a challenge, especially for those who sought to construct commonality, as occurred with the attempts to introduce "*Jumma* nationalism" as a unifying program in identity politics in the CHT (Schendel 1992: 128), the translocal activist constellation is far more inclusive in two ways. First, the shift away from demanding autonomy for the CHT and towards the adoption of global concepts of indigeneity has also opened new ways for linking up with and integrating the concerns of *adivasi* living on the plains. Nevertheless, despite the attempts activists have made to incorporate the demands of all indigenous people living in Bangladesh into one political program, frictions persist, for example between those living on the plains and in the hills. Second, Bengali intellectuals, academics, and members of local and national NGOs have joined the activist movement, because they have resources at their disposal that may serve the purposes of the movement. This is attractive, because the number of well-educated Bengalis with respective (rhetoric) competencies is greater than that of indigenous people, and at the same time, many Bengali activists have contacts with elites and decision makers in politics, the military, and transnational networks. One Bengali human rights activist I interviewed in 2010 defined three core competencies that encourage Bengali sympathizers to help the indigenous movement. First, they may foster the inclusion into national (civil) society and provide "psychological support." Second, Bengali activists might be able to better pursue the strategic interest of tapping into the existing networks evolving within patron–client relationships, which exist all over Bangladesh (see Lewis 2011: 22). Third, the participation of Bengali activists enhances the movement's legitimacy. This is especially true of those who are respected for their opinion qua social status and are entitled to speak on behalf of marginalized populations.

Such cross-ethnic alliances may be attained in two ways, either by incorporating Bengali activists into the movement or by merging indigenous peoples' issues into larger activist realms. The women's rights movement, which places itself firmly in the national civil society sphere (Kabeer 1991), for example, has incorporated women's rights concerns of indigenous groups into their catalogue of claims and integrates local, indigenous, women's organizations into their activities. Well-known women's rights activists frequently take part in the annual 9 August celebrations in order to publicly espouse the safeguarding of indigenous interests; they particularly focus on gender-specific aspects in the discrimination of indigenous people. In this case, two separate movements, both supported by global rhetoric and nationally anchored, encounter each other, and this overlap suggests interesting dynamics yet to be explored.

Enlarging the boundaries of belonging also becomes relevant in activist collectives across national borders. While some indigenous Bangladeshis who live in Korea, the United States, Australia, and elsewhere support the campaigns in Bangladesh and thus form transnational networks that can be found in various contexts, claims also find their way to international organizations and the governments of Western countries via organizations and coalitions with a broader agenda and membership. Apart from well-known human rights advocates such as Amnesty International, the International Work Group for Indigenous Affairs (IWGIA), or Survival International, my own fieldwork within a German-based lobby network offered yet another perspective.[22] The network establishes contacts between German politicians and activists in Bangladesh, and organizes conferences and lobby tours to address policy makers in Europe. These advocacy networks seek to accomplish occasional successes regarding political decisions and developmental initiatives. They rely upon relationships between individuals built up over many years and blur the boundaries between "us" and "them."

Mutual trust is one of the core characteristics of these constellations and vital for the cohesion of social formations promoting indigenous claims in different parts of the world. Usually, representatives are chosen based on strategic interests in a particular context. As a result of this, it is often non-indigenous actors who present the concerns to representatives of the state, because if state representatives know the advocate from a different context, the necessary basis of trust is already present. Where authenticity is demanded, folklore groups from rural areas are invited and the potentially appealing exotic character of such events is used purposefully to generate sympathy. By bringing in non-indigenous representatives as experts, the movement hopes to increase the chances of realizing its demands in the national context.

Boundary Confinement

Activists without "indigenous" backgrounds may be legitimized to represent the matters of the movement, which, as we have seen, brings several potential benefits. An important precondition is that the activist is accepted by the collective of activists as well as those who are supposedly being represented. "Being accepted" depends not only on strategic considerations, but on other characteristics such as sympathy, reliability, and the individual's ability to relate to people's concerns. Proving that someone is empathetic to the movement's claims, and shows a real commitment, is as important as a certain openness concerning cultural practices. Only when one is accepted by the movement is one entitled to speak for it, and discussions about acceptance can be very controversial.[23] Therefore, supposedly well-minded Bengalis can become the subject of trash talk rather quickly. Regardless of whether the criticism is justified or not, interviewees reported that individuals may be excluded because of their political leanings or immoral practices, such as corruption. In one case, local people complained that a Bengali activist was primarily led by his personal career aspirations. The activists I talked to expressed concerns that such an attitude would lead to more domination, and even exploitation—a concern that can be interpreted in light of the existing inequalities between the Bengali and the indigenous population. In other cases, critical voices referred to the person's political affiliation. Boundaries that define belonging to the activist movement are thus rigidly maintained, especially when it comes to alliances with activists belonging to the Bengali majority.

Conversely, it may be possible that even "biologically indigenous" persons, as one activist phrased it in an interview, may appear as opponents. They may not back the demands of the movement, or may position themselves as belonging to "the other side," for example by supporting or representing a Bengali-dominated political party. Repeatedly, activists have voiced their resentment against individuals holding ministerial posts or posts in local administration. Whereas some local politicians who acquired powerful positions were accepted, others were labeled as "traitors." Being squeezed between the obligations derived from representing the state on the one hand and loyalty to one's "group"—often expressed in intimate personal relationships—on the other, being accused of treachery by one side is an obvious danger for these individuals (see Kelly and Thiranagama 2010). At the same time, various political factions within the indigenous movement itself restrict its boundaries.

Apart from ethnic differences, categories such as class, generation, and gender also entail exclusionary potential. Concerning women, for example, current discourses have been dominated by victimizing overtones, whereas the movement itself is dominated by male representatives. This reflects existing patriarchal gender orders, and brings with it the danger of silencing women as actors in the issues that concern them. Major differences that may reinforce exclusion are linked to origin and lifestyle. Similar to Kaushik Gosh's examples from Indian Jharkhand (Ghosh 2006), cosmopolitically oriented *adivasi* are demonstratively differentiated from the majority of the indigenous population. During my fieldwork, people in the villages criticized the socioeconomic gap between them and those who seek to represent them, and argued that such would-be representatives had no idea of the rural lifestyle anymore. Living in Bangladesh's capital Dhaka, or abroad, alienated them from the rural lifestyle because their habits were more oriented in the direction of the Bengali elite or Western role models. Their would-be rhetoric, emphasizing the rural idyll and traditional ways of cultivation as characteristic of the indigenous population, would therefore become implausible. Such a lack of legitimacy is mostly related to class differences, but may also spill over to ethnic categories, in that some "groups" are considered to be better off than others.

Enlarging and confining of boundaries takes place at, and spans across, spatial scales. On the one hand, constellations of belonging based on emotionally reasoned fundaments like "togetherness" clash with ethnic categories, as inclusion may be strategic in character, and activists know precisely how to use this. The movement's heterogeneity enables them to oppose various addressees in promising ways, by choosing the most suitable representatives, depending on the respective "stage" on which these representations are to be performed. On the other hand, acquiring a membership status is not an easy venture, and contrarily, even "biologically indigenous" individuals may find their membership reneged if they do not behave correctly.

Global Rhetoric, Translocal Linkages, and Belonging

Global representations of indigeneity have considerably changed the demands voiced by the indigenous movement in Bangladesh in recent years. Specifically, they have provided additional legitimacy and transnational support, as they open new venues for networking within and across national borders. Perhaps the adaptation and translation of the global language of indigeneity into local idioms and systems of meaning enabled the formation of the movement on a national level, but this process has been an ambivalent one. Whereas local actors make use of the language of indigeneity to reinforce their political positions, translocal coherence of interaction stands out, due to coalitions that cross ethnic borders. Indigenous representatives from all over Bangladesh have joined forces across local borders and built national networks. Activists with various ethnic, linguistic, and religious backgrounds have formed alliances to give more importance to the claims of the movement. The networks of solidarity stretch out in translocal space, which creates new formations.

Belonging is closely interwoven with societal structure formation. At this junction, increasing divergence between ethnic belonging as a category of representation on the one hand, and its relevance for contexts constituting activism on the other, can be observed. Indigeneity as a societal category of differentiation is (re)constituted and turned into a resource by actors who, seen through the ethnic lens, do not belong to it themselves. This chapter has shown that multiethnic, strategically oriented alliances evolve, while at the same time contributing to maintaining ethnical demarcations. However, this process is riddled with contradictions, as the activist representations rely upon images of indigeneity that allocate societal spaces to them that are then marginal to the mainstream. It is one of the central dilemmas of such movements today that in order to legitimize themselves and to make their demands heard in public, they are forced to reproduce exoticizing images. Quite sadly, it is the global notion of indigeneity, which has been established with emancipatory expectations, that provides new ground for the essentialization of the indigenous population.

Eva Gerharz (Dr.phil., Bielefeld) is Professor of Sociology with a special focus on globalization at Fulda University of Applied Sciences, Germany. She previously held the position of Junior Professor for Sociology of Development and Internationalization at Ruhr-University Bochum, and Interim Professor of Development Sociology at Bayreuth University from 2017 to 2018. Until 2010, she was a researcher in the Department of Social Anthropology, Faculty of Sociology at Bielefeld University, Germany, and also Associate Scientist at the International Centre for Integrated Mountain Development (ICIMOD), Kathmandu. With a major focus on South Asia (Bangladesh and Sri Lanka), her research deals with indigeneity, ethnicity and conflict, development and reconstruction, political activism, and transnationalism. Eva has published in several academic journals, including *Mobilities, Conflict and Society, Asian Ethnicity*, and *Indigenous Policy Journal*. As well as her monograph, *The Politics of Reconstruction and Development in Sri Lanka* (Routledge, 2014), she has co-edited *Governance, Development and Conflict in South Asia* (Sage, 2015, with Siri Hettige) and *Land, Development and Security in South Asia* (SAMAJ, 2016, with Katy Gardner).

Notes

This is a revised version of the article "Indigenous Activism in Bangladesh: Translocal Spaces and Shifting Constellations of Belonging," published in *Asian Ethnicity* 15(4): 552–70.

1. See http://www.un.org/en/events/indigenousday/background.shtml (accessed 1 July 2017).
2. See http://www.un.org/esa/socdev/unpfii/index.html (accessed 1 July 2017).
3. Apart from participating in several activist events, I have had (repeated) conversations with indigenous activists, human rights campaigners, jour-

nalists, and social science scholars. I also conducted several months of ethnographic field research in the Chittagong Hill Tracts in the southeastern part of Bangladesh in 1999 and 2000.
4. The German lobby network Bangladesh-Forum comprises non-governmental development organizations, human rights organizations, diaspora groups, and some individual members, who gather on a regular basis to advocate for human rights and developmental issues in Bangladesh. As a member, I have been able to combine research and activist commitment in the last few years.
5. In the Indian and Bangladeshi context alike, *adivasi* is a local term that people make use of in their everyday lives. In India, the notion also became a political catchword, somewhat earlier than in Bangladesh.
6. The notions *pahari* and *jumma* refer to the indigenous people of the Chittagong Hill Tracts only, whereas those populations living in the plains have adopted "plainland *adivasi*" as a common denominator.
7. With the partition of the Indian subcontinent in 1947, two states, India and Pakistan, were formed, with East Bengal being allocated to Pakistan (East Pakistan). In 1971, the war of independence in East Pakistan led to the formation of Bangladesh.
8. With the Chittagong Hill Tracts Regulation of 1900, the CHT was made an excluded area. The idea behind this act was to protect the indigenous population from interference. However, as van Schendel points out, it fostered the isolation of the hills and a "process of 'enclavement' in which the hill people were denied access to power and were subordinated and exploited directly by the British overlords" (Schendel 1992: 111). Against the background of the recent conflict, some activists argue that the regulation serves as an important reference for the protection of hill people's minority rights.
9. In his analysis of the causes of poverty, Shapan Adnan (2004) discusses the demographic transformation in detail. According to his estimates, in 2004, the ratio was 51.43 percent (*pahari*) to 48.57 percent (Bengali). He also highlights that the growth rate among the Bengali population has been much higher.
10. The Chakma Raja is one of the three traditional chiefs presiding over the administrative system in the CHT.
11. See Gerharz (2002) on the commitment of German development cooperation after the Chittagong Hill Tracts peace treaty in 1997.
12. See http://www.undp.org.bd/projects/proj_detail.php?pid=54 (accessed 1 July 2017).
13. Aside from the European Commission, the Danish embassy is also financially committed.
14. The Bangladeshi government has not always reacted favorably to utterances by foreign partners. When the foreign minister of the EU criticized violent outbreaks in the Chittagong Hill Tracts in spring 2010, the government of Bangladesh reacted with a brusque rejection.
15. Unfortunately, it is beyond the scope of this chapter to further explore this interesting but complicated relationship.
16. The International Chittagong Hill Tracts Commission seeks to promote respect for human rights, democracy, and the restoration of civil and polit-

ical rights, participatory development, and land rights in the Chittagong Hill Tracts in Bangladesh, including examination of the implementation of the CHT Peace Accord of 1997. The CHT Commission will build on the work undertaken by the original CHT Commission between 1990 and 2001. See http://www.chtcommission.org/ (accessed 1 July 2017). The first CHT Commission was formed in 1990 when, with intensifying militarization, human rights violations became more frequent. It was initiated by the Amsterdam-based Organising Committee CHT Campaign (OCCHTC) and the International Work Group for Indigenous Affairs (IWGIA) in Copenhagen. The Commission carried out a number of field investigations, on the basis of which it produced reports documenting the human rights violations. The Commission was reformed in 2008 with the mandate quoted above, in light of the changing conditions after the signing of the peace agreement, as well as the increased awareness of the situation in the CHT in Bangladesh and internationally. As of 2012, the CHT Commission consists of four Bangladeshi members, of whom two are very well-known and respected lawyers and all are respected activists, and four non-Bangladeshi members.

17. See http://bdnews24.com/politics/2011/06/18/no-indigenous-reiterates-shafique (accessed 1 July 2017).
18. See http://bdnews24.com/bangladesh/2011/07/26/indigenous-people-a-misnomer-moni (accessed 1. July 2017).
19. The Indian case, however, is different because special provisions for so-called Scheduled Castes and Scheduled Tribes have been safeguarded in the Indian constitution for a long time.
20. Colonialist interventions were geared towards the abolishment of *jhum*, which was considered "backward." This discourse persists, as *jhum* is labor intensive and the relative output is considered to be low. Opinions vary as to whether this agricultural model could be improved or optimized.
21. Throughout many years of exchange with indigenous activists from Bangladesh, I have often been approached by them. In 1999, several indigenous activists and politicians requested that I impart messages to European governments, and write and publish on the subject. As a member of the German network Bangladesh-Forum, which is involved in lobbying work for Bangladesh in Europe, I have been repeatedly contacted with specific advocacy concerns, such as the necessity to foster networking among organizations and individuals worldwide.
22. See http://www.bangladesh-forum.de/ (accessed 1 July 2017).
23. For the sake of the anonymity of my respondents, it is not possible to provide more details here.

Bibliography

Adnan, Shapan. 2004. *Migration, Land Alienation and Ethnic Conflict: Causes of Poverty in the Chittagong Hill Tracts of Bangladesh*. Dhaka: Research and Advisory Services.

Adnan, Shapan and Ranajit Dastidar. 2011. *Alienation of the Lands of Indigenous Peoples in the Chittagong Hill Tracts of Bangladesh.* Dhaka/Copenhagen: Chittagong Hill Tracts Commission and International Work Group for Indigenous Affairs.

AIPP (Asia Indigenous Peoples Pact) (ed.). 2009. *Indigenous Peoples' Human Rights Report in Asia 2008.* Chiang Mai: Human Rights Campaign.

Anthias, Floya. 2002. "Where Do I Belong? Narrating Collective Identity and Translocational Positionality." *Ethnicities* 2(4): 491–514.

Arens, Janneke. 1997. "Winning Hearts and Minds: Foreign Aid and Militarisation in the Chittagong Hill Tracts." *Economic and Political Weekly* 32(29): 1,811–24.

Aziz-al Ahsan, Syed and Bhumitra Chakma. 1989. "Problems of National Integration in Bangladesh: The Chittagong Hill Tracts." *Asian Survey* 29(10): 959–70.

Barkat, Abul, Mozammel Hoque, Sadeka Halim, and Asmar Osman. 2009. *Life and Land of Adibashis: Land Dispossession and Alienation of Adibashis in the Plain Districts of Bangladesh.* Dhaka: Pathak Shamabesh.

Bates, Crispin. 1995. "'Lost Innocents and the Loss of Innocence': Interpreting Adivasi Movements in South Asia." In *Indigenous Peoples of Asia*, ed. Robert H. Barnes, Andrew Gray, and Benedict Kingsbury, 103–120. Ann Arbor, MI: University of Michigan.

Bierschenk, Thomas, Jean-Pierre Chaveau, and Jean-Pierre Olivier de Sardan. 2001. "Lokale Entwicklungsmakler: Zur Soziologie von Zivilgesellschaft und Partizipativer Entwicklungshilfe." In *Markt, Kultur und Gesellschaft: Zur Aktualität von 25 Jahren Entwicklungsforschung,* ed. Heiko Schrader, Markus Kaiser, and Rüdiger Korff, 211–238. Münster: Lit Verlag.

Bleie, Tone. 2005. *Tribal Peoples, Nationalism and the Human Rights Challenge.* Dhaka: University Press Limited.

Brubaker, Rogers. 2002. "Ethnicity without Groups." *Archives Européennes de Sociologie* XLIII(2): 163–89.

Chakma, Bumitra. 2010. "The Post-Colonial State and Minorities: Ethnocide in the Chittagong Hill Tracts, Bangladesh." *Commonwealth and Comparative Politics* 48(3): 281–300.

Chittagong Hill Tracts Commission (ed.). 2009. "Report of the Chittagong Hill Tracts Commission's Mission in Bangladesh." Copenhagen and Dhaka: Chittagong Hill Tracts Commission.

Comaroff, John L. and Jean Comaroff. 2009. *Ethnicity Inc.* Chicago, IL and London: The University of Chicago Press.

Dahl, Jens. 2012. *The Indigenous Space and Marginalized Peoples in the United Nations.* New York: Palgrave Macmillan.

della Porta, Donatella and Sidney Tarrow (eds). 2005. *Transnational Protest and Global Activism: People, Passions, and Power.* Lanham, MD: Rowman & Littlefield Publishers.

Gellner, David. 2009. "Introduction: How Civil are 'Communal' and Ethno-nationalist Movements?" In *Activism and Civil Society in South Asia: Governance, Conflict, and Civic Action: Volume 2,* ed. David N. Gellner, 1–26. New Delhi: Sage.

Gerharz, Eva. 2002. "Dilemmas in Planning Crisis Prevention: NGOs in the Chittagong Hill Tracts of Bangladesh." *The Journal of Social Studies* 97(1): 19–36.
———. 2012. "Approaching Indigenous Activism from the Ground Up: Experiences from Bangladesh." In *Beyond Methodological Nationalism: Research Methodologies for Cross-Border Studies*, ed. Anna Amelina et al., 129–152. New York and London: Routledge.
Ghosh, Kaushik. 2006. "Between Global Flows and Local Dams: Indigenousness, Locality and the Transnational Sphere in Jharkhand, India." *Cultural Anthropology* 21(4): 501–34.
Gray, Andrew. 1995. "The Indigenous Movement in Asia." In *Indigenous Peoples of Asia*, ed. Robert Harrison Barnes, Andrew Gray, and Benedict Kingsbury, 35–58. Ann Arbor, MI: University of Michigan.
Hale, Charles R. 2001. "What Is Activist Research?" *Social Science Research Council* 2(1–2): 13–15.
Jahangir, Burhanuddin Khan. 1986. *Problematics of Nationalism in Bangladesh*. Dhaka: Centre for Social Studies.
Kabeer, Naila. 1991. "The Quest for National Identity: Women Islam and the State of Bangladesh." In *Women, Islam and the State*, ed. Deniz Kandiyoti, 115–143. Philadelphia, PA: Temple University Press.
Karim, Lamia. 1998. "Pushed to the Margins: Adivasi Peoples in Bangladesh and the Case of Kalpana Chakma." *Contemporary South Asia* 7(3): 301–16.
Karlsson, Bengt G. 2003. "Anthropology and the 'Indigenous Slot'." *Critique of Anthropology* 23(4): 403–23.
Keck, Margaret E. and Kathryn Sikkink. 1998. *Activists beyond Borders: Advocacy Networks in International Politics*. Ithaca and London: Cornell University Press.
Kelly, Tobias and Sharika Thiranagama. 2010. "Introduction: Spectres of Treason." In *Traitors*, eds. Tobias Kelly and Sharika Thiranagama, 1–23. Philadelphia, PA: University of Pennsylvania Press.
Kuper, Hilda. 2003. "The Language of Sites in the Politics of Space." In *The Anthropology of Space and Place: A Reader*, ed. Lawrence-Zúñiga Low, 247–63. Oxford: Blackwell.
Lachenmann, Gudrun. 2008. "Transnationalisation, Translocal Spaces, Gender and Development-Methodological Challenges." In *The Making of World Society: Perspectives from Transnational Research*, ed. Remus Gabriel Anghel et al., 51–74. Bielefeld: transcript.
———. 2010. "Globalisation in the Making: Translocal Gendered Spaces in Muslim Society." In *Translocality: The Study of Globalising Processes from a Southern Perspective*, ed. Ulrike Freitag and Achim von Oppen, 335–367. Leiden and Boston: Koninklijke Brill.
Lewis, David. 2011. *Bangladesh: Politics, Economy and Civil Society*. Cambridge: Cambridge University Press.
Li, Tanja Murray. 2000. "Articulating Indigenous Identity in Indonesia: Resource Politics and the Tribal Slot." *Comparative Studies in Society and History* 42(1): 149–79.
Merry, Sally Engle. 2006. "Transnational Human Rights and Local Activism: Mapping the Middle." *American Anthropologist* 108(1): 38–51.

Mohsin, Amena. 1997. *The Politics of Nationalism: The Case of the Chittagong Hill Tracts, Bangladesh*. Dhaka: University Press Ltd.
Muehlebach, Andrea. 2001. "'Making Place' at the United Nations: Indigenous Cultural Politics at the UN Working Group on Indigenous Populations." *Cultural Anthropology* 16(3): 415–48.
———. 2003. "What Self in Self-Determination? Notes from the Frontiers of Transnational Indigenous Activism." *Identities: Global Studies in Culture and Power* 10(2): 241–68.
Oldham, Paul and Miriam Anne Frank. 2008. "'We the Peoples…': The United Nations Declaration on the Rights of Indigenous People." *Anthropology Today* 24(2): 5–9.
Pelican, Michaela. 2009. "Complexities of Indigeneity and Autochthony: An African Example." *American Ethnologist* 36(1): 52–65.
Pfaff-Czarnecka, Joanna. 2007. "Challenging Goliath: People, Dams, and the Paradoxes of Transnational Critical Movements." In *Social Dynamics in Northern South Asia, Volume 2: Political and Social Transformations in North India and Nepal*, ed. Hiroshi Ishii, David N. Gellner, and Katsuo Nawa, 399–433. Delhi: Manohar.
———. 2010. "'Minorities-in-Minorities' in South Asian Societies: Between Politics of Diversity and Politics of Difference." In *Minorities in South Asia and in Europe*, ed. Samir Kumar Das, 100–131. Kolkata: Samya.
Pfaff-Czarnecka, Joanna and Gérard Toffin. 2011. "Introduction: Belonging and Multiple Attachments in Contemporary Himalayan Societies." In *The Politics of Belonging in the Himalayas: Local Attachments and Boundary Dynamics*, ed. Joanna Pfaff-Czarnecka and Gérard Toffin, xi–xxxviii. New Delhi: Sage.
Roy, Rajkumari Chandra Kalindi. 2000. "Land Rights of the Indigenous Peoples of the Chittagong Hill Tracts, Bangladesh," Copenhagen: International Working Group for Indigenous Affairs.
Schendel, Willem van. 1992. "The Invention of the 'Jummas': State Formation and Ethnicity in Southeast Bangladesh." *Modern Asian Studies* 26(1): 95–128.
———. 2001. "Who Speaks for the Nation? Nationalist Rhetoric and the Challenge of Cultural Pluralism in Bangladesh." In *Identity Politics in Central Asia and the Muslim World: Nationalism, Ethnicity and Labour in the Twentieth Century*, ed. Willem van Schendel and Erik J. Zürcher, 107–47. London and New York: I.B. Tauris Publishers.
———. 2011. "The Dangers of Belonging: Tribes, Indigenous Peoples and Homelands in South Asia." In *The Politics of Belonging in India: Becoming Adivasi*, ed. Daniel J. Raycroft and Sangeeta Dasgupta, 19–43. London and New York: Routledge.
Shah, Alpa. 2007. "The Dark Side of Indigeneity? Indigenous People, Rights and Development in India." *History Compass* 5/6: 1,806–32.
Tarrow, Sidney. 2005. *The New Transnational Activism*. Cambridge: Cambridge University Press.
Tsing, Anna. 2007. "Indigenous Voice." In *Indigenous Experience Today*, ed. Marisol de la Cadena and Orin Starn, 33–67. Oxford: Berg Publishers.

Uddin, Nasir. 2010. "Politics of Cultural Differences: Ethnicity and Marginality in the Chittagong Hill Tracts of Bangladesh." *South Asian Survey* 17(2): 283–94.

Vanderkerckhove, Nel. 2009. "'We Are Sons of This Soil': The Endless Battle over Indigenous Homelands in Assam, India." *Critical Asian Studies* 41(4): 523–48.

White, Sarah C. 1999. "NGOs, Civil Society, and the State in Bangladesh: The Politics of Representing the Poor." *Development and Change* 30(2): 307–26.

Wimmer, Andreas. 2008. "Elementary Strategies of Ethnic Boundary Making." *Ethnic and Racial Studies* 31(6): 1,025–55.

Yuval Davis, Nira. 2006. "Belonging and the Politics of Belonging." *Patterns of Prejudice* 40(3): 197–214.

 5

In Search of Self

Identity, Indigeneity, and Cultural Politics in Bangladesh

Nasir Uddin

Introduction

> When I was born, I was given a name, Pailung, and was called that same name by the villagers. When I went to school, and studied with other Mru and Marma students, people started calling me adding by my group name: Pailung Khumi. When I went to study in Bandarban town and met Bengalis, I was addressed by different names: Pahari, tribe and *upajatee* [sub-nation]. When I got involved in regional politics in the Chittagong Hill Tracts, I myself started using a new name: *jumma*. When I crossed the state boundary of Bangladesh, I was branded with another name: that used for the indigenous people of Bangladesh. Sometimes, I become confused thinking about who I really am.
> —Pailung Khumi, 6 October 2012

While discussing *adivasi rajniti* (indigenous politics), this is how Pailung Khumi, an educated Khumi youth who is involved with various human rights movements for indigenous people in Bangladesh, explained to me how multiple identities compete and negotiate with each other using complex networks of positioning in local and translocal spaces. In addition to revealing various terms of reference, the statement develops the changing notions of identity in relation to space and across time. It prompts many questions about the construction of ethnic categories, the political implications of identity formation, and the spatial interweaving of identity transformation. This chapter addresses these issues with empirically informed analysis on how a particular group of people, known as the Khumi, position themselves within the local and national politics of identity and the transnational politics of indigeneity.

Using the case of Khumi people, whom I have been researching for several years, this chapter engages with the debate on identity, indigeneity, and cultural politics in Bangladesh. It also takes part in debates about various forms of identity politics and escalating activism over indigenous issues, which have been expressed in academia in terms of political and cultural articulation as the "indigenous slot" (Karlsson 2008; Li 2000), "return of the native" (Kuper 2003), "different selves in different contexts" (Hodgson 2011), "Kalahari revisionism" (Barnard 2006), "global ethnoscape" (Ghosh 2006), "the dark side of indigeneity" (Shah 2007), and "multiple attachments and belongings" (Pfaff-Czarnecka and Toffin 2011).

As stated in the introductory quote, the Khumi, a group of people culturally different to the majority Bengali population and sharply distinct from other indigenous groups in Bangladesh, experience multiple identities—Khumi, Pahari, *upajatee* (sub-nation), tribal, *adivasi*, indigenous people, *jumma* (people who are involved in swidden cultivation), and *khudra nrigoshti* (small ethnic group)—amidst the nationalist politics of identity and the global politics of indigeneity. Here, by identity I mean a kind of cultural and political category that makes a particular group of people distinct from and recognized by others (see Barth [1954] 1998). As such, multiple identities refer to people belonging to various forms of sociocultural and political categories (see Pfaff-Czarnecka and Toffin 2011) while simultaneously depending on certain sociocultural and spatial contexts. Because people are now connected with the global community while living in local spaces, they experience multiple identities through their attachments, networks, and connections, which play a significant role in identity formation, involving as it does local cultural politics, translocal political discourses, and transnational politics of indigeneity. Critical analysis of how the Khumi belong to a given category, with which considerations, and under what circumstances, will provide us with an empirical foundation to examine various established notions of cultural politics in Bangladesh, in connection with transnational politics of indigeneity. Khumi experiences of identity politics in Bangladesh also reveal inter- and intra-dynamics of indigenous activism as a bargaining space for various social, economic, and civil rights of indigenous people. The Khumi conceptualization of indigeneity, through the critical examination of various terms of reference that are prevalent in the Chittagong Hill Tracts (CHT) and in Bangladesh, will also be shown to challenge the politics of indigenous activism in another way, as a sort of imposition of identity—albeit one that differs from that imposed upon colonized people by colonizers (see also Uddin 2009, 2016). This analysis also uncovers how a given type of people in a given type of situation are also subject to discrimination and marginalization, determined by transnational politics of indigeneity and local politics of identity, along with the politics of modern nation-states (see Shah 2007). Using the case of the Khumi, this chapter examines the idea of indigeneity, politics of identity, the sense of belonging, notions of statehood, and the politics of nationalism in Bangladesh within the larger canvas of the Chittagong Hill Tracts, in contrast with the state relations that have been historically shaped across times and regimes — from the colonial (British), through the semi-colonial (Pakistan), to the post/neocolonial (Bangladesh) era.

Who Are the Khumi? Identity Formation through Khumi Mythology

There is no written information on how the Khumi became the Khumi, why they are called "Khumi," or when they appeared in the demographic composition of the CHT. For the first time, I recorded Khumi mythology about their "origin," which I published elsewhere (see Uddin 2008a, 2008b). Despite this, Thomas H. Lewin ([1870] 2004), a British colonial administrator in the CHT, tried to trace the "origins" of the Khumi by looking at their dress and the meaning behind the name "Khumi." He wrote:

> "Kwey" or "Khwee" in Arakanese language means "a dog" and "mee" is an affix conveying the idea of man; "Khwey mee" therefore means "dog man." Now the "Kumi" wear a very scanty breech cloth, which is so adjusted, that a long end hangs down behind him in a manner of a tail; add to this that the dog is a favourite article of food among them, and the derivation of name seems pretty clear. (Lewin [1870] 2004: 220)

This is indeed consistent with the British colonial view, sketching an image of colonized people as "exotic others." This "dog thesis" seems very simple today, yet several ethnographic accounts—from St. John (1873), Robert Hutchinson (1906), George A. Grierson (1927), and Lucian Bernot (1964)—supported the idea that the orthography of "Khumi" is somehow connected with a dog's tail (see Uddin 2008a: 35). A century later, a few Bangladeshi writers—Abdus Sattar (1983: 336; 2000: 206), Benu Prasad Barua (2001: 56), and Amena Mohsin (2002: 17)—have argued that the Khumi believe they are the best human "race" in the world. I wrote elsewhere "They explain the rationale behind this conviction by arguing that, in Khumi language, '*Kha*' means 'man,' and '*mi*' means 'best race'. They are, therefore, *Khami*, the best human 'race.' These Bangladeshi writers neither had direct contact with the Khumi—who live in remote and inaccessible areas of the CHT—nor were familiar with the Khumi language" (2008a: 35). Consequently, they followed the legacy of Lewin in trying to trace the origin of a group of people through the etymology of their name, a near impossible task. My fieldwork[1] reveals that the Khumi themselves are not aware of this discourse, but some of them have heard that Bengalis sometimes refer to the Khumi as the people of the "dog race."

Through my fieldwork over several years, I learned that in the Khumi language, *"khumi"* means human, male is *"nemchu,"* female is *"nempu,"* and a child is *"khumi-chu."* The Khumi themselves have a very popular myth about their origin and appearance in the world. I have written about this in detail in other publications (Uddin 2008a, 2008b). According to the myth:

> The Khumi are the third creation of Thuram (God in Khumi language). Thuram created the world, the trees and reptiles first, then the dog, and finally the Khumi. After creating the world, trees and reptiles, Thuram, in fact, tried to create the human body with clay, but could not complete it in a day. When Thuram went to sleep at night, a big snake came and devoured the half-finished model of the human body. It happened twice, thrice, and it was continuing the following day. Then Thuram decided to create a dog to guard the model of the human during the night. Thuram created a dog and put life into it. In addition, Thuram made half a human body for the day. When Thuram went to sleep, the snake came but could not commit any harm. When the watchful dog barked, the snake was frightened and ran away. On the following day, Thuram completed the half-finished human body in full shape and put life into it. This is the creation of Khumi, "the Human," and they appeared in the world. There is, according to the Khumi belief, an invisible relationship between dog and human. The Khumi believe that the dog therefore howls when a human dies. According to the Khumi oral tradition, human beings owe their creation to a dog. Because the dog had saved humans from total annihilation, they accordingly pay homage to it. (Uddin 2008b: 35–36)

Although Lewin claimed, the Khumi do not eat dog as it has some specific ritual values as I observed during my fieldwork. According to the 1991 Government of Bangladesh (GoB) population survey, 1,241 Khumi live in Bangladesh; 1,150 (92.67 percent) of these live in Bandarban, and 91 (7.33 percent) live in Rangamati (see Uddin 2008a). However, during my dissertation fieldwork (2005–2007), and subsequent follow-up fieldwork (2008–17), I could not find any Khumi living in Rangamati. In fact, the Khumi live in only three sub-districts of Bandarban, namely Rowangchhari, Ruma, and Thanchi. It is reported that during the 1950s, a large number of Khumi (re)migrated to Myanmar, crossing the border because of political unrest and the economic crisis in the CHT, in what was then East Pakistan.[2] Though there is no such official record in support of this claim, the survey records discussed above demonstrate the possibility of such mass migration. The Khumi were first recorded in a British population survey in 1872, when the number of Khumi living in this region was 534. In the next survey, conducted in 1901, the number had increased to 1,053. During the time of East Bengal's inclusion in the Pakistan federation, two surveys were conducted and published in 1951 and 1956, in which the numbers of Khumi stood at 1,951 and 2,500 respectively (see Uddin 2008a). In the modern era of the Bangladeshi Republic, three successive surveys were conducted in 1981, 1991, and 2011, in which the number of Khumi was recorded as 1,000 (1981) and 1,241 (1991), with no separate number of Khumi recorded in 2011. The decrease in the number of Khumi from 2,500 in 1956 to 1,000 in 1981 indicates that during the Pakistan period a considerable number of Khumi may have crossed the border into Myanmar. At the time this chapter was written in 2016, there was no official record of exactly how many Khumi people live in Bangladesh. However, there is an unofficial record, counted by village, published by a local NGO, prepared with active support from educated Khumi.[3] I also visited most of the Khumi-inhabited areas of Ruma, Rowangchhari, and Thanchi and roughly estimated the number of households in each village. I used these figures of the number of households in each village to try and verify this unofficial record, and most of the time I found the figures to be consistent, although there were large differences in some villages. According to my estimate, there were about 2,300–2,400 Khumi living in different villages in three sub-districts of Bandarban— Ruma, Thanchi, and Rowangchhari—in 2007, and now in 2017 there are about 4,500 living in Bangladesh.

Notions of Pahari: Postcolonial Practice of Colonial Fantasy

During my fieldwork in 2008, an aged Khumi named Pewsai (aged seventy-nine), who unfortunately died in 2015, explained to me: "When we became Pahari, we even didn't know, but now we are simultaneously Pahari and Khumi." He continued: "It was [during the] British period, or may be in the early Pakistan period, [that] we started meeting one or two Bengalis in and around the *bazar* [marketplace]. Ordinary Bengalis and the Bengalis working in the administration and law-enforcing agencies started calling us Pahari, along with others of Marma, Chakma, Kheyang, and Bawm etc." This simple statement reveals the complex notions of identity that were formed in Bangladeshi government agencies based on British colonial administrative policy. Even though the people living in the CHT were distinct from each other in terms of "social organizations of cultural differences," as Fredrik Barth ([1954] 1998) phrased it, and even though each group has its own name, language, religion, beliefs and rituals, foods, costumes, and distinctive social institutions, it was difficult for British administrators to identify each group with a particular name or using a particular set of criteria for identification because all groups apparently looked alike. Therefore, the British administration introduced a generalized and sweeping term of reference—"hill people"—to indicate those people who lived in the hills and were distinct from Bengalis. This reference contains colonial connotations of imagining "colonized peoples" as exotic, primitive, and wild people. The Bengali translation of "hill people" is "Pahari," which is still used to brand the indigenous people of the CHT, including the Khumi. In fact, "the terminology and ideology set forth by British colonial administrators laid down the foundation of the ethnic identity of the CHT people, which was carried out as part of the colonial legacy in Bangladesh" (Uddin 2010: 286). Therefore, terming CHT peoples as "Pahari" is a Bengali (postcolonial) practice from British (colonial) discourse, as it has strong colonial connotations—Prashanta Tripura (1992) refers to it as "colonial fantasy," but I prefer to phrase it as "Bengali imagination of savage people"—which persists in the postcolonial era, in the form of a Bengali mindset. Tripura has written: "As an ideal type of humans, the 'hill men' were an invention, they existed not so much in real time and places as in the imagination of British" (1992: 1). One more critical aspect of Pewsai Khumi's statement is the claim that the Khumi became Pahari following the colonial fantasy, without even knowing why, how, when, or in what context their identity was transformed. So, identity is framed, constructed, and invented according to the administrative policy of the state, even without the consent and knowledge of the people involved. Although global academia is obsessed with the idea of indigeneity, many indigenous people, like Pewsai Khumi, who meet the criteria of being indigenous set by the United Nations and the International Labour Organization (ILO), do not even know they are indigenous. Therefore, as Adam Kuper has rightly said, "the notion of 'indigenous peoples' is an ideological makeover of the old idea of primitive people" (2006: 21).

In the village where I conducted my research, the majority of villagers thought of themselves as both Khumi and Pahari. According to their view, not all Pahari are Khumi, but all Khumi are Pahari. This means Pahari is a collective category that encompasses eleven indigenous groups living in the CHT, including the Khumi. Although the etymological meaning of "Pahari" is "the people who live in the *pahar* (hill)," it is in fact an identity made up of social, cultural, and political categories. For example, people who live in the Sylhet hill, North Bengal hill, and Shitakundu hill areas of Bangladesh are not identified as Pahari, whereas people belonging to Chakma, Marma, Tripura, Khumi, and other ethnic groups who live in towns, urban centers, big cities, plainland and even in the capital are still identified as Pahari, even though they do not live in the *pahar*. Therefore, the Pahari is a majoritarian imagining and colonial category of a group of people who inhabit the CHT.

The Khumi are "Khumi" within the Khumi world, but they become Pahari during interactions with Bengalis. According to the Barthian framework ([1954] 1998), the identity of Khumi and Pahari is formed in association with other peoples, in this particular case Bengalis, as such associations demarcate a clear social boundary. The question of transnational notions of indigeneity matters little in the formation of identity at the village level, where an ethnic mosaic exists. The position of the Khumi in the formation of identity at a local and regional level challenges the assumption that relatively isolated groups whose members are far away from metropolitan settings and markets and who lack the knowledge of nation-state politics, are rarer today than two or three decades back (see Barnard 2006). There still exist many groups of people worldwide who are branded as indigenous yet know little about the notions of indigeneity that inform transnational politics of indigenous rights and privileges.

The Category of Tribe and *Upajatee*: A Discourse for "Uncivilized" People

When British India was divided into two separate nation-states based on religious belonging—the Hindu majority area that would be included within the Republic of India or Hindustan, and the Muslim majority areas that would become part of Pakistan—the CHT was also incorporated into Pakistan, despite being a non-Muslim majority area. The Pakistani state abolished the CHT Manual of 1900, enacted by the British, "against the wishes of the CHT people in order to find a legal excuse for the migration of non-Paharis into the CHT" (Uddin 2010: 287). As part of state policy, Pakistan changed the official status of the region, categorizing it as a "tribal area." Philosophically and practically, the area in which "tribal" people live is called a "tribal area." But state policy also stigmatized the people of the CHT within a sociocultural category that was "exotic," "primitive," "wild," and "uncivilized." This demonstrates a continuation of colonial policy in the postcolonial era by the Pakistani state, as they treated the CHT people in the same way that the British had. Van Schendel explains:

> For the first time, "tribe" became part of comparative taxonomy: contemporary societies that Europeans considered to be farthest behind in time were designated as "tribe," primitive and aborigines or savage. First in colonial South Asia, the term "tribe" came to refer to groups that were given a low rank in a hierarchical system based upon civilisation and modernity. They were uncivilized (hence wild, primitive and savage) and unmodern (hence backward and ruled by custom). Second, those South Asians who came to be defined as "tribe" were seen as members of a universal category: in the nineteenth century Europeans were discovering "tribe" all over the world. (Van Schendel 2011: 20)

So, during the Pakistan period the Khumi people became "tribe" as inhabitants of a "tribal area" without any understanding of the political dynamics between the CHT and the Pakistani state. Now, the Khumi were the Khumi, the Pahari, and the tribe. However, I noted that among the villagers only a few young Khumi—those who have regular contact with urban centers, an irregular connection with the regional politics of *Jana Samhati Samiti* (JSS) or Peoples' Solidarity Association, and represent the Khumi in the political forum at various levels—sometimes refer to "tribal" as one of the groups to which the CHT people belong. Poire Khumi (aged thirty-two) explained to me how tribal identity is perceived among the Khumi. Poire is an NGO worker, educated, and has a relatively clear idea about the political dynamics between the JSS and the state. He said:

> We become Pahari when we are among Bengalis. We have little idea about why we are tribes. We don't even understand why other people call us tribe. I have little idea about tribal since I have some experience of attending meetings called by military, government officials, NGOs and international organizations like UNDP, UNICEF, UNESCO, Red Crescent, CARITAS, DANIDA and ILO. When they read out some papers, work on papers and show up some papers, they commonly use "tribal" to indicate Pahari people. In that context, the Khumi become tribal as Pahari. So, it seems to me, "tribe" is an official and administrative language of Pahari and in that sense Pahari and tribe are two names of the same people. Since when Pahari people became tribal, I don't know. So far I know the majority of the Khumi people haven't heard of the word "tribe" until recently. We are only few among the Khumi, those who have access to outer world and administrative dealings, and are familiar with the word "tribe." In fact, whether the Khumi people are identified as Pahari or tribe, it matters nothing in Khumi life, since it doesn't change anything in our everyday course of life. (Poire Khumi, 26 May 2010)

This narrative unveils three important aspects of identity politics. First, identity is a form of branding, constructed not by the desire of the people themselves, but by the people who hold state power. However, people negotiate a new identity for the sake of community interests, as commonality matters to individual identity. For example, the Khumi do not understand why they are identified as a tribe, but, if necessary, they use the term as a collective category, along with other ethnic groups, conforming to other Pahari people. Second, identity is not a fixed and static concept; it changes and transforms based on locations and situations. This narrative suggests that the same people can be Khumi, Pahari, and tribe, both together and separately, depending on the context of their positioning in particular spaces. For example, the Khumi are Khumi within the Pahari, but they are simply Pahari beyond the Pahari world. On the other hand, the Khumi are tribal when they are dealt with officially in bureaucratic and administrative frameworks. Third, self-identity is a mostly normative phenomenon, based on sociocultural sameness and difference, within and beyond the people concerned. For example, the self-identity of being a Khumi is related to "social organizations of cultural difference" that are the markers of Khuminess. However, "Pahari" and "tribe" are categories that involve political discourse, colonial ideology, and complexities of modern nation-states.

Tribe is generally translated in Bengali as *upajatee*, a term that emerged during the Bangladeshi period. "The term is used as synonymous to 'tribal' people. Bengalis frequently call them *upajatee*—antonym of *jatee* (nation) or branch of *jatee* but not a complete *jatee*—implying that the Pahari people are incomplete, or half-human and half-wild or a sub-nation" (Uddin 2010: 290). Eventually the Khumi became *upajatee* along with their already existing Pahari and tribal identity. The spirit of the Bengali nationalist movement, which started in 1952 as a language movement, led to the liberation and independence of Bangladesh in 1971. Since then, Bangladeshi political leaders have attempted to build a homogeneous nation-state based on Bengali nationalism, excluding "cultural others" such as the Khumi.[4]

In fact, the politics of nationalism gave birth to a discourse of "*jatee*" versus "*upajatee*." *Jatee*, a Bengali word, means "nation," and *upajatee* means "sub-nation." The ideology behind the construction of this discourse was to position the Bengali and the Pahari within the framework of the modern nation-state. Because the majority of nationals forms the state, regulates state machineries, and leads the management of the state, this majority always feels empowered and superior; because Bengalis, as the dominant majority, are *jatee*, the Pahari are not entitled to be *jatee*, but *upajatee*. The term therefore holds strong colonial connotations, as *upajatee* is the Bengali translation of "tribe," which was first used during the time of the Pakistan federation and carries the legacy of British colonial fantasy. Within this dominant majority notion of nationhood, which led the formation of the state of Bangladesh, the Khumi people became, therefore, *upajatee*. But *upajatee* is also a category-turned-identity, imposed by the state, as they quite often refer to themselves as Khumi-*jatee,* or "Khumi nation." A popular perception among Khumi people is that they are a distinctive group of people who live in a particular territory, have distinctive social, cultural, economic, and political systems of their own, and feel a sense of belonging to a particular group of people known as the Khumi. The Khumi in this sense do not subscribe to the state discourse of *upajatee,* because they believe that they are a *jatee* (see Uddin 2008a; Uddin 2008b).

One day in November 2006, while undertaking fieldwork, I was talking with the Karbari, or village head of Rongeo Para. He was sixty-six years old. After working all day in the *jhum* field, he used to visit me at my *machan* (small bamboo house) to check whether I was alright and spend some time for chatting. This was almost a daily routine for him. As part of our discussion, he explained to me very clearly how the Khumi people conceptualize *jatee*. He explained: "We are the people of same kind. We speak and communicate in the same language, our lifestyle, rules, and regulations are the same. We feel amongst each other that we are the people of same kind. So, aren't we the same *jatee*?" This quote neatly captures why the Khumi people define themselves as a *jatee*. Within the framework of majority and minority politics in the discourse of the nation-state, however, the Khumi are identified as *upajatee.* In government documents, official records, and—until recently—the textbooks of the Bangladesh national curriculum, the Pahari, including the Khumi, were described as *upajatee.* "The invention of *upajatee* reflects the state's policy of building a homogenous nation state for only Bengalis, who are seen as occupying a superior position[,] whilst the Pahari belong to a lower grade" (Uddin 2010: 290). This can be seen as a byproduct of the dominating sense of nationhood, which Amena Mohsin (2002) calls "the politics of nationalism." In recent years, however, the frequency with which the term *upajatee* has been used has fallen due to the growing political and critical awareness of the Pahari indigenous people, as well as the voices of human rights workers and the support of civil society in Bangladesh. In 2010, the Bangladeshi government was compelled to enact a law to change the Pahari's official identity from *upajatee* to *khudra nrigoshti,* which I will discuss in more detail later.

Jumma as Commonality: The Political Identity of Collective Space

The Pahari people are represented by a regional political organization called the Chittagong Hill Tracts People's Solidarity Association, or *Parbatya Chattagram Jana Samhati Samiti* (PCJSS or JSS). Soon after Bangladesh became independent, on 15 February 1972, a Pahari delegation, under the leadership of M.N. Larma, called on the then prime minister of Bangladesh to demand the constitutional recognition of their separate ethnic identity. This call was rejected, which then resulted in the formation of the JSS in 1972, and an armed wing, the *shanti bahini* (peace troops), in 1973. The state regarded the formation of these groups as separatist activity and attempted to control it through the full militarization of the region, which eventually resulted in violent conflict between the two parties. The conflict officially ended in 1997 with the signing of a peace treaty, but the Pahari still live with multifaceted conflicts (see Uddin 2005, 2010).

After the formation of the JSS, the Pahari continued their struggle for what they call regional autonomy, self-determination, and separate ethnic identity. However, it became difficult for them to frame a common platform for all Pahari indigenous groups, who are distinct from each other with regards to their language, social organizations, beliefs and rituals, costumes, and material culture. Because "Pahari" has British colonial connotations, and "tribe" or *"upajatee"* reflects a primitive and therefore derogatory ideology, they introduced a new identity, *jumma*, reflecting commonality, belonging, and mutual attachment, to bring all diversified ethnic groups under what van Schendel (1992: 121) calls a "social umbrella," but I prefer to call a "culturally embedded political space." *Jumma* is derived from *zomia*, a geographical area whose inhabitants' perennial occupation is *jhum* (swidden, or slash-and-burn) cultivation (see Scott 2009). Despite the above-mentioned distinctions between the groups, all Pahari ethnic groups by and large practice *jhum* cultivation, and therefore the JSS decided upon this as a basis of commonality and a symbol of unity in diversity. Van Schendel explains:

> A remarkable cultural innovation occurred which was reflected in the emergence of a new term to designate the people of the Chittagong hills. They were now called *"Jumma."* An old pejorative term for "swidden cultivator" in the Chittagonian dialect of Bengali, it has been appropriated by the JSS in its attempt to unify all hill people under one social umbrella. It is remarkable that this term came up at a time when many hill people had been forced to give up swidden cultivation. (Van Schendel 1992: 120–21)

Jhum is the common means of livelihood of all Pahari indigenous groups. Not only that, but Pahari life, their many rituals, traditions and customs, marriages, family organization, and different festivals are based on the rules, calendar, and operation of *jhum* cultivation.[5] Therefore, Pahari political leaders proposed *jhum* as their collective political identity, with the thought that *jhum* could truly represent all Pahari indigenous groups. Soon after they proposed *jumma* to indicate all Pahari people, the CHT became *"jumma* land" and the Pahari political movement morphed into the *"jumma* movement." However, there is a debate regarding the *jumma* people in academia, as, in addition to the Pahari people of the CHT, huge numbers of people across the South Asian and Southeast Asian uplands also practice *jhum* cultivation (see also Scott 2009). The basic argument is that if the *jumma* movement is for the people of the CHT, how does the term relate to people who are not living in the CHT, but live in *zomia*, the "land of *jhum* cultivation"?[6] It is therefore argued that the use of the term *jumma* as a collective identity and a common political platform does not pertain only to the Pahari people living in the CHT (see also van Schendel 1992). Despite this, the JSS continue to claim the term *jumma*, and describe themselves as *jumma* people, even as the indigenous movement has assumed a transnational form.

When the JSS introduced the idea of *jumma* as a political identity of a shared collective space, the Khumi gained a new identity to add to their existing three (Pahari, tribal, and *upajatee*). Yet the majority of the Khumi people do not understand the intended political spirit of *jumma* identity and its connotations for political bargaining, perhaps with the exception of those Khumi youths who study in schools and colleges, or have contacts with regional political organizations, or who work in different local, national, and international NGOs, that is, those who have knowledge about the political dynamics of the CHT versus the state. This segment of people in Khumi society deliberately started using *jumma* in their everyday language. Though small numbers of Khumi people talk about *jumma* and refer to *jumma* people, many villagers are now gradually becoming aware of the political connotations of *jumma* as a collective category and space of the struggle for Pahari rights. However, as a group identity, the majority of Khumi people do not subscribe to the idea of *jumma* to a substantial extent. In the villages, inhabitants rarely use the term *"jumma* people." I have spent almost three years— in different phases—living among the Khumi during the last decade, and I hardly ever heard "jumma people" used as a phrase, a discourse, or as a form of identity in everyday interactions and conversations among villagers. However, I heard it frequently during discussions with Peyang Khumi (an NGO worker), Poire Khumi (who was working with Médecins Sans Frontières or MSF), Row Khumi (a Khumi representative at the local government office), Shoilo Master (a primary school teacher), Lelung Khumi (a highly educated Khumi who represents the Khumi *jatee* in various forums), and Poippa Khumi (a local NGO worker and college student), because all of these people are somehow connected with indigenous activism in the CHT. This reflects the premise that people connected with the outside world are more likely to subscribe to the political discourse on identity, while others, more confined within their communities, tend to stick to sociocultural categorizations of identity. In local-level elections in the CHT, *jumma* is a very effective and motivating sense of identity in terms of gaining votes in favor of Pahari candidates (see Uddin 2010). Sometimes, Pahari candidates from Marma, Mru, and Tripura use the identity *"jumma* people" in elections to campaign against Bengali candidates, with effective results. Although Marma and Tripura are not Khumi, these candidates establish a connection and collective space by using *"jumma* people," so that Khumi people feel they are their own candidates. In these ways, Khumi people negotiate the identity of *jumma* people in specific contexts.

Adivasi versus *Khudra Nrigoshti*: A New Debate

The *adivasi* issue is a very recent intervention in the field of indigeneity in Bangladesh. The indigenous rights movement in Bangladesh was primarily triggered by the international recognition of indigenous people's rights by the United Nations. It also brought a new form of identity, *adivasi,* to the realm of identity politics in Bangladesh. Considering the socioeconomic and political positioning of indigenous people around the world, a general perception has been established of indigenous people as "poor, marginalized, colonized, [and] exploited indigenous populations must be protected, their cultures must be preserved, and their rights must be enshrined in UN Human Rights legislation" (Shah 2007: 1,807). As in many other countries, the indigenous people of Bangladesh also felt encouraged and motivated by this international recognition, and hence adopted the ideas of the UN declaration.[7] They formed the Bangladesh Indigenous People's Forum, or the Bangladesh Adivasi Forum (BAF), in 2001 with Shantu Larma, the then president of the JSS, as president and Sanjeeb Drong, a Garo indigenous activist, as general secretary. This can be seen as a local articulation of international indigenous politics and a national adaptation of transnational identity politics (see Gerharz 2014). Under the BAF, many people of various ethnic groups, living in both the plains and the hill areas, were given a voice to speak out about their constant suffering, everyday forms of discrimination, and confrontation with local agents of the state. The movement of the JSS gained a new spirit, a new voice, and a new dimension as it became a major part of the BAF, while simultaneously continuing as a separate movement for the Pahari people. The JSS gained momentum from its involvement with the BAF for at least two main reasons: (1) Shantu Larma, the president of the JSS, became the president of the BAF, and hence CHT issues became the priority agenda of the BAF; and (2) CHT issues were adopted by various other indigenous peoples living on the plains, as they all now shared the same platform—the BAF. With the formation of the BAF, CHT issues were more frequently noticed in the capital, due to support from academics, the country's civil society, left-leaning political organizations, and progressive media. Furthermore, CHT issues garnered more international support as the BAF formed new connections with many international rights organizations. Eva Gerharz wrote:

> The Forum is an official member of the Asia Indigenous Peoples' Pact (AIPP), a Forum member is currently employed as the Coordinator for the Human Rights Campaign and Policy Advocacy at AIPP's headquarters in Chiang Mai, Thailand. The Forum also networks with a variety of other regional organisations, particularly in India. The Forum is frequently invited to UN meetings, such as the Permanent Forum consultations in New York. For the International Working Group on Indigenous Affairs and the European Commission, the Forum serves as a major contact partner. Although some foreign organisations contact smaller groups directly, such as women's groups, the Indigenous People's Forum serves as the contact institution for globally operating institutions and represents Bangladeshis at the meetings called by the UN bodies directly concerned with indigenous people's issues. (Gerharz 2013: 13)

Because the JSS became actively involved in the BAF and its regular activism, the Khumi people, like many other Pahari indigenous groups, also systematically became part of the BAF movement and thereby gained a new identity as *adivasi* or indigenous people. *Adivasi* is not their own innovation; like many other forms of identity, it, too, was imposed from outside.

However, the majority of the Khumi do not understand the politics of indigeneity as such and therefore are not quite aware of what kind of benefits they can gain through international recognition, endorsement, and support. The engagement of the Khumi with the *adivasi* issue is limited, and hence it matters little to their daily lives whether they are identified as *adivasi* or not. The Khumi have three levels of engagement in *adivasi* activism. First, they engage by attending different *adi-*

vasi cultural programs organized by various Pahari organizations, local administrations, *adivasi* rights organization, the JSS, and the BAF. On the International Day of the World's Indigenous Peoples in August every year, the Khumi present themselves with their traditional costumes, perform typical Khumi dances, and engage in a symbolic display of Khumi warfare with traditional war instruments. Second, a few educated Khumi youths participate in different meetings of the JSS and the BAF, representing the Khumi people as one of the *adivasi* groups living in Bangladesh. Third, they participate in various meetings on *adivasi* rights set up by international organizations, various NGOs, civil society, and human rights organizations; in such meetings, it is generally the same educated Khumi individuals who represent the Khumi people. In my research, I found that most villagers are unconcerned with whether they are *adivasi* or not, because they cannot detect any difference since the identity of *adivasi* appeared in Khumi life. This illustrates that the politics of indigeneity is in some ways a kind of elite politics of relatively privileged *adivasi* groups and people, who have access to urban centers, education, markets, and international networks.

Also in recent times, indigenous activism and the *adivasi* debate has been freshly fueled by the introduction of a new identity, *khudra nrigoshti*, imposed by the government of Bangladesh in 2011, with the fifteenth amendment to the Bangladeshi constitution. While the BAF, along with many other *adivasi* organizations such as Adivasi Odhikar Andolon (Adivasi Rights Movement), with the support of civil society, left-leaning political parties, many academics, and intellectuals, demanded their constitutional recognition as *adivasi* or indigenous people, the Awami League (AL) government categorically denied this demand. The state's intention, with the introduction of the term *khudra nrigoshti* (small ethnic minority people), is motivated by the ideology of considering culturally different groups of people as demographic, economic, and political minorities within the state framework of Bangladesh. The AL government came to power in Bangladesh in 2008, and it was expected that, as the AL had a reputation as a secular party that was compassionate towards *adivasi* people, the AL would confer a constitutional recognition of indigenous people as *adivasi*. Even in their electoral manifesto, the AL pledged to meet the demands of indigenous people. Furthermore, in the years that followed their election, i.e., from 2008 onwards, the AL government showed great support for the International Day of the World's Indigenous Peoples, held on 9 August in 2008, 2009, and 2010. In order to mark the day, the AL government officially made a public statement pronouncing the inclusion of "indigenous people" in the official program of the government. Respective district administration, as part of government policy, officially celebrated the day as an internationally acknowledged day of indigenous people. Suddenly in 2011, however, the AL government completely reversed their position and declared that there are no indigenous people in Bangladesh. The then foreign minister, Dr Dipu Mony, declared in 2011 that Bangladesh has no *adivasi* people.[8] In 2011, the AL government circulated an official bulletin that was sent to all district administrations and sub-district administrations, instructing them not to celebrate the International Day of the World's Indigenous Peoples and not to support any indigenous peoples' programs or any program marking the International Day of the World's Indigenous Peoples (see Uddin 2014, 2016). This decision generated huge criticism, and the AL government provided no convincing clarification on their change in stance. The government merely emphasized two main arguments supporting their new position: the Bangladeshi constitution, following the fifteenth amendment, does not recognize any indigenous people in Bangladesh; and Bangladesh is not a signatory to the Declaration on the Rights of Indigenous Peoples adopted in 2007 by the United Nations General Assembly.

The indigenous people of Bangladesh, including the Pahari, have been fighting for inclusion in the constitution since *khudra nrigoshti* was introduced in 2010, but the fight has taken on a seemingly chaotic nature. Indigenous people, the media, and some left-leaning political organizations arrange seminars, symposia, sit-in programs, and public demonstrations. A procession takes place in August every year to mark the International Day of the World's Indigenous Peoples and to demand the constitutional recognition of indigenous people or *adivasi*. Yet, after these events are concluded, there is little follow-up discussion about the issues they raise. Some academics and indigenous activists sometimes post about related issues on social media, but it has had very little impact on any discussion in wider society (see Wilson and Stewart 2008), despite increasing use of the internet.

The Khumi people themselves have very little awareness of *khudra nrigoshti*. They are relatively unaware of the conceptual battle and intellectual debates over their identity and whether they are *khudra nrigoshti* or *adivasi*. It is their understanding that their lives are scarcely influenced by this sort of critical intellectual debate and conceptual fight. Despite being relatively unaware of this issue themselves, the Khumi are included in the category of *khudra nrigoshti* from a statist perspective, and they are *adivasi* or indigenous people from the viewpoint of indigenous activists. The inhabitants of the village where I conducted my research, for example, are still not certain of the merits and disadvantages of being either *khudra nrigoshti* or *adivasi*. However, several villagers believe that if they have an official status, and the status is recognized by the state constitution, it could be of some benefit to them. They have gained this idea through their interaction with Khumi youths who are engaged in *adivasi* politics in Bangladesh. Though a large number of Khumi people are not interested in this new form of ethnic identity, whether it is *khudra nrigoshti* or *adivasi*, a few educated and political Khumi are actively involved in the politics of rejecting the state-induced idea of *khudra nrigoshti*, and are instead actively involved in the demand for recognition as indigenous people.

Conclusion

From the above discussion, it is clear that within the local, translocal, national, and transnational politics of indigeneity, the position of the Khumi people is not definite. This is because, at various levels of Khumi society, many Khumi people subscribe to and unsubscribe from different forms of identity depending on their level of education, their degree of connectivity and contact with the outer world, their access to political circles, and their engagement in *adivasi* politics. The differing identities—hill people, Pahari, tribal, *upajatee*, and *khudra nrigoshti*—imposed by the state and state power holders have always been problematic because they carry colonial connotations, implying colonial fantasy and a colonial legacy in depicting the colonized people—although they now live in a decolonized and independent country—within a framework of primitive, uncivilized, exotic, and savage people. However, the Khumi people have gained several other identities—*jumma* and *adivasi* or indigenous people—which are also in some ways imposed upon them from outside. The basic difference between these two sets of identities is that while earlier identities relate to state policies of domination, exclusion, subjugation, and derogation, newer identities contain the hopes of political empowerment, an ambition for dignity, and privileges stemming from the transnational politics of indigeneity. As the Khumi people are largely "uneducated," have irregular contact with the outside world, and have little access to the regional politics of the JSS, the centralized politics of the AL and the Bangladesh Nationalist Party (BNP), or the transnational politics of indigeneity, they sometimes find themselves in a very ambivalent situation with regards to understanding their own identity, as well as that imposed upon them.

The Khumi people have acquired identities based on the commonality and community spirit of belonging within a framework of cultural difference and sameness between Bengalis and non-Bengalis. Therefore, identities imposed from outside and/or within the forum of *adivasi* politics appear to Khumi people in very complex and complicated ways. In fact, under the practice and existence of multiple identities, the Khumi people search out identities for themselves based on their own social organizations, cultural practices, language, beliefs, ethnic background, and everyday interactions among themselves and in contact with others. Multiple identities indeed create spaces for the Khumi to lose their own "self." Rechen Khumi, who has some knowledge of the national and transnational politics of indigeneity and *adivasi* issues, explained it to me during an afternoon walk in a *jhum* field as follows:

> Everybody is doing politics of *adivasi*. The state is doing politics so that *adivasi* people can't claim any rights and privileges. *Adivasi* politicians are doing politics so that they can gain some political power and privilege. Academics are doing politics for their own professional establishment by writings on *adivasi* people. NGOs are doing politics as NGO officials need to justify the funds they receive from outside. International organizations are doing their politics to pretend that they have great sympathy for *adivasi* people. But, we people who live in hills, involve ourselves in *jhum* to ensure meals every day, know little about what is happening outside our world, are confined within our own social and cultural settings in the hill, and are imposed various identities as part of the politics of indigeneity. Sometimes we accept some since we think it could bring some good to us but sometimes we just don't bother since we think it doesn't make any difference whether we bother or not. But, the big problem is that within these multiple identities, we are gradually losing our "self" which we believe is our real identity. (Rechen Khumi, 21 June 2012)

Nasir Uddin (PhD, Kyoto) is a cultural anthropologist based in Bangladesh, and Professor of Anthropology at Chittagong University. He studied and carried out research at the University of Dhaka, the University of Chittagong, Kyoto University, the University of Hull, Delhi School of Economics, Ruhr-University Bochum, VU University Amsterdam, Heidelberg University, and the London School of Economics (LSE). His research interests include indigeneity and identity politics; dialectics between colonialism and postcolonialism; refugee, statelessness, and citizenship; notions of power and the state in everyday life; the Chittagong Hill Tracts; and South Asia. His latest book is *Life in Peace and Conflict: Indigeneity and State in the Chittagong Hill Tracts* (Orient BlackSwan, 2017).

Notes

1. I performed ethnographic fieldwork among the Khumi for more than a year between 2005 and 2007 during my dissertation research. Consequently, I spent a further fifteen months doing fieldwork in the CHT in different periods from 2008 to 2014.
2. During the time of the Pakistan Republic, i.e., until 1971, the official name of Bangladesh was East Pakistan.
3. The name of the local NGO is the Jhum Aesthetic Council (JAC). In 2004, it published a special bulletin on the Khumi called "LAANG." The JAC published another bulletin in 2003, called "AMANG," in which an unofficial survey of the Khumi population was recorded (pp. 27–28).
4. In the 1972 constitution—and in the first move of its kind—Article 1(6) declared that "citizens of Bangladesh shall be identified as Bengalis," which constitutionally excluded non-Bengali people, including the Pahari and thereby the Khumi. For details, see Uddin (2008b).
5. For details, see Bassaignet (1958) and Uddin (2008a).
6. Scott (2009: ix) wrote: "Zomia is a new name for virtually all the lands at altitudes above roughly three hundred meters all the way from the Central Highlands of Vietnam to northeastern India and traversing five Southeast Asian nations (Vietnam, Cambodia, Laos, Thailand, and Burma) and four provinces of China (Yunnan, Guizhou, Guangxi, and parts of Sichuan). It is an expanse of 2.5 million square kilometers containing about one hundred million minority peoples of truly bewildering ethnic and linguistic variety."
7. For example: (1) the formation of the UN Working Group on Indigenous Populations (WGIP) in 1982; (2) the introduction of the first international legal mechanisms for the protection of indigenous peoples in 1989 in the form of ILO Convention 169; (3) the declaration of the UN International Decade of the World's Indigenous Peoples from 1995 to 2004; (4) the formation of a Permanent Forum on Indigenous Issues in 2000; (5) the appointment of a UN Special Rapporteur on the Rights and Fundamental Freedoms of Indigenous People in 2001; (6) the adoption of the UN Declaration on the Rights of Indigenous Peoples in 2007 in the UN General Assembly.
8. See *The Daily Star*, 27 July 2011; *bdnews24.com*, 26 July 2011; *The Daily Independent*, 27 July 2011.

Bibliography

Barnard, Alan. 2006. "Kalahari Revisionism, Vienna and the Indigenous Peoples' Debate." *Social Anthropology* 14(1): 1–16.

Barth, Fredrik. [1954] 1998. *Ethnic Groups and Boundaries: The Social Organization of Culture Difference.* Long Grove, IL: Waveland Press.

Barua, Benu Prasad. 2001. *Ethnicity and National Integration in Bangladesh: A Study of the Chittagong Hill Tracts.* New Delhi: Har-Anand.

Bassaignet, P. 1958. *Tribesmen of the Chittagong Hill Tracts.* Dhaka: Asiatic Society of Pakistan.

Bernot, Lucien. 1964. "Ethnic Groups of Chittagong Hill Tracts." In *Social Research in East Pakistan*, ed. Pierre Bessaignet, 137–71. Dhaka: Asiatic Society of Pakistan.
Gerharz, Eva. 2013. "Beyond and Beneath the Nation-State: Bangladeshi Indigenous People's Activism at the Crossroads." *Working Papers in Development Sociology and Social Anthropology*, no. 372. Bielefeld: University of Bielefeld.
———. 2014. "Indigenous Activism in Bangladesh: Translocal Spaces and Shifting Constellations of Belonging." *Asian Ethnicity* 15(4): 552–70.
Ghosh, Kaushik. 2006. "Between Global Flows and Local Dams: Indigenousness, Locality, and the Transnational Sphere in Jharkhand, India." *Cultural Anthropology* 21(4): 501–34.
Grierson, George A. 1927. *Linguistic Survey of India*. Vols. I–VI. Calcutta: Government Press.
Hodgson, Dorothy. 2011. *Being Maasai, Becoming Indigenous: Postcolonial Politics in a Neoliberal World*. Bloomington, IN: Indiana University Press.
Hutchinson, Robert H.S. 1906. *An Account of Chittagong Hill Tracts*. Calcutta: Bengal Secretariat Book Depot.
Karlsson, Bengt. 2008. "Anthropology and the 'Indigenous Slot': Claims to and Debates about Indigenous Peoples' Status in India." *Critique of Anthropology* 23(4): 403–23.
Kuper, Adam. 2003. "The Return of the Native." *Current Anthropology* 44(3): 389–402.
———. 2006. "The Concept of Indigeneity: Discussion." *Social Anthropology* 14(1): 21–22.
Lewin, Thomas H. [1870] 2004. *Wild Race of the Eastern Frontier of India*. London: Allen.
Li, T.M. 2000. "Articulating Indigenous Identity in Indonesia: Resource Politics and the Tribal Slot." *Comparative Studies in Society and History* 42(1): 149–79.
Mohsin, Amena. 2002. *The Politics of Nationalism: The Case of the Chittagong Hill Tracts*. Dhaka: The University Press.
Pfaff-Czarnecka, Joanna and Gerard Toffin. 2011. "Belonging and Multiple Attachments in Contemporary Himalayan Societies." In *The Politics of Belonging in the Himalayas: Local Attachments and Boundary Dynamics*, ed. Joanna Pfaff-Czarnecka and Gerard Toffin, xi–xxxviii. Delhi: Sage.
Sattar, Abdus. 1983. *In the Sylvan Shadows*. Dhaka: Bangla Academy.
———. 2000. *Research on Tribal People in Bangladesh*. Dhaka: Nasas. [In Bengali]
Scott, James. 2009. *The Art of Not Being Governed: An Anarchist History of Upland Southeast Asia*. New Haven, CT and London: Yale University Press.
Shah, Alpa. 2007. "The Dark Side of Indigeneity?" *History Compass* 5/6: 1,806–32.
St. John, R.F.A. 1873. "A Short Account of the Hill Tribes of North Arakan." *Journal of Anthropological Institute of Great Britain and Ireland* 2: 233–47.
Tripura, Prashanta. 1992. "The Colonial Foundation of Pahari Ethnicity." *The Journal of Social Studies* 68: 1–16.
Uddin, Nasir. 2005. "History is the Story for Existence: A Case Study of Chittagong Hill Tracts." *Asian Profile* 33(4): 391–412.
———. 2008a. "Homeless at Home: An Ethnographic Study on Marginality and Leadership among the Khumi in the Chittagong Hill Tracts of Bangladesh," unpublished PhD dissertation. Kyoto University.

———. 2008b. "Living on the Margin: The Positioning of the Khumi within the Socioeconomic, Political and Ethnic History of the Chittagong Hill Tracts." *Asian Ethnicity* 9(1): 33–53.

———. 2009. "Colonial (Re)presentation of Colonised People: A Case Study of the Chittagong Hill Tracts." Unpublished research monograph funded by the British Academy.

———. 2010. "Politics of Cultural Difference: Identity and Marginality in the Chittagong Hill Tracts of Bangladesh." *South Asian Survey* 17(2): 283–94.

———. 2014. "Beyond Political and Cultural Binary: Understanding Indigenous Activism from Below." Paper presented at a workshop titled *Indigenous Activism in Bangladesh: A Critical Perspective* organized by the Department of Anthropology, the London School of Economics and Political Sciences, 18 March 2014.

———. 2016. "Identity Politics and Indigenous Activism in the Chittagong Hill Tracts." In *Bangladesh: History, Politics, Economy, Society and Culture,* ed. Mahmudul Huque, 319–340. Dhaka: The University Press Limited.

Van Schendel, Willem. 1992. "The Invention of the 'Jummas': State Formation and Ethnicity in South Eastern Bangladesh." *Modern Asian Studies* 26(1): 95–128.

———. 2011. "The Dangers of Belonging: Tribes, Indigenous Peoples and Homelands in South Asia." In *The Politics of Belonging in India: Becoming Adivasi,* ed. Daniel Rycroft and Sageeta Dasgupta, 19–43. London and New York: Routledge.

Wilson, Pamela and Stewart, Michelle (ed.). 2008. *Global Indigenous Media: Cultures, Poetics and Politics.* Durham, NC and London: Duke University Press.

PART III

INDIGENEITY AS A POLITICAL RESOURCE

 6

DIFFERENT TRAJECTORIES OF INDIGENOUS RIGHTS MOVEMENTS IN AFRICA
Insights from Cameroon and Tanzania
Michaela Pelican

Introduction

"Indigeneity" has been a highly contested concept, particularly in Africa (and Asia) where the indigenous rights movement has only recently gained significance. Over the past twenty years, many ethnic and minority groups in Africa have laid claim to "indigeneity" on the basis of their political marginalization and cultural distinctiveness in their country or region of residence. They have drawn inspiration from the United Nations definition of "indigenous peoples" as a legal category with collective entitlements, and have linked up with the global indigenous rights movement. Concurrently, there has been an extensive debate within Africanist anthropology on the analytical usefulness of the concept. Moreover, several African governments have questioned its applicability to the African continent, arguing that all population groups may be considered "indigenous." However, after the adoption of the United Nations Declaration on the Rights of Indigenous Peoples in 2007, this conceptual criticism has somewhat abated, and many African governments have made attempts to integrate the indigenous rights discourse in their policies and development programs—with varied results.

In this chapter I wish to outline different trajectories of indigenous rights movements in Africa and discuss the factors that may contribute to their ascent or decline. In particular, I will draw on two case studies. The first is that of the Mbororo of Cameroon, a pastoralist group that joined the global indigenous rights movement in 2005, and whose socioeconomic and political trajectory I have followed since the 1990s.[1] The second is the case of Maasai pastoralists of Tanzania, whose involvement in the global indigenous rights movement dates back to the late 1980s. Here I rely on the research of the anthropologist Dorothy Hodgson and her comprehensive review of twenty years of Maasai advocacy and development activities (Hodgson 2001, 2002, 2009, 2011).

Controversies over Indigeneity: Academic and Political Debates

In his comprehensive study on the history of the global indigenous rights movement, Ronald Niezen (2003, 2010) makes clear the constructed nature of indigeneity; in fact, he prefers the term "indigenism" so as to highlight its character as a political movement. As he argues, "Indigenous Peoples were first the citizens of an idea before they became members of an international community with distinct rights" (Niezen 2010: 135). Thus, the term "indigenous peoples" was initially introduced as a legal category and only later filled with meaning. Understood primarily as a political notion, the term may refer to different subjects in different historical and regional contexts.

The application of the indigenous rights discourse to the African continent instigated much debate, among both academics and political actors. While in the Pacific and the Americas, indigenous activism has a long history and the status of "first peoples" is generally uncontested, the situation in Africa—as well as in many parts of Asia (see Baird's and Uddin's chapters in this volume)—is different. Here, defining which groups may be considered "indigenous" is more problematic and controversial, as the African continent has long and complex histories of migration, assimilation, and conquest. Furthermore, as Kopytoff (1987) demonstrated in his classic essay, African societies tend to reproduce themselves at their internal frontiers, continuously creating and recreating a dichotomy between "original inhabitants" and "latecomers" along which political prerogatives are negotiated. This recurring process does not allow for permanent and clear-cut distinctions between "first nations" and "dominant societies" as is implied by the universal notion of "indigenous peoples." Accordingly, some anthropologists have criticized the concept of "indigenous peoples" as inapplicable to the African context, and as promoting an essentialist ideology of culture and identity (e.g., Kuper 2003, 2005). Conversely, others have claimed that these complexities have effectively been reflected in the working definitions of the International Labour Organization (ILO) and the

United Nations (UN), which emphasize cultural distinctiveness, political marginalization, and self-identification as fundamental criteria. In their view, the above criticism is not only unjustified, but counterproductive both to the anthropological endeavor and to "indigenous realities" (e.g., Kenrick and Lewis 2004: 8). A reconciliatory approach has been suggested by Barnard (2004, 2006), who questions the validity of "indigenous peoples" as an anthropological concept while recognizing its utility as a political and legal tool in the struggle for collective rights. I agree with Barnard. Moreover, I contend that by now—more than ten years after the initial debate—the focus has shifted from debating the validity of the concept to studying the social dynamics of the indigenous rights movement in different parts of Africa. This chapter is a contribution to this aim.

Concurrent to the academic debate of the 2000s, many African governments had been opposed to the concept of "indigenous peoples" and their entitlement to land, arguing that all Africans are "indigenous" and should have equal access to natural resources (Lutz 2007). While the deliberative process in the United Nations began in 1971, it was only in 2007 that it finally culminated in the adoption of the Declaration on the Rights of Indigenous Peoples. A critical moment occurred in 2006, when a group of African states (in particular Namibia, Botswana, and Nigeria) took exception to some of the formulations in the declaration (Oldham and Frank 2008; Pelican 2009). Subsequently, the African UN member states ("African Group") agreed to maintain a united position and issued a *draft aide mémoire*, specifying their concerns regarding the definition of "indigenous peoples," issues of self-determination, ownership of land and resources, establishment of distinct political and economic institutions, and national and territorial integrity (African Group 2006). Moreover, they stated that for some member states the declaration may pose fundamental constitutional and political problems, rendering its implementation impossible. Faced with these objections, the Global Indigenous Peoples' Caucus engaged in a series of negotiations, and the African Commission on Human and Peoples' Rights (ACHPR) of the African Union issued an advisory opinion in 2007 (ACHPR 2007). Eventually, the African Group within the United Nations agreed to nine amendments to the declaration, two of which specifically addressed the issues of the definition of the term "indigenous peoples," and possible misinterpretations of the right to self-determination. Finally, in September 2007, the Declaration on the Rights of Indigenous Peoples was adopted by the General Assembly of the United Nations, with the support of the African Group, and four countries opposed: Canada, Australia, New Zealand, and the United States.

As rightly noted by Oldham and Frank (2008), the objections of the African Group typify the anthropological controversy over the concept of "indigenous peoples." As argued by Suzman (2002) and others, the adoption of the Declaration on the Rights of Indigenous Peoples has been particularly problematic for southern African states, such as Botswana and Namibia, who—as a way of distancing themselves from apartheid politics—excluded the provision for differential treatment of their citizens on the basis of race or ethnicity. Conversely, in countries like Cameroon, where ethnic and regional favoritism have long been vital features of national politics (Bayart 1984; Kofele-Kale 1986; Mehler 1993), the concept of "indigenous peoples" is much less problematic. However, as I will show in this chapter, the declaration's implementation has not been without problems both in Cameroon and in other parts of the continent.

Studying Indigenous Rights Movements in Africa

Over the past twenty years, the global indigenous rights movement has gained traction in many parts of Africa. Southern Africa in particular, with its complex history of settler colonialism, has been a hotbed of controversies—over the concept of "indigenous peoples" and their purported needs, as well as the role of international organizations in the indigenous rights movement (e.g., Marshall 2002; Pelican and Maruyama 2015; Sapignoli and Hitchcock 2013; Saugestadt 2011). Here, for example, the case of the San hunter-gatherers has received much attention, while other cases, such as Afrikaners' claims to indigeneity, have been neglected, due to their opposition both from popular opinion and political sensibilities (see also Kuper 2003).

In this chapter, I will focus on two examples from West and East Africa: the case of Mbororo in Cameroon and of Maasai in Tanzania. Both are pastoralist groups that have undergone similar experiences of marginalization and are minorities in their respective sites of settlement. Both engaged with the global indigenous rights movement as a way to strengthen their claims vis-à-vis their national governments. Their political trajectories and achievements, however, have been somewhat different. As I will argue, in Cameroon the indigenous rights discourse has largely retained its currency. The same does not apply to Tanzania, and Maasai activists have turned to alternative development frameworks. Thus, rather than assuming the existence of a single and coherent indigenous rights movement in Africa, I suggest speaking of indigenous rights movements in the plural, which, while drawing on the same global discourses and international legal frameworks, are confronted with divergent national and local contexts.

This chapter aims to outline the factors that have contributed to the movements' divergent outcomes by expounding and comparing the two case studies. I will first present in detail the Mbororo case, which I know firsthand from fieldwork conducted in northwest Cameroon since the 1990s. To elucidate the situation of Maasai pastoralists in Tanzania, I will draw on the comprehensive work of Dorothy Hodgson, who has followed Maasai economic development and political activism since the mid 1980s (Hodgson 2001, 2002, 2009, 2011).

In her recent book *Being Maasai, Becoming Indigenous* (2011), Hodgson uses the concept of "positionings" to analyze observed shifts in orientation among Maasai activists. She relates these shifts to the need of local institutions, organizations, and individuals to respond and position themselves in relation to changing discourses, shaped by the international community and development establishment. As she argues, the turn to neoliberalism in the 1980s was accompanied by a focus on civil society as a self-governing body. By the late 2000s, however, the role of national governments was reconsidered, and governmental institutions have increasingly been integrated in the conception and realization of developmental programs and, most importantly, in the channeling of funds. In Tanzania, this resulted in the repositioning of Maasai nongovernmental organizations as civil society organizations, and in the reframing of their political struggles from the language of indigenous rights to that of pastoralist livelihoods (Hodgson 2011: 157–58).

Hodgson's findings serve as a conceptual starting point to compare the trajectories and achievements of the indigenous rights movements in Cameroon and Tanzania. The concept of "positionings" will inform the analyses of both case studies and provide a framework for their comparison. Finally, it will help us to identify alternative strategies and to develop tentative ideas about the possible futures of indigeneity in Africa.

The Indigenous Rights Movement in Cameroon: The Example of Mbororo Pastoralists

With regard to Cameroon, the term "indigenous peoples" is generally associated with two population groups: Baka and Bagyeli hunter-gatherer societies (also known as Pygmies) and Mbororo cattle pastoralists. Occasionally, the Montagnards, or Kirdi, in the country's Far North are also mentioned as an "indigenous people" of Cameroon (e.g., IWGIA 2014: 453–58). The focus of this chapter is on Mbororo pastoralists, whose recognition as an "indigenous people" has been fraught with a number of complexities, but who, of the three groups mentioned above, have capitalized most actively on this status.

The Mbororo belong to the ethnic category of Fulbe, whose members are dispersed over the Sahel and Savannah belt from West to East Africa. Substantial Mbororo populations are found in Cameroon, Nigeria, Niger, Chad, and the Central African Republic. They are cattle pastoralists who identify with distinct Fulbe lineages and speak distinct Fulfulde dialects. In Cameroon, Mbororo communities are found in many parts of the country suitable for cattle grazing, including the northern area (*le grand nord*), the Northwest, West, and East administrative regions. In addition, a growing number of educated and entrepreneurial Mbororo have moved to the country's southern cities. Generally speaking, the Mbororo constitute an ethnic minority, accounting for, at most, 10 per cent of the population in each of the regions they inhabit. In this case study, I will focus on the Mbororo in the Northwest Region. They have been at the forefront of Mbororo political activism and engagement in the global indigenous rights movement and thereby constitute the most assertive section of Mbororo society in Cameroon.

Mbororo Establishment and Ethnic Coexistence in Northwest Cameroon

Cameroon is a multiethnic and multilingual country, inhabited by more than 250 ethnic and linguistic groups (Mbaku 2005: 1). It looks back on a complex precolonial and colonial history characterized by population movement and changing colonial administrations. The country was first colonized by the Germans (1884–1914), then split and placed under French and British mandates (1919–60/61). While the larger part went to France, the western region was annexed to the British colony of Nigeria. In 1960, French Cameroon attained independence, and Ahmadou Ahidjo became its first president. The British mandate ended in 1961 with a plebiscite organized by the United Nations, which resulted in the northern part being integrated with Nigeria, while the southern part joined the Republic of Cameroon (Ardener 1962; Njeuma 1995). Today, Cameroon is officially a bilingual country with distinct administrative and legal frameworks in its francophone and anglophone regions.

The Northwest Region is located in the anglophone part of the country. Due to its grassy vegetation, it is also known as the Bamenda Grassfields. It is home to many ethnic and linguistic groups that share common features of economic and sociopolitical organization and which here are conflated into the category of Grassfields societies. While most

Grassfields societies have been present in this region for several hundred years, Mbororo pastoralists only arrived in the early twentieth century. Originating from the Kano region in present-day Nigeria, they slowly migrated southwards over the course of the nineteenth century in search of more favorable ecological and political conditions (Boutrais 1995/96: 15–210; Dognin 1981). Attracted by the fertile pastures of the Bamenda Grassfields, many Mbororo families settled there and gradually adopted a more sedentary lifestyle (Pelican 2015: 80–98).

In the first half of the twentieth century, when the population density was still low, Mbororo were generally welcomed both by local Grassfields chiefs and the British colonial administration. Grassfielders treated them as guests on their land and as subjects of their rulers. The British colonial administration—applying the policy of indirect rule—endorsed this system of accommodation and classified the Mbororo as "strangers" and subordinates to "native" Grassfields authorities. Subsequently, under the regime of Cameroon's first president, Ahmadou Ahidjo, which lasted from 1960 to 1982, the Mbororo qualified as Cameroonian citizens (Njeuma and Awasom 1990). However, on account of their Muslim identity and Fulbe ethnicity, they were subsumed under the cultural category of "northerners." Consequently, Mbororo who were born and grew up in northwest Cameroon were still considered "strangers" to the area with limited rights to the region's natural resources and state support.

While Mbororo pastoralists put up with their precarious legal status for several decades, during which land for grazing and farming was still abundant, the situation changed in the 1990s. With growing competition for natural resources and a new era of national politics, Mbororo individuals began to question the status quo, and to claim political representation in their own right. I argue that Mbororo strategies of political activism can be divided in three phases, starting with the formation of ethnic and regional elite associations in the early 1990s, followed by international lobbying as an "indigenous people" in the 2000s, to the recent repositioning of Mbororo activists and the diversification of their lobbying strategies.

The Rise of Ethnic Elite Associations

With Cameroon's democratization in the 1990s, a new era evolved, characterized by party political struggles as well as ethnic and minority politics (Nyamnjoh and Rowlands 1998; Takougang and Krieger 1998). Encouraged by newly gained freedoms and government policies, many population groups began to establish ethnic or regional elite associations, which acted as their representatives to the state. This novel political avenue was also explored by young, mostly educated Mbororo who, in 1992, founded the Mbororo Social and Cultural Development Association (MBOSCUDA) (Davis 1995; Hickey 2007; Pelican 2008). While other organizations promoting Mbororo and pastoralists' interests were also founded during this period, MBOSCUDA soon became the most vocal and effective organ of Mbororo self-representation to the Cameroonian government and international development organizations. It designed a number of regional programs aimed at the revitalization of Mbororo cultural practices, the improvement of Mbororo women's socioeconomic situation, the promotion of education for Mbororo children, and the improvement of pastoral conditions (Duni et al. 2009). Several of these programs were realized with the support of local communities, as well as national and international organizations and funding bodies.[2] Moreover, on account of MBOSCUDA's continuous lobbying, the Mbororo eventually attained the status of a regional and national minority, with rights to natural resources and political representation in their home areas. These developments also led to a change in Mbororo self-understanding. While initially associated with backwardness and superficial Islamization, the ethnonym "Mbororo" gained new, positive meanings. As Mbororo interviewees explained to me, they no longer saw themselves as marginalized pastoralists but as an empowered Cameroonian minority. On the basis of these achievements, MBOSCUDA consolidated its credibility with relation to both its Mbororo constituency and the Cameroonian government.

In the 2000s, MBOSCUDA expanded its political lobbying to the international arena by establishing links with global human rights and indigenous rights movements. Thanks to personal connections with European researchers and development workers, contacts were formed with the International Work Group for Indigenous Affairs (IWGIA). In 2005, MBOSCUDA was granted special consultative status by the Economic and Social Council of the United Nations, which resulted in the international recognition of the Mbororo as one of the "indigenous peoples" of Cameroon. While, in view of MBOSCUDA's political engagement, this step could be seen as completely reasonable, from a critical anthropological perspective Mbororo claims to "indigeneity" are ambiguous, as they collide with local conceptions of "autochthony" (Pelican 2009).[3]

The Complexities of Indigeneity and Autochthony in Cameroon

In Cameroon—as in other parts of Western Africa—notions of "indigeneity," "autochthony," "firstcomers," or "natives" have a long history and frame local conceptions of political hierarchy and legal entitlement (Bayart, Geschiere, and Nyamnjoh 2001; Geschiere 2009; Lentz 2006). In the Northwest Region of Cameroon, it is local Grassfields societies that consider themselves "natives" and "guardians of the land" and regard Mbororo pastoralists as "strangers" and "latecomers" with limited rights to land and landed resources. While this conception is rooted in precolonial notions of political power based on being the first group to have settled in an area, it has also been informed by colonial and postcolonial policies. At the national level, discourses of autochthony came to be highlighted in the context of Cameroon's democratization. As stipulated in the country's revised constitution of 1996, priority is given to the protection of the rights of "minorities" and "indigenous populations."[4] In this national political framework, "indigenous populations" are meant to refer to local groups that consider themselves "firstcomers," "natives," or "autochthones." This is different from the UN and ILO conception of "indigenous peoples," which prioritizes the criteria of self-identification, historical or contemporary experience of marginalization, and cultural difference from the majority population (Daes 1996; ILO 1989).

As confirmed by Tchoumba (2005) in his ILO pilot study on Cameroon, Mbororo pastoralists as well as Baka and Bagyeli hunter-gatherers of southern and southeastern Cameroon (also known as Pygmies) fulfill the ILO and UN criteria, and thus may be considered "indigenous peoples" of Cameroon. Conversely, the Cameroonian government has never officially endorsed the two groups' classification as "indigenous peoples," but instead utilizes the notion of "vulnerable" or "marginal populations" (in French, *populations marginales*). This complexity of concepts with some resemblances but different political and legal implications has resulted in the puzzling situation in which the Mbororo are recognized internationally as an "indigenous people," yet in the lo-

Table 6.1. Illustration of parallel and partly conflicting categories.

	Local categories	Colonial categories	Postcolonial categories	Current government categories	UN categories
Mbororo	latecomers	strangers	*allochthon*	marginal population, marginalized minority	indigenous
Grassfields societies	firstcomers	natives	*autochthon*	majority	non-indigenous

Table 6.2. Perspectives on primary entitlement to land on the basis of the categorizations in Table 6.1.

	Local perspective	Colonial perspective	Postcolonial perspective	Perspective of current government	Perspective of United Nations
Mbororo				(x)	x
Grassfields societies	x	x	x	x	

cal and national context they are seen as "latecomers," "allochthones," or a marginalized minority. We thus have a situation in which international and local interpretations of "indigeneity" are irreconcilable and engender a new potential for competition and conflict. Despite these conceptual and terminological complexities, the international recognition of the Mbororo as an "indigenous people" did initiate a new era in their identity politics.

Ambivalent Experiences and Changing Strategies of Mbororo Activists

With the adoption of the Declaration on the Rights of Indigenous Peoples in 2007, expectations were high among many activists and organizations that the precarious situation of minority groups may gradually be improved. The same hopes were shared by Mbororo activists, in particular MBOSCUDA leaders, who promoted this new, supra-ethnic identity in the hope of capitalizing on its political weight. Yet their subsequent recourse to the new indigenous rights discourse produced ambivalent and at times unforeseen results. Here I wish to outline two developments that seem representative of the learning processes of many indigenous and human rights activists in Africa and beyond: a progression from enthusiasm to disillusionment and then pragmatism; and recent ventures into alternative spaces of political lobbying, namely social media.

To me and many of my interlocutors, the Sabga leadership crisis of 2007 was a crucial test case to assess the applicability and efficacy of the indigenous rights discourse with regard to Mbororo in Cameroon (for a detailed analysis, see Pelican 2010). The crisis emerged over the procedure to select a new community leader, with Mbororo activists claiming their right to political and territorial integrity as an "indigenous people." The issue began in the summer of 2007, when government representatives forcefully intervened in Sabga, the main Mbororo settlement in northwest Cameroon. Through the influence of a wealthy and well-connected entrepreneur, the community-elected leader was administratively deposed and replaced by a Mbororo ruler of the entrepreneur's choice. Members of the Sabga community protested against this interference, to which the government reacted with military intervention. The Mbororo elite in Sabga eventually decided to use its international connections to pressure the government. Fearing for their lives, the deposed leader and his supporters sought refuge at the United States embassy in the capital, Yaoundé. Mbororo women staged a protest at the prime minister's office and demanded the deposition of the imposed ruler and the reinstatement of their rightful community leader. Moreover, with the help of MBOSCUDA, they reported the case to national and international human rights organizations as well as to the UN Human Rights Council. For a short while, government officials seemed willing to reconsider the case. On the initiative of the prime minister, an investigative team was sent to Sabga. Its members reported their findings to the presidency, but no action was taken. Mbororo human rights activists further publicized the issue and solicited national and international bodies to issue official letters of concern. Moreover, in 2007, Rodolfo Stavenhagen, at the time Special Rapporteur on the situation of human rights and fundamental freedoms of indigenous peoples, visited Cameroon and included the Sabga leadership crisis in his report, demanding a response from the Cameroonian government and the resolution of the issue (Stavenhagen 2007). Yet, while government officials were obliged to deliver opinion statements on the reported infringements of Mbororo human and indigenous rights, no factual consequences materialized. The imposed leader remained in place, and the Mbororo community had to come to terms with the political dynamics and internal frictions that the protracted issue had caused.

To fully understand the relevance of this case, let me further qualify its key features. It was one of the few occasions of near-unanimous community action, when Mbororo women, youths, and men took to the streets in Sabga to publicly protest against the intervention of the regional administration in the selection procedure of their community leader. It was also unprecedented in the sense that community members—including illiterate women and men, rather than just educated Mbororo activists—took action and traveled to the capital, Yaoundé, to seek both national and international assistance. Finally, this was also the first time that MBOSCUDA's report to the Special Rapporteur on the situation of human rights and fundamental freedoms of indigenous peoples and the Human Rights Council effected an intergovernmental exchange and follow-up. However, these interventions ultimately produced no significant actions, and the queries of the Human Rights Council remained largely unresolved. Eventually, the initial hopes of Mbororo activists, whereby UN instruments and the discourse on human and indigenous rights would work in their favor, were dashed. The ensuing repercussions were twofold. They included governmental sanctioning of Mbororo development actors, as well as disagreement within the Mbororo community on the efficacy of international intervention, and, more profoundly, the rightfulness of Mbororo claims to indigeneity. Critical voices emerged among members of the economically progressive Mbororo elite. In their view, classifying the Mbororo as an "indigenous people" was inaptly suggestive of Mbororo backwardness and poverty. Conversely, they saw their personal trajectories as evocative of Mbororo advancement and integration, on equal terms with other population groups.

The Sabga leadership crisis thus initiated a phase of general disenchantment with global advocacy and the indigenous rights discourse. At the same time, it occasioned a reorientation of Mbororo activists away from overt criticism of the state towards a more pragmatic approach and collaboration with governmental institutions (Pelican 2013). As mentioned earlier, the Cameroonian government has integrated the indigenous rights discourse in its developmental agenda, albeit under the moniker of "marginal populations." Thus, Mbororo organizations continue to employ the indigenous rights discourse, while at the same time seeking to engage with government officials. This is reflected in a number of workshops, initiated by Mbororo organizations, which are aimed at generating dialogue and cooperation between representatives of indigenous groups, relevant government institutions, academics, and NGOs. These events are also remarkable in the sense that they illustrate the repeated efforts of educated and visionary Mbororo actors to engender a self-understanding that transcends the narrow boundaries of Mbororo ethnicity and embraces the broader categories of "indigenous peoples" or "ethnic minorities."

New Spaces of Mbororo Advocacy and Development

In recent years, the number of Mbororo individuals who have moved from rural areas to study or work in urban centers has increased considerably. This has been accompanied by a proliferation of Mbororo community organizations in Cameroon's urban centers, some initiated by university students, others by professionals. While the majority of these NGOs focus on community development, some engage in indigenous rights and are also active on an international level. Among them was Lelewal, a self-proclaimed indigenous peoples' non-governmental organization. Its founder regularly participated in UN meetings and, together with MBOSCUDA representatives, gave weight to Mbororo complaints.[5] Another is the Laimaru Network, created in 2011, whose aim is to support NGOs working in the field of indigenous and minority rights by providing information about fundraising, capacity building, advocacy, and social entrepreneurship.[6] As these examples illustrate, there has been a growing interest and expertise in community development and advocacy among Mbororo in Cameroon, particularly among educated youths. This has also been reflected in their recent ventures into virtual and social media as a new space for political lobbying. Here I will cite the example of the Justice and Dignity Campaign, an advocacy initiative launched in 2011 by Mbororo individuals based both in Cameroon and abroad.

The initial spark to set up the campaign was a broadcast by a private television station that slandered the development programs of Mbororo and the so-called Pygmies (Baka and Bagyeli hunter-gatherers in southern and southeastern Cameroon). Taking offense at the broadcast's racist undertones, and drawing inspiration from the growing popularity of social media, a small group of Mbororo activists decided to launch an internet campaign, setting up an online petition, followed by a Facebook page, a corresponding website, a YouTube channel, and a Twitter account. Unlike in previous strategies of political lobbying and advocacy where the focus was on the malpractice of the Cameroonian state, the campaign highlighted the misdoings of a particular individual who also played a crucial role in the Sabga leadership crisis. To the surprise of its initiators, the Justice and Dignity Campaign—in particular its Facebook page—attracted considerable attention among Cameroonians abroad as well as back home. Despite still rather rudimentary internet services, Mbororo youths—particularly in urban areas—are fully conversant with Facebook and also use it to keep their non-literate and rural relatives updated. For the campaign's supporters, it was a sign of success when they learned that their opponent was astounded by his inability to control this online flow of information and, for the first time in a long history of Mbororo grievances, publicly responded to their accusations. Consequently, the campaign's focus has broadened and now addresses various issues related to human and indigenous rights violations, such as the mass abduction of Nigerian schoolchildren by Boko Haram in April 2014, the abuse of Baka hunters by wildlife officers in October 2014, and the forcible appropriation of land inhabited by Mbororo herders by the Catholic Church in northwest Cameroon. The latter was eventually resolved in the summer of 2014 with an official retraction from the Catholic Church in response to media pressure and legal follow-up.

As the Justice and Dignity Campaign illustrates, venturing into virtual and social media has proven rather effective, as it has helped to publicize critical information and engender new sensibilities. At the same time, while the campaign initiators are well aware that online advocacy cannot replace more conventional forms of political lobbying, it may lend credibility and legitimacy to their cause and position. In this sense, Mbororo individuals continue to lobby on an international, national, and local scale. They participate in the yearly meetings of the United Nations for Indigenous Peoples (UNFPII), submit reports to the Human Rights Council, and collaborate with government representatives on joint programs. Concurrently, they run social media campaigns, denouncing individual and institutional malpractices. And even though the Cameroonian government has not fully subscribed to the concept of "indigenous peoples" and its legal implementation, the indigenous rights discourse has retained its place in the national and international political domains.

The Indigenous Rights Movement in Tanzania: The Case of Maasai Pastoralists

In Tanzania, two population groups are generally associated with the term "indigenous peoples": Maasai cattle pastoralists and Hadza hunter-gatherers. In this section, I will focus on Maasai engagement in the global indigenous rights movement and its impact on the community's development. Similar to the exposition of the Mbororo case, I will embed Maasai activism in the national historical context and outline different phases in its political trajectory. While drawing on the comprehensive work of Dorothy Hodgson, my explorations will be selective and aimed at providing a basis for the subsequent comparison of the two cases.

Maasai Pastoralists and the Tanzanian State

Like most African countries, Tanzania is linguistically and ethnically diverse. While Swahili and English are the country's official languages, there are some 120 different linguistic and ethnic groups, with the Sukuma, Nyamwesi, Chagga, and Haya being the largest among them (Otiso 2013: 4). Maasai pastoralists belong to the group of Maa-speakers. They live on arid and semi-arid lands in northern Tanzania and across the border in southern Kenya. In Tanzania, they are concentrated in the Arusha and Manyara Regions which, until the 1970s, were administered as a single unit, the Masai District, and today are known as "pastoralist" districts (Hodgson 2011: 65–66, 150).

As Hodgson outlined in her earlier book *Once Intrepid Warriors* (2001), the (self-)identification of Maa-speaking pastoralists as Maasai has largely been the product of colonial and postcolonial policies. Many of these policies were aimed at regulating the mobility of semi-nomadic herders and taking control of their natural resources. Concurrently, the policies oscillated between the goals of preserving Maasai "culture", by limiting their access to education and healthcare, and "modernizing'" Maasai herders, so as to integrate them into Tanzanian mainstream society. The elites of the postcolonial era pursued the latter and introduced modernizing measures, such as a dress code for Maasai men and women (Hodgson 2001: 149–50; Schneider 2006). As Hodgson (2011: 66) argues, this contributed to the alienation of Maasai citizens from the state as well as increasing their hostility vis-à-vis the "Swahili," a term used by her Maasai interlocutors to denote all non-Maasai. This situation was aggravated during President Julius Nyerere's socialist regime from the time of Tanzania's independence in 1960 until 1985, when large areas of grazing land in the district designated to Maasai pastoralists by the colonial administration were redistributed to people and institutions that were considered more economically "productive." Concurrently, a national villagization scheme was introduced, and dispersed Maasai herders were forcibly relocated into settled villages (Hodgson 2001: 148–59). While dissatisfied with these measures, Maasai herders at the time had few or no means with which to protest state actions or demand changes, as all political activities were then under the control of the single party Chama Cha Mapiduzi (CCM), a party they considered to be firmly in the hands of the "Swahili."

This situation changed rapidly in the late 1980s and early 1990s. After Nyerere's retirement in 1985, his successor Ali Hassan Mwinyi consented to structural adjustment programs; he endorsed the introduction of multiple political parties and neoliberal economic policies. As Hodgson explains, there was "a radical restructuring of the Tanzanian economy from one based on socialist principles of Ujamaa, collective wellbeing, and communally owned resources to one based on the capitalist principles of a free market economy, privatization of resources, individual success, and profit maximization" (Hodgson 2011: 68). Hodgson outlines the effects of increased competition for land and landed resources and names cases of major land grabs, the most glaring example being the leasing of the Loliondo Game Controlled Area to an army brigadier from the United Arab Emirates to create a private hunting park (Hodgson 2011: 69; MERC 2002). Moreover, private and state attempts at land appropriation were accompanied by new government policies aimed at encouraging the resettling of pastoralists and intensifying the pastoral economy. These measures contributed to exposing Maasai pastoralists to increasing hardship and deprivation, and in alienating them from their lands, their neighbors, and the state.

Yet, concurrent with the introduction of these neoliberal economic policies, there was an opening of spaces for political participation, which for the first time enabled Maasai and others to organize themselves collectively, and to openly voice their claims and grievances. This is the context in which Maasai political activism and their engagement with the indigenous rights movement emerged.

Maasai (Re)positionings: From Indigenous Rights to Pastoralist Livelihoods

Maasai pastoralists from Tanzania were among the first African groups to join the global indigenous rights movement. In 1989, the Maasai activist Moringe ole Parkipuny participated in the United Nations Working Group on Indigenous Populations (UNWGIP) in Geneva, Switzerland. He was the first African to address the UN Working Group. Together with a Hadza compatriot, he represented the interests of "indigenous peoples" in Africa in general and Tanzania in particular. Together with other Maasai men, Parkipuny formed one of the first non-governmental Maasai organizations in Tanzania, the Korongoro Integrated People Oriented to Conservation (KIPOC).

Maasai political lobbying and associated NGO activities can be divided into three phases. The first phase, occurring during the late 1980s and early 1990s, was characterized by the emergence of non-governmental Maasai organizations. Two major NGOs emerged, which pursued somewhat different approaches. Inspired by the vision of its founder, Parkipuny, KIPOC actively advocated for indigenous rights. By challenging governmental policies aimed at "modernizing" Maasai pastoralists and their economic practices, the NGO adopted a confrontational strategy vis-à-vis the state. Inyuat e Maa (the Maa Pastoralists Development Organization) was founded during the same period. In contrast to KIPOC, it followed a more conciliatory approach by focusing on the cultural survival and development of Maasai pastoralists. The primary aim of both organizations was to secure international as well as national recognition of Maasai cultural and political rights, and most importantly their access to land. While Maasai activists never claimed the status of a "first people," they declared Maasai pastoralists an "indigenous people" on the grounds of their cultural and political marginalization.

The second phase, during the mid 1990s, saw the consecutive formation of two umbrella organizations. First, PINGOs Forum (Pastoralists Indigenous Non-Governmental Organization Forum) was created to represent the interests of not only Maasai pastoralists but also other pastoralist and hunter-gatherer groups in Tanzania, all of whom considered themselves indigenous and marginalized peoples. After a time, however, PINGOs became riddled with internal frictions. During this time of assumed demise of PINGOs, a second umbrella organization was created, the Tanzania Pastoralists and Hunter Gatherers Organization (TAPHGO). As Hodgson (2002, 2011: 137–44) argues, both umbrella organizations were driven mainly by donor agendas, and so were mainly concerned with securing their own survival. Only secondarily did they respond to the needs of the people they claimed to represent. This engendered distrust within their constituencies as well as rivalries with government institutions who felt sidelined by both the NGOs and the international donors.

The third phase, taking place in the early 2000s, entailed the reorientation of Maasai NGOs from the international to the national arena. While, over the past two decades, Maasai activists had been highly successful in increasing their international visibility and attracting donor funding, their activities were not winning the backing of government officials. Similar to many African countries, the Tanzanian state was critical of the UN notion of "indigenous peoples" and did not respond favorably to Maasai claims to indigeneity and their entitlement to land and resources. Attempts by Maasai activists to validate their claims via the support of international institutions and court actions were met with rebuttals and hostility.

Facing failure after failure, Maasai NGOs eventually decided to change strategies: to become more pragmatic and less political, and to seek ways to engage with, rather than fight, the government. As Hodgson argues, "Maasai activists and NGO leaders reframed their political struggles from the language of 'indigenous rights' to that of 'pastoralist livelihoods' and started calling themselves civil society organizations (CSOs) instead of NGOs" (Hodgson 2011: 157). In 2003, for example, PINGOs contributed to formulating the proposal for Tanzania's second Poverty Reduction Strategy by framing pastoralism as a "sustainable livelihood strategy" and supplanting its original understanding of the merely economic rationale of livestock production (Hodgson 2011: 162–65). Similarly, TAPHGO participated in designing the new National Livestock Policy. However, when President Jakaya Kikwete came to power (2005–15), he prioritized livestock production over pastoralist development (Hodgson 2011: 165–72).

Overall, Maasai and pastoralist organizations have had limited influence on government policies. Yet through their engagement with the international community and the Tanzanian government, Maasai activists and organizations have developed a new array of skills and lobbying strategies (Hodgson 2011: 172–80). These include the cultivation of informal relations with sympathetic donors and government officials, the use of the independent media and internet-based communication networks in order to circulate information and mobilize support, and the gradual integration of Maasai individuals into government services.

Reassessment of Maasai Livelihood and Development

In the last chapter of *Being Maasai, Becoming Indigenous* (2011), Hodgson reviews the changes in the lives of pastoralists over the past twenty years. Based on interviews conducted in 2005–06 with a large sample of Maasai women and men in the pastoralist districts of Tanzania, as well as her own assessment from having visited these areas two decades earlier, Hodgson comes to a rather disappointing conclusion. She contends that "the presence of these [Maasai and pastoralist] organizations has, in general, helped some community members diversify, secure, and improve their livelihoods in modest ways, but done little to help them address the structural inequalities (such as lack of sufficient quality schools and healthcare facilities) impeding their collective progress" (Hodgson 2011: 182).

Throughout the chapter, Maasai interlocutors voice their dissatisfaction with the Tanzanian government and its failure to provide basic infrastructure, such as clean water, adequate healthcare, and quality education. Their statements convey a feeling of deep economic insecurity, which is reflected in the frequent allusion to poverty (*enkaisinani* in the Maa language) and hunger (*esumash*) (Hodgson 2011: 199). Moreover, comparing statistical data on healthcare facilities in different parts of the country, Hodgson (2011: 201–3) confirms the existent disparity between pastoralist and non-pastoralist districts.

Thus, taking into account pastoralists' enduring neglect by the Tanzanian government, Maasai and other pastoralist organizations faced an enormous challenge in promoting development for and the rights of the people they represented. Evidently, they could not meet the expectations of their purported base. Moreover, despite national and international visibility, many organizations were unable to garner the awareness and support of pastoralist community members (Hodgson 2011: 205). Notwithstanding these institutional shortcomings, Hodgson emphasizes the vital learning effect of engaging with the global indigenous rights movement. That is, by identifying as "indigenous," Maasai pastoralists experienced new ways of belonging that embraced both the local and the global, and which helped them to transform themselves from "subjects" to "citizens" within their nation-state (Hodgson 2009: 23; 2011: 215).

At the same time, Hodgson (2011: 8) draws our attention to recent policy changes in the world of international development, which increasingly channels funds no longer via civil society, but through government institutions. Hence, despite an emphasis on civil society and international law, the nation-state has retained its position as a crucial player in shaping the realities and development of its populace.

Indigenous Rights Movements in Cameroon and Tanzania: A Comparison

In the following, I will compare and discuss the two case studies with the aim of outlining the trajectories of the relative indigenous rights movements and the factors that account for their variation. I thus hope to derive insights that are applicable to the general study of indigenous rights movements in Africa and beyond. I will structure my comparison along three lines. First, I will compare the two groups' historical and economic situations within their national contexts. Second, I will outline similarities and differences in the two movement's political strategies and their repositionings in relation to changing national and international development frameworks. Third, I will reconsider the impact of the movements on the lives of Mbororo and Maasai pastoralists and provide tentative ideas about the future of indigeneity in the two countries.

Historical and Economic Situation

I will begin by outlining structural and historical parallels between the two case studies. Both Mbororo and Maasai are cattle pastoralists and have occupied territories that cut across national boundaries. Both are ethnic minorities in their settlement areas and see themselves as distinct from the respective majority populations, the Grassfields societies in northwest Cameroon, and the population groups termed "Swahili" by Maasai in northern Tanzania. Moreover, both groups were exposed to colonial and postcolonial policies inspired by the goal of "modernization." These included measures promoting pastoralists' sedentarization and their participation in the market economy, as well as policies aimed at integrating them into mainstream society, thereby disregarding their distinct livelihoods and cultures.

Despite these commonalities, there are significant differences between the two cases that relate to their distinct ecological and economic conditions. While Mbororo pastoralists can look back on a history of social and political marginalization, their economic situation has been relatively promising. Many prospered upon settlement in northwest Cameroon in the first half of the twentieth century, as a result of the region's favorable climate and low population density. Since that time, the situation has changed, and competition for pastoral land has increased considerably. Nonetheless, the Mbororo are in a relatively privileged position compared with their Maasai counterparts. The Cameroonian government generally acknowledges Mbororo herders' contribution to the region's alimentation and economy, and their competitors are mostly members of neighboring Grassfields societies, with whom they tend to be on a par.

Based on Hodgson's work (2001, 2011), and without having visited Tanzania myself, I conclude that the situation of Maasai pastoralists in northern Tanzania is more tenuous, in both economic and ecological terms. Moreover, they have had to contend with powerful competitors for land and natural resources, such as state enterprises, and national and international investors, who, in the government's modernist neoliberal perspective, have been viewed as more economically productive and as contributors to the country's overall development. Consequently, Maasai pastoralists have repeatedly been confronted with government attempts at land appropriation and resettlement, as well as with a general disregard for their pastoralist way of life.

In an attempt to simplify the cases' complexity, I therefore wish to highlight these two significant varying factors. The first is the groups' economic power in their national contexts, which also has implications for their political leverage; the second is the presence of powerful competitors for land and, importantly, the role of the government in mediating the competitors' claims. Both factors seem to be more important in the Maasai case and work to their detriment.

The Movements' Political Strategies and (Re)positionings

In comparing the trajectories of Mbororo and Maasai political activism, a number of similarities are evident, despite a slight time gap between the initiation of the two movements (Maasai activism started in the late 1980s, and Mbororo activism in the early 1990s). First, both movements were initiated by visionary individuals who were members of the then newly emerging educated Maasai and Mbororo elites. They capitalized on the opening of political spaces in the context of their countries' liberalization and formed ethnically based non-governmental organizations. As the movements grew, they widened their ethnic and regional constituencies and diversified their activities. Moreover, they passed through a developmental cycle that was rather typical for the professionalizing of non-governmental organizations. That is, with increasing donor funding, they shifted their focus to capacity building, while gradually disengaging from grassroots communities—a process that engendered internal frictions and disappointment among local pastoralists.

In terms of political activism, both movements took inspiration from the discourses promoted by the international development and human rights establishments. While Maasai activists identified with the international indigenous rights movement early on (with Parkipuny's participation in the UNWGIP meeting in 1989), Mbororo representatives joined more than a decade later (with MBOSCUDA gaining special consultative status with the UN Economic and Social Council (ECOSOC) in 2005). Both movements went from states of initial enthusiasm to disillusionment to pragmatism as they were confronted with their governments' disapproval of their use of the UN indigenous rights framework to make claims to land and political self-determination. Thus, Maasai and Mbororo activists came to realize the sovereignty of the nation-state vis-à-vis the international community as well as the need to reposition themselves in relation to changing government discourses. Yet it is in how they repositioned themselves that the two cases diverge. Whereas Maasai activists shifted to a discourse about livelihoods, Mbororo activists retained the indigenous rights discourse while diversifying their lobbying strategies.

In her comprehensive analysis of the Maasai case, Hodgson (2011: 9–12) emphasizes the vital role of the international community and donor agencies in shaping national and international development policies. I support her point. However, as the comparison of the two case studies illustrates, we also need to pay attention to nation-states and variations between them in selectively adopting development discourses; that is, whereas the Tanzanian government prioritizes the country's economic development through neoliberal policies, the Cameroonian government favors ethnically and minority-based politics, which tie in well with global rights discourses. Hence, I argue that the variation between the countries' political frameworks is a vital factor, accounting for the different trajectories of their indigenous rights movements.

Impacts of Indigenous Rights Movements and Visions for the Future

In the third and last part of this comparison, I wish to assess the impacts of the two indigenous rights movements on the lives of Mbororo and Maasai pastoralists and to provide tentative ideas of the movements' future outlooks. Both are challenging tasks, which require that divergences between the two cases as well as those between researchers' approaches be taken into account.

Hodgson (2011: 181–209) places her analysis of the impact of the indigenous rights movement in Tanzania in a development framework. She is primarily interested in the question of whether or in which ways Maasai involvement in the global indigenous rights movement has benefitted Maasai pastoralists in improving their livelihoods and their access to basic services such as education and healthcare. She shares this interest with her Maasai interlocutors living in Tanzania's pastoralist districts. Their, and her, answers to the above concerns were rather bleak: few individuals had benefitted, poverty was still rife, and the privatization of land was an ongoing issue. As it transpires from Hodgson's account, it was primarily the Tanzanian government and its failure to invest in the region's economic development and infrastructure that accounted for the precarious situation of the Maasai people. Against this background, the achievements of non-governmental organizations in terms of political recognition and global advocacy were dwarfed by the absence of tangible economic improvements. Moreover, the NGOs' activities—mostly at the national and international level—only reached the grassroots communities in a limited way and attracted little attention among members of local pastoralist groups.

Thus, based on Hodgson's assessment, I assume that Maasai activists' disengagement from the global indigenous rights movement continues—despite the occasional participation of Maasai individuals at the UN Permanent Forum (Hodgson 2011: 213). Furthermore, I suspect that in the context of Tanzania's current policy framework, indigeneity—as a political discourse and identity—has no valid future. However, predicting the future has never been a major aim or strength of anthropologists.[7] Recent developments in the ongoing controversy over the Loliondo Game Controlled Area may also attest to the continued relevance of the global rights discourse and the Tanzanian government's occasional willingness to respond to international pressure.[8]

Turning to the Mbororo case, my predictions are just as tenuous. My research on the indigenous rights movement was informed by my primary interest in interethnic relations and identity politics in Cameroon (Pelican 2006, 2015). While the question of pastoralist development was also relevant, it was not my main focus.[9] However, from the perspective of Mbororo activists and the majority of Mbororo interlocutors living in rural areas, political self-representation and access to development projects were the main concerns of Mbororo pastoralists in Cameroon. In contrast to the situation in Tanzania, Mbororo herders live in various regions of the country, none of which has been particularly neglected in terms of infrastructure or economic development. The marginalization of Mbororo herders was primarily blamed on their lack of civic participation and political self-representation. Mbororo NGOs, such as MBOSCUDA, effectively addressed these issues. Moreover, by combining advocacy work and development activities, MBOSCUDA gained the recognition and support of many members of local Mbororo communities as well as of related non-Mbororo NGOs, government representatives, and international organizations. It is important to note that the engagement of Mbororo activists in the global indigenous rights movement was but a corollary of their earlier advocacy work. Thus, when their expectations of the efficacy of the indigenous rights discourse failed to be realized, they could fall back on previous lobbying and development activities while still diversifying their strategies and networks. Ultimately, the impact of Mbororo advocacy work on the lives of Mbororo pastoralists has been significant, not so much in economic terms, but in political and social terms, as it has transformed their relationship to the state and to neighboring population groups.

How the Mbororo indigenous rights movement will develop in the future is difficult to say. A crucial player in defining valid lobbying strategies is the Cameroonian government and its policy choices.[10] Most likely, Mbororo activists will continue to identify with global discourses on human, minority, and indigenous rights as long as it proves beneficial to their cause. At the same time, there is a slow but noticeable increase of educated Mbororo individuals being involved in government services, as well as an increase of Mbororo businesspeople. Hence, in the long term, Mbororo pastoralists may gradually cease to be a marginalized minority and become politically on a par with other majority population groups. Whether indigeneity is still a valid category of political identification when that time comes remains to be seen.

Conclusion

It was the aim of this chapter to provide insights into the indigenous rights movements in Africa by drawing on different case studies, to make clear that there is no single and coherent movement but a variety of movements that are shaped by their divergent national and local contexts. By comparing the cases of the Mbororo in Cameroon and Maasai in Tanzania, I attempted to outline the movements' different trajectories and to identify the factors that account for these divergences. Among these factors were differences in the groups' historical and economic situations within their national frameworks, as well as the divergent approaches of the two governments in relation to indigenous and minority rights discourses. While this comparison drew on specific cases, I believe its findings are applicable more generally to indigenous rights movements in Africa and beyond. Finally, I attempted to formulate tentative ideas about the possible futures of indigeneity as a political discourse in Africa. Obviously, these prognoses can only be tentative, and may soon be overturned by political and economic changes on the national or international level, whose unpredictability is part and parcel of contemporary realities.

Michaela Pelican (Dr.phil., Halle-Wittenberg) is Professor of Cultural and Social Anthropology at the University of Cologne, Germany. She was also the Director of the University of Cologne Forum "Ethnicity as a Political Resource: Perspectives from Africa, Latin America, Asia, and Europe" (2013–16). Ethnicity has been one of the central themes guiding much of her research. In particular, she has been interested in the expression of ethnicity as a collective identity, its use in political and economic contexts, as well as its role in conflict. Two projects grew out of this thematic focus: firstly, a study on interethnic relations and identity politics in northwest Cameroon; secondly, a critical examination of recent claims to indigeneity in Africa, centering on the case of the Mbororo-Fulbe in Cameroon. Both studies have resulted in a number of publications. Her book *Masks and Staffs: Identity Politics in the Cameroon Grassfields* was published by Berghahn in 2015.

Notes

The research leading to this chapter was realized with the support of the Max Planck Institute of Social Anthropology in Halle/Saale, the University of Zurich, and the University of Cologne. I appreciate the intellectual and institutional support provided by my colleagues and members of the University of Cologne Forum "Ethnicity as a Political Resource: Perspectives from Africa, Latin America, Asia, and Europe." An earlier version of this chapter was presented at the workshop "Futures of Indigeneity: Spatiality, Identity Politics and Belonging" in Bochum in November 2013. My thanks go to Dorothy Hodgson and to the anonymous reviewers for their valuable comments.

 1. This contribution is based on long-term familiarity with the situation of Mbororo pastoralists in northwest Cameroon. It follows up on earlier analyses where some of the arguments presented here have been explored in more detail (Pelican 2006, 2008, 2009, 2010, 2013, 2015).
 2. Several of MBOSCUDA's programs have been funded by Village AiD, a British non-governmental organization (Duni et al. 2009).
 3. Obviously, there are a number of examples in other parts of the world dealing with multiple and overlapping claims to indigeneity with contingent competing claims to land and resources, such as the case of the Labrador Inuit (Procter 2016).
 4. While the English version of the constitution uses the wording "indigenous peoples," the French version prefers the term *peuples autochtones*. The same applies to the United Nations Declaration on the Rights of Indigenous Peoples, due to the derogatory connotations of the French colonial term *indigène*.
 5. Due to the untimely death of Lelewal's founder, Ibrahim Njobdi, the organization was disbanded in 2014.
 6. See http://laimaru.org/ (accessed 18 January 2015).
 7. For example, Philip Burnham (1996) ended his excellent study on interethnic relations and conflict in northern Cameroon with a rather bleak and violent vision of the future, which fortunately did not materialize. Similarly, in his conceptual study *How Enemies Are Made* (2008), Günther Schlee provided a tentative prognosis of the resolution of the Somalia conflict that was soon invalidated by historical events.
 8. The controversy over the Loliondo Game Controlled Area started in 1993 with the minister of tourism leasing the area to a hunting firm owned by an army brigadier from the United Arab Emirates (Hodgson 2011: 69; MERC 2002). Since then, there has been an ongoing tug of war between the Tanzanian government and Maasai activists, whose claims have been backed by international advocacy groups. The latest developments are as follows. As IWGIA (2014: 208) reports, in 2013 the Tanzanian government responded to national and international pressure by confirming the land rights of pastoralist communities. In September 2014, the British newspaper *The Guardian* announced that the government had changed its stance and ordered Maasai pastoralists to vacate the area by the end of the year so as to make room for the planned "wildlife corridor," to be managed by a Dubai-based safari company (Smith 2014a). Two months later, the same newspaper reported that thanks to a petition launched by the global web movement Avaaz and signed by 2.3 million people, the Tanzanian president, Jakaya Kikwete, tweeted that Maasai pastoralists' fears of being evicted from their ancestral

lands were unfounded (Smith 2014b). As these news reports illustrate, the issue has not yet been fully resolved, and as an outsider, it is rather difficult to assess its long-term outcome.

9. The subject of Mbororo development was at the heart of an earlier study on the transformation of women's socioeconomic role in Mbororo society (Pelican 1996).

10. In 2009 the Cameroon government set about revising its land tenure system in response to the new priorities of the world of international development, which are aimed at enhancing food security and resource governance (USAID 2011). In this context, Mbororo representatives have been involved in the administrative process of devising a pastoral code. Concurrently, they have made efforts to familiarize their constituencies with the implications of the new pastoral code for pastoral livestock production (Django, Shei, and Duni 2011). In the view of Mbororo activists, these and other activities are compatible with lobbying for the indigenous and minority rights of their people.

Bibliography

ACHPR (African Commission on Human and Peoples' Rights). 2007. Advisory Opinion. Retrieved 17 February 2017 from http://www.achpr.org/files/special-mechanisms/indigenous-populations/un_advisory_opinion_idp_eng.pdf.

African Group. 2006. Draft Aide Memoire. Retrieved 17 February 2017 from http://www.iwgia.org/images/stories/int-processes-eng/decl-rights-ind-peop/docs/AfricanGroupAideMemoireOnDeclaration.pdf.

Ardener, Edwin. 1962. "The Political History of Cameroon." *The World Today* 18(8): 341–50.

Barnard, Alan. 2004. "Indigenous Peoples: A Response to Justin Kenrick and Jerome Lewis." *Anthropology Today* 20(5): 19.

———. 2006. "Kalahari Revisionism, Vienna and the 'Indigenous Peoples' Debate." *Social Anthropology* 14(1): 1–16.

Bayart, Jean-François. 1984. *L'état au Cameroun*. Paris: Presses de la foundation nationale des sciences politiques.

Bayart, Jean-François, Peter Geschiere, and Francis Nyamnjoh. 2001. "Autochtonie, Démocratie et Citoyenneté en Afrique." *Critique Internationale* 1(10): 177–94.

Boutrais, Jean. 1995/96. *Hautes terres d'élevage au Cameroun*. Paris: ORSTOM.

Burnham, Philip. 1996. *The Politics of Cultural Difference in Northern Cameroon*. Edinburgh: Edinburgh University Press.

Daes, Erica. 1996. *Working Paper on the Concept of Indigenous Peoples*. UN doc. E/CN.4/Sub.2/AC.4/1996/2. Retrieved 15 January 2015 from http://ap.ohchr.org/documents/alldocs.aspx?doc_id=7620.

Davis, Lucy. 1995. "Opening Political Space in Cameroon: The Ambiguous Response of the Mbororo." *Review of African Political Economy* 22(64): 213–28.

Django, Sali, William Shei, and Jeidoh Duni. 2011. *Legal Framework for the Regulation of Access to, and Management of Pastoral Resources in Cameroon*. Bamenda: MBOSCUDA/PASOC.
Dognin, René. 1981. "L'installation des Djafoun dans l'Adamaoua camerounais: La djakka chez les Peul de l'Adamaoua." In *Contribution de la recherche ethnologique à l'histoire des civilisations du Cameroun*, ed. Claude Tardits, 139–157. Paris: CNRS.
Duni, Jeidoh, et al. 2009. "Exploring a Political Approach to Rights-Based Development in North-West Cameroon: From Rights and Marginality to Citizenship and Justice." In *BWPI Working Paper* 104. Manchester: Brooks World Poverty Institute.
Geschiere, Peter. 2009. *The Perils of Belonging: Autochthony, Citizenship, and Exclusion in Africa and Europe*. London: University of Chicago Press.
Hickey, Samuel. 2007. "Caught at the Crossroads: Citizenship, Marginality and the Mbororo Fulani in Northwest Cameroon." In *Making Nations, Creating Strangers: States and Citizenship in Africa*, ed. Sara Dorman, Daniel Hammett, and Paul Nugent, 81–104. Leiden: Brill Publishers.
Hodgson, Dorothy. 2001. *Once Intrepid Warriors: Gender, Ethnicity, and the Cultural Politics of Maasai Development*. Bloomington, IN: Indiana University Press.
———. 2002. "Precarious Alliances: The Cultural Politics and Structural Predicaments of the Indigenous Rights Movement in Tanzania." *American Anthropologist* 104(4): 1,086–97.
———. 2009. "Becoming Indigenous in Africa." *African Studies Review* 52(3): 1–32.
———. 2011. *Being Maasai, Becoming Indigenous: Postcolonial Politics in a Neoliberal World*. Bloomington, IN: Indiana University Press.
ILO (International Labor Organization). 1989. *Convention (No. 169) Concerning Indigenous and Tribal Peoples in Independent Countries*. Retrieved 21 June 2017 from http://www.ilo.org/dyn/normlex/en/f?p=NORMLEXPUB:12100:0::NO::P12100_ILO_CODE:C169
IWGIA (International Workgroup for Indigenous Affairs). 2014. *The Indigenous World 2014*. Edison: Transaction Publishers.
Kenrick, Justin and Jerome Lewis. 2004. "Indigenous Peoples' Rights and the Politics of the Term 'Indigenous'." *Anthropology Today* 20(2): 4–9.
Kofele-Kale, Ndiva. 1986. "Ethnicity, Regionalism, and Political Power: A Post-mortem of Ahidjo's Cameroon." In *The Political Economy of Cameroon*, ed. Michael Schatzberg and William Zartman, 53–82. New York: Praeger Publishers.
Kopytoff, Igor. 1987. "The Internal African Frontier: The Making of African Political Culture." In *The African Frontier: The Reproduction of Traditional African Societies*, ed. Igor Kopytoff, 3–84. Bloomington, IN: Indiana University Press.
Kuper, Adam. 2003. "The Return of the Native." *Current Anthropology* 44(3): 389–95, 400–401.
———. 2005. *The Reinvention of Primitive Society: Transformations of a Myth*. London and New York: Routledge.
Lentz, Carola. 2006. "First-Comers and Late-Comers: Indigenous Theories of Land Ownership in the West African Savanna." In *Land and the Politics of*

Belonging in West Africa, ed. Richard Kuba and Carola Lentz, 35–56. Leiden: Brill.
Lutz, Ellen. 2007. "Indigenous Rights and the UN." *Anthropology News* 48(2): 28.
Marshall, John. 2002. *A Kalahari Family*. DER Documentary.
Mbaku, John M. 2005. *Culture and Customs of Cameroon*. Westport, CT: Greenwood Press.
Mehler, Andreas. 1993. *Kamerun in der Ära Biya: Bedingungen, erste Schritte und Blockaden einer demokratischen Transition*. Hamburg: Institut für Afrikakunde.
MERC (Maasai Environmental Resource Coalition). 2002. *The Killing Fields of Loliondo: The Hunting Operations of the Ortello Business Company and Their Impact on Maasai Rights, Wildlife, and the Environment*. Washington, DC: MERC.
Niezen, Ronald. 2003. *The Origins of Indigenism: Human Rights and the Politics of Identity*. Los Angeles, CA: University of California Press.
———. 2010. *Public Justice and the Anthropology of Law*. Cambridge: Cambridge University Press.
Njeuma, Martin. 1995. "Reunification and Political Opportunism in the Making of Cameroon's Independence." *Paideuma* 41: 27–37.
Njeuma, Martin and Nicodemus Awasom. 1990. "The Fulani and the Political Economy of the Bamenda Grasslands, 1940–1960." *Paideuma* 36: 217–33.
Nyamnjoh, Francis and Michael Rowlands. 1998. "Elite Associations and the Politics of Belonging in Cameroon." *Africa* 68(3): 320–37.
Oldham, Paul and Miriam A. Frank. 2008. "'We the Peoples…': The United Nations Declaration on the Rights of Indigenous Peoples." *Anthropology Today* 24(2): 5–9.
Otiso, Kefa. 2013. *Culture and Customs of Tanzania*. Westport, CT: Greenwood Press.
Pelican, Michaela. 1999. *Die Arbeit der Mbororo-Frauen früher und heute: eine Studie zum Wandel der sozio-ökonomischen Situation semi-nomadischer Fulbe-Frauen in Nordwest Kamerun*. Bayreuth: Universitätsbibliothek Bayreuth.
———. 2006. *Getting along in the Grassfields: Interethnic Relations and Identity Politics in Northwest Cameroon*. Halle, Saale: Universitäts- und Landesbibliothek Sachsen-Anhalt.
———. 2008. "Mbororo Claims to Regional Citizenship and Minority Status in Northwest Cameroon." *Africa* 78(4): 540–60.
———. 2009. "Complexities of Indigeneity and Autochthony: An African Example." *American Ethnologist* 36(1): 149–62.
———. 2010. "Umstrittene Rechte indigener Völker: das Beispiel der Mbororo in Kamerun." *Zeitschrift für Ethnologie* 135: 37–58.
———. 2013. "Insights from Cameroon: Five years after the Declaration on the Rights of Indigenous Peoples." *Anthropology Today* 29(3): 13–16.
———. 2015. *Masks and Staffs: Identity Politics in the Cameroon Grassfields*. New York: Berghahn Books.
Pelican, Michaela and Junko Maruyama. 2015. "The Indigenous Rights Movement in Africa: Perspectives from Botswana and Cameroon." *African Study Monographs* 36(1): 49–74.
Procter, Andrea. 2016. "Uranium and the Boundaries of Indigeneity in Nunatsiavut, Labrador." *The Extractive Industries and Society* 3: 288–96.

Sapignoli, Maria and Robert Hitchcock. 2013. "Indigenous Peoples in Southern Africa." *The Commonwealth Journal of International Affairs* 102: 355–65.

Saugestad, Sidsel. 2011. "Impact of International Mechanisms on Indigenous Rights in Botswana." *The International Journal of Human Rights* 15(1): 37–61.

Schlee, Günther. 2008. *How Enemies Are Made: Towards a Theory of Ethnic and Religious Conflict.* New York: Berghahn Books.

Schneider, Leander. 2006. "The Maasai's New Clothes: A Developmentalist Modernity and Its Exclusions." *Africa Today* 53(1): 100–31.

Smith, David. 2014a. "Tanzania Accused of Backtracking over Sale of Masai's Ancestral Land." *The Guardian*, 16 September. Retrieved 18 January 2015 from http://www.theguardian.com/world/2014/nov/16/tanzania-government-accused-serengeti-sale-maasai-lands.

———. 2014b. "Tanzania's Masai 'Breathe Sigh of Relief' after President Vows Never to Evict Them." *The Guardian*, 25 November. Retrieved 18 January 2015 from http://www.theguardian.com/world/2014/nov/25/tanzania-masai-eviction-uturn.

Stavenhagen, Rodolfo. 2007. *Report on the Situation of Human Rights and Fundamental Freedoms of Indigenous Peoples; Addendum: Summary of Cases Transmitted to Governments and Replies Received, 20.09.07.* UN doc. A/HRC/6/15/Add.1. Retrieved 13 October 2014 from http://www2.ohchr.org/english/bodies/hrcouncil/docs/6session/A.HRC.6.15.Add.1.pdf.

Suzman, James. 2002. "Kalahari Conundrums: Relocation, Resistance and International Support in the Central Kalahari Botswana." *Before Farming* 4(12): 1–10.

Takougang, Joseph and Milton Krieger. 1998. *African State and Society in the 1990s: Cameroon's Political Crossroads.* Boulder, CO: Westview Press.

Tchoumba, Belmond. 2005. *Indigenous and Tribal Peoples and Poverty Reduction Strategies in Cameroon: Project to Promote ILO Policy on Indigenous and Tribal Peoples (PRO 169).* Publication of the International Labor Organization. Retrieved 21 June 2017 from http://staging.ilo.org/public/libdoc/ilo/2005/105B09_90_engl.pdf.

USAID. 2011. *Property Rights and Resource Governance: Cameroon. USAID Country Profile.* New York. Retrieved 18 January 2015 from http://usaidlandtenure.net/sites/default/files/country-profiles/full-reports/USAID_Land_Tenure_Cameroon_Profile.pdf.

7

POLITICS OF INDIGENEITY IN THE ANDEAN HIGHLANDS

Indigenous Social Movements and the State in Ecuador, Bolivia, and Peru (1940–2015)

Olaf Kaltmeier

Although rarely used by indigenous movements themselves, indigeneity has become a fashionable concept in academic discussions on the indigenous question; we can observe a strong effort to internationalize the issue of "indigeneity," as shown by its documentation in the UN Declaration on the Rights of Indigenous Peoples in 2007. As a social categorization, indigeneity presupposes a commonality among different indigenous peoples worldwide, often defined in contrast to other identitarian groups. Within the Latin American context, the catch-all category *"indio"* does not say anything about what is signified; instead it must be conceived as a mirror, or a negative puzzle of white, Western self-identifications. The "Indians" were seen as traditional, passive, backwards, or minor, in contrast to the Spanish conquistadors and British settlers who identified themselves as modern, active, progressive, and educated. Indian is thus a multiethnic category that allows a broad range of self-ascriptions and ascriptions by others. Nevertheless, the term has been appropriated by the discriminated, and at different conjunctures it has been reframed and subverted to challenge established power systems.

Looking at the semantic field of indigeneity, we see that the adjective "indigenous" can be derived from the Latin term *"indigenus,"* meaning "native, born in a country," which comes from "indi" or "indu," originally derived from "in" and "gen"—the root of "gigno" ("to give birth to"). To indigenous we add the suffix "-ity," which denotes the state, property, or quality of an adjective, in our case "indigenous."

This conception of indigeneity as a "state of being" evokes a whole series of discursive practices to define criteria for the assumed ontological quality of "indigenous," with such definitions as language, traditions, natural religion, special way of life, and so on. In this sense, indigeneity tends to define, delimitate, and essentialize a specific social group consisting of different peoples, with different historical experiences, and with internal processes of fragmentation and social differentiation.

Against this approach towards indigeneity, I would like to propose a constellational approach to identity politics (Kaltmeier and Thies 2012), which understands indigeneity as an ongoing process and a relational category that includes both self-identification and identification by others, such as colonizers, settlers, the church, the state, and—with a great deal of symbolic capital—scholars. From a similar standpoint, Marisol de la Cadena and Orin Starn (2007: 3) have defined indigeneity as "a relational field of governance, subjectivities, and knowledges that involve us all—indigenous and non-indigenous—in the making and remaking of its structures of power and imagination." Thereby, indigeneity is intrinsically related to history, like concepts such as indigenous, native, aboriginal, and first nations: "all refer etymologically to priority in time and place" (Pratt 2007: 398). The relational construction of the term itself is embedded in struggles about recognition and redistribution. As Andrew Canessa (2012: 207) succinctly puts it: "Indigeneity is about history and power."

Nevertheless, indigeneity remains an indistinct concept, which can be explored in two dimensions. From a synchronic perspective, the hype around indigeneity is related to the emergence of a transnational conjuncture of the "indigenous question." In order to increase their influence with supranational political institutions, indigenous movements began to organize beyond their nation-states (Kemner 2013; Niezen 2003). By the 1970s, the World Council of Indigenous Peoples and the International Indian Treaty Council were accredited as international representatives of indigenous peoples by the United Nations and were included in their list of official NGOs. The internationalization of indigenous demands has been strengthened by new alliances with the rise of ecological and human rights movements in the Western Hemisphere, some of whom have specialized in—or at least have an emphasis on—campaigning for indigenous peoples (e.g., the International Work Group for Indigenous Affairs [IWGIA], Cultural Survival, Survival International, Society for Threatened Peoples). The global demands of the ecological movement, such as sustainable development, are often articulated with local actions by indigenous peoples, portrayed as "keepers of our earth."

Facing the political pressure of indigenous movements and their allies, especially NGOs, an international consensus on the necessity for addressing the indigenous question began, finding its expression in the United Nations International Year of the World's Indigenous People in 1993, the UN International Decade of the World's Indigenous People (1995–2004 and 2005–14), international norms and conventions (ILO Convention 169 in 1989, and the UN Declaration on the Rights of Indigenous Peoples in 2007), and supranational fora like the UN Working Group on Indigenous Populations (1982–2006) or the Permanent Forum on Indigenous Issues. These global networks have given shape to a new transnational identification of a "Pan-Indigenismo" (Bengoa 2000: 138).

Indigeneity thus offers a global platform for identification for ethnically discriminated groups worldwide. This global concept of indigeneity has been an important tool in overcoming discrimination due to colonialism and imperialism. But the self-reflexive, fluid, and strategic use of the concept has led to a situation in which even settler groups, such as the Boers in South Africa, have tried to frame their demands for cultural autonomy and land in the language of indigeneity. This synchronic and fluid understanding of indigeneity reveals much about contemporary post-multicultural identity politics and patterns of conflict, but is not very useful for grasping diachronic and geopolitically rooted conflicts.

In this chapter I introduce an alternative approach towards indigeneity, one that can be characterized as diachronic, geopolitically located, and related to structural power relations. This approach will be exemplified with regard to indigeneity in the Americas. In the case of the Americas, the meaning of indigeneity cannot be separated from the colonial situation (Bonfil Batalla 1972). Together with the "invention of America," the process of European colonial expansion and conquest also saw the invention of the ethno-racial category of the *"indio."* This invention can be attributed to Christopher Columbus, who, in a letter about his first voyage to the Americas in 1492, gave a brief description of the native Arawaks, whom he called simply *"indios."* In short, in 1491 there were no Indians in the Americas; in 1492 there were tens of millions (Bonfil Batalla quoted after Canessa 2012: 207).

Anthropologists and historians such as José Bengoa and Guillermo Bonfil Batalla have argued that this conquest was the first and most significant rupture in the Americas, as no continuity can be constructed between the pre-Hispanic cultural and political dynamics of the peoples, nations, and empires in the pre-Columbian America, and the new reality of coloniality afterwards. With the concept of "coloniality of power," Peruvian sociologist Aníbal Quijano (2008) has pointed out that the emergence of the capitalist world system in the late sixteenth century, which has been analyzed by Immanuel Wallerstein in geopolitical and economic terms, also created a new political-cultural matrix. A cultural system of classification based on racism was established that also had material and socio-structural consequences, as it structured the ethnic division of labor in the world system, where the indigenous and Afro-American population was subordinated to the white colonizer.

Coloniality can thus be interpreted as a temporal structure of *longue durée* that is ongoingly renewed and rearticulated in different circumstances after conquest. Thus, coloniality is not only reconstructed but also contested by decolonializing conjunctures. This is particularly the case in the field of indigeneity in the Americas. Indigeneity here is a conflictive terrain that is relevant in terms of political representation, citizenship rights, and programs of development. From colonial times until today, indigenous peoples in the Americas have been important actors in the process of state and nation building (Becker 2008; Canessa 2012; Clark 2007). In this sense, an underlying working hypothesis of this chapter is inspired by social movement theories and approaches of neo-operaism that argue that social movements are the driving force behind social change (Fuchs 1999; Hardt and Negri 2000). This means, in political terms, that social movements have a creative potential to subvert or even overthrow the established orders of political/cultural representation, while state organizations mainly react in order to integrate these movements into the established power constellations. This interplay of action and reaction, and its historical conjunctures in the field of indigeneity, will be explored in the context of developments in the Andean highlands in the twentieth and twenty-first century.[1]

The Birth of Indigenism

In colonial times, the problem of how to deal with the indigenous population in the conquered territories was solved by the Spanish Crown through the establishment of a segregated political system of two republics, one for the white conquerors and one for the indigenous conquered population (Thurner 1997). Although this segregated system subordinated the indigenous population to the Spanish Crown, the simultaneous recognition of indigenous authorities established channels of political communication that allowed the indigenous population to address problems like discrimination and exploitation. After independence, this system of two republics was replaced by a unified notion of the nation, a single republic, which was formally based on ideas of republican citizenship but which de facto excluded the indigenous population from political participation. In the postcolonial state, the indigenous population lost the particular political status it had enjoyed in colonial times, and was denied citizenship rights, thereby experiencing politics of extinction (Larson 2004). Until the beginning of the twentieth century, alternative channels of political mediation did not exist, so the indigenous population was doomed to a "subaltern voicelessness" (Kaltmeier 2016).

In Latin America, the emergence of socialist and communist movements at the beginning of the twentieth century offered new possibilities to form interethnic alliances that could articulate important claims of the rural indigenous population. In the Andes in particular, strong indigenous peasant movements emerged that had the organizational capacity to carry out agenda setting on a nationwide scale and foster the process of constructing collective identities. Nationwide social movement organizations placed the fragmented local experiences of discrimination and exploitation in a national frame. The high concentration of indigenous populations in the Andean highlands and historical structures of exploitation, in a system of internal colonialism based around indigenous labor on haciendas and mines, led to the emergence of a strong articulation of ethnic and class-based identifications and demands. In parallel, and often in reaction to the growing influence of socialist and communist indigenous peasant movements, *indigenismo* emerged as a political and cultural movement of non-indigenous activists and state agencies that developed social and cultural policies towards indigenous peoples.

While *indigenismo* in Mexico—especially after the end of the government of Lázaro Cárdenas (1934–40)—turned out to be more of a program of assimilation and acculturation, in some Andean countries the field of indigenism was influenced by the Marxist positions of José Carlos Mariátegui. In general terms, *indigenismo* placed the indigenous population in the center of the imagined national community, aiming for a profound process of assimilation in the name of *mestizaje*.[2] In spite of its assimilationist undertones, it challenged conceptions of the nation based on whitening and established a field of practice and intervention that put the indigenous question on the political agenda of the postcolonial nation-states.

Indigenism cannot therefore be limited to a single national experience; it must be conceived as a field of practice that had a transnational—or better hemispheric—range. The most visible aspect of inter-American indigenism was the foundation of the Inter-American Indigenist Institute (III), which was first discussed at the Octava Conferencia Panamericana in Lima (1938) in the context of a renewed reinforcement of inter-American relations. The III was officially founded at the Primer Congreso Indigenista Interaméricano, which took place in 1940 in Pátzcuaro in Mexico, as an independent international organization with its seat in Mexico City (Giraudo 2006). Branches of the III were additionally formed in most of the American republics, and in the Andean countries. The III disseminated its ideas on *indigenismo* through its journals, *América Indígena* and *Boletín Indigenista* (later renamed *Anuario Indigenista*). In 1953, it was integrated into the OAS (Organization of American States), and in 2009—after a significant loss of importance since the 1970s—it was closed.

The general dynamics in the field of indigeneity in the first half of the twentieth century in Latin America differed from country to country. In relation to the inter-American indigenist movement, Ecuador was among the first countries to create a national indigenist institute (1943); the central figure in this process was Alvaro Pío Jaramillo. Official political support for the Instituto Indigenista Ecuatoriano was weak, however, so we cannot speak of a significant process of institutionalization (Becker 2012). Rather, interethnic relations with socialist and communist movements shaped indigenous organization processes in Ecuador in the first half of the twentieth century. We can identify the first step towards socialist organization in Ecuador at the beginning of the twentieth century, with the founding of the Socialist Party in 1926 and the Communist Party in 1931. In 1944, a nationwide communist workers' union was founded, encompassing several gremial branches, among them the Federación Ecuatoriana de Indios (FEI, Ecuadorian Federation of Indios, founded in 1944), which became the main platform for the demands of highland Indians in Ecuador until the 1970s (Becker 2008). The actions of these socialist and communist organizations took place within a legal framework of cases for labor rights and the denunciation of mistreatments. Direct actions, such as land occupations, were not part of the FEI's repertoire.

Bolivia witnessed a series of indigenous uprisings between the 1910s and 1920s that remained of local importance. After Bolivia's defeat in the Chaco War (1932–35), a new nationalist consciousness arose, which included the indigenous peasants of the highlands, and as a result a host of nationalist, socialist, and communist parties were founded—among them the Trotskyist Partido Obrero Revolucionario (POR), the Stalinist Partido de Izquierda Revolucionaria (PIR), and the Movimiento Nacionalista Revolucionario (MNR, Revolutionary Nationalist Movement). An indigenous peasant self-consciousness arose. In 1942, the first congress of Quechua-speaking indigenous people was organized by the PIR-oriented peasant movement, where the abolishment of the *pungaje*,[3] the restitution of communal lands, and lower taxes were the main demands (Rivera Cusicanqui 1987). With the indigenous peasant organization forming one pillar, Bolivia faced an accelerated organizational and institutional dynamic, which culminated in the national revolution of 1952.

In Peru, too, several indigenous peasant uprisings took place in the 1910s and 1920s, especially in the Cuzco region—the former capital of the Inca empire. In this period, several pro-indigenous organizations were founded by mestizo activists, partly with the direct participation of indigenous leaders. The liberal presidentship of Augusto Leguía (1919–30), influenced by early Andean indigenism, answered the demands of these mobilizations with the formation of a National Bureau for Indigenous Affairs (de la Cadena 2000). These measures aimed to pacify the rural protest movement and to redirect their organizational basis into the channels of state-run indigenism. However, the movement's main demands for recognition and indigenous citizenship remained unfulfilled, and later the rural protest movement took on a class-based form in the emerging trade union movement. In 1946, after the Pátzcuaro conference, a National Indigenist Institute (IIP) was founded in Peru. The foundation took place in the midst of a struggle between two discursive strains of *indigenismo*, one that argued that the indigenous presence constituted an obstacle to the constitution of the Peruvian nation, i.e., implying an assimilationist and ethnocidal policy, and the other that argued that the nation had indigenous foundations. The IIP followed a compromise between these two positions, by proposing a gradual, state-led process of assimilation, focused on cultural and educational elements (Gonzales 2012). Thereby it served as an instrument for the co-optation of critical voices into a moderate program of gradual social change.

In spite of particular local and regional dynamics, it is possible to identify a general trend of indigenism in the Andes in the first half of the twentieth century. With the growing influence of socialist and communist groups in the Andean highlands and their alliances with indigenous peasants, social movements emerged that possessed the organizational resources to carry out national agenda setting with regard to the recognition of indigenous and workers' rights. By their merging of the different, fragmented local experiences into a national frame, these organizations were eminently important in the construction of collective identities. In contrast to our contemporary understanding of indigeneity, which is mainly based on ethnic identification, indigenous collective identity in the first half of the twentieth century in the Andes was based on an articulation of ethnic and class-based elements (Becker 2008; Kaltmeier 2007, 2016). This class-based positioning permitted access to the political field, as Mercedes Prieto (2004) has argued with regard to Ecuador. While indigenous people were excluded from the political system, proletarians, who were not ethnically marked, could demand certain rights as integral parts of the nation. Thus, for indigenous people, class-based identification was a strategic intermediate step on the path to obtaining citizenship rights.

In another sense, *indigenismo* could also be interpreted as a fragmented version of citizenship. While excluded from full citizenship in terms of political participation (especially the right to vote), indigenism created a contradictory field of intervention within an array of national and international development projects in health, agriculture, education, and so on. The III provided a conceptual point of reference for the international development project Misión Andina of the International Labour Organization (ILO), which since 1952 covered several countries in the Andean region. Although excluded from full political citizenship and from civil society, the indigenous population—politically invisible since the middle of the nineteenth century—now became a subject of the *political* society (see Chatterjee 2006). In the Andean region, the establishment of *indigenismo* as a dispositive to control indigenous populations was without doubt a governmental reaction to the growing politicization of the indigenous question, but it also opened the door for new counter-governmental practices.

From *Indios* to Peasants

After World War II, the inter-American dynamics of indigenism had weakened, and only some national indigenisms remained important, especially in Mexico. In the context of modernization theories and the quest for development, there was no place for indigenous citizenship. Consequently, indigenous communities reinforced their identitarian political strategy, to position themselves in terms of class-based identifications. In the Andean countries, indigenous peoples formed the most important base of peasant movements, which increasingly aimed at not only the improvement of workers' rights but the redistribution of land and agrarian reform.

In the 1960s and 1970s, the struggle for redistribution in Latin America reached its peak in the mobilizations for agrarian reforms. Historian Tulio Halperin Donghi (1991) characterized the period between 1960 and 1970 as the "decisive decade"; while revolutionary movements campaigned to overcome the traditional, "feudal" power relations through agrarian reform, liberal reformers sought to modernize the agricultural sector and thereby intensify capitalist relations.

One of the most notable and impactful changes to agrarian relations was the Bolivian revolution of 1952, which was related—as noted above—to the mobilization cycle of the 1930s. The revolution changed the political context structure enabling the indigenous peasant sectors of society to gain access to the political field via trade union-based corporativism. Trade unions became the main points of articulation between the state and society. The indigenous peasant population benefitted from the revolution in several ways, including gaining class-based citizenship rights and recognition as peasants, the restitution of land,[4] and the provision of health and education. In political-cultural terms, the overall aim of the Bolivian revolution was a mestization of society in which indigenous positionings had no place. Nevertheless, indigenous highland communities organized themselves relying on their *ayllu*-communities and the traditional "Indian law" against the processes of forced syndicalization and modernization (Ari 2014).

With the passing of time, however, the initial social revolutionary ambitions were replaced by the politics of capitalist restoration. The rural trade union movement lost more and more of its autonomy and eventually became subordinated to the MNR-run state. After the degradation of the MNR government, General Barrientos (1964–69) carried out a coup d'état and instrumentalized the previous government's established connection with peasant syndicates for anti-communist politics that left little space for social movement agency.

In Ecuador, an agrarian reform was first passed in 1964. This reform abolished the traditional system of exploitation, *huasipungaje*, and allocated small plots of land to indigenous peasants in the highlands. At the same time, inspired by the US-driven Alliance for Progress, another major aspect of the reform was the modernization of agriculture, supporting agro-industrial complexes in the fertile Andean valleys. Although the actual land allocations were quite limited, the *political* impact of the agrarian reform—which had not in fact been demanded by the indigenous peasant organizations—cannot be overstated. The end of the hacienda regime left a political vacuum in the central Andean highlands, which was filled by emergent indigenous self-organizations (Kaltmeier 2007, 2016).

In Peru since the 1950s, there has been an ambivalent coexistence of indigenist symbolic and peasant trade unionist organizational forms. In the 1950s and 1960s, an increase in class-based conflicts in the rural highlands found its expression in local uprisings and guerrilla activities, such as the Trotskyist movement of Hugo Blanco. It was in this context that General Juan Velasco Alvarado came to power in 1968. His political project was the construction of a new left-wing nationalism that expressed itself in agrarian reform and the nationalization of industries. In terms of indigeneity, the Velasco government was highly remarkable in that it prohibited the use of the term *"indio,"* which was replaced by *"campesino,"* in its agrarian reforms. In addition, it repeatedly used references to Incan symbolism and, in 1972, recognized Quechua as an official language of the Peruvian state.

Although we can observe an accelerated process of transformation in the 1960s and 1970s, the basic patterns of coloniality remained unchanged. In no Latin American country did the "decisive decade" culminate in a social revolution. In Ecuador, social movements did not have the power base to lead a general transformation; in Bolivia, the revolution lost its transformative impact; and in Peru, the "third way" was abandoned after the overthrow of Velasco. Instead of redistributive policies, an increase in citizenship rights, and the recognition of ethnic and/or class-based rights, the 1980s were characterized by a wave of anti-communist authoritarian regimes that limited the space for maneuvering of the social movements through repressive measures. The class-based cycle of mobilization and the fight for redistribution of economic resources ended, and a new cycle of neoliberal politics began.

The indigenous communities and organizations perceived the end of the class-based cycle of mobilization to different extents. On the one hand, interethnic alliances with urban, mestizo, socialist, and communist activists did not lead to the goal of a general transformation of society, but they were quite successful with regard to citizenship rights, social assistance, the modernization of infrastructure, and a limited redistribution of land. On the other hand, the organizational forms of trade unions, gremial organizations, and corporativism did not necessarily correspond to the indigenous political structures in the *comunidades* (rural communitites) and *ayllus*. In terms of identity politics, the unionized organizational form of indigenous people in the Andean highlands, such as the *sindicato* in Bolivia, or the *comunas* (subject to the Ley de la Comunas of 1937) in Ecuador, could be understood as forms of postcolonial mimicry. On the one hand, they are copies of postcolonial forms (i.e., occidental, class-based trade unions); on the other hand, they are—to use the phrase of postcolonial thinker Homi Bhabha (1994: 86)—"almost the same but not quite," because they are ultimately driven by Andean subject positions. There is always an ambivalent excess of meaning between regulation and the "unappropriated." The end of these forms of interest mediation, such as indigenism, and the end of the leftist cycle of mobilization opened a vacuum of power to be filled by ethnic indigenous organizational processes.

The end of the left-wing cycle of mobilization spelled the beginning of a deep crisis for *indigenismo*. Social anthropologists, especially those related to the new left students' movements, criticized the politics of assimilation at the end of the 1960s and in the 1970s as ethnocide. The first declaration of Barbados produced by critical anthropologists, with the lemma "For the Liberation of the Indian," stated in 1971:

> The analysis we have made has shown that the indigenist politics of the Latin American nation-states has failed for its action as well as for its omission. For omission, because of its incapacity to guarantee every single indigenous group the specific protection that the state has to offer and to impose the law on the fronts of national expansion. For action, because of the colonialist and classist nature of its indigenist politics. This failure makes the state directly guilty for or an accomplice to several crimes of genocide and ethnicide that we could prove.[5]

The end of these two periods, namely the end of the class-based cycle of indigenous peasant mobilization and the critique of essentialist *indigenismo*, opened the space for autonomy-based projects of ethnic indigenous mobilization.

The Politicization of the Indigenous Question in the 1990s

The indigenous uprising in Ecuador in 1990 and protests by indigenous groups in response to the celebrations marking the 500th anniversary of the European conquest of Latin America by Christopher Columbus in 1992 marked a turning point in the field of indigeneity and initiated a new politicization of the indigenous question in Latin America. A new visibility of the indigenous question, the introduction of ethnic symbols and semantics into public spaces, and the reinvention of ethnic identities shaped the political culture of Latin American countries from the 1990s onwards, and raised questions about principles of vision and division in a social world based on coloniality. The high degree of organization—from local communities connected by regional alliances, to nationwide umbrella organizations—is one of the most important factors in explaining the strength of this new movement. This notwithstanding, due to the ethnic diversity of the various indigenous peoples and nations involved, there is a need to explain how this massive process of ethnogenesis, based on indigeneity, has come about. In other words, why and how do different peoples and communities choose to position themselves as indigenous? Social anthropologist Carola Lentz

(1994) has argued that the experience of racism in their migration work in the coastal plantations in the 1960s is one reason why peoples might identify themselves as *"indio."* Another aspect that I want to highlight is the interchange of experiences between different communities in the former left-leaning indigenous peasant organizations, especially the FEI, which led to a nationwide self-identification as *indios*.

Using these historical experiences as a basis, in the 1990s the emerging indigenous movement managed to introduce new aspects to the understanding of indigenous self-identification. Here we have to mention the use of concepts such as nations, nationalities, and peoples. These concepts are applied to overcome discriminatory and limiting concepts such as "ethnic minorities," and allow strategic references to international law (e.g., ILO Convention 169). We can also note a persistence of left-wing concepts, such as the Leninist-Stalinist concept of the right of national self-determination, and associated national liberation movements, among others. In this sense, it would be too simplistic to reduce indigenous movements to only "pure" ethnic demands. In fact, demands for social services, redistribution of wealth, agrarian reform, anti-imperialism, national sovereignty, and the critique of free trade and neoliberalism are also concerns for other non-indigenous subaltern populations. Especially in the Andean region, for example in Bolivia and Ecuador, indigenous movements filled the "political vacuum" that appeared after the end of the socialist mobilization cycle, and which was reinforced by socioeconomic structural changes, resulting from neoliberal privatization policies and the ideological crisis of the left after the collapse of the Soviet Union.

As fresh and innovative political actors, with high degrees of credibility, indigenous movements were able to win the support of middle-class urban mestizo intellectuals. Furthermore, they were seen as "ecological natives," and thus as "natural" preservers of the environment, a topic that gained importance after the Rio Conference for Sustainability and Development in 1992. Additionally, due to their anti-neoliberal stance, indigenous movements also addressed the topic of national sovereignty, thereby gaining further support from like-minded movements.

A general trend towards the politicization of the indigenous question took various paths in the Andean region. Firstly, we will look at Bolivia, where the Katarista movement emerged at the end of the 1960s. This movement was formed by young urban Aymaras whose parents had migrated from rural areas to the city suburb of El Alto, La Paz. Central to the cultural politics of the Katarista was the appropriation of the (symbolic) figure of Tupac Katari (Julián Apaza), who together with Tupac Amaru II was the leader of the indigenous revolution in Peru in the 1780s. With their "Manifiesto de Tiwanaku" of 1973, the movement gained national and international attention—in spite of the dictatorship of Hugo Banzer. It was a cornerstone in a new dynamic of decolonization, and put autonomy in the center of the political organization process: "We do not believe in the preaching of those parties who call themselves left-wing and yet do not allow the peasantry to determine its own future. If a political party is to be a means to freedom for the peasants it must be established, led, and sustained by us peasants. Our political organizations must reflect our values and our own interests."[6] Strategically, the Kataristas established themselves in the trade union movement, where they successfully introduced their program. In 1978, the Kataristas divided into two fractions: one popular, supported by the Movimiento Revolucionario Tupac Katari (Revolutionary Movement Tupac Katari), which advocated strategic alliances with other left-wing organizations; and another, more ethnic-orientated, which rallied around the Movimiento Indio Tupac Katari (Indigenous Movement Tupac Katari or MITKA). In 1979, the Kataristas merged with other trade unions into the Confederación Sindical Única de Trabajadores Campesinos de Bolivia (CSUTCB, Unified Syndicalist Confederation of Rural Workers of Bolivia) in order to oppose the Banzer military dictatorship (Schilling-Vacaflor and Schorr 2011).

In Ecuador, the ethnic indigenous mobilization cycle has its roots in the Amazonian lowlands, where the Indian Asociación Shuar was founded in 1962, supported by the Catholic Church. Consequently, many more Indianist organizations were founded in the Amazonian lowlands, culminating in their merging into the CONFENIAE (Confederation of Indigenous Nationalities of the Ecuadorian Amazon) in 1980. In the highlands, the political vacuum left by the abandonment of the hacienda regime was also filled by newly founded ethnic peasant organizations, who were supported by progressive sectors of the Catholic Church, themselves inspired by liberation theology (Martínez Novo 2007). In 1972, a highland umbrella organization, Ecuarunari (in Kichwa: Ecuador Runakunapak Rikcharimuy, or Movement of the Indigenous People of Ecuador) was founded, and in 1986 the main regional indigenous organizations of the highlands, the coast, and the Amazonian lowlands created a nationwide umbrella organization, the CONAIE (Confederation of Indigenous Nationalities of Ecuador), which shaped indigenous mobilizations and demands for recognition and redistribution in the following decades (CONAIE 1989; Guerrero and Ospina Peralta 2003; Zamosc 2004). A first uprising organized by CONAIE took place in 1990, and rocked the ethno-political fundaments of Ecuadorian society. Since 1992, several uprisings have managed to successfully overthrow anti-popular and/or neoliberal governments.

In terms of indigenous mobilization in the Americas in the 1990s, Peru is considered an exceptional case, due to the lack of any major organizational efforts in the country. Due to an ongoing civil war between guerrilla movements (of Sendero Luminoso and the Movimiento Revolucionario Tupac Amaru, MRTA) and the state, there was little room for indigenous political participation. Villanueva (2013: 79) states: "An 'Indigenous agenda' was basically absent from public discussion until the mid-2000s and currently has little visibility." Some first steps towards indigenous self-organization have been made, but only in the Amazonian lowlands.

With regard to the mobilization processes in the Andean region in the 1990s, certain similarities can be noted. The main actors in these new Indianist mobilization processes were young indigenous, who had passed through the modern education system and adopted the codes of conduct of modern occidental society, as well as retaining the norms of the indigenous communities. These "organic intellectuals" —to use Gramsci's words—used indigenous identities in order to improve their positions and those of their groups. As mediators between the two worlds, they were essential for enabling indigenous concerns to be "heard" and "understood" in mestizo society.

Despite being formally recognized as citizens, and having the right to vote since the end of the 1970s, indigenous peoples in the Americas were de facto excluded from real political and cultural participation, as well as political representation. In this context, the indigenous movements put the question of indigenous citizenship on the political agenda through mobilizations and protests (García 2005; Yashar 2005). Indigenous movements also intervened directly in the political field. In the mid 1990s, political parties emerging from indigenous social movements were particularly successful in local elections, where they won seats in several municipalities (Ospina Peralta 2006). These political parties and movements also gained varying influence in the national arena (Van Cott 2005). In Bolivia, the Movimiento Revolucionario Tupaj Katari de Liberación (MRTKL), in alliance with the more traditional MNR (in the mid 1990s a neoliberal orientated party), won the Vice-Presidency of the Republic with their candidate, Aymara Victor Hugo Cárdenas, in 1996. Today, the Movimiento al Socialismo (MAS) of the current president, Evo Morales, and the Indianist Katarist party MIP (Movimiento Indígena Pachakuti), are the most important political parties in Bolivia. In Ecuador, the CONAIE founded the left-wing political movement Movimiento de Unidad Plurinacional Pachakutik-

Nuevo País (MUPP-NP) in 1995, and in 2002 managed to install three indigenous ministers.

In only a few cases did indigenous political movements limit themselves to acting solely as pressure groups for indigenous peoples; generally, they were multiple-issue movements and/or represented more than one group. In the Andean region in particular, indigenous political movements became spokespeople for general multiethnic subaltern demands, addressing questions of economic politics, neo-imperialism, democratization, social rights, racism, and ecological justice.

Neo-*indigenismo*

The political outcomes from this new cycle of indigenous mobilization were overwhelming. In the 1990s, there were several constitutional changes in Colombia (1991), Peru (1993), Bolivia (1994), Ecuador (1998), and Venezuela (1999) that recognized the specific cultural rights of indigenous peoples. Furthermore, ILO Convention 169, which recognizes cultural rights and limited autonomy for indigenous peoples, was signed by nearly all Latin American governments: Colombia (1991), Bolivia (1991), Peru (1994), Guatemala (1996), Ecuador (1998), Brazil (2002), and Venezuela (2002).

All this does not imply, however, that multiculturalism in the Americas should be assumed to be an unproblematic success story, in terms of increasing the inclusion of formerly excluded "minorities," or promoting broader understandings of cultural rights and respect for cultural difference. These politics of recognition by the state took place against a background of neoliberal government policies, which deepened socioeconomic disparities. It is somewhat remarkable that indigenous demands for cultural recognition were partially fulfilled while claims for social justice and redistribution of wealth were largely ignored.

One main critique of the transnational expansion of multiculturalism concerns the articulation of multiculturalism and neoliberal politics in the 1990s (Bretón Solo de Zaldívar 2001, 2005; Postero 2007). Inspired by the Foucauldian concept of governmentality, this critical vein of thought postulates that indigenous communities can be infiltrated and employed as instruments of new governmental techniques— techniques that can be described as "government through community" (Kaltmeier 2008).

The Ley de Participación Popular in Bolivia is a case in point, illustrating the articulation of neoliberal politics and the politics of recognition by the government of Gonzalo Sánchez de Lozada (1993–97). In the context of a new generation of structural adjustment programs, a project of political decentralization with the Ley de Participación Popular as its cornerstone became a central government issue. Here, reform-oriented sections of indigenous movements formed a collaboration with neoliberal technocrats (Postero 2006).

In Ecuador, where the state demonstrated a great openness towards demands for ethnic recognition without taking into account demands of redistribution, the World Bank executed a pilot project for indigenous peoples (PRODEPINE) in cooperation with the state and CONAIE, the biggest national indigenous organization. Promoting the concept of social capital, PRODEPINE aimed to empower indigenous communities by integrating them into self-defined development projects. However, in 2005 CONAIE rejected a second phase of the program, arguing that it would lead to a "de-ideologization" of the indigenous movement and to a co-optation of its leaders (ICCI 2005).

Across Latin America, new neo-indigenist state institutions were founded in the 1990s and 2000s that replaced traditional indigenist instances of mediation. Here we have to mention CONADI in Chile and CODENPE in Ecuador. In Mexico, the Comisión Nacional para el Desarrollo de los Pueblos Indígenas even replaced the famous Instituto Nacional Indigenista, the most important bastion of traditional *indigenismo*. In Peru, the Instituto Indigenista Peruano was dissolved exactly fifty years after it was founded in 1946, under the Fujimori government. In 2005, the Peruvian government of Alejandro Toledo founded the Instituto Nacional de los Pueblos Andinos, Amazónicos y Afroperuanos (INDEPA) to coordinate indigenous politics. In most cases, these institutions are not the equivalent of a government ministry; rather they are subordinate to the president, and place "*etno-desarrollo*" (ethno-development) at the center of their activities. These new state institutions can be understood as an expression of neo-indigenism, a rebirth of indigenist politics in a context of neoliberal hegemony and indigenous self-organization.

This articulation of multiculturalism and neoliberal politics reflects the growing interest of international development corporations like USAID, the Inter-American Development Bank, and the World Bank in indigenous peoples. Part of this increased interest is without a doubt due to the increased mobilization capacities of indigenous movements, whom CIA reports in the 1990s labeled as more dangerous for liberal capitalist systems than even the last existing guerrilla movements. Although programs funded by these corporations were basically designed to pacify and integrate these movements, they also produced new knowledge and practices in the field of development. After the strong critique of the Washington Consensus, and the neoliberal politics of the governments of its "first generation," new social and culturally sensitive programs were needed. Empowerment, social capital, political decentralization, and reforms of the educational and judicial systems were the new preferred areas of intervention (Bretón Solo de Zaldívar 2005; Walsh 2009).

Together with nation-states, these agencies established a regime of vision and division, which Charles Hale (2005: 24) ironically refers to as "indio permitido (permitted Indian)." Thus, indigenous people who engaged in projects of ethno-development were able to gain social recognition, while those who opposed and protested against them were marked as criminals or terrorists, especially after 9/11. This was the case, for example, in the *cocalero* movement with its leader Evo Morales, the now president of Bolivia.

Futures of Indigeneity

Political culture in Latin America nowadays is barely conceivable without the inclusion of indigenous peoples. Throughout the region, we can observe far-reaching institutional and constitutional politics of recognition, which challenge the exclusion of the indigenous populations in the postcolonial era, a period that dominated the political culture of Latin American countries from the nineteenth until the end of the twentieth century. The dimension of this rupture in Latin American political culture differs from country to country. While some countries have not gone further than cosmetic changes, which have brought existing political regimes in line with international agreements, others have advocated for a decolonization and nothing less than the "refoundation of the nation."

Earlier we stated that neoliberalism and neo-indigenism have gone hand in hand. This has had impacts not only in terms of political rationalities, but also in terms of changes in social structures. The Ecuadorian case is particularly striking. From 1998 to 2006, the poverty rate declined from 44.64 percent to 38.28 percent, and the rate of indigence decreased from 18.68 percent to 12.86 percent. Nevertheless, there is an ethnic bias to these numbers—indigenous poverty has actually dramatically increased from 45.84 percent to 69.46 percent, and indigence among the indigenous population has also increased from 17.63 percent to 43.07 percent (Jijón 2013: 55). To summarize, in the same period in which indigenous people have gained important rights, their socioeconomic situation has actually worsened. While the white mestizo population has benefitted from the neoliberal reforms of the late 1990s, the indigenous population has been the clear loser.

After twenty-five years of massive indigenous mobilization (if we take the protests in 1992, marking 500 years after Columbus's arrival in the Americas, as a point of reference), it seems necessary to take stock of the political outcomes and future perspectives. We answer the question by pointing to a threefold rupture: first, of the postcolonial *longue durée* of exclusion; second, of the neoliberal political-economic era; and third, of the dominating elites.

This reflection seems even more pertinent when we consider that the global cycle of indigeneity reached its peak in 2007 with the UN Declaration on the Rights of Indigenous Peoples. In fact, several international indigenous groups, such as the UN Working Group on Indigenous Populations, have now been dissolved, the two UN International Decades of the World's Indigenous People came to an end in 2015, and, in general terms, we can see a paradigm shift from "indigenous recognition" to "cultural diversity" in the UN system. This transnational dynamic has been mirrored by increased internal fragmentations of indigenous peoples due to migration and social mobility, the latter surely an outcome of the mobilization cycle. In terms of the future of indigeneity in the Andean region, I would like to present the following three scenarios.

Scenario 1: From Indigenismo to Decolonization

Without any doubt, Bolivia underwent the deepest transformation process of any Andean country in its political culture. After massive protests against the neoliberal course of the Gonzalo Sánchez de Lozada government and the privatization of gas and water, Evo Morales, the leader of the Movimiento al Socialismo, emerged as the face of the protest movement and was elected as president in 2005 (García Linera 2006; Postero 2007). He advocated anti-neoliberal politics and a "refoundation of the nation," calling for a constituent assembly, with a broad participation of indigenous and popular movements, in 2006. In 2009, a new constitution was approved by plebiscite. In 2014, Evo Morales was re-elected as president until 2020.

The constitution defines Bolivia as a pluri-national, yet at the same time unitary state. It introduces several mechanisms of local and regional autonomy, especially for indigenous communities, and recognizes thirty-six indigenous languages as official languages of the state. The constitution is inspired by ideas of decolonization and places the concept of *Buen Vivir*, derived from indigenous cosmovisions, at the center of the nation's development.[7] The central goal of a break with the historical form of the state, and the project of the refounding of the nation, is explicitly expressed in the preamble of the constitution:

> We have left the colonial, republican and neo-liberal State in the past. We take on the historic challenge of collectively constructing a Unified Social State of Pluri-National Communitarian law, which includes and articulates the goal of advancing toward a democratic, productive, peace-loving and peaceful Bolivia, committed to the full development and free determination of the peoples. ... We found Bolivia anew, fulfilling the mandate of our people, with the strength of our Pachamama and with gratefulness to God.[8]

The project of decolonization is epitomized in the foundation of a Vice Ministry of Decolonization. The renationalization of central industries, such as petrol and gas, has been a cornerstone in an economic strategy that has also enabled the increased financing of social welfare programs. Furthermore, limited agrarian reforms have been implemented. These policies cannot be interpreted simply in terms of an indigenization of the Bolivian state, because they are also related to class-based struggles and forms of organization (we should not forget that Morales was a former syndicate leader and no great authority on ethnic matters). This decolonization project distinguishes itself from traditional multiculturalism, as the decolonization of society and the proposed new model of *Buen Vivir* involve all segments of the Bolivian society. We can in part claim that a revolutionary change in the elite ruling structure has taken place, insofar as there exists a clear break with the *longue durée* cycle of coloniality. The extension of full citizenship and political participation rights to the indigenous population—who were previously specifically excluded and therefore reverted to a system of clientelism—is a process that seems to have been successful and also irreversible. Indigeneity is nowadays officially defined and considered an integral part of Bolivia's political culture. However, there are also continuities with the economic model. The exploitation of natural resources is still the main foundation of the Bolivian economy, and one can observe several examples of conflicts between the state and its partners and local communities. The most emblematic case is the planned highway in the TIPNIS national park, which—against the wishes of the surrounding indigenous communities—aims to provide a link between Brazil and the Pacific Ocean. This neo-*desarrollismo* perspective—one that contradicts the government discourse "to protect Pachamama" (Mother Earth)—is also found in the recently announced plan to build Bolivia's first nuclear plant.

Scenario 2: A Renaissance of Modernization and National Identity

In Ecuador, the indigenous movement was characterized by high degrees of unity and a capacity to mobilize in the 1980s and 1990s. The movement managed to put topics on the political agenda that went far beyond the recognition of particular ethnic groups. In 2006, the CONAIE organized protests against the planned bilateral free trade agreement with the US and the exploitation of oil resources by the transnational company Occidental. These protests culminated in a new movement led by Rafael Correa, who was elected to the presidency in 2007. Correa's anti-neoliberal politics were supported by the CONAIE, especially in regard to the organization of a constitutional assembly—one of the main demands of the CONAIE. In October 2008, a new constitution was approved, which—similar to the Bolivian constitution—defines the state as pluri-national, and focuses on the concepts of development and *Buen Vivir*. Furthermore, it is the first constitution worldwide that recognizes the rights of nature (Quintero 2009).

Paradoxically, it is precisely the anti-neoliberal, new hegemonic project represented by Rafael Correa that threatens the gains of ethnic recognition made over the last decade. Since the middle of 2008, there has been a growing political gap between Correa and CONAIE, the latter of which argues that indigenous peoples have not been recognized sufficiently in the writing of the new constitution. In January 2009, the three main national indigenous organizations—the CONAIE, the evangelist organization FEINE, and the socialist organization FENOCIN—united in a protest against Correa, criticizing the planned mining law, and oil policy in the Amazonian lowlands, especially in the Yasuní National Park.

This left-wing, development-style course followed neo-extractivist policies that could be seen as a continuation of the traditional extractivism of the previous neoliberal government, the main difference being that a greater part of revenues are nationalized.[9] This, however, does little to lessen conflicts between the state and indigenous peoples. Another conflict is related directly to the established forms of neo-indigenist politics in Ecuador. While the indigenous movement had previously followed the neo-corporativist model of the state (Ospina Peralta 2011), which combined individual personal rights with collective rights, the new Correa government opted for a liberal model of citizenship, based on individual citizenship rights rather than collective or corporate ones. Departing from the previous model, Correa abolished all political institutions concerned with "ethnic recognition" that had been established in the neo-indigenist cycle of the 1990s. For example, he dissolved the

Dirección Nacional de Educación Intercultural y Bilingüe (DINEIB, National Board of Intercultural and Bilingual Education), an educational institution with the status of a ministry, with indigenous leadership. And he limited the powers of the neo-indigenist CONDENPE, an institution for indigenous development, run by indigenous leaders and based in organizational terms on the CONAIE's ethnic classification system. During these changes, Correa accused the indigenous movements of "[making] another state, where the legitimate and elected authorities, and the institutions are not recognized, but only the indigenous leadership. This is barbarism" (Correa, quoted in Santos 2010: 182, translation by the author). In this defense of a nation-state, unified against corporativism and pluralism, Correa did not even shy away from using the racist comparison of "civilization" versus "barbarism." Here we see a structural conflict with the state, which relates to concepts of citizenship. While Correa defends a liberal definition of rudimental individual citizenship rights only, the indigenous movement advocates for "post-liberal citizenship" (Yashar 2005), which considers collective rights as an integral element of the Ecuadorian state. In fact, in contrast to the idea of *Buen Vivir*, expressed in the Ecuadorian constitution, Correa's economic policies are guided by the principles of *desarrollismo*, and a liberal model of individual citizenship subjected to a central state. In this sense, there is a conflict between the approved, but not sufficiently detailed, rights in the constitution and the de facto policy of Correa. The situation is quite conflicted for the indigenous movement. On the one hand, the indigenous movement is in a state of *recession*, and it does not appear that there will be any resurgence in the near future; on the other hand, the indigenous movement continues to be the most powerful social movement in Ecuador.

Scenario 3: Defense of Indigenous Livelihoods

The third possible outlook for indigeneity is related to regional cases of an economic model based on the exploitation of natural resources, which social scientist Eduardo Gudynas (2009) has called neo-extractivism. Indigenous peoples in particular are greatly affected by accelerated accumulation processes, i.e., those that rely on the exploitation of natural resources (oil, forests, minerals, and water), as they mainly live in areas that have been largely excluded from the processes of capitalist accumulation. This neo-extractivist development regime often goes hand in hand with big infrastructure projects, such as highways, that in turn open the door for the unplanned neo-colonization of landless peasants. This is especially the case for the indigenous communities in the

Amazon regions. In the case of the highland communities, which have been historically better integrated into local and regional commerce, the threat comes from new mining projects and proposed controls of water reserves.

Here, conflicts arise independent of governments' differing political orientations. As previously detailed, Bolivia currently faces the TIPNIS conflict, Ecuador has to deal with the ITT conflict (named after the three oil sources Ishpingo, Tambococha und Tiputini in the National Park Yasuní in the Amazonian lowlands), and in 2009, Peru experienced its most violent confrontation since the end of the civil war, when indigenous protests against petroleum exploitation and a new free trade agreement with the US broke out and led to clashes with military forces.

The pressures of an economic model based on extractivism find indigenous communities increasingly involved in struggles to defend their basic rights, and their livelihoods. The discussion around concepts like *Buen Vivir* reveals the importance of defining alternative economic models; the outcome of such discussions will be a key element for the future of indigenous peoples.

With regard to the political field, it seems that the fight for recognition has lost its previous dynamic, due to gains for indigenous peoples in constitutional changes, particularly in the Bolivian and Ecuadorian constitutions. The legal and political basis of indigenous rights is now greater than it has ever been under any previous government or in any constitution. This does not necessarily mean, however, that these rights are equally implemented. Procedural methods for the execution of laws have to be found, as well as adjustments to actually live with new formal autonomies. The implementation of these procedures is something that many social movements, originally formed to rally people to create change, are familiar with. After the high expectations that arose in the cycle of indigenous politicization, reaching their high point in the electoral victories of Evo Morales and Rafael Correa, the following political realities have disillusioned many indigenous social movements and their advocates. In Ecuador, the concept of *sumak kawsay* granted in the constitution has been reduced to little more than political rhetoric, and is now subordinate to Correa's modernization and liberal state-building project. In Bolivia, in contrast—despite neo-extractivist tendencies—we can observe a clear turning point in the political culture: the introduction of state-sponsored social programs, and the emergence of new indigenous elites. The differences from the cycle of multicultural neoliberalism and neo-indigenism in the 1990s are obvious, but this "left-wing turn" in Andean countries is not without its economic and political contradictions.

Olaf Kaltmeier (PhD, Bielefeld) is Professor of Ibero-American History and Director of the Center for InterAmerican Studies (CIAS) at Bielefeld University. He is also Director of the Maria Sibylla Merian Center for Advanced Latin American Studies (CALAS). He has published on issues of indigeneity, postcoloniality, space, and identity politics. Among his recent publications are *Konjunkturen der (De-)Kolonialisierung: Indigene Gemeinschaften, Hacienda und Staat in den ecuadorianischen Anden von der Kolonialzeit bis heute* (transcript 2016), *Entangled Heritages: Postcolonial Perspectives on the Uses of the Past in Latin America* (edited with Mario Rufer; Routledge 2017), and *Selling EthniCity: Urban Cultural Politics in the Americas* (Ashgate 2011, 2nd ed. 2016).

Notes

1. This area covers predominantly the pre-Colombian Tahuantinsuyo Inca Empire, and comprises the actual nation-states of Ecuador, Peru, and Bolivia. Most of the population lives in regions between 2,000 and 3,500 meters above sea level, where subsistence agriculture and mining are the main economic activities. Since colonial times, this area has comprised various zones of contact and transculturation, not least in the main urban centers, such as Quito, Cuzco, Arequipa, Sucre, and La Paz. In colonial times, Potosí—with the well-known "silver mountain"—was the most populous city in the world, while nowadays El Alto in Bolivia is considered to be the first postcolonial indigenous metropolis in the world, with nearly one million inhabitants.
2. *Mestizaje* is a Latin American ideology, which is based on the idea that the fusion of various cultural traditions (especially indigenous and Spanish ones) leads to the creation of a new mestizo race. This idea is best presented in José Vasconcelos' 1925 essay *La raza cósmica* (The Cosmic Race).
3. *Pungaje, yanaconaje* (in Bolivia and Peru), or *huasipungaje* (in Ecuador) is a kind of bonded debt that linked an indigenous workforce to a hacienda. It has its roots in colonial times, but it was practiced in Latin American republics until the middle of the twentieth century.
4. Particularly in the Amazonian lowlands, a junker way of Agrarian modernization was practiced, which led to the formation of large agro-industrial complexes, and the colonization of land that was conceived as "empty" space.
5. "Primera Declaración de Barbados: Por la liberación del indígena," 1971, http://servindi.org/pdf/Dec_Barbados_1.pdf (accessed 18 January 2015). Translation by the author.
6. "Tiwanaku Manifesto," 1973, http://www.nativeweb.org/papers/statements/identity/tiwanaku.php (accessed 18 January 2015).
7. *Buen Vivir* (Good Living), *sumak kawsay* in Kichwa, and *suma qamaña* in Aymara, are conceptions of social order, formulated by indigenous movements as a critical response to neoliberal and other capitalist paths of de-

velopment. These conceptions are based on indigenous cosmovisions, and principles of reciprocity and complementarity, or indigenous understandings of the natural world. Recently, these conceptions have been included in the Bolivian and Ecuadorian constitutions. For a broader definition, see Báez and Cortez (2012).
8. Bolivian constitution, 2009, https://www.constituteproject.org/constitution/Bolivia_2009.pdf (accessed 18 January 2015).
9. Extractivism refers to an economic model that is based on the extraction of natural resources (primary sector) for exportation to the world market. In contrast to traditional extractivism, contemporary discussions focus on neo-extractivism, which refers to the efforts of left-leaning governments to use revenues from resource extraction to finance social programs for the poor and middle classes in their respective countries. Critics highlight the environmental degradation and social costs, especially for indigenous populations, associated with this economic model. For a broader definition, see Matthes and Crncic (2012).

Bibliography

Albó, Xavier. 1994. "And from Kataristas to MNRistas? The Surprising and Bold Alliance between Aymaras and Neoliberals in Bolivia." In *Indigenous Peoples and Democracy in Latin America*, ed. Donna L. Van Cott, 55–82. New York: St. Martin's Press.
Ari, Waskar. 2014. *Earth Politics: Bolivia's AMP Indigenous Intellectuals 1921–1971*. Durham, NC: Duke University Press.
Báez, Michelle, and David Cortez. 2012. "Buen Vivir, Sumak Kawsay." In *Social and Political Key Terms of the Americas: Politics, Inequalities, and North-South Relations*, Version 1.0 (2012). Retrieved 18 January 2015 from http://elearning.uni-bielefeld.de/wikifarm/fields/ges_cias/field.php/Main/Unterkapitel11.
Becker, Marc. 2008. *Indians and Leftists in the Making of Ecuador's Modern Indigenous Movements*. Durham, NC: Duke University Press.
———. 2012. "The Limits of Indigenismo in Ecuador." *Latin American Perspectives* 39(186): 45–62.
Bengoa, José. 2000. *La emergencia indígena en América latina*. Santiago: Fondo de Cultura Económica.
Bhabha, Homi K. 1994. *The Location of Culture*. Cambridge: Routledge.
Bonfil Batalla, Guillermo. 1972. "El concepto de indio en América: una categoría de situación colonial." *Anales de Antropología* 9: 105–24.
Bretón Solo de Zaldívar, Víctor. 2001. *Cooperación al desarrollo y demandas étnicas en los Andes ecuatorianos*. Quito: Flacso.
———. 2005. *Capital social y etnodesarrollo en los Andes*. Quito: Centro Andino de Acción Popular.
Breuer, Martin. 2017. "The Nexus of *Indigenismo* and International Development Cooperation in Peru: The Examples of the *Vicos-Cornell* and the *Puno-Tambopata* Projects in the 1950s and 1960s." In *Politics of Entanglement*, ed. Olaf Kaltmeier, Jochen Kemner, and Lukas Rehm. Trier: WVT.

de la Cadena, Marisol. 2000. *Indigenous Mestizos: The Politics of Race and Culture in Cuzco, Peru, 1919–1991*. Durham, NC: Duke University Press.
de la Cadena, Marisol and Orin Starn (eds). 2007. *Indigenous Experience Today*. New York: Berg.
Canessa, Andrew. 2012. "New Indigenous Citizenship in Bolivia: Challenging the Liberal Model of the State and Its Subjects." *Latin American and Caribbean Ethnic Studies* 7(2): 201–22.
Chatterjee, Partha. 2006. *The Politics of the Governed: Reflections on Popular Politics*. New York and Chichester: Columbia University Press.
Clark, A. Kim. 2007. "Shifting Paternalism in Indian-State Relations, 1895–1950." In *Highland Indians and the State in Modern Ecuador*, ed. A. Kim Clark and Marc Becker, 89–104. Pittsburgh: University of Pittsburgh Press.
CONAIE (ed.). 1989. *Las nacionalidades indígenas en el Ecuador: Nuestro proceso organizativo*. Quito: Ediciones Tinkui.
Fuchs, Martin. 1999. *Kampf um Differenz: Repräsentation, Subjektivität und soziale Bewegungen das Beispiel Indien*. Frankfurt a.M.: Suhrkamp.
García, María E. 2005. *Making Indigenous Citizens: Identity, Development, and Multicultural Activism in Peru*. Stanford, CA: Stanford University Press.
García Linera, Á. 2006. "State Crisis and Popular Power." *New Left Review* 37: 73–85.
Giraudo, Laura. 2006. "No hay propiamente todavía Instituto: los inicios del Instituto Indigenista Interamericano (abril 1940–marzo 1942)." *América Indígena* 62(2): 6–32.
Gonzales, Osmar. 2012. "The Instituto Indigenista Peruano: A New Place in the State for the Indigenous Debate," *Latin American Perspectives* 39(5): 33–44.
Gudynas, Eduardo. 2009. "Diez tesis urgentes sobre el nuevo extractivismo: Contextos y demandas bajo el progresismo sudamericano actual." In Centro Andino de Acción Popular (CAAP) and Centro Latinoamericano de Ecología Social (CLAES) (eds), *Extractivismo, política y sociedad*. Quito: CAAP/CLAES, pp. 187–225.
Guerrero Cazar, Fernando and Pablo Ospina Peralta. 2003. *El poder de la comunidad: Ajuste neoliberal y movimiento Indígena en los Andes ecuatorianos*. Buenos Aires: Consejo Latinoamericano de Ciencias Sociales.
Hale, Charles R. 2005. "Neoliberal Multiculturalism: The Remaking of Cultural Rights and Racial Dominance in Central America." *PoLAR* 28(1): 10–28.
Halperin Donghi, Tulio. 1991. *Geschichte Lateinamerikas von der Unabhängigkeit bis zur Gegenwart*. Frankfurt a.M.: Suhrkamp.
Hardt, Michael and Antonio Negri. 2000. *Empire*. Cambridge, MA and London: Harvard University Press.
ICCI (Instituto Científico de Culturas Indígenas) (ed.). 2005. "La CONAIE, dice no al Banco Mundial." *Boletín ICCI-ARY Rimay* 7(76). Retrieved 18 January 2015 from http://icci.nativeweb.org/boletin/76/editorial.html.
Jijón, Víctor H. 2013. "The Ecuadorian Indigenous Movement and the Challenges of Plurinational State Construction." In *Indigenous and Afro-Ecuadorians Facing the Twenty-First Century*, ed. Marc Becker, 34–70. Newcastle: Cambridge Scholars Publishing.

Kaltmeier, Olaf. 2007. "Politización de lo étnico y/o etnización de lo político en el Ecuador en los años noventa." In *Etnicidad y poder en los países andinos*, ed. Chistian Büschges, Guillermo Bustos, and Olaf Kaltmeier, 195–216. Quito: Corporación Editora Nacional.

———. 2008. "Neoliberalismo, el Estado, y los Indígenas: Sobre la gubernamentalización de la comunidad indígena en Chile, Bolivia y Ecuador." In *E pluribus unum? National and Transnational Identities in the Americas*, ed. Sebastian Thies and Josef Raab, 93–110. Münster and Tempe AZ: Lit Verlag.

———. 2016. *Konjunkturen der (De-)Kolonialisierung: Indigene Gemeinschaften, Hacienda und Staat im ecuadorianischen Hochland von der Kolonialzeit bis heute*. Bielefeld: transcript.

Kaltmeier, Olaf and Sebastian Thies. 2012. "Specters of Multiculturalism: Conceptualizing the Field of Identity Politics in the Americas." *Latin American and Caribbean Ethnic Studies* 7(2): 223–40.

Kemner, Jochen. 2013. "'We the Indigenous Peoples of the World': Pan-ethnic Unity and the Challenge of Diversity for the Early Transnational Indigenous Movement." In *Mobilizando etnicidad: Políticas de identitad en contienda en las Américas: pasado y presente*, ed. Eric Javier Bejarano et al., 201–224. Madrid: Vervuert.

Larson, Brooke. 2004. *Trials of Nation Making: Liberalism, Race, and Ethnicity in the Andes, 1810–1910*. Cambridge: Cambridge University Press.

Lentz, Carola. 1994. "Die Konstruktion kultureller Andersartigkeit als indianische Antwort auf Herrschaft und Diskriminierung: eine Fallstudie aus Ecuador." In *Kosmos der Anden. Weltbild und Symbolik indianischer Tradition in Südamerika*, ed. Max P. Baumann, 412–446. Munich: Diederichs.

Martínez Novo, Carmen. 2007. "Evangelización y movilización étnica: El aporte de la misión salesiana al movimiento indígena de Cotopaxi." In *Etnicidad y poder en los países andinos*, ed. Chistian Büschges, Guillermo Bustos, and Olaf Kaltmeier, 261–271. Quito: Corporación Editora Nacional.

Matthes, Sebastian and Zeljko Crncic. 2012. "Extractivism." In *Social and Political Key Terms of the Americas: Politics, Inequalities, and North-South Relations*, Version 1.0 (2012). Retrieved 18 January 2015 from http://elearning.uni-bielefeld.de/wikifarm/fields/ges_cias/field.php/Main/Unterkapitel53.

Mignolo, Walter D. 2000. *Local Histories/Global Designs: Coloniality, Subaltern Knowledges, and Border Thinking*. Princeton, NJ: Princeton University Press.

Niezen, Ronald. 2003. *The Origins of Indigenism: Human Rights Issues and the Politics of Identity*. Berkeley, CA: University of California Press.

Ospina Peralta, Pablo (ed.). 2006. *En las fisuras del poder: Movimiento indígena, cambio social y gobiernos locales*. Quito: Instituto de Estudios Ecuatorianos.

———. 2011. "Corporativismo, estado y revolución ciudadana: el Ecuador de Rafael Correa." In *Culturas políticas en la región andina*, ed. Christian Büschges, Olaf Kaltmeier, and Sebastian Thies 85–118. Madrid and Frankfurt a.M.: Iboamericana and Vervuert.

Postero, Nancy. 2006. *Now We Are Citizens: Indigenous Politics in Postmulticultural Bolivia*. Stanford, CA: Stanford University Press.

———. 2007. "Andean Utopias in Evo Morales's Bolivia." *Latin American and Caribbean Ethnic Studies* 2(1): 1–28.

Pratt, Mary L. 2007. "Indigeneity Today." In *Indigenous Experience Today,* ed. Marisol de la Cadena and Orin Star, 397–404. New York: Berg.
Prieto, Mercedes. 2004. *Liberalismo y temor: imaginando los sujetos indígenas en el Ecuador postcolonial, 1895–1950.* Quito: FLASCO.
Quijano, Aníbal. 2008. "Coloniality of Power: Eurocentrism and Social Classification." In *Coloniality at Large: Latin America and the Postcolonial Debate,* ed. Mabel Morana, Enrique Dussel, and Carlos A. Jáuregui, 181–224. Durham, NC: Duke University Press.
Quintero, Rafael. 2009. "Las innovaciones conceptuales de la Constitución de 2008 y el Sumak Kawsay." In *El buen vivir: Una vía para el desarrollo,* eds. Alberto Acosta and Esperanza Martínez, 75–92. Quito: Ediciones Abya-Yala.
Rivera Cusicanqui, Silvia. 1987. *Oppressed But Not Defeated: Peasant Struggles among the Aymara and Qhechwa in Bolivia, 1900–1980.* Geneva: United Nations Research Institute for Social Development.
Santos, Boaventura de Sousa. 2010. *Refundación del estado en América Latina: Perspectivas desde una epistemología del Sur.* Lima: Instituto Internacional de Derecho y Sociedad and Programa Democracia y Transformación Global.
Schilling-Vacaflor, Almut and Bettina Schorr. 2011. "Desenredando el nudo: movimientos sociales, identidades culturales y estrategias políticas en Bolivia." In *Culturas políticas en la región andina,* ed. Christian Büschges, Olaf Kaltmeier, and Sebastian Thies, 247–268. Madrid and Frankfurt a.M.: Iberoamericana and Vervuert.
Thurner, Mark. 1997. *From Two Republics to One Divided: Contradictions of Postcolonial Nationmaking in Andean Peru.* Durham, NC: Duke University Press.
Van Cott, Donna L. 2005. *From Movements to Parties in Latin America: The Evolution of Ethnic Politics.* Cambridge: Cambridge University Press.
Vasconcelos, José. 1925. *La raza cósmica.* Madrid: Agencia Mundial de Librería.
Villanueva M, Aída. 2013. "Political Representation of Indigenous Peoples in Peru: Perceptions of Indigenous Leaders and Characteristics of the Peruvian Model." In *Cases of Exclusion and Mobilization of Race and Ethnicities in Latin America,* ed. Marc Becker, 78–103. Newcastle: Cambridge Scholars Publishing.
Walsh, Catherine. 2009. "Estado e interculturalidad: Reflexiones críticas desde la coyuntura andina." In *Los Andes en movimiento: Identidad y poder en el nuevo paisaje político,* ed. Pablo Ospina, Olaf Kaltmeier, and Christian Büschges, 217–248. Quito: Corporación Editora Nacional.
Yashar, Deborah J. 2005. *Contesting Citizenship in Latin America: The Rise of Indigenous Movements and the Postliberal Challenge.* Cambridge and New York: Cambridge University Press.
Zamosc, León. 2004. "The Indian Movement in Ecuador: From Politics of Influence to Politics of Power." In *The Struggle for Indigenous Rights in Latin America,* ed. Nancy Postero and León Zamosc, 131–157. London: Sussex Academic Press.

 8

CONFLICTING DIMENSIONS OF INDIGENEITY AS A CONTESTED POLITICAL RESOURCE IN CONTEMPORARY MEXICO

Gilberto Rescher

In the communal elections that took place in 2005 in the Mexican state of Hidalgo, the oppositional Partido de la Revolución Democrática (PRD)[1] surprisingly won most of the municipalities, clearly defeating the Partido Revolucionario Institucional (PRI),[2] which had formerly been regarded as the dominant state party. One focal point of this electoral swing was the Valle del Mezquital, a region that was previously considered to fully support the PRI.[3] This turn of events created a great deal of surprise as much among local citizens and politicians as among external observers, as it did not fit into common perceptions of how politics in this region, assumed to be mainly clientelist, was done. The consequences were twofold, spreading discourses that processes of democratization had finally prevailed, and a widespread skepticism about the possibility of "real" change. Such discourses are paradigmatic of ideas about politics in rural areas of Mexico, especially for those labeled as indigenous, based on a common assumption that rarely, if ever, does any meaningful social or political change take place in these areas and, duly, there is little change in the local and regional political system.[4] These opinions were present in the public discourse that was reflected in local media, the discourses of local politicians, and in statements given to me by interview partners. However, as I will discuss, this political development, rather than being obstructed, was actually fostered by the indigenous background of the region's inhabitants. In fact, there are several subtle political processes that are related to the ideas and practices of indigeneity, with quite controversial implications.

Common Views on Indigenous People in Mexico

As in most parts of the world, public discourses on indigenous people in Mexico frequently emphasize their supposed backwardness, and as a consequence, they conceptualize indigenous groups as marginalized and trapped in clientelist relations. However, my findings from extensive ethnographic fieldwork in the Valle del Mezquital suggest that indigenous villages are social arenas in which local and translocal processes intersect, facilitating the negotiation of social, economic, and political transformations.

Rural areas in Mexico are usually seen as backward and underdeveloped; they are associated with stagnation rather than development. This perception tends to be accentuated if the region is predominantly inhabited by members of indigenous groups. The notions of isolation and traditionalism add to this perception, in which indigenous people are, in contrast to empirical evidence, seen as being cut off from the nation and from modernity, or even as anti-modern. These prejudices have an additional political component. It is often presupposed that under these imagined conditions, political rule is conducted in a clientelist manner, with strong groups of local and regional *caciques* (powerful local bosses, commonly related to political parties) controlling the region and dominating everyone. In this sense, the state and its institutions are conceived as a kind of property of the ruling party and its leaders. Thus, political and especially democratic change is believed to be unachievable in such indigenous rural areas. Furthermore, it is often informally stated that citizens in these areas do not care about democratic change, and are even unable to obtain a more democratic system.

The Valle del Mezquital can be seen as a paradigmatic case for this kind of rural area with a large indigenous population. For a long time, it was seen as marginalized, poor, and underdeveloped, and has therefore been the target of a large number of development interventions and experiments by the Mexican state. One reason for this is the fact that, of those regions viewed as underdeveloped, it is the closest to Mexico City (ca. 120 km). Thus, for members of the urban middle class, "poverty" here became more visible. Because this poverty was located so close to the capital, it was considered to be a source of shame. Moreover, since the 1960s, social movements have been in force in this region, often drawing on discourses that integrated subalternity and indigeneity. The social pressure manifested by these movements was mitigated through developmental programs and projects, and the region was turned into a kind of social laboratory. For this purpose, a specialized organization, the Patrimonio Indígena del Valle del Mezquital (Indigenous Patrimony of the Valle del Mezquital), was founded. It was intended to be an institution to represent and assist the rural population. At the same time, in accordance with Mexican paternalistic ideas of politics, it aimed at co-optation of the local population into the political system. The Valle del Mezquital eventually gained a reputation as a region extremely loyal to the (former) state party PRI and thoroughly penetrated by clientelist networks (see Martínez Assad and Sarmiento Silva 1991). Accordingly, it is subjected to stereotypical views and perceptions about its loyalty and clientelist politics, which are prevalent even in the self-perceptions of its inhabitants. Contrary to these impressions, during my research I found that a process of social and political change is underway that could possibly lead to democratization in local and regional political fields, in the sense of the increased participation of common citizens. Indigeneity is strikingly important in this development, as the conceptualization of these citizens as indigenous peoples is relevant in several related processes.

In this chapter, I discuss several pertinent dimensions of the interwovenness of ethnic categorizations and political change in the rural communities of the Valle del Mezquital, which can be seen as exemplary of transformations in rural areas in central Mexico. My focus will be on political negotiation, community representation, and the strategic use of indigeneity in this region. I analyze these transformations using Long's (1989; see also Long and Long 1992) interface approach, in order to interpret political practices and analyze political logics that form the basis for interactions in political arenas.

Indigenous Communities: Institutions of Self-Representation and Self-Organization

In Mexico, villages with predominantly indigenous inhabitants normally present themselves as indigenous communities for several reasons. As in other regions, villages in the Valle del Mezquital are characterized by a special kind of organization; they form so-called *comunidades* (communities) that are supposed to comprise all villagers.[5] These units form the basis for most aspects related to the social life of the village and its interaction with external actors. At the same time, this community is the foundation of identity constructions of the village as a we-group, and it encompasses the institutions for self-organization and representation. Every *comunidad* has a village assembly, where local citizens meet to debate and vote on current concerns, and where community members are elected for local posts. These posts are part of the structure of local self-organization, and among them the most important and recognized is the so-called *delegado* (literally, "delegate"). The *delegado* is a kind of village head who acts as a mediator in internal conflicts and as a representative to the "outside world." The main body of the organization is formed by committees, whose members are also elected by the village assembly. These committees manage diverse areas, such as water supply, schools, and current projects. Both the *delegado* and the committees are responsible for the organization of *faenas,* a further basic institution of the local organization. *Faena* is the communitarian work that mainly takes care of the maintenance of the village's infrastructure and the realization of new projects. Every citizen has to fulfill a certain amount of *faenas* and in the same manner is obliged to pay local dues, which are used for community projects and festivities. A citizen who does not comply with these duties can be sanctioned by losing some or all of the local rights for himself and his family. This could mean, for example, having their water supply cut off, or being denied the right to be buried in the village's graveyard, a sanction that very few would dare to risk.

This kind of organization is related to the indigenous background of these villages and is part of the so-called *usos y costumbres* (ways and customs) that are frequently criticized as a kind of indigenous self-rule, supposedly offensive to national laws and individual rights.[6] Though mainly present in rural areas, the basic idea of this kind of self-organization is also reflected in the urban centers in the Valle del Mezquital. However, there the means of representation and organization, which is done through vicinity committees, is less elaborate than in indigenous communities. It is important to stress that this kind of village organization is not a sign of isolation and traditionalist ideology, nor should it be misunderstood as egalitarian grassroots democracy, in accordance with idealized notions and romanticism about indigenous groups. It is in fact a very pragmatic response to a situation of public disregard that led to a minimal level of state assistance. As the state did not provide sufficient assistance, villagers had to self-organize to achieve infrastructural improvements, provide schooling, and so on. Moreover, they had to present themselves as a collective, represented by a *delegado,* to be included in and have some control over interventions. Therefore, in our thematic context, the *comunidad* has two relevant features that make it important for the political realm. These are, firstly, of being a unit of intermediation between the village population and external actors, especially at higher levels of social organization, and secondly, its potential for unifying the villagers as a we-group (Elwert 1997, 2002) and displaying a collectivity, whether or not it ultimately exists. In the following section, I will analyze this central position of the community in relation to local/regional politics.

The Community's Key Position for the Political System

As previously pointed out, in rural indigenous villages, the community is the focal point for most collective interactions with external actors. It is a central institution, for all kinds of approaches that aim to address the villagers as a collective, or those that address certain subgroups within the community. Thus, political negotiations, especially those intended to gain collective support, are channeled through the community, as is nearly every single development intervention, at least in their initial phase. In short, the *comunidad* as an institution is the main mediator between the rural population and higher levels of societal organization. Anyone planning to address villagers must first approach the community and its authorities, which shows its importance.[7] Moreover, these communities can be seen as an important basis of the overall political system, because they can be thought of as a potential unit of political mobilization favoring specific political actors. This allegiance to specific parties or politicians was thought to be secured through a classic clientelist exchange of (state) resources for political loyalty. Thus, the community organization is often seen as facilitating this co-optation. However, on the contrary, there are several aspects of this kind of organization that can strengthen the community's position with respect to external actors, if properly employed.

First of all, through its organizational dimension the *comunidad* offers a social space that is controlled or at least can be appropriated by its members. This can be a space for constructing their own visions of political relations or even putting into practice their "own" ideas, through internal negotiations between different groups in the community. This process is influenced by a broad range of external transfers, especially those related to education, but also new life experiences, and the flow of symbols and resources in transnational social spaces, among others. The community and its institutions are the main arena in which such ideas and visions are negotiated, often resulting in new collective positions. Thus, most external influences are first received and negotiated in the *comunidad*, creating in return the basis for further interactions as a unified community with external actors.

This way of communitarian organization carries with it the potential to enact a relatively strong sense of autonomy, especially concerning interventions by state agents. The community has certain room for maneuver in accepting or, more commonly, renegotiating propositions from the outside. In united communities that have access to alternative resources, their position of negotiation is so strong that they even have the ability to choose whether or not to accept assistance, or whether or not to partake in a certain development program. This kind of strategic negotiation with state agents definitely does not fit into common ideas about indigenous communities that are supposed to be totally dependent on assistance from the outside. In some villages in the Valle del Mezquital, their autonomy goes as far as a kind of tacit agreement by which state forces, especially the police and the military, are not allowed to enter the community's territory without having asked the *delegado* for permission beforehand. This is the result of experiences of abuses of power by the local police in the 1950s and 1960s, which led to the first social movement in the region and finally, despite periods of strong repression, to the acceptance of the aforementioned de facto autonomy in several *comunidades*. In the 1990s in particular, this notion of autonomy was enforced by sometimes violent but mostly peaceful social protest activities. These included demonstrations, the occupation of administrative buildings, and the blockading of the Panamericana highway that crosses the Valle del Mezquital, and also in several cases the short-term kidnappings of public servants and politicians. These actions reflect the common repertoire of protest activities in Mexico, and all over the country they are frequently employed as part of a strategy of escalation in cases in which citizens find themselves aggrieved or ignored by state agents or politicians. In an extreme example, villagers I interviewed from a specific part of the Valle del Mezquital frequently made reference to the burning of a local federal police station that occurred as the end of a complex, escalating regional conflict.

Even in cases where the community's position is not so strong or where the villagers do not exercise such a sweeping use of autonomy, the very existence of communitarian self-organization indicates that it is widely accepted, that its members, through community organization, largely control their own affairs. Such forms of self-rule are predominantly based on mainly unwritten communitarian rules and on decisions made by the village assembly or elected authorities. Hence, there is a strong awareness among villagers of the value of this self-organization and autonomy. This is why local politicians, as well as state actors concerned with development programs, are eager to achieve and maintain a good working relationship with communities that are no longer (fully) integrated into the above-mentioned classic clientelist networks of control. At the same time, any social change is first seen and negotiated in the communities. This refers to a wide range of dimensions of change, such as gender relations, ideas about economic development, education, new perspectives, and/or alternative outlooks on life, and certainly ideas about politics. Finally, through interfaces with external actors, these local changes might be transferred to regional and even national settings and intermingle with processes deriving from other localities.

Thus, communities are purportedly using their own spaces for their own benefit. In several aspects of their day-to-day life, they rely upon cooperation and cohesion among themselves to achieve certain aims, ranging from gaining assistance for a specific local infrastructure or development project to successfully supporting a political candidate whom it is believed will be favorable to the community. This is normally seen as the only available option to achieve a particular level of social, economic, and infrastructural development in a village, a perception based on past experiences, when almost no assistance reached rural villages. The inhabitants of such villages thus had to organize themselves to carry out necessary work and reach decisions on community affairs. But even in the 1960s and 1970s, when the first institutions began to offer support to the *comunidades*, these institutions expected to work with well-established and organized communities, increasing the need for the villages to be formally organized, that is, with a village head, committees, and so on. Historically, therefore, it has been important, for various reasons, for villagers to work together as a relatively coherent group. The construction of a communitarian identity as a we-group is therefore essential, as it helps maintain or enforce social cohesion.

This kind of self-organization and self-confidence allows the communitarian organization to be maintained as an owned space that is protected from external interventions. This protection can be interpreted as hidden transcripts in the sense of Scott (1985, 1990). In day-to-day interactions with external actors, especially institutional ones, many elements of these interactions go uncontested and are seemingly accepted. It often appears, therefore, as if every aspect is adopted and internalized by the villagers, something that has contributed to the kinds of assumptions about clientelism mentioned above. This can also be attributed to the apparent representation of loyalty towards a certain party. In reality, most villagers are acutely aware of their own position, and the conditions for their political interaction are shaped by this self-awareness. In this manner, the community is an important element in doing politics and in the negotiation of their development. At the same time, these two fields (politics and development projects) are the main areas in which the *comunidad* interacts as a collective, and form the main spaces for interaction and negotiation with external institutions and actors. Hence, transformations in communities can be adequately analyzed with reference to these two fields.

Representation as Indigenous Communities

It is noteworthy that in day-to-day interactions the communities are rarely represented as indigenous. Such representation is regularly embedded in formalized political interactions. At larger political events, the supposed support of indigenous people is orchestrated by the attendance of persons labeled as indigenous and often wearing purportedly traditional dress as an ethnic marker. This representation has its roots in clientelist logic, and the mainly non-indigenous party leaders clearly seek to appropriate indigeneity as a political resource. In a similar vein, party politicians and holders of formal state posts attempt to portray themselves as assisting indigenous people or make accordant promises in their campaigns. Owing to the aforementioned public conceptions of indigeneity, such politicians can rely upon these prejudices to present themselves as being concerned with the poorest sections of Mexican society. Later I will touch on some such interactions in which party-affiliated political actors attempt to employ indigeneity as political resource.

However, even without highlighting their categorization as indigenous, representatives of communities themselves allude to commonly held imaginaries and views of indigenous peoples, often in subtle ways. They strategically enact suitable representations in political negotiations, without actually employing the term indigenous. This is often done in a very subtle manner, as local demands are never overtly presented in relation to an indigenous background.[8] This means that the communities might present themselves as underdeveloped, even marginalized, or as having a lack of opportunities that must be ameliorated by state projects and material transfers. As these self-descriptions conform to the aforementioned common stereotypes of indigenous people, those receiving such messages relate them to the ethnic background of the specific community, without indigeneity having to be explicitly mentioned in negotiations. The relevant imaginaries are implicitly alluded to. In this sense, local community leaders stress the commonly held stereotypes about indigenous communities, reproducing (prejudiced) mainstream notions about them, as a strategic concession that allows them to gain access to state resources.

This means of negotiation is deeply rooted in the logic of *indigenismo*, which, from the 1930s onwards, defined relations between indigenous groups and the Mexican state. *Indigenismo's* basic premise was that instead of ignoring the specific situation of indigenous peoples as it did previously, the state should offer institutional assistance to integrate them into "modern" post-revolutionary Mexican society and, ultimately, to assimilate them (Korsbaek and Sámano Rentería 2007; Sánchez 1999: 19–83; Stavenhagen 2002: 27–28). This was seen as a way to offer Mexicans with an indigenous background an opportunity to share in the social justice promised by the revolution (Boyer 2003: 188–222). In return, indigenous communities had to show their allegiance to the state and its representatives. During its beginnings, this was seen as an attempt to convert a relatively large part of the Mexican population into a political power base for the then president, Lázaro Cárdenas. Later, it was seen as a means to integrate the indigenous population into the state's power structure (Dawson 2004: 96–126). Thus, it was foremost a political strategy defined by ideas of assimilation and modernization, with an overwhelmingly paternalistic stance on indigenous people. This notwithstanding, it should be acknowledged that, for the first time, public policies were specifically oriented, in an institutionalized manner, towards a group of Mexican citizens who had previously been largely ignored. Moreover, it was recognized that the socioeconomic position of indigenous peoples was not "given" but socially constructed, and could therefore be altered by state interventions.

A part of *indigenismo* politics was the advancement of opportunities for formal education. To this end, young indigenous men and women were trained as teachers, first in residential schools and later in specialized colleges. These so-called *maestros bilingües* (bilingual teachers), being deeply influenced by the *indigenismo* ideology, were supposed to act as a sort of broker between "modern" Mexican society and the indigenous groups (cf. Kugel 1995). As a result of their position in the *comunidades*, many of these teachers also became community spokespersons and were often recruited by the then dominant state party, the PRI. To this extent, most community leaders and local politicians still follow the political logic of *indigenismo* and are used to an exchange of state resources in return for political loyalty. Ultimately, this means they are accustomed to the corresponding means and rules of interaction (that follow *indigenismo* logic), and engage in them accordingly because they can more accurately predict the reaction of state actors and thus can generally expect to succeed with their demands. One crucial element to this strategy is the aforementioned presentation of the *comunidad* as vulnerable, marginalized, and in need of assistance, while at the same time being prepared to be loyal to the politicians and state actors that may provide any aid. In this sense, the communities are also constructed as grateful and incapable of rebellion. This purported allegiance is often publicly staged on diverse occasions as mass mobilizations, involving as many community members as possible.

Turning the Conceptualization Around: The Community's Displayed Unity as Menace

Despite the problematic reproduction of mostly pejorative stereotypes, it should be noted that the *indigenismo* model of interaction between the state and indigenous groups fostered the creation of the abovementioned internal institutions in the communities to act as counterparts to state structures. It is now accepted that such communities are at least partly able to govern themselves. This facilitated the preservation of the community as a quasi-autonomous social space, in the sense of hidden transcripts. Though often presented as compliant with the ideas of state actors, the community constitutes a protected space that is defended by its members in the case of an overt intrusion. Accordingly, the capability to collectively stage a community mobilization can be turned against outsiders, and used as a threat in political interactions. This potential threat is facilitated by a transformation of the community's bargaining position in political negotiations, based on the entanglement of local and migration-influenced translocal processes like the transfer of resources, but also ideas, knowledge, and experiences, that foster social change and alter forms of dependency.

One important implication of these new local and translocal processes is that the relative worth of state assistance has declined. In the past, any kind of aid was considered a great help, and in general crucial, as it would make up a considerable portion of the total available resources. For this reason, it was of great importance to be included in programs such as *Solidaridad* and *Oportunidades,* which delivered food parcels or petty financial assistance, for example through so-called stipends for pupils on a family level. On the communitarian level, financial assistance through agricultural extension services, small business projects (often targeting women), or material assistance to communitarian projects was seen as indispensable. Over the past few years, however, the perception of these kinds of grants has changed. This is mainly due to the widespread labor migration, mostly undocumented, to the USA. By the 1990s at the latest, every village in the Valle del Mezquital had been incorporated into this migration process (see Quezada Ramírez 2004; Rivera and Quezada Ramírez 2011; Serrano Avilés 2006), which ended up transnationalizing most of the communities.[9] Based on my field experiences, I estimate that there are very few, if any, families in the Valle del Mezquital that do not have at least one relative living in the USA. In most cases, this means that those family members who remain at home are able to benefit materially to some extent through the remittances sent back by migrants, despite the numerous problems related to the migration process. These financial transfers have gained great importance in family economics, as they may represent large increases in income relative to those amounts formerly available. At the same time, with increasing remittances, the communities benefitted from a growing potential to fund communitarian projects. In summary, the relative worth of any kind of state assistance has declined, and is thus no longer as indispensable as it was before. Mostly, however, the perception of the relatively small stipends and food parcels has changed, and they are no longer so highly valued by most rural dwellers in the Valle del Mezquital. This has resulted in a decreased dependency on public assistance, on the part of *comunidades* as a whole and by single rural households, especially compared to ten or fifteen years ago. Hence, the promise of governmental material assistance is losing its appeal, and is less and less of a motive for providing political support in order to receive such assistance in exchange.

The waning appeal of promises of government assistance is typified by the following occurrence. In the 1990s, the government initiated a new national program of social assistance, *Progresa* (now called *Oportunidades*). As part of its introduction, a village in the countryside of the Valle del Mezquital was selected for the official act of inauguration.[10] At the time, most of the villagers qualified for the new program and were solemnly inducted as part of the ceremony. About eight years later, however, only a few of the original recipients remained in the program. Migration promised greater financial rewards and so the program lost its attraction. A final reason to abstain from accepting government assistance through such programs is the severe conditions imposed on recipients. These duties, such as additional *faenas*, obligatory participation in seminars, and medical checks, are now perceived as too harsh, laborious, and/or time-consuming for the perceived returned value. It is this imbalance, between the assistance offered and the dedication expected in return, that is the basis upon which a lot of former beneficiaries chose to withdraw their participation.

At the same time, other processes led to a subtle but nonetheless fundamental transformation in the situation of the members of *comunidades* I have studied. Among these is the fact that many locals, especially women, have achieved higher educational levels than the previous generation, and gained formal posts with regular and secure incomes, often as teachers. Additionally, villagers have benefitted from new ideas, values, norms, skills, and knowledge, which have entered the villages through diverse channels. In a similar vein, the migration-based transnationalization not only increased the achievable material resources, but also transferred social remittances (Lamba-Nieves and Levitt 2011; Levitt 1998), which combined enabled a social repositioning of the beneficiaries. The increase in self-confidence and the lessening dependence of indigenous groups enables the stereotypical concept of relatively homogeneous and easily mobilized communities to be transcended. If a community is no longer dependent on assistance and the "benevolence" of politicians, then the unity of indigenous communities, and their displayed ability to mobilize en masse, can be employed as a threat to politicians who do not keep their promises or renege on agreements, or are seen to be abusing their power as state authorities. Overall, this means that indigeneity can be employed as a resource to enhance the bargaining position of the communities.

Portrayed Community Unity and Indigeneity as a Political Resource

In both the strategies previously analyzed, it is essential to be able to show how the community's unity underscores compatible concepts of indigeneity. The fundamental relative unity of the communities is achieved by social cohesion, based as much on differing forms of pressure as on the day-to-day practices that enhance community belonging. Local leaders, especially, try to enforce this cohesion through neotraditional discourses, or by demanding the fulfillment of community duties. So *faenas* and financial contributions are not just means to realize community projects; they also foster social cohesion. In practice, villagers themselves, and not just leaders, support the idea that an indigenous community per se must be united. Therefore, the (often prejudiced) conceptions of indigenous communities are also embodied by their members, and these affiliations are displayed internally and externally, on the one hand to confront external actors—for instance public servants, politicians, or those with economic interests—and on the other to foster internal unity.

Hence indigeneity and presenting oneself as a united community are important political resources, even though in reality these groups, far from being homogeneous, are often affected by internal conflicts and power hierarchies. These internal heterogeneities can be related to disputes among members over resources, especially water or land, or more generally they can be a byproduct of social transformations, as in the case of changing gender relations (cf. Rescher 2008). Another example of the growing heterogeneity, and how it can trigger disputes, is what is locally known as envy. These conflicts are, above all, because a village's social reality is far from the ideal of a homogeneous one, as the distribution of income, the level of education, occupations, and so on are somewhat disproportional. Even people within these communities are inclined to believe they are still a homogeneous group, and thus being confronted with their own growing heterogeneity may also be a cause of conflicts.

It is important to acknowledge that despite all these common internal problems, the vast majority of community members are aware of the importance of demonstrated and purported unity towards outsiders, as this positioning allows for a more favorable standing during interactions with other sections of Mexican society. Due to these strategic concessions that make use of imaginaries of indigeneity, the social positioning of indigenous groups is initially reinforced. Nevertheless, indigenous communities can successfully utilize this (self-) representation to redefine their place in political (and also social) relationships.

The Other Side: Indigeneity in Attempts at Re-establishing Clientelist Networks

Representatives of indigenous villages are not the sole actors seeking to benefit from indigeneity as a political resource. As described above, with the establishment of *indigenismo* politics in the 1930s, several organizations were founded that were to attend to the needs of indigenous people, to develop indigenous regions, and even to create spaces for indigenous representation and participation. This happened in the Valle del Mezquital and in other indigenous regions in Mexico. Alongside the renowned Patrimonio Indígena del Valle del Mezquital, an organization that for several years had a higher project budget than the entire state of Hidalgo, the so-called Consejo Supremo Hñähñu (CSH, Supreme Hñähñu Council) was also founded. A similar organization was established for nearly every (major) indigenous group in Mexico, as a supposed high council of its leaders. However, most of these institutions, like *indigenismo* politics in general, were not intended just to be a medium to assist and to give indigenous peoples a voice, but also as a means of co-optation. Indigenous people were offered an improved position in Mexican society, and in return were expected to grant the ruling political party their unconditional political allegiance.

The formation of these *indigenismo* institutions could also be seen as a response to the social unrest in various indigenous regions at the time. In most parts of Mexico, these organizations eventually vanished and often even the general idea of *indigenismo* did not work out well, due to continuing social conflicts, based on discrimination against indigenous and rural peoples, which fueled organized opposition towards ruling local and regional officials. In the Valle del Mezquital, however, the co-optative dimension of *indigenismo* was largely successful. There, therefore, the CSH still exists, and for a long period held an important political position.

It was not until recently that the power and significance of the CSH began to wane, and this occurred for several reasons. The most important for the argument presented here is that the effectiveness of these organizations, whose task as defined by the ruling political party was to maintain clientelist networks, to co-opt and control the local rural and indigenous population, was weakened by increasing migration processes. When transnational migration to the USA became more widespread, many members of the established networks just "disappeared." As members physically left, and as my empirical data indicate, this meant a demise of previous clientelist relationships and a loss in their importance. As my informants stated, people also noticed they were not as dependent on these relationships as they had previously thought, a fact related to their aforementioned growing self-confidence, and the declining material dependence on various forms of state assistance. This, in turn, caused the CSH to lose its political significance, to which it reacted by developing strategies to re-establish networks of co-optation—by transnationalizing them. It implemented this on the one hand by offering migrants and their relatives services related to migration, such as the legalization of imported cars, the return of deceased family members, and the organization of convoys intended to facilitate a secure "homecoming" of returning migrants. On the other hand, the CSH has tried to establish formal migrant organizations in the United States itself, which are designed to assist and represent migrants there. As an additional part of its engagement in the United States, reciprocal visits by mayors, police chiefs, and politicians between cities in the United States and the Valle del Mezquital have been organized, and there is even a kind of ID handed out by the CSH and accepted in the Tampa Bay Area in Florida.

A central aspect of this engagement is that this intent by the CSH to transnationally revive clientelist networks is strongly framed in ethnic terms. One important element in discourses on this topic is the accentuation of a supposed overall ethnic identity—with the image of an entire group with a common culture, interests, and needs—achieved through the stressing of a supposed "brotherhood" of all Hñähñu.[11] In these discourses, migration forms an important element, discursively including migrants as part of this ethnic group and emphasizing a sense of their belonging to the communities and families in the Valle del Mezquital. Through this discourse, the CSH claims to represent "the Hñähñu people," stressing a pretended shared ethnic identification or "essence." "We as the Hñähñu people..." is a common refrain in discourses by political actors allied with the CSH. Recently, a *"bastón de mando"* ceremony was even invented in which a local PRI politician, being a candidate for the governor's post, was nominated as a trusted representative of "the Hñähñu people" during an electoral rally (co-)organized by the CSH. This was done with a large ceremony, during which a "ruler's bar" was handed over to the politician, alluding to an indigenous tradition, one that apparently never actually existed in the Valle del Mezquital. Rather, it seems to be an adaptation of the staged inauguration ceremony of Bolivia's president-elect Evo Morales, in which he was legitimized in a supposedly traditional, indigenous manner. In addition to these activities in Mexico, the CSH presents (irregular) migrants from the Valle del Mezquital to officials in the United States as part of an indigenous collective that is culturally distinct from *mestizo* migrants, though in reality this distinction is not that marked.

There are many difficulties associated with these strategies of reclientalization by the CSH. Though many citizens utilize the services of the CSH, this does not mean they automatically accept being reincorporated into a clientelist relationship. As previously stated, many no longer feel that they need to commit themselves to a certain political group in exchange for required services or goods. Obviously, there are still many people who do willingly participate in the political activities of such organizations, and even more who simply make use of the services offered. But it is important to note that the beneficiaries, seen by the political parties as potential clients, do not actually perceive themselves as such. This is most probably the decisive change from past years. People from the Valle del Mezquital use services and accede to the offices of the respective organizations for advice in particular and diverse situations, but do not thereby feel an obligation to support the corresponding political party. Statements from my interview partners clearly show that part of their strategy includes benefitting from all the offers that might be useful to them, without giving their unconditional support in exchange, or feeling bound or in debt. Thus, the strategy of villagers contradicts and undermines that of the organizations trying to recreate the dominance of clientelist relations. At the same time, the migrant organizations, established by the CSH, seem to have only limited support from active migrants themselves. The CSH can therefore legitimize its existence in front of its political patrons, but this does not necessarily point to a lack of democratic consciousness among local citizens. Moreover, local citizens are frequently aware of the CSH's intentions, and are therefore generally skeptical towards formal migrant organizations such as so-called "home town associations." So while these migrant organizations are generally envisaged in migration studies as the main field for migrants' political engagement (see Bada 2014; Escala Rabadán, Bada, and Rivera Salgado 2006), migrants from the Valle del Mezquital tend to see them as facilitators of co-optation and therefore distrust them. Hence, they prefer to rely on their *comunidades* for political representation and participation.

Even within the communities, however, there is a group of politicians that can potentially benefit from indigeneity as political resource—politicians who are often assisted by the CSH and similar organizations. They are frequently members of the former state party PRI, which ruled Mexico for more than seventy years and still governs the state of Hidalgo. They represent themselves as indigenous politicians and move in diverse political spheres. At the local and regional levels, voters often prefer a candidate to be indigenous, have roots in the region, and be aware of what their life is like. At the national level, these candidates rely upon their reputation as indigenous members of parliament to be seen as representatives of the indigenous groups in their respective regions, and thereby maintain a certain political importance. Here politics has clearly become ethnicized, and indigeneity has become an important resource in the political system.

Indigeneity: A "Double-Edged Sword"

In conclusion, indigeneity can be an important political resource in central Mexico, especially if employed by villages that present themselves as strong and unified communities. In this manner, they may take advantage of commonly held ideas about indigenous communities, despite such ideas being based on prejudiced conceptualizations. This appropriation of a prejudicial (self-) image facilitates a transformation of the community's bargaining position in political negations, and offers opportunities to foster political change. However, at the same time, this strategic use of indigeneity and the presentation of a *comunidad* perpetuates the stereotypical views that they are based on or allude to. Moreover, as the example of party-associated, clientelist organizations shows, indigenous *comunidades* are not the only actors trying to benefit politically by using the ideas and terms of indigeneity. Thus, indigeneity can be both part of practices that enhance political transformation possibilities, and a discursive instrument in attempts to revive clientelist modes of political interaction, and even to transnationalize clientelism.

Gilberto Rescher (Dr., Bielefeld) is coordinator of the Latin-American Studies Programmes at the University of Hamburg, Germany. He was previously a lecturer at the Ruhr-University Bochum and the University of Bielefeld. He is trained as a sociologist and received his doctoral degree from the University of Bielefeld. His dissertation is based on an ethnographic study on the entanglements of processes of democratization, migration-led transnationalization, transforming gender relations and ethnic positioning, and more general social change in the Valle del Mezquital, a rural and indigenous area in central Mexico. His research interests include (local) politics, development, migration/transnationality, indigenous/ethnic groups, gender issues, and qualitative methodologies, and he has conducted extended empirical fieldwork in Mexico, Nicaragua, and the Philippines. Based on these, he has published several articles inter alia on political transformations in Mexico and is co-editor of the anthology *The Making of World Society: Perspectives from Transnational Research* (transcript 2008, co-edited with Remus Anghel, Eva Gerharz and Monika Salzbrunn).

Notes

1. A center-left party that was founded in the late 1980s, during a split from the then-ruling party, PRI.
2. The PRI was founded in the aftermath of the Mexican Revolution and then formed the government of Mexico, a reign which lasted, without a change in the ruling party, for seventy-two years.
3. This region is located about 120 kilometers north of Mexico City. Valle del Mezquital means "Valley of the Mesquite Grove."
4. These juxtaposed extreme interpretations of change in the political realm in Mexico are very close to those experienced in the aftermath of the presidential elections in 2000, when a non-PRI candidate was elected as president for the first time in history. There were conflicting opinions in the aftermath of this historic occasion, ranging from the claim that Mexico had finally been democratized, to the statement that the system would remain unaltered, and only the party and its candidates had been substituted.
5. However, only those who are designated with local citizenship status have full rights concerning the communities' self-organization. This applies

mostly to male villagers, who are supposed to be representatives for their family. Usually, the main characteristic of community "citizens" is that they are able to pay the communitarian fees, and thus women with formal employment are quite often offered citizen status (see Mendoza 1999; Rescher 2008; Rivera Garay 2006).
6. This criticism is part of a constant discussion in Mexican newspapers, and one that also occurs in (mainly local) politics.
7. This is also expected and often mandatory for doing fieldwork in such communities.
8. An exception to this exists when institutions are addressed that ought to specifically support indigenous people, such as the case of the CDI (Comisión Nacional para el Desarrollo de los Pueblos Indígenas—National Commission for the Development of Indigenous People), a national institution that supports inter alia economic projects in indigenous regions.
9. Concerning the concepts of transnationality, transnationalism, and so on, see Faist (2000), Glick Schiller, Basch, and Szanton Blanc (1992), and Pries (1999); in relation to the transformation of indigenous communities, see Besserer and Kearney (2006); and concerning transnational migration from the Valle del Mezquital, see Schmidt and Crummett (2004).
10. This procedure is quite common, as it can be used for positive publicity for political parties by bringing together the "helpful" president and the supposedly indigent and grateful indigenous rural dwellers. Villages in the Valle del Mezquital are well suited to this purpose, as the region is renowned for being poor and underdeveloped. And due to its closeness to Mexico City, it can be reached quickly by the president's helicopter.
11. The indigenous people in the Valle del Mezquital refer to themselves as Hñähñu as a rejection of the pejorative term Otomí from precolonial times. Remarkably, the name Hñähñu has been promoted in villages in the Valle del Mezquital by the same bilingual teachers who were trained as part of *indigenismo* politics and therefore often had close ties to the CSH or the PRI. This shows that in past decades, too, indigeneity was frequently used as a political resource.

Bibliography

Bada, Xóchitl. 2014. *Mexican Hometown Associations in Chicagoacán: From Local to Transnational Civic Engagement*. Piscataway, NJ: Rutgers University Press.
Besserer, Federico and Michael Kearney. 2006. *San Juan Mixtepec: Una comunidad transnacional ante el poder clasificador y filtrador de las fronteras*. Mexico D.F.: Juan Pablos.
Boyer, Christopher R. 2003. *Becoming Campesinos: Politics, Identity, and Agrarian Struggle in Postrevolutionary Michoacán, 1920–1935*. Stanford, CA: Stanford University Press.
Dawson, Alexander S. 2004. *Indian and Nation in Revolutionary Mexico*. Tucson, AZ: University of Arizona Press.

Elwert, Georg. 1997. "Boundaries, Cohesion and Switching. On We-Groups in Ethnic National and Religious Forms." In *Rethinking Nationalism and Ethnicity: The Struggle for Meaning and Order in Europe*, ed. Hans-Rudolf Wicker, 251–72. Oxford: Berg.

———. 2002. "Switching Identity Discourses: Primordial Emotions and the Social Construction of We-Groups." In *Imagined Differences: Hatred and the Construction of Identity*, ed. Günther Schlee, 33–56. Münster: Lit.

Escala Rabadán, Luis, Xóchitl Bada, and Gaspar Rivera Salgado. 2006. "Mexican Migrant Civic and Political Participation in the US: The Case of Hometown Associations in Los Angeles and Chicago." *Norteamérica* 1(2): 127–72.

Faist, Thomas. 2000. "Transnationalization in International Migration: Implications for the Study of Citizenship and Culture." *Ethnic and Racial Studies* 23(2): 189–222.

Glick Schiller, Nina, Linda Basch, and Christina Szanton Blanc (eds). 1992. *Towards a Transnational Perspective on Migration: Race, Class, Ethnicity, and Nationalism Reconsidered*. New York: New York Academy of Sciences.

Korsbaek, Leif and Miguel Ángel Sámano Rentería. 2007. "El indigenismo en México: Antecedentes y actualidad." *Ra Ximhai* 3(1): 195–224.

Kugel, Verónica. 1995. "Normatividad étnica y normatividad nacional: Maestros del Valle del Mezquital." In *Sociedad y derecho indígenas en América Latina*, ed. Thomas Calvo and Bernardo Méndez, 103–123. México D.F.: Centro de Estudios Mexicanos y Centroamericanos.

Lamba-Nieves, Deepak and Peggy Levitt. 2011. "Social Remittances Revisited." *Journal of Ethnic and Migration Studies* 37(1): 1–22.

Levitt, Peggy. 1998. "Social Remittances: Migration Driven Local-Level Forms of Cultural Diffusion." *International Migration Review* 32(4): 926–48.

Long, Norman (ed.). 1989. *Encounters at the Interface: A Perspective on Social Discontinuities in Rural Development*. Wageningen: Wageningen University.

Long, Norman and Ann Long (eds). 1992. *Battlefields of Knowledge: The Interlocking of Theory and Practice in Social Research and Development*. London: Routledge.

Martínez Assad, Carlos R. and Sergio Sarmiento Silva (eds). 1991. *Nos queda la esperanza: El valle del Mezquital*. México D.F.: Consejo Nacional para la Cultura y las Artes.

Mendoza, Silvia. 1999. "Estructura y relaciones familiares ante la migración de los padres y jefes de familia a los Estados Unidos 1986–1997: Estudio de caso del Maye Ixmiquilpan Hidalgo," Master's thesis. Universidad Nacional Autónoma de México, Mexico D.F.

Pries, Ludger. 1999. *Migration and Transnational Social Spaces*. Aldershot: Ashgate.

Quezada, Maria Felix. 2004. "La migración Hñähñu del Valle del Mezquital, Estado de Hidalgo," Master's thesis. Universidad de Tijuana.

Rescher, Gilberto. 2008. "Transnational Citizenship, Local Politics and Development: The Case of a Rural Community in Central Mexico." In *The Making of World Society: Perspectives from Transnational Research*, ed. Remus Anghel, Eva Gerharz, Gilberto Rescher and Monika Salzbrunn, 195–218. Bielefeld: Transcript.

Rivera Garay, María Guadalupe. 2006. "La Negociación de las Relaciones de Género en el Valle del Mezquital: Un Acercamiento al Caso de la Participación Comunitaria de Mujeres Hñähñus." *Estudios de cultura otopame* 5: 249–66.

Rivera Garay, Maria Guadalupe and María Félix Quezada Ramírez. 2011. "El Valle del Mezquital, Estado de Hidalgo: Itinerario, balances y paradojas de la migración internacional de una región de México hacia Estados Unidos." *Trace—Travaux et Recherches dans les Amériques du Centre* 60: 85–101.

Sánchez, Consuelo. 1999. *Los pueblos indígenas: Del indigenismo a la autonomía.* México D.F.: Siglo Veintiuno Editores.

Schmidt, Ella and María Crummett. 2004. "Heritage Re-created: Hidalguenses in the United States and Mexico." In *Indigenous Mexican Migrants in the United States,* ed. Jonathan Fox and Gaspar Rivera-Salgado, 401–415. La Jolla: Center for US-Mexican Studies.

Scott, James C. 1985. *Weapons of the Weak: Everyday Forms of Peasant Resistance.* New Haven, CT: Yale University Press.

———. 1990. *Domination and the Arts of Resistance: Hidden Transcripts.* New Haven, CT: Yale University Press.

Serrano Avilés, Tomás. 2006. *Migración internacional y pobreza en el Estado de Hidalgo.* Pachuca: Universidad Autónoma del Estado de Hidalgo.

Stavenhagen, Rodolfo. 2002. "Indigenous Peoples and the State in Latin America: An Ongoing Debate." In *Multiculturalism in Latin America: Indigenous Rights, Diversity, and Democracy,* ed. Rachel Sieder, 24–44. Houndmills and New York: Palgrave Macmillan.

PART IV

INDIGENEITY AND THE STATE

 9

Intimate Antagonisms
Adivasis and the State in Contemporary India
Uday Chandra

Introduction

It is commonplace in academic and popular discourses in contemporary India to see populations described variously as tribes, scheduled tribes, adivasis, *vanvasis,* or indigenous peoples as being locked in perpetual combat with the modern state.[1] Indeed, some even argue that if the state in India represents the forces of modernity, adivasis represent an amodern, counter-modern, or even premodern social formation. As a consequence, adivasis are sometimes believed to exhibit the "elementary aspects" of rural insurgency in colonial India (Guha 1983; for a critique, see Bates and Shah 2014) as quintessential subaltern radicals defending older, nobler ways of life in "arcadian spaces" with "visions of alternative moralities" (Shah 2010: 190). At other times, adivasis are simply taken to be the hapless victims of state-directed development, dispossession, and "everyday tyranny" (Kela 2012; Nilsen 2010; Padel 2009). Moreover, those seeking to critique modernity and its forms in India have found adivasis "good to think with," in Claude Lévi-Strauss's terms, calling into question the ways of states, archives, and the public sphere all at once (Banerjee 2006a; Chakrabarty 2011; Visvanathan 2006). None of the above ought to be seen as peculiar to present-day India: the prose of otherness associated with the seductive figure of the tribal or indigene has its origins in the colonial past (Chandra 2013a), and its imprint on the modern social sciences is widespread (see, e.g., Clastres 1987; Lévi-Strauss 1969; Scott 2009; van Schendel 2002).

At the same time, the politics of representing adivasis in contemporary India speaks to a wider conundrum that students of indigeneity now face globally (Chandra 2013b; Hodgson 2011; Jung 2006; Li 2010; see also Chapter 6 in this volume). The "strategic essentialisms" (Spivak 1988) on which indigenous activism rely are, as Renée Sylvain

(2014) has recently argued, at least as limiting as they are enabling. On the one hand, activists and scholars rallying around the indigenous acknowledge the hard-nosed instrumental actions that prove necessary to achieve their ends. Yet, on the other hand, the same defenders of indigenous rights are compelled to speak in the explicitly non-instrumental and affect-laden language of authenticity and belonging. As Adam Kuper (2003) perceptively noted a decade or so ago, indigeneity talk in today's world has revived racialized notions of the primitive Other from a bygone era, and the "return of the native" can hardly be regarded as an unproblematic matter (Béteille 1998; Mamdani 2013; see also Chapter 3 in this volume). Writing about indigenous or adivasi politics thus turns out to be fraught with many dangers, of which racial stereotyping, essentializing, and speaking for silent subalterns are among the most common. In fact, a number of social scientists have recently asked whether discourses of indigeneity, deployed strategically or not, are actually part of a global neoliberal regime of "hypermarginality" that makes the so-called indigenous even more vulnerable than ever before (Bessire 2014; Hale 2004, 2005; McCormack 2012; Muehlmann 2009; see also Chapter 4 in this volume).

In India today, where a Maoist insurgency has raged since 2004, some scholars and activists see adivasis as victims in need of protection (Guha 2007; Nigam 2010; Simeon 2010), while others, and society at large, see them merely as savages to be civilized or "developed" through a mix of educational and commercial initiatives (Chaudhury 2009; Patel 2012; Planning Commission of India 2008; Verghese 2010). In this scenario, adivasi politics is represented either in terms of tragedy or triumphalism. These contradictory representations place the modern adivasi subject in an "irresoluble double bind" (Banerjee 2006b). Playing the victim connects adivasis to an ever-expanding universe of sympathetic officials, activists, and scholars who are all too keen to write on "tribal issues." Equally, however, invoking the "savage slot" (Rolph-Trouillot 2003) can help remake local communities through violent means that defy the many civilizing missions that prey on adivasi life. In this manner, the politics of representing adivasis are tied inextricably, albeit uneasily, to the politics that adivasi men and women pursue in India today.

In interrogating adivasi politics in contemporary India, this chapter departs sharply from dominant representations of adivasi politics today. It does so by challenging the easy binary between the modern state and adivasis in India, based on three years of doctoral research on the relations between colonial and postcolonial states and rural adivasi communities since the late eighteenth century, in the forest state of Jharkhand in eastern India. In my doctoral dissertation (Chandra 2013c), I show how the "state" and "tribe," paradoxically, constitute each other over time in the margins of modern India. The "state" here is both an idea and a set of governmental practices (Abrams 1988; Mitchell 1991) just as the "tribe," too, is an ideological as well as material formation. My argument here is, briefly, that the two are isomorphic, and that subaltern resistance, whether violent or peaceful, is best understood as the negotiation, not negation, of modern state power. This argument necessarily runs against a dominant strand of scholarship on South Asia that regards adivasis as subalterns *par excellence*, and identifies adivasi politics as primarily one of negating or opposing modern state structures (see, e.g., Bhadra 1985; Guha 1983; Mayaram 2003; Skaria 1999). Yet it also stands in solidarity with other scholars who have, in their distinctive ways, questioned these dominant logics of representing adivasi politics vis-à-vis the modern Indian state (Béteille 1974; Chatterjee 2013; Guha 1999; Prasad 2003; Sivaramakrishnan 1999; see also Chapter 11 in this volume). The two case studies in this chapter zoom in on intergenerational and gender divides within rural adivasi communities, and highlight how these intracommunity divides mirror divisions within modern state imaginaries. I rely here on my fieldwork in contemporary Jharkhand as well as a critical reading of secondary sources on Jharkhand and other "tribal" regions in India and beyond. Might the apparent opposition between "state" and "tribe," I ask, be better characterized as an intimate antagonism? If so, what might be the implications of such a characterization of adivasi–state relations for global debates over indigeneity and its futures?

Case Study 1

"Sacrifice your today for the nation's brighter tomorrow." This was Prime Minister Jawaharlal Nehru's call to his fellow citizens in the first decade after independence. "We have to make them [adivasis] progress," he proclaimed. "What is good in the rest of India will, of course, be adapted by them gradually" (Singh 1989: 125). At the same time, Nehru hoped to avoid "dispossessing the tribal people" and causing "the economy of the tribal areas to be upset" (ibid.: 124). A delicate balance between the demands of economic modernization and those of cultural conservation thus characterized Nehruvian policy on the "tribal" areas demarcated by the last colonial constitution for India in 1935, as well as the subsequent postcolonial constitution of 1950. But if adivasis in the margins of the fledgling postcolony had to sometimes suffer during the process of modernization, Nehru believed, they ought to "suffer in the interest of the country" (cited in Ghosh 2006: 65). Since Nehru's time, the "greater common good" of the postcolony has remained the principal justification for displacing and dispossessing adivasi populations in the course of what Marx (1967: 714–15) called the "primitive accumulation of capital" (Roy 1999). In the context of Jharkhand, some writers have gone so far as to invoke the notion of "internal colonialism" (Hechter 1975) to describe the relations between the postcolonial Indian state and its adivasi margins (Das 1992; Devalle 1992; Sinha 1973). Elsewhere, on India's northeastern frontier, the question has been raised whether the "postcolonial" has truly begun (Kar 2009).

One of the earliest public sector undertakings in postcolonial India, Heavy Engineering Corporation (HEC) was established in 1958 on the outskirts of the city of Ranchi, now capital of Jharkhand (then south Bihar). Roylen Gudiya of Lohajimi village recalled in a conversation with me what happened then: "They did not care that our *sasandiris* [burial stones] and *sarnas* [sacred groves] mean everything for us Mundas. They dispossessed the villagers, stomped all over their lands, and desecrated their ancestral faith. No one protested, no one resisted; they kept quiet because they did not know better."

Around the same time, the government of the state of Bihar, within which Jharkhand was then subsumed, began surveying villages on the banks of the Koel and Karo rivers. This was the first step taken towards a major hydroelectric power project that promised to bring electricity to this "backward" adivasi region. Little else happened until 1976, when the headman of Lohajimi, Soma Munda, returned to his ancestral village. Soma had served as a mechanic in the Indian army for twenty-one years, traveling to the frontiers of the postcolony in Kashmir and the equally contentious areas bordering Bangladesh and China. He recalled for me an occasion when the army was setting up a camp in Kashmir and simply "kicked out" the local villagers in order to go about their business. He, like Roylen, also knew about the fate of those displaced by HEC in the Nehruvian era. But Soma was determined that his people would not suffer the same fate as those victims.

In 1976, the Bihar state government sent in engineers and workers to the villages along the Karo river. They were supposed to complete survey and measurement work in the area before embarking on dam-building activities there and along the Koel river farther north. As the village headman or *munda*, Soma exercised his traditional authority to mobilize villagers in what he called the "inherently consensual and democratic ways of adivasi communities" to protest and resist the proposed hydroelectric project. This traditional authority had been shored up since the late colonial period by officials who had worked alongside adivasi headmen and elders to compile, codify, and enforce regimes of customary law in Jharkhand and elsewhere in "tribal" or scheduled areas (Cederlöf 2008; Karlsson 2011; Sen 2012). Faced with the proposed submergence of 256 villages by two dams on the Koel and Karo rivers, 44 and 55 meters respectively in height, and connected by a 34.7-meter canal (Ghosh 2006: 67), villagers were instructed by Soma Munda and his companions to resist peacefully. Initially, they demanded that all labor be done by local workers alone, not by Bihari plainsmen from superior caste backgrounds, which prevented them from dining with villagers. This demand went unmet. Then, the Karo Jan Sangathan, headed by Soma, declared a curfew, to prevent anyone from entering or exiting the villages in the proposed dam area. Mimicking state actions in this manner, Soma ensured that the government engineers and workers, who would not accept food or water from adivasi villagers, were compelled to ask for supplies from the subdivisional headquarters, over ten kilometers away. "They would bring water in tanks that would stop at the village boundary, from where the junior officers had to carry it in containers into their camps. It was great fun watching them toil in the sun," says Soma. "We were determined to resist and protest, but peacefully. No arms or violence. If we got violent, they'd brand us as extremists [*ugravadi*], kick us out in an instant, and lay claim to all our lands."

As dam building proceeded slowly but surely, new forms of organization and protest strategies evolved. The Jan Sangathans ("Popular Fronts") on the Koel and Karo rivers were merged into a single antidam movement. The new Koel-Karo Jan Sangathan began to invoke adivasi customs strategically to oppose dam building, fully aware of the nature of customary laws that were in force locally as well as the state's view of them as nature-worshipping, forest-dwelling primitives. Soma explained to me: "We told them that we, adivasis, have only three things: *sasan*, *sarna*, and the CNT Act." The last of these is the Chota Nagpur Tenancy Act, a colonial-era law dating back to 1908, which prescribes rules for the ownership as well as the sale and transfer of adivasi lands. "These are tribal lands," Soma proceeded, "defined by our religious customs and protected by law. We cannot allow them to be submerged. Koel-Karo *alo thalouka* [must stop]." Forced into negotiations by 1987, the Bihar state government offered to re-create adivasi villages elsewhere along with their *sasans* and *sarnas* as well as schools and hospitals. The offer followed a Nehruvian script of modernity: dams, as "temples of modern India," would bring electricity, employment, education, and healthcare in their wake. In response, Soma told government officials: "Choose one village along each river, and resettle them according to proper tribal rites and customs. If you can do it, we will let you proceed with your work. Otherwise, you must leave." The government failed to keep its side of the promise, of course. But it also refused to leave.

The Koel-Karo Jan Sangathan was far from daunted, however. They shrewdly invoked customary arrangements to combat the government's obstinacy. The Sangathan instructed villagers to plant corn around government camps. "They were outwitted," recalls Roylen Gudiya. "If they stepped on our corn, we could lodge a case against them and demand compensation." Government officials had no choice but to tiptoe in and out of their camps every day. Next, the Sangathan passed a resolution to prevent these officials from accessing the nearby forests for firewood or purchasing it from villagers. It argued that forest regulations and customary laws assigned adivasi villagers the exclusive right to such use of the forests. Non-adivasis claiming the same rights would be designated as encroachers and subject to punishment under law. Soon after, the Sangathan, under Soma's leadership, passed another resolution to state that anyone living in government camps could not defecate in the village because that would necessarily pollute the *sarnas*. "We compelled them to basically cook, eat, and shit inside their camps," said Soma. In the light of these indignities, the Bihar government engineers and their staff beat a hasty retreat under the cover of darkness. Soma could barely suppress his smile when he told me that the Sangathan had "made the *sarkar* [state] bend to [their] will" through their reliance on custom, law, and clever but peaceful protest tactics.

In 2003, the chief minister of Jharkhand, Arjun Munda, officially scrapped the Koel-Karo project, though the specter of a possible return continues to loom today. For a movement led by and for adivasi villagers, its success contrasts strikingly with the celebrated Narmada anti-dam movement, led by middle-class activists and celebrity cheerleaders (Nilsen 2010; Whitehead 2010). As an anthropologist who participated in and studied the Koel-Karo movement extensively, Kaushik Ghosh (2006: 69) writes:

> For journalists, the presence of urban middle-class activists at the heart of the NBA [Narmada Bachao Andolan] has been a key point of attraction, identification and communication. This presence could catch their imagination, they could relate to the middle-class leadership packaged into the familiar narrative of sacrifice where a privileged, elite person "gives up" his or her privileges and goes to awaken and mobilize the oppressed masses. This narrative form has direct continuity with the form of the

Indian nationalist biography of the nation's leaders: the unconscious, pre-political phase of life, the coming into awareness and the eventual assumption of leadership in mobilizing the people against the (colonial) state.

Soma, too, exclaimed with more than a small measure of pride: "We don't need to hold any meetings or rallies in Ranchi or Delhi. We are not like Narmada Bachao of Medha Patekar [sic]. Our politics is local. We will resist them here on our turf."

Soma and his companions had talked back to the state in its own language of "primitivism" (Chandra 2013a), itself the product of negotiations between adivasi headmen and paternalistic state officials since the mid nineteenth century. Strategic essentialism, in Spivak's sense, is alive and well in such circumstances. But the Koel-Karo Jan Sangathan went a step further, by reading the law back to the postcolonial state too, reminding it of a binding constitutional commitment to protect adivasi lands from alienation. This kind of claim making from below by rural subjects has been termed "rightful resistance" in the context of contemporary China by Kevin O'Brien and Lianjiang Li (2006). It is a classic instance of a "within-system form[s] of contention in the reform, not revolution, paradigm" (O'Brien 2013: 1,058). Contentious politics of this kind do not seek to negate, but to negotiate with the political authority represented by modern states. There is more than a slight resemblance, of course, between rightful resistance and another within-system form of contention, James Scott's (1985) "weapons of the weak" or everyday forms of peasant resistance against landed superiors. Rightful resistance adapts traditional weapons of the weak by the rural poor to a new context of claim making vis-à-vis the modern state. The performance of subaltern resistance-as-negotiation invokes and deploys adivasi customs and history creatively against a powerful state, yet "off stage," participants joke about how their ancestors, who formed these villages two or three centuries ago, did not bring any *sasans* and *sarnas* with them at all (cf. Scott 1990). The logic of resistance-as-negotiation is, therefore, endogenous to that of power, which is, ironically, what makes it effective in achieving its aims (Chandra 2015b; Haynes and Prakash 1992; Mitchell 1990). This is how tribe and state constitute each other in the margins of modern India.

Case Study 2

It is important to realize that the Koel-Karo Jan Sangathan's success is not appreciated by everyone locally. Kalyan, for instance, is a young man from the nearby village of Tapkara, who resents the celebration of custom by older activists such as Soma and Roylen.[2] In a long diatribe against the village elders who led the Sangathan, Kalyan said: "What has the CNT Act done for us? We have been dispossessed again and again for the past century. Our elders keep acting like the *junglis* the government thinks we are: venerating ancestor spirits [*bhuts*], drinking rice beer [*hanria*], making sacrifices of fowl at the time of sowing and harvest. You are an educated person from the city: does anyone in Delhi believe that killing a chicken will bring more rain to the fields?" Another young Christian Munda man, Benjamin, points to widespread discontent with the elders in Munda villages: "In every village, the young and the old are at odds with each other nowadays. Our tradition is simply to listen to what the elders say. We must farm for them, our wives and sisters must cook and prepare rice beer for them. What is so good about such traditions?"

These voices of discontent, I found, point to deep-seated intergenerational and gendered conflicts within rural adivasi communities in Jharkhand. These intracommunity conflicts within villages are anything but new in the region: there is plenty of evidence of the same conflicts in the colonial archives (see, e.g., Sinha 2005). Nor is it the case that such conflicts are peculiar to rural Jharkhand: the Narmada valley in western India, for instance, exhibits strikingly similar tendencies with vital consequences for social movements and resettlement operations there (Thakur 2014). Even outside India, say, in West Africa, there is ample evidence of intergenerational and gender divides at the heart of civil wars and iconoclastic movements directed against the traditional authority of male elders in "tribal" society (McGovern 2012; Richards 1996; Sarró 2008). Young men and women thus form "war machines," as Danny Hoffman (2011) explains with the help of a term drawn from Gilles Deleuze's writings, as they seek to overturn established authority and replace it with new models of legitimate authority cast in their own irreverent image.

The politics of youth and gender have been at the heart of the Maoist movement in rural Jharkhand. Young women have typically comprised a clear majority among the armed Maoist cadres in Jharkhand, a significant anomaly in its overall operations across central and eastern India. This state of affairs in Jharkhand could not be more different from those in the Maoists' strongholds in the plains of central and south Bihar, where men from subordinated caste backgrounds have taken the fight to their oppressors from the landed dominant castes since the 1980s (Bhatia 2005; Kunnath 2012). In Jharkhand, over the past decade, the Maoists have offered non-farm, non-traditional livelihood options for young men and women. Where young men are keen to move away from farming and where women are prohibited by patriarchal custom from even touching agricultural implements, Maoism and migration to megacities have emerged as the two principal alternatives for adivasi youth. Victoria, an Oraon domestic worker in Delhi, pointed this out to a researcher recently: "Young women like me only have two ways of coming out of the household before marriage, to migrate for domestic work to a large city or join the Maoist movement" (Wadhawan 2013: 47). Alpa Shah (2006) has found that seasonal migrants from rural Jharkhand, especially women, discover spaces of freedom in big cities, away from the taboos and restrictions of traditional adivasi village life. On these trips away from rural Jharkhand, love affairs are common, although in most cases they would be deemed illicit by elders back in the village. As we can learn from the recent gang rape of a Santal woman, accused of having an affair with a Muslim man from a neighboring town, so-called "traditional" sanctions against errant women are imposed with a vengeance, especially when patriarchal honor and community pride are at stake (Chandra 2014). The "traditional" or customary gerontocratic order places clear restrictions on sexual and marital unions within clans of a tribe and across tribes. By contrast, the Maoists not only do not object to, but actively encourage marriages across class, ethnic, and religious lines. The simplicity of Maoist marriages, too, contrasts with the more ritually elaborate traditional ceremonies overseen by the *pahan* or village priest. In matters of domesticity and work alike, therefore, powerful incentives have attracted young women and men to the Maoist "war machine."

Within Maoist ranks, adivasi youth enter a parallel universe of "modern" comradeship, in and of itself a critique of traditional village society. Maoist cadres participate in campaigns to raise the minimum wage, to ensure MNREGA (Mahatma National Rural Employment Guarantee Act) funds are paid fully and in a timely fashion, to help build homes for the poorer villagers, and to redistribute lands that are illegally held by non-tribals among the poorest. In Chatra district, at one point, the Maoists were even offering cheap loans at 2 percent interest per annum (*Hindustan Times* 2009). NGOs working in central and southern Jharkhand have rarely, if ever, been prevented by the Maoists from working for grassroots development, including in cases when their activities dovetail nicely with New Delhi's counter-insurgency plans. The fiscal structure depends almost entirely on local forms of taxation (*rangdari*), especially on high-value forest products such as the lac resin and *tendu* leaves (Chandra n.d.; Suykens 2010). The need to resort to the "selective elimination" of an odd policeman, forester, or local trader is actually less common than is often assumed. Fear of the gun typically works just as well, if not better, than the gun itself. Unsurprisingly, the greatest critics of Maoist youth are the village elders, natural defenders of the traditional Munda way of life. When discussing the raging Maoist insurgency in rural Jharkhand in 2009–10, Soma Munda, the Lohajimi-based leader of the Koel-Karo anti-dam movement, spoke to me of "misguided youth" and the "romance of violence." Others, such as Sukhram Hao, a retired schoolteacher in the nearby town of Khunti, adopted a harsher tone to condemn the adivasi youth who joined the Maoists: "These party people are destroying our culture [*sanskriti*]. They don't care at all for the past or for us elders. When we were young, we always listened to our parents. But our children will not do so. This is the sad state of affairs today." There can be little doubt that village elders, recognized by colonial and postcolonial states as bearers of customary or traditional authority, have found themselves under attack from young men and women who refuse to accept their authority as legitimate. The elders' politics must, perforce, be anti-Maoist.

The story of Masi Charan Purty, one of the best-known Maoist icons in central Jharkhand, neatly illustrates the aforementioned points about adivasi youth politics and the desire to erect new forms of legitimate political authority. Masi's fame ascended to the status of folklore after he contested the Jharkhand state elections in December 2009. A shy, intelligent boy educated by Catholic missionaries in the highland village of Bandgaon in West Singhbhum district, Masi moved to the capital city of Ranchi to pursue a Bachelor's degree in Commerce. By all accounts, he was a good student, and a bright future lay ahead of him. However, in 2003, a couple of years into his degree, he found his family embroiled in a land dispute with the village headman or *munda*. With the headman's contacts in the local police, the Purty family faced the risk of losing its family plot. The legal system in these adivasi villages, as elsewhere in India, was so far skewed in favor of the dominant lineages of rural society that a fair fight in court would have been nearly impossible. So, when the local Maoist unit offered its help, Masi could hardly refuse. He took on the village headman, literally, and ensured his family could hold onto their land. But there was no going back for Masi. He joined the Maoists in Khunti district, and rose swiftly to become a key lieutenant of the area commander, Kundan Pahan.

A couple of years into his new job, Masi led a Maoist operation to rescue female comrades from a detention facility for women in Hatia, barely five kilometers from the state capital of Ranchi. These young women, mostly adivasis from nearby villages in Ranchi and Khunti districts in central Jharkhand, had been arrested for their participation in local Maoist party activities. Like Masi, they too had escaped the traditional patriarchal and gerontocratic set-up of their rural homes, in pursuit of new forms of comradeship within the Maoist movement. One of the women arrested and then rescued in the Masi-led break-in at the Hatia detention facility was Masi's future wife, Protima. Unlike the other women, Protima came from a village in Northeast India on the border between the states of Assam and Meghalaya. After running away from home as a teenager and working in Shillong and Delhi as a domestic worker, she had ended up with the Maoist women by sheer chance. They had rescued her from the rail tracks, where she was attempting to commit suicide because, as Masi put it, "life had nothing left to offer [her]." She had been abused as a domestic worker in Delhi and had no home to go back to. The Maoist women took Protima under their wing, nursing her back to health and teaching her the party's basic gospel of personal and social liberation.

Both Masi and Protima had seemingly entered the local Maoist ranks by accident rather than design, a fact that both have repeatedly emphasized to me. Theirs was a shotgun marriage. Protima could not, as she put it, refuse him. Masi, by this time, had run into a glass ceiling within the local Maoist organization. He had served as deputy to the area commander, Kundan, who himself had not risen up the organizational ladder in nearly two decades. With his ambitions frustrated within Maoist ranks, Masi was keenly seeking alternatives. Protima, in turn, was not looking forward to a life dictated by Maoist discipline and jungle warfare. She told me: "We couldn't even talk to each other like we are now. We didn't feel a personal connection with them. One day, five of us, including Masi and me, ran away from the [Maoists] and came back to our village here in Bandgaon. We started our own [rebel] group, settling old scores with the local *munda* and ensuring people like us could hold onto their land without the elders deciding everything."

This new breakaway group was named the Jharkhand Liberation Tigers (JLT), though they now call themselves the People's Liberation Front of India (PLFI) to indicate their national ambition. In reality, however, the PLFI operates in Khunti and West Singhbhum districts, where it enjoys an uneasy, fractious relationship with its parent organization. Masi has been in jail since 2008; the PLFI supports his wife and two sons, paying for their daily expenses and school fees.

Many locals believe that Masi actually won the Khunti seat on a Jharkhand Mukti Morcha (JMM) ticket in the state election in December 2009, but bribery and vote rigging helped his Bharatiya Janata Party (BJP) rival, Nilkanth Singh Munda, win officially by 438 votes. Protima told me, "we were celebrating at the election center at 4.30 [p.m.], and went off to the village to tell everyone. Later, we were told that cash-filled boxes meant for sweetmeats were taken into the [counting] office by BJP party workers, and the ballot boxes [sic] were subsequently tampered with."

By Indian standards, 438 votes is a slender margin of victory, and popular rumors of electoral fraud say as much about how Mundas see the state today (Shah 2007) as about the actual course of events on election day. Today, Masi is a modern Munda youth icon: he married whom he wished, regardless of ethnicity or religion; he used the power of his gun to fight for the poor; he settled land disputes extra-judicially against the interests of the rural elite and policemen in their pay; he avoided what his followers call "mind-numbing" rituals. This is the example through which the PLFI wishes to remake village communities in central Jharkhand. Despite being in jail, Masi was certain that he would contest the next state election, and remained confident of an outright victory.

It is important to recognize that Masi and other adivasi youth in rural Jharkhand are as much in dialogue with the postcolonial Indian state as with the elders of their own communities. As Philip Abrams pointed out long ago, the state–society binary is itself illusory: "[T]he state is not the reality which stands behind the mask of political practice. It is itself the mask which prevents our seeing political practice as it is" (Abrams 1988: 82). Students of power and resistance have thus sought to transcend this binary by examining how state and society shape each other in everyday life (Fuller and Bénéï 2001; Migdal 2001). Accordingly, the logic of resistance, conceptualized as the negotiation of everyday relations of power in society, cannot be regarded simply as a governmental affair. It is, equally, about the constitution of a social "field of struggles" (Bourdieu 1984: 244) and contestation therein, whether on the basis of class, ethnicity, gender, or, as in this instance, generational differences. The rural adivasi "community" we encounter today is far from a vestige of a pristine precolonial past, but an artifact of the constitution of modern state–society relations in India with its peculiar set of intergenerational conflicts that define the nature and limits of governmentality. Intergenerational conflicts within this "community," therefore, map onto competing statist visions of adivasi communities as well as the ways by which adivasi subjects negotiate the modern Indian state today.

Conclusion

In this chapter, I have shown two different ways in which adivasi subjects respond to two faces of the postcolonial Indian state. They can play helpless victim before the state and civil society in order to make claims on them vis-à-vis the complementary domains of custom and law. Yet they can also fit the savage slot by invoking the bloodthirsty image of the tribal rebel. Academic scholarship and media coverage routinely replicate, circulate, and legitimize these images, reifying them as the "truth" about adivasis as quintessential subaltern actors. Scraping beneath the surface, however, we can appreciate how this two-faced "tribal" subject promoted by our pundits may be a mirror image of the duplicitous state in the margins of postcolonial India (Nelson 2004). The state pledges to protect adivasi land rights and empower local democratic institutions, yet it also covets the minerals and forests around their dwellings and auctions off their lands to the highest bidder. Thereafter, the adivasi tribal subject is constituted as "poor," and hence a worthy object for the multi-million dollar poverty industry. Cunningly, the state is often described as being "absent" from tribal areas (Misra and Pandita 2011), whereas it may, in fact, be omnipresent. It suffuses the processes of self-making and community-making for adivasi subjects, causing them to mirror the two-facedness of the state.

The gender and intergenerational struggles within Munda villages in Khunti district today blur the distinction between what Chris Fuller and Véronique Bénéï (2001) term "the everyday state and society." Whereas village elders resort to their customary privileges to defend a "traditional" anthropological vision of community, young adivasi men and women are determined to remake the community in their own "modern" image. These everyday social antagonisms are intimate, and so, too, are the negotiations of power within the governmental realm that follow. Peaceful and violent repertoires of resistance-as-negotiation compete with each other within rural adivasi communities, but they are also interlocking political strategies that enable adivasis to negotiate the terms of their subjecthood in postcolonial India.

Quite apart from romanticized representations of adivasis as subaltern rebels *par excellence,* we find, in Jharkhand and beyond, empirical cases of adivasi resistance, both violent and peaceful, negotiating rather than negating modern state power. Thus, we see adivasi youth enter the electoral fray after their Maoist adventures, even as their elders invoke colonial anthropological notions of the "tribe" to talk back to the state in its own languages of customary law. The contradictory tropes and images of modern state making in these tribal margins have defined adivasi subjectivities recursively. In turn, these political subjects have reworked the logics and languages of the modern state to remake it from below, thereby remaking their own "communities" in the course of resistance-as-negotiation. The antagonisms between adivasis and the postcolonial state in India today are, therefore, far more intimate than they are often taken to be. Students of indigeneity worldwide will find that this thesis carries relevance far beyond the South Asian region. My argument resonates strongly with those of Latin Americanists such as Gilbert Joseph and Daniel Nugent (1994) and Wolfgang Gabbert (2001), Africanists such as Paul Richards (1996) and Mahmood Mamdani (1996), and Southeast Asianists such as Anna Tsing (1993) and Tania Li (2007). If "state" and "tribe" are mutually constituted, this is far from an arcane academic discovery. The centrality of the modern state in adivasi/indigenous lives is an inescapable empirical reality that no amount of anthropological romanticizing can wish away.

Uday Chandra (PhD, Yale) is Assistant Professor of Government at Georgetown University, Qatar. He holds a PhD in political science from Yale University, and received the 2013 Sardar Patel Award for writing the best dissertation in a US university on any aspect of modern South Asia. His research lies at the intersection between critical agrarian studies, political anthropology, postcolonial theory, and South Asian studies. His work has been published in the *Law & Society Review, Interventions, Critical Sociology, Social Movement Studies, New Political Science, The Journal of Contemporary Asia, Contemporary South Asia,* and the *Indian Economic & Social History Review*. Chandra has co-edited volumes and journal special issues on the ethics of self-making in modern South Asia, subaltern politics and the state in contemporary India, caste relations in colonial and postcolonial eastern India, and social movements in rural India today.

Notes

1. For deeper discussion of these terms and the politics associated with each of them, see Chandra (2015a). In this chapter, I use the term "adivasi" consistently throughout because it is most widely accepted across academic and activist milieus.
2. Here and elsewhere in this section, the real names of my interlocutors have been changed to protect their identities.

Bibliography

Abrams, Philip. 1988. "Notes on the Difficulty of Studying the State." *Journal of Historical Sociology* 1(1): 58–89.

Banerjee, Prathama. 2006a. *Politics of Time: "Primitives" and History-Writing in a Colonial Society.* New Delhi: Oxford University Press.
———. 2006b. "Culture/Politics: The Irresoluble Double-Bind of the Indian Adivasi." *Indian Historical Review* 33: 99–126.
Bates, Crispin and Alpa Shah (eds). 2014. *Savage Attack: Adivasis and Insurgency in India.* New Delhi: Social Science Press.
Bessire, Lucas. 2014. "The Rise of Indigenous Hypermarginality: Native Culture as a Neoliberal Politics of Life." *Current Anthropology* 55(3): 276–95.
Béteille, André. 1974. "Tribe and Peasantry." In *Six Essays in Comparative Sociology.* New Delhi: Oxford University Press, pp. 58–74.
———. 1998. "The Idea of Indigenous People." *Current Anthropology* 39(2): 187–92.
Bhadra, Gautam. 1985. "Four Rebels of Eighteen Fifty-Seven." In *Subaltern Studies IV,* ed. Ranajit Guha, 229–275. New Delhi: Oxford University Press.
Bhatia, Bela. 2005. "The Naxalite Movement in Central Bihar." *Economic and Political Weekly* 40: 1,536–43.
Bourdieu, Pierre. 1984. *Distinction: A Social Critique of the Judgment of Taste.* Cambridge, MA: Harvard University Press.
Cederlöf, Gunnel. 2008. *Landscapes and the Law: Environmental Politics, Regional Histories, and Contests over Nature.* Ranikhet: Permanent Black.
Chakrabarty, Dipesh. 2011. "History and the Politics of Recognition." In *Theorizing the Present: Essays for Partha Chatterjee,* ed. Anjan Ghosh et al., 21–34. New Delhi: Oxford University Press.
Chandra, Uday. n.d. "The State, Popular Resistance, and the Political Economy of Forests in Contemporary Eastern India," Unpublished manuscript.
———. 2013a. "Liberalism and Its Other: The Politics of Primitivism in Colonial and Postcolonial Indian Law." *Law & Society Review* 47(1): 135–68.
———. 2013b. "Going Primitive: The Ethics of Indigenous Rights Activism in Contemporary Jharkhand." *SAMAJ* 7. Special issue on "The Ethics of Self-Making in Postcolonial India." Retrieved 11 December 2016 from http://samaj.revues.org/3600.
———. 2013c. "Negotiating Leviathan: Statemaking and Resistance in the Margins of Modern India," (PhD dissertation, Yale University, New Haven, CT).
———. 2014. "Rashomon Revisited: Contesting the 'Tribe' in Contemporary India." *Economic & Political Weekly* 49(17): 15–17.
———. 2015a. "Adivasis in Contemporary India: Engagements with the State, Non-state Actors, and the Capitalist Economy." In *Routledge Handbook of Contemporary India,* ed. Knut A. Jacobsen, 297–310. London and New York: Routledge.
———. 2015b. "Rethinking Subaltern Resistance." *Journal of Contemporary Asia* 45(4): 563–73.
Chatterjee, Indrani. 2013. *Forgotten Friends: Monks, Marriages, and Memories in Northeast India.* New Delhi: Oxford University Press.
Chaudhury, Shoma. 2009. "Halt the Violence! Give me 72 Hours." *Tehelka* 21 (November).
Clastres, Pierre. 1987. *Society against the State: Essays in Political Anthropology.* New York: Zone Books.

Das, Victor. 1992. *Jharkhand: Castle over Graves*. New Delhi: Inter-India Publications.
Devalle, Susanna B.C. 1992. *Discourses of Ethnicity: Culture and Protest in Jharkhand*. New Delhi: Sage Publications.
Fuller, Chris J. and Véronique Bénéï (eds). 2001. *The Everyday State and Society in Modern India*. London: C. Hurst & Co.
Gabbert, Wolfgang. 2001. "Social Categories, Ethnicity, and the State in Mexico." *Journal of Latin American Studies* 33(3): 459–84.
Ghosh, Kaushik. 2006. "The Modernity of Primitive India: Adivasi Ethnicity in Jharkhand and the Formation of a National Modern," PhD dissertation. Princeton University.
Guha, Ramachandra. 2007. "Adivasis, Naxalites and Indian Democracy." *Economic and Political Weekly* 42: 3,305–12.
Guha, Ranajit. 1983. *Elementary Aspects of Peasant Insurgency in Colonial India*. New Delhi: Oxford University Press.
Guha, Sumit. 1999. *Environment and Ethnicity in India, 1200–1991*. Cambridge: Cambridge University Press.
Hale, Charles. 2004. "Rethinking Indigenous Politics in the Era of the Indio Permitido." *NACLA Report on the Americas* 38(2): 16–21.
———. 2005. "Neoliberal Multiculturalism." *POLAR* 28(1): 10–19.
Haynes, Douglas and Gyan Prakash. 1992. "Introduction." In *Contesting Power: Resistance and Everyday Social Relations in South Asia*. Berkeley, CA: University of California Press.
Hechter, Michael. 1975. *Internal Colonialism: The Celtic Fringe in British National Development, 1536–1966*. London: Routledge and Kegan Paul.
Hindustan Times. 2009. "Now Naxals Offer Hassle-Free Banking for Poor." 21 May.
Hodgson, Dorothy. 2011. *Being Maasai, Becoming Indigenous: Postcolonial Politics in a Neoliberal World*. Bloomington, IN: Indiana University Press.
Hoffman, Danny. 2011. *The War Machines: Young Men and Violence in Sierra Leone and Liberia*. Durham, NC: Duke University Press.
Joseph, Gilbert and Daniel Nugent (eds). 1994. *Everyday Forms of State Formation: Revolution and the Negotiation of Rule in Modern Mexico*. Durham, NC: Duke University Press.
Jung, Courtney. 2006. *The Moral Force of Indigenous Politics: Critical Liberalism and the Zapatistas*. New York: Cambridge University Press.
Kar, Bodhisattva. 2009. "When Was the Postcolonial? A History of Policing Impossible Lines." In *Beyond Counter-insurgency: Breaking the Impasse in Northeast India*, ed. Sanjib Baruah, 49–77. New Delhi: Oxford University Press.
Karlsson, Bengt G. 2011. *Unruly Hills: A Political Ecology of India's Northeast*. New York: Berghahn Books.
Kela, Shashank. 2012. *A Rogue and Peasant Slave: Adivasi Resistance, 1800–2000*. New Delhi: Navayana Publishers.
Kunnath, George. 2012. *Rebels from the Mud Houses: Dalits and the Making of the Maoist Revolution in Bihar*. New Delhi: Social Science Press.
Kuper, Adam. 2003. "The Return of the Native." *Current Anthropology* 44(3): 389–402.

Lévi-Strauss, Claude. 1969. *The Raw and the Cooked.* New York: Harper & Row.
Li, Tania M. 2007. *The Will to Improve: Governmentality, Development, and the Practice of Politics.* Durham, NC: Duke University Press.
———. 2010. "Indigeneity, Capitalism, and the Management of Dispossession." *Current Anthropology* 51(3): 385–414.
Mamdani, Mahmood. 1996. *Citizen and Subject: Contemporary Africa and the Legacy of Late Colonialism.* Princeton, NJ: Princeton University Press.
———. 2013. "What Is a Tribe?" *London Review of Books* 34(17): 20–22.
Marx, Karl. 1967. *Capital: A Critique of Political Economy,* Vol. I. New York: International Publishers.
Mayaram, Shail. 2003. *Against History, against State: Counterperspectives from the Margins.* New York: Columbia University Press.
McCormack, Fiona. 2012. "Indigeneity as Process: Māori Claims and Neoliberalism." *Social Identities* 18(4): 417–34.
McGovern, Mike. 2012. *Unmasking the State: Making Guinea Modern.* Chicago, IL: University of Chicago Press.
Migdal, Joel S. 2001. *State in Society: Studying How States and Societies Transform and Constitute One Another.* Cambridge: Cambridge University Press.
Misra, Neelesh and Rahul Pandita. 2011. *The Absent State: Insurgency as an Excuse for Misgovernance.* Gurgaon: Hachette.
Mitchell, Timothy. 1990. "Everyday Metaphors of Power." *Theory and Society* 19: 545–77.
———. 1991. "The Limits of the State: Beyond Statist Approaches and Their Critics." *American Political Science Review* 85(1): 77–96.
Muehlmann, Shaylih. 2009. "How Do Real Indians Fish? Neoliberal Multiculturalism and Contested Indigeneities in the Colorado Delta." *American Anthropologist* 111(4): 468–79.
Nelson, Diane M. 2004. "Anthropologist Discovers Legendary Two-Faced Indian! Margins, the State, and Duplicity in Postwar Guatemala." In *Anthropology in the Margins of the State,* ed. Veena Das and Deborah Poole, 117–140. Santa Fe, NM: School of American Research Press.
Nigam, Aditya. 2010. "The Rumour of Maoism." *Seminar* 607.
Nilsen, Alf Gunvald. 2010. *Dispossession and Resistance in India: The River and the Rage.* Abingdon and New York: Routledge.
O'Brien, Kevin J. 2013. "Rightful Resistance Revisited." *The Journal of Peasant Studies* 40(6): 1,051–62.
O'Brien, Kevin J. and Lianjiang Li. 2006. *Rightful Resistance in Rural China.* New York: Cambridge University Press.
Padel, Felix. 2009. *Sacrificing People: Invasions of a Tribal Landscape.* New Delhi: Orient Blackswan.
Patel, Aakaar. 2012. "The Ghost's in the Details, Ma'am." *Outlook,* 30 April.
Planning Commission of India. 2008. *Development Challenges in Extremist Affected Areas: Report of an Expert Group.* New Delhi: Government of India.
Prasad, Archana. 2003. *Against Ecological Romanticism: Verrier Elwin and the Making of an Anti-modern Tribal Identity.* New Delhi: Three Essays Collective.
Richards, Paul. 1996. *Fighting for the Rain Forest: War, Youth and Resources in Sierra Leone.* London: International African Institute.

Rolph-Trouillot, Michel. 2003. "Anthropology and the Savage Slot: The Poetics and Politics of Otherness." In *Global Transformations: Anthropology and the Modern World*, 7–28. New York: Palgrave Macmillan.

Roy, Arundhati. 1999. "The Greater Common Good." *Outlook*, 24 May.

Sarró, Ramon. 2008. *The Politics of Religious Change on the Upper Guinea Coast: Iconoclasm Done and Undone*. Edinburgh: Edinburgh University Press.

Scott, James C. 1985. *Weapons of the Weak: Everyday Forms of Peasant Resistance*. New Haven, CT: Yale University Press.

———. 1990. *Domination and the Arts of Resistance: Hidden Transcripts*. New Haven, CT: Yale University Press.

———. 2009. *The Art of Not Being Governed: An Anarchist History of Upland Southeast Asia*. New Haven, CT: Yale University Press.

Sen, Asoka Kumar. 2012. *From Village Elder to British Judge: Custom, Customary Law and Tribal Society*. New Delhi: Orient Blackswan.

Shah, Alpa. 2006. "The Labour of Love: Seasonal Migration from Jharkhand to the Brick Kilns of Other States in India." *Contributions to Indian Sociology* 40: 91–118.

———. 2007. "'Keeping the State Away': Democracy, Politics, and the State in India's Jharkhand." *Journal of the Royal Anthropological Institute* 13: 129–45.

———. 2010. *In the Shadows of the State: Indigenous Politics, Environmentalism, and Insurgency in Jharkhand, India*. Durham, NC: Duke University Press.

Simeon, Dilip. 2010. "Permanent Spring." *Seminar* 607.

Singh, K.S. 1989. *Jawaharlal Nehru, Tribes, and Tribal Policy: A Centennial Tribute*. Calcutta: Anthropological Survey of India.

Sinha, Sachchidananda. 1973. *The Internal Colony: A Study in Regional Exploitation*. New Delhi: Sindhu Publications.

Sinha, Shashank Shekhar. 2005. *Restless Mothers and Turbulent Daughters*. Kolkata: Stree.

Sivaramakrishnan, K. 1999. *Modern Forests: Statemaking and Environmental Change in Colonial Eastern India*. Stanford, CA: Stanford University Press.

Skaria, Ajay. 1999. *Hybrid Histories: Forests, Frontiers and Wildness in Western India*. New Delhi: Oxford University Press.

Spivak, Gayatri Chakravorty. 1988. "Can the Subaltern Speak?" In *Marxism and the Interpretation of Culture*, ed. Cary Nelson and Lawrence Grossberg. London: Macmillan, 271–313.

Suykens, Bert. 2010. "Diffuse Authority in the Beedi Commodity Chain: Naxalite and State Governance in Tribal Telangana, India." *Development and Change* 41: 153–78.

Sylvain, Renée. 2014. "Essentialism and the Indigenous Politics of Recognition in Southern Africa." *American Anthropologist* 116(2): 1–14.

Thakur, Vikramaditya. 2014. "Unsettling Modernity: Resistance and Forced Resettlement Due to Dam in Western India," PhD dissertation. Yale University, New Haven, CT.

Tsing, Anna L. 1993. *In the Realm of the Diamond Queen: Marginality in an Out-of-the-Way Place*. Princeton, NJ: Princeton University Press.

van Schendel, Willem. 2002. "Geographies of Knowing, Geographies of Ignorance: Jumping Scale in Southeast Asia." *Environment and Planning D* 20(6): 647–68.

Verghese, B.G. 2010. "Daylight at the Thousand-Star Hotel." *Outlook*, 3 May.
Visvanathan, Shiv. 2006. "The Tribal World and the Imagination of the Future." *India Together*, 14 November. Verrier Elwin Memorial Lecture. Retrieved 11 December 2016 from http://indiatogether.org/verrier-society.
Wadhawan, Neera. 2013. "Living in Domesti-City: Women and Migration for Domestic Work from Jharkhand." *Economic & Political Weekly* 48(43): 47–54.
Whitehead, Judy. 2010. *Development and Dispossession in the Narmada Valley.* New York and New Delhi: Pearson International.

10

INDIGENEITY, CULTURE, AND THE STATE
Social Change and Legal Reforms in Latin America
Wolfgang Gabbert

Introduction

"Indigeneity" and "indigenous peoples" have become hotly debated concepts in both political and academic circles in the last decades.[1] The Americas have played a crucial part in these debates, not least for the Amerindian activists' pioneering role in the international indigenous rights movement.[2] In addition, it has seemed easier to decide who was to be considered indigenous here than in other world regions. This was due to the Americas' colonial past and the subordinated role Amerindians have played in the states that came into being after independence from the European colonial powers in the late eighteenth (the United States) and early nineteenth centuries (the Latin American countries). In contrast to most Asian and African countries, the ruling groups of the independent states were culturally and, more or less, physically the heirs of the former colonizers in the Americas.[3]

Since the 1980s, constitutions have been reformed to acknowledge the multicultural and ethnically diverse character of the nation, and recognize the existing indigenous legal and political practices in many Latin American countries. Thus, a first step in creating a more accessible and more adequate legal system has been taken. However, the debate on indigenous rights in general and these legal reforms in particular touches on problematic issues such as the reification of culture. This chapter starts with a brief discussion of the state's influence on ethnic categorization, and an introduction to the historical development of colonial ethnic categories in Latin America. Then, several topics that are of key importance for understanding the implications of recent legal and constitutional changes and the character of indigenous movements are examined. These are: the notions of indigeneity and peoplehood; the political fragmentation of the Amerindian populations in Latin America; their cultural and social heterogeneity; the relationship between law and social structure; and the incidence of power relations in customary law. It is argued that much of the current debate on autonomy and the recognition of so-called indigenous customary law applies the earlier model of the nation-state, thereby running the risk of fostering new forms of cultural homogenization and sustaining the current relations of inequality and domination. Current debates about indigenous rights often ignore the recency of ethnogenesis and the increasing social differentiation within the Amerindian population that is a crucial factor for explaining the emergence of indigenous organizations on the local, national, and international levels. Thus, indigenous social movements are not the result of an "awakening" of existing units, but rather a product of recent social change. Constitutional and legal reforms in Latin America (and elsewhere) do not preserve or revive age-old traditions, but lead to the emergence of new forms of political participation and legal practice.

The State, International Organizations, and Social Categories

The state and, increasingly, international organizations (IOs), such as the United Nations and the World Bank, have played a major role in shaping ethnicity and interethnic relations in most parts of the world. They also have a profound influence on the prevailing discourse on ethnicity and rights in a society. The state and the IOs are not merely dealing with existent social or ethnic categories but frequently create new ones with their own administrative regulations. As is widely known, many "tribes" of Africa and Asia are not relics of some distant past but the outcome of administrative action by the colonial states.[4] Furthermore, the state and IOs are major distributors of resources. The criteria applied by an administration for the allocation of resources are frequently of the utmost importance for the expression of ethnicity. As Paul Brass puts it:

> Many categories and groups are not even recognized by the census authorities, that is, groups are not even counted in the literal sense of the term and, in such cases, do not "count" politically in the figurative sense of the term. Some categories and groups are singled out for special protection or privilege by the state, given or denied citizenship, given or denied proportional or extra representation in electoral constituencies

or government bodies or in government service. Some categories and groups are entitled to special protection of their language or religion or personal laws, some are not. (Brass 1991: 271)[5]

The activities and programs of governments and, more recently, of IOs play a major part in shaping the possibilities and constraints of individual actors. They may strengthen existing relations of domination by backing local elites or weaken them by directly or indirectly taking sides with subordinate groups at the local level (e.g., Brass 1991: 272–74). Therefore, social categorization (of which ethnic classification is only a part) is not simply an intellectual game. To be classed as belonging to a certain social category means to occupy a specific status position. Thus, social categories are not neutral but respected and valued differently. *Who* is allowed or obliged to occupy some social position denoted by a category is frequently as much disputed as the evaluation of the category as such. Bourdieu referred to these facts as "a forgotten dimension of class struggles" ([1979] 1987: 755).

Colonial Categories in Latin America

Iberian colonialism in Latin America, which began in the late fifteenth century, was based on a social structure consisting of groups of supposedly common ancestry (*castas*, English "castes") each endowed with legally recognized rights and duties.[6] Affiliation to the social categories of Spaniard (or Portuguese), Indian (*indígena, indio*), mestizo, or mulato was held to be determined by descent or biological criteria.[7] In reality, however, wealth and cultural adaptation occasionally permitted mobility into categories of higher status, so that a number of mestizos and Indians with sufficient property and language skills in Spanish, for example, were legally accepted as Spaniards.[8] Some Indian artisans and tradesmen in the cities became quite prosperous. Many donned European dress and became culturally Hispanicized to such a degree that by the end of the colonial period they were indistinguishable from Spaniards or mestizos. Phenotypic clues to differentiate between the various groups in colonial society had always been quite unreliable and even lost in significance when miscegenation between Iberians and Amerindians became widespread in the course of the colonial period. Status symbols such as descent, phenotype, occupation, and wealth were distributed inconsistently, making ascription of legal and social status difficult (e.g., Gabbert 2004a: 18–23; McAlister 1963: 355).

In the course of the colonial period, the mestizo group expanded enormously as a result of the miscegenation of people of different ancestries as well as the cultural Hispanicization of large parts of the indigenous population. After independence in particular, the indigenous nobility and urban artisans and tradesmen dissolved into the mestizo population. Wealth differences within the Indian village populations decreased. The category Indian became a term used more and more by urbanites and elites to refer to the poor, uneducated, and supposedly backward rural population. In the nineteenth century, racism became the leading ideology and postcolonial progress-oriented elites came to view "the Indians" as the quintessence of barbarism, to be "redeemed" either by miscegenation or civilization. Such views have survived up to the present day.

With independence, the state was conceived of as unitary and its citizens as equal before the law, and the discriminatory legal system was to be abandoned, although frequently not in practice.[9] The presence of populations from different cultural backgrounds, such as the Amerindians, was considered an obstacle to national development. Thus, government policies mostly aimed at the acculturation and assimilation of indigenous groups through education and integration into capitalist agricultural practices, in order to overcome the fundamental backwardness allegedly rooted in the culture of (indigenous) peasants.[10] Nevertheless, large sections of the population remained economically, politically, and socially excluded from mainstream society.[11]

While Amerindians in the colonial core areas (Mexico, Guatemala, and the Andean region) were freed from colonial legal restrictions, they had to face new and intensified assaults on their communal lands, propelled by expanding capitalist agriculture. Those laws of the Spanish Crown that had provided at least some protection of indigenous land rights in the colonial period were restricted or annulled. Thus, the nineteenth and early twentieth centuries were characterized not by less, but by more collective violence than most other periods in the colonial era. The expansion of haciendas and plantations, and the expropriation of village lands as part of the so-called Liberal Reforms,[12] provoked large-scale Amerindian peasant rebellions all over Latin America.[13]

Since the 1950s, living conditions in many rural areas of Latin America have further declined. Amerindian lands have been invaded by enterprises seeking to exploit oil, wood, mineral, or other resources. The advancement of cattle ranchers and poor peasants into indigenous areas has increasingly provoked conflicts. Government policies fostering the colonization of allegedly unused lands, and major infrastructure projects, such as hydroelectric dams, have contributed to these processes. Indigenous population growth has further intensified the pressure on lands and natural resources. Neoliberal government policies, fostering land privatization, the cultivation of export crops (e.g., soya), and the exploitation of natural resources have further worsened the social and economic marginalization of the indigenous population, not to mention the lower classes in general.[14] However, development policies have also had some unintended consequences, such as the emergence of an Amerindian middle class (see below), and three major changes in the general political situation in the last decades: (1) indigenous social movements, demanding political autonomy and an end to discrimination, have grown almost everywhere (e.g., Gabbert 1999a); (2) international organizations, such as the United Nations, have promoted democratization, decentralization, and respect for cultural diversity (e.g., ILO 1989; UN 2007; see also Anaya 2004: 58–72); and (3) Latin American governments have tried to regain the legitimacy they lost due to a severe economic crisis and increasing poverty (Assies 1999; van Cott 2000a). These factors facilitated a change in government attitudes to the ethnic question. Constitutional reforms took place in many countries to acknowledge the multicultural and ethnically diverse character of the nation, and to recognize indigenous autonomy rights.[15]

Indigeneity and Peoplehood

The spread of the term indigenous (French *indigène*; Spanish *indígena*) across the globe is closely related to the colonial expansion of European powers from the late fifteenth century onwards. As in Latin America, it was mainly used to distinguish the colonized from the colonizers (Daes 1996: 5). This distinction was frequently linked to the idea that the colonized had to be civilized. Article 22 of the Covenant of the League of Nations, for example, obliged the members to further the well-being and development of the "natives" or "indigenous populations" in the former "colonies and territories" of the states defeated in World War I (Daes 1996: 6; League of Nations 1919). Colonized groups as well as minorities within independent states were mostly referred to as "native inhabitants" or "indigenous populations" in need of protection due to "the deficiency in their physical and intellectual development," as the Pan-American Union put it, in its resolution XI from 21 December 1938 (cited in Daes 1996: 7; see also Lüdert 2013: 341–44). Their complete integration and assimilation into the states' national life remained the main objective of governments and IOs for several decades. An important discursive shift can be detected when comparing two ILO conventions. While Convention 107 of 1957 is directed at the "Protection and Integration of Indigenous and Other Tribal Populations in Independent

Countries," Convention 169 from 1989 refers to "Indigenous and Tribal Peoples in Independent Countries." In the discourse of indigenous movements, international organizations, and much of the recent legislation on multicultural issues in Latin America, "indigenous peoples" have become the subject of claimed or granted rights. Thus, the 2007 United Nations Declaration on the Rights of Indigenous Peoples, for example, states:

> *Article 3.* Indigenous peoples have the right to self-determination. By virtue of that right they freely determine their political status and freely pursue their economic, social and cultural development.
>
> *Article 4.* Indigenous peoples, in exercising their right to self-determination, have the right to autonomy or self-government in matters relating to their internal and local affairs ... (UN 2007: 4)

The Mexican constitution establishes:

> This Constitution recognizes and guarantees the right of the indigenous peoples and communities to their free determination and, consequently, autonomy to:
>
> I. Decide their internal forms of living together and social, economic, political, and cultural organization.
>
> II. Apply their own normative systems in the regulation and solution of their internal conflicts adhering to the Constitution, respecting the individual rights, the Human Rights and ... the dignity and integrity of the women. (Constitución ... Unidos Mexicanos, Art. 2)[16]

However, the implementation of these and similar stipulations poses serious problems, possibly the most fundamental of which is how to identify the bearers of these granted rights. Who should be considered "indigenous peoples"? While the recent UN Declaration on the Rights of Indigenous Peoples (UN 2007) avoids this issue entirely, the following paragraph provides a UN Sub-Commission's attempt at a definition, which is accepted by many activists and scholars. It states:

> Indigenous communities, peoples and nations are those which, having a historical continuity with pre-invasion and pre-colonial societies that developed on their territories, consider themselves distinct from other sectors of the societies now prevailing in those territories, or parts of them. They form at present non-dominant sectors of society and are determined to preserve, develop and transmit to future generations their ancestral territories, and their ethnic identity, as the basis for their continued existence as peoples, in accordance with their own cultural patterns, social institutions and legal systems. (UN Sub-Commission on Prevention of Discrimination and Protection of Minorities, UN Doc. E/CN.4/Sub.2/1986/7/Add.4, para. 379 [1986], quoted in Anaya 2004: 10n2)

As James Anaya (2004: 5) rightly points out, within international law and institutions a "common set of experiences rooted in historical subjugation by colonialism, or something like colonialism," is the central criterion for recognizing certain populations as "indigenous." Beyond this, indigenous movements and their "organic intellectuals" have developed a concept of indigeneity based on core values (such as reciprocity, responsibility, redistribution, and a sense that human beings are related not only to each other, but to all animals, plants, and things) common to all indigenous peoples (e.g., Harris and Wasilewski 2004).

However, the concepts of "indigenous" and "indigeneity" have come under attack from anthropologists such as Adam Kuper for "relying on obsolete anthropological notions and false ethnographic vision," and for "fostering essentialist ideologies of culture and identity, [which] may have dangerous political consequences" (2003: 395). Kuper especially criticizes the assumptions of an "authentic culture" and of a cultural and genetic continuity with an ancient past that, in the indigenous peoples' movement, forms "the bedrock of collective identity" (2003: 390, 392). He also questions the assumption, made implicitly or explicitly, in the discourse of indigenous movements that "indigenous peoples" were the descendants of the *original* inhabitants of a country, and therefore should have privileged access to its resources (Kuper 2003: 390; cf., for example, Sanders 1977: 12).[17] International organizations and many members of international law circles see "indigenous peoples" not necessarily as the first inhabitants of their habitat, but stress their occupation before the arrival of a colonizing population. ILO Convention 169, for example, states:

> This Convention applies to:
>
> (a) tribal peoples in independent countries whose social, cultural and economic conditions distinguish them from other sections of the national community, and whose status is regulated wholly or partially by their own customs or traditions or by special laws or regulations;
>
> (b) peoples in independent countries who are regarded as indigenous on account of their descent from the populations which inhabited the country, or a geographical region to which the country belongs, at the time of conquest or colonisation or the establishment of present state boundaries and who, irrespective of their legal status, retain some or all of their own social, economic, cultural and political institutions. (ILO 1989, Art. 1)

Anaya makes the point even more clearly: "They are *indigenous* because their ancestral roots are embedded in the lands in which they live, or would like to live, much more deeply than the roots of more powerful sectors of society living on the same lands or in close proximity"

(2004: 3, original emphasis). This seems to imply that the occupation by the colonists is relatively recent. While this assumption does not fit many cases in Africa, India, China, or certain Nordic countries, where the majority populations have also occupied the lands in question for millennia (e.g., Karlsson 2003: 407–15; Waldron 2002: 10), it does reflect the situation in some former European colonies, such as Canada, the US, New Zealand, Australia, and Latin America, quite correctly. In Latin America, then, there is a general consensus that the "indigenous peoples" are the descendants of the populations that the Spanish and Portuguese invaders encountered in the sixteenth century. This is evident in much of contemporary Latin American legislation. The Law of Indigenous Rights of the Mexican State of Campeche, for example, defines "indigenous peoples" as follows: "Human collectivities that, for continuing the political, economic, social, and cultural institutions of their pre-Cortesian [i.e., before the Spanish conquest by Hernán Cortés] ancestors, possess their own economic, social, cultural, and political forms of organization, and freely assert their membership in the ethnies established in the territory of the State" (Ley de Derechos ... Campeche, Art. 5-X). The respective law of the State of Chiapas considers as an "indigenous people" "one formed by persons who descend from populations that inhabited the State's territory at the time of the conquest and who speak the same language and preserve their culture and social, political, and economic institutions and practice particular habits, customs, and traditions" (Ley de Derechos ... Chiapas, Art. 3). Bolivia's constitution asserts: "A native indigenous peasant nation and people are all human collectivities that share a cultural identity, language, historical tradition, institutions, territory, and worldview that derived their existence from before the Spanish colonial invasion" (República de Bolivia 2008, Art. 30.I).

It comes as no surprise that Kuper's attack on the concept of "indigenous peoples" has triggered a lively debate between critics and defenders. However, discussions have focused mostly on indigeneity, while the problematic status of peoplehood has been generally ignored.[18]

In international political discussions, "peoplehood" has been a problem because of its association with the right to self-determination, established in the United Nations Charter. Therefore, governments only reluctantly, and after long controversies, agreed to the use of the term "peoples" in the ILO Convention 169, and then only after a clause was introduced excluding its use as having any implications regarding the rights attached to it under international law (ILO 1989, Art. 1.3; see also Anaya 2004: 59–61; Karlsson 2003: 407–10). In addition, the notion of "people" is important for suggesting the entity to which collective rights correspond (see below).

While colonial laws recognized a special category of "Indians" or indigenous people (*indios* or *indígenas*), as has been said already, the legal separation from the non-Indians fell into disuse in most Latin American countries after independence. Without a legal definition, language has become the most important trait employed in defining the so-called indigenous "peoples."[19] The categories delimited according to this criterion vary considerably in size. While there were more than a million Nahuatl speakers in Mexico around the year 2000, and almost 2.9 million people in Bolivia whose mother tongue was Quechua, Papago was spoken by fewer than 200 individuals in Mexico (LASR 2003: 9, 11). Each of the large language categories consists of several mutually incomprehensible languages and numerous local dialects. In addition, the members of the larger language categories frequently live in widely dispersed areas (Díaz-Couder 1991: 143f.; Smailus 1990: 263).

Although these language categories are generally considered "peoples" by indigenous movements, international organizations, NGOs, many governments, and the public, an ethnic consciousness encompassing all speakers, particularly in the large and medium-sized language categories (i.e., with more than 10,000 members), does not exist. Most members still consider themselves as belonging primarily to a village, local community, or region. Violent conflicts over land or water rights are quite frequent between neighboring communities.[20] Processes of ethnogenesis are relatively recent phenomena (see, e.g., Albó 1979; Gabbert 2004a).

The dominance of the local community as the key institution of social integration and as a focus of identification results from Spanish colonial policy. It destroyed all forms of indigenous political integration beyond the local level, such as the pre-conquest empires, kingdoms, and chiefdoms. Each indigenous local community ("Indian republic") was treated as an autonomous administrative unit, directly responsible to the Spanish institutions, in most Latin American regions.[21]

Due to this historical fragmentation of indigenous groups, any political institution beyond the local community that might be the bearer of autonomy rights would be a novel creation, in most cases.[22] Their legitimacy could not be derived from being rooted in tradition, but must rest on a capacity to represent broad sectors of the indigenous population. Thus, although current autonomy policies in Latin America frequently claim to preserve existing communities and their traditions, they are in fact contributing to processes of national (or ethnic) consciousness building, not unlike those of Europe in the nineteenth century.[23] In both cases, small elite groups (see below) try to disseminate an awareness of belonging to a community of fate among fairly heterogeneous aggregates of people, and base their political claims on the assumption that these communities were already present in the ancient past.[24] By claiming a century-long history for the Amerindian "peoples" or "nations" (as in the case of the Miskito, Sumu, or Rama), Miskito nationalists, for example, have tried to establish a historical continuity with earlier indigenous groups that inhabited the Atlantic coast of Nicaragua:

> We are indigenous peoples, since we are descendants of our ancestors who were the original inhabitants of this territory ... they were living in this region in the tenth century .... We inherited particular social, economic, and cultural customs from our ancestors which we have preserved up to this day and by which we are identified as a people. (MISURASATA 1982: 134f.; cf. also CNI 2001)

Up to now, Latin American legislation has on the whole avoided defining the political institutions that could administer indigenous autonomy rights beyond the local level in the future. The laws concerning the rights, culture, and organization of the Maya-speaking population in the Mexican states of Campeche and Quintana Roo are noteworthy exceptions. The laws declare a "Great Maya Council" and a "Maya Congress" as the highest bodies of political representation for the "Maya Indians" in both states (as far as Maya rights and culture are concerned) (Ley de Derechos ... Campeche, Art. 46ff.; Ley de Derechos ... Quintana Roo, Art. 51ff.). Neither the "Great Maya Councils" nor the "Maya Congresses" have historical precursors. The Maya-speaking population of the Mexican Yucatán peninsula was never politically unified. It was organized in several political entities in pre-Hispanic times, and became even more fragmented in the colonial and postcolonial eras (Gabbert 2004a: 6, 10f., 28–31, 57f., 79, 161f.; Quintal 2003: 305). In addition, the delimitation of the spheres of competence of the above-mentioned institutions does not correspond to any cultural logic, but instead follows the political boundaries of Mexican federal states created in the nineteenth and twentieth centuries. While on the one hand, Campeche and Quintana Roo are somewhat exceptional in defining higher-level indigenous institutions of representation, at the same time they exemplify the general trend in Latin American autonomy policies; that is, although the laws were passed in 2000 and 1998 respectively, the representative bodies have not yet materialized.

Cultural Heterogeneity

Echoing key elements of classical nationalist thought, the global discourse of autonomy and self-determination suggests that each indigenous "people" is characterized by a common language, culture, and social institutions. Political claims are also frequently based on these assumptions. As an indigenous leader from Mexico argued: "If we indigenous peoples are a cultural unit we should also be a political unit" (Regino 2001). Essentialist arguments often characterize the discussion about the recognition of indigenous legal practices. Not unlike the German historical school of *Jurisprudence,* founded by, among others, Karl von Savigny in the nineteenth century, it is implied that indigenous (customary) law is an expression of the spirit of the people (*Volksgeist*), and not the result of power struggles in society (cf. Savigny 1815: 6). Indigenous activists, scholars, politicians, and the wider public often assume that a coherent corpus of traditional norms, shared by all members of a people, exists, and must simply be recognized by the government (cf., e.g., CNI 2001; ECPI 1990: 2, 7–8; Ríos Morales 2001: 73–75). Cabedo Mallol, for example, suggests: "The law is a reflection of a particular culture, a worldview, which in the case of indigenous peoples ... differs substantially from Western society. Therefore, we will always find in indigenous legal systems a substrate that is an expression of these peoples' values" (2004: 78). Consequently, customs or traditions frequently play major roles in legislation on "indigenous justice." The Law on Indigenous Justice in the Mexican State of Quintana Roo, for example, determines: "The traditional judges and magistrates apply the norms of the indigenous customary law" (Ley de Justicia Indígena ... de Quintana Roo, Art. 10). And the Law for the Protection of the Maya Community of the State of Yucatán (Mexico) stipulates that Mayan law will be administered according to "their habits, customs, and traditions" (Ley para la Protección ... Yucatán, Art. 23). According to the Campeche Law on the Rights, Culture, and Organization of Indigenous Peoples and Communities, it is the responsibility of the "Great Maya Council ... to safeguard the habits, customs, traditions, and language of the Maya ethnie" (Ley de Derechos ... Campeche, Art. 48).[25] These examples not only disclose a wholly conservative view of indigeneity, but also imply an assumption of cultural homogeneity in the indigenous population. Between communities of the same language group, however, there are often major discrepancies in legally relevant norms, in addition to gender and generational differences. Important cultural institutions, such as kinship systems, may vary even between hamlets in the same community.[26]

Therefore, a recognition of indigenous customary law cannot be grounded on shared norms either at the language group level (i.e., one that defines an "indigenous people") or the community level. A *compromise* or *consensus* on practices and norms within indigenous groups is only conceivable as the result of a democratic political process. As John Haviland (2001: 188) aptly puts it, custom is neither statute nor code but a process, and frequently, I should add, a conflictive one. Any codification of customary law would not lead to its preservation, as many activists would have it, but to a fundamental change in its character.

Power Relations and Customary Law

As already stated, indigenous customs and traditions are frequently considered the source of an alternative legal system in the current autonomy debate.[27] It is assumed that there is consensus on the norms and procedures of conflict management, and that applying customary law leads to a re-establishment of "social harmony" in indigenous communities.[28] This assumption, however, neglects existing conflicts within indigenous populations. These conflicts are not, as several authors suggest (e.g., Gómez 1995: 214; Hamel 1990: 209), merely due to the weakening of community cohesion and traditional norms as a result of growing state penetration. Instead, at the heart of many traditions are relations of power. As Laura Nader has rightly pointed out, compromise, and more generally the "harmony model" stressed by many indigenous groups, may be the means to various ends. It can be used to protect the group from encroaching superordinate power holders, as well as to defend established internal power structures against subordinates (Nader 1989: 337f.; 2005: 207f.). Consequently, recognition of the so-called customary law in indigenous communities does not simply acknowledge a coherent corpus of fixed and shared "traditions," but supports the interpretation and interests of certain social or local power groups.

As critical Marxist approaches have argued, law in capitalist societies is an arena for and a result of class struggle and thus has an ambivalent character. While legitimizing existing relations of domination on the one hand, it incorporates the interests of the non-ruling classes, to a certain extent, on the other. Therefore, law should not be reified as a power above and outside society (e.g., Hunt 1976). Although many indigenous groups, in which customary law is important, are not class stratified, conflicts of interest and relations of domination between different social groups, age groups, sexes, or spatially separated groups are far from unknown.[29] Thus, customary law, as well as state law, has to be interpreted and evaluated in the context of existing power relations (see also Starr and Collier 1989: 12, 24f.). Both forms of law are not neutral in their effects, but strengthen or weaken the rights and social positions of different actors. If we acknowledge, for example, the customary practices in the Tzotzil community of Zinacantan, Chiapas, in southern Mexico, where only male descendants can inherit agricultural land, we inherently support the interests of men to the disadvantage of women (Collier 1976: 116f.; Köhler 1975: 48; Laughlin 1969: 166; Rosenbaum 1993: 49f.). On the other hand, agrarian reform laws in Latin America have also been frequently gender-biased, while the majority cede land rights only to household heads who are male (Deere and León 2001: 3, 99–106). Thus, from a normative perspective, the relevant questions to be asked are—both in the case of customary and state law—which interpretation fosters the democratization of local communities and national society, and how representative and legitimate are the authorities or political actors involved? An examination of the indigenous movement's emergence in the last decades shows that different living conditions (such as working in agriculture or as a professional), and the resulting material interests (e.g., land reform or the creation of jobs in the public sector), do not necessarily lead to irreconcilable contradictions, but may in some cases be a necessary condition for strategic alliances between actors occupying different social positions.

Increasing Social Differentiation: The Hidden Side of the Indigenous Movement's Rise in the Twentieth Century

In the 1970s, major participants of the Barbados Group, a circle of mostly Latin American anthropologists and indigenous representatives, pleaded for the integration of the indigenous struggle for liberation to be included as part of the debate around broader social conflicts in Latin America.[30] They assumed, somewhat optimistically, that Amerindians and the Latin American lower classes had the same interests, due to their shared economic exploitation and political marginalization, and that common political action would easily be possible. Hence, in spite of his otherwise detailed analysis of social differentiation among indigenous people, the anthropologist Stefano Varese concluded at the beginning of the 1970s that "any heightening of [ethnic] group consciousness is accompanied by the intensification of class consciousness in Latin America today" (1982: 41). More recently, Gerardo Otero has treated indigenous movements as indigenous peasant mobilizations, and argues in the same vein that "class and identity struggles are actually inseparable" (2003: 249).

The Barbados Group members had already recognized the strategic importance of the emergence of an indigenous middle class and bourgeoisie for ethnic mobilization.[31] However, the marginalization of Marxist approaches in academic debate as a consequence of the disintegration of the Communist Bloc has lamentably led to a decreasing interest in class analysis. Some laudable exceptions notwithstanding (e.g., Adams and Bastos 2003), most recent treatments of indigenous movements neglect the emerging stratification within indigenous groups. They concentrate on the indigenous lower class, or take the "indigenous peoples" as their point of reference, thus obscuring the increasing diversity of living conditions, interests, and expectations among Amerindian populations. The stereotypical view of the Amerindian as a poor peasant, landless farmhand, or, in the lowland areas, as a hunter and gatherer has thus survived up to this day. Anthropologist Harry Sanabria, for example, stresses the association of "indigenous peoples" with rural landscapes, and attributes the rise of indigenous movements to the failure of ideologies and policies related to *mestizaje* (race mixture), which "largely did not lead to the fulfilment of promises of upward economic mobility" (2006: 135). Other scholars consider Amerindians as the poorest and most destitute part of Latin America's population (Davis and Partridge 1994, cited in Yashar 1996: 97). Political scientist Deborah Yashar explains the rise of indigenous movements as a result of "the structural conditions [that have] disadvantaged indigenous communities for centuries," and increased political opportunities as a result of democratization and growing support by international organizations and NGOs (1996: 97–101). While conflicts between highland and lowland groups are sometimes addressed, the issues of demography, changes of ethnic identification (passing), miscegenation, and internal class differentiation, which might lead to economic contradictions and conflicts of interest, are generally neglected. Internal differentiation is mostly reduced to questions of leadership and the role of indigenous intellectuals (cf., e.g., Otero 2003: 265). As a consequence, most recent academic discussions related to indigenous movements focus on politics, rights, citizenship, discourse, culture, and identity.

I would argue that growing internal stratification[32] is a key factor for the emergence of indigenous movements, and has a major influence on the form and content of their demands. Following Joseph Rothschild and Paul Brass, I see a close relationship between increasing resource competition between social or ethnic groups or categories and the emergence of ethnicity. Both authors stress the importance of elite groups for the ideologization of ethnicity, and for the mobilization of the sharers of ethnic markers (Brass 1991: 13–15, 25–30, 270–93; Rothschild 1981: 27–29).

The emergence of numerous indigenous organizations on the local, regional, national, and international stages can be attributed to a variety of factors, such as a greater openness by national governments and international organizations to address ethnic demands. In addition, opportunities for communication among members of the same language group have increased due to better infrastructure—particularly roads, further migration, and the establishment of radio programs in indigenous languages. However, the two most important causes are, in my view, firstly, the capitalist expansion into the previously rural peripheries, and critically the development of land tenure in these regions, which has resulted in massive social conflicts (see above). Therefore, the issues of land tenure and the right to natural resources have become the central demands of most indigenous organizations. Secondly, public policies have accelerated social change in the indigenous subsocieties since the 1950s, producing a new, educated social group among Amerindians that has provided leadership for many organizations.[33]

Since the 1950s, many Latin American governments and international institutions have introduced development policies aimed at integrating marginal, frequently indigenous regions and their inhabitants into the capitalist economy, and additionally assimilating them into the national culture. These parties considered the language and culture of the various indigenous groups as "barriers to integration" that had to be overcome. National and international organizations launched numerous projects, using a strategy that was quite modern at the time: "community development." Members of alleged "backward" communities were themselves expected to become the carriers of "modernization." Education played a key role in this concept, one of the intentions of which was to change the value system of the local population. Thus, a multitude of "cultural promoters," health workers, and rural teachers were trained as "agents of change" within their communities (Aguirre Beltrán 1966; Münzel 1984: 71–73; Schüren and Gabbert 2013). Several figures illustrate the dimensions of this new social group within the indigenous population. The number of indigenous bilingual teachers and cultural promoters in Mexico, for example, increased from approximately 3,400 in 1970 to more than 30,000 in the early 1990s and almost 49,000 in the year 2000. This represents an increase of more than 1,400 per cent in merely thirty years.[34]

It is a historical irony that it was precisely this group, created to promote assimilation, that became one of the most vital forces in the emerging indigenous movements that were to be found all over Latin America. Development policies after the 1950s initially provided new opportunities for upward social mobility, such as education, professional training, and jobs. However, it did not take long for these indigenous teachers, cultural promoters, university students, and nurses to recognize that their possibilities for social mobility were extremely limited. They were rarely able to compete successfully with whites or mestizos for the desired middle- or high-level positions. Not only was their training frequently of a lesser quality, but more significantly here, they met with the open contempt and discrimination of the national majority.[35] Now mindful that assimilation was not always possible, the indigenous men and women became aware that belonging to a minority was important.[36]

The social psychology of intergroup relations shows that attempts to attain collective social change will inevitably occur when individual social mobility becomes difficult or even impossible (e.g., Tajfel 1981: 238–53, 312–15). Thus, the rise of indigenous movements can be seen, in part, as an expression of educated Amerindians' ambitions for social advancement. The movements' demands for bilingual education, for instance, cannot be comprehended simply as an attempt to preserve native languages. It should also be seen as a means of securing jobs for indigenous bilingual teachers who can (in contrast to their non-indigenous colleagues) teach in the native idiom. It is no mere coincidence that the rise of indigenous movements runs roughly parallel to the spread of neoliberal policies in Latin America. These reduced the public sector and downsized bureaucracies, fostering the competition for jobs, which probably intensified the discrimination against indigenous professionals by their non-indigenous peers—in spite of the formers' advanced acculturation.

To enable the mobilization of significant parts of the indigenous population, the interests in social advancement of the member elites must be linked to key problems of the rural masses (usually the protection of land rights). The demand for political autonomy and indigenous territories is a case in point. Its fulfilment would offer suitable positions for educated Amerindians, and at the same time solve the land problems of the rural indigenous population.

The educated elites need the indigenous masses as a potential power base if they are to succeed in regulating their (quite particular) interests. The rural natives, for their part, require the elites to effectively articulate their demands. They depend on elites to translate their political activities into forms that are acceptable to the dominant "Western" culture, forms such as peasant unions, cooperatives, or indigenous organizations with associational structures. Beyond that, an organizational connection between the different local communities is necessary to focus, structure, and channel their otherwise isolated discontent.[37] Hence, elites can contribute to solving the structural problems of organization in rural populations, such as the lack of communication or coordination issues related to scattered settlement patterns. The rhetoric of indigenous organizations emphasizes "common" issues such as language, culture, tradition, and descent, since it needs to unify people of different social standings and, at least partially, divergent interests. However, what unites the different sectors of indigenous groupings, apart from the above-mentioned functional necessities, is the attitude of the dominant sectors of Latin American societies towards indigenous peoples, which even today is often one of contempt and discrimination.

Indigenous movements have also begun to counter discrimination on an ideological level by appropriating the term "Indian" (*indio, indígena*), hitherto defined almost exclusively in negative terms. Following the example of the US civil rights movement in the 1960s, they strive to make the category a positive symbol, one with which all indigenous people can identify, their remaining differences and conflicts notwithstanding. In this sense, "Indian" is no longer seen as a foreign category imposed by the Iberian colonialists, but instead is filled with new content independent of colonial domination. Indigenous movements invoke tradition, language, and culture in their "Indian" discourse, celebrating a worldview with a high degree of spirituality, a peaceful relationship to nature, and a strong ideal of communalism—attributes supposedly shared by all indigenous groups. In contrast to "the West," with its destruction of nature, exploitation, egoism, and alienation, they invoke the myth of a pan-American indigenous personality characterized by solidarity, respect, honesty, and love (cf., e.g., Bonfíl Batalla 1981: 35–44).

Membership criteria have changed in many indigenous groups to allow the reintegration of "social climbers" and of the growing number of Amerindians living in cities.[38] The Miskito of eastern Nicaragua are a case in point. The Miskito have a long history of intermarriage with foreigners. Since the seventeenth century at least, Miskito women established alliances with European sailors or traders, fugitive African slaves, or US workers, among others. These men then frequently advanced their social positions in the villages. Outsiders and their offspring were integrated into the Miskito communities by the establishment or construction of kin relationships.[39] Up until the second half of the twentieth century, a system of generalized reciprocity, including mutual aid among kin and fellow villagers, and a generous distribution of food (especially meat), were the principal mechanisms used to integrate members into Miskito communities. Villagers defined themselves as "the poor," and only those newcomers who participated in this system of generalized reciprocity were then accepted by the community as fellow Miskito. Upward social and economic mobility often resulted in a change of this ethnic categorization. For example, shop owners or traders of Miskito descent who began to favor their commercial interests at the expense of the expected generosity towards kinsmen were no longer considered in-group members (Gabbert 1992: 268f.). The prominent role of descent as the chief determinant of individual identity is a more recent development—the result of missionary work and growing social differentiation that weakened relations of reciprocity, even back in the 1960s and 1970s.

Favoring descent and language as the main criteria for group membership facilitates the reintegration of the elite into Amerindian society, and sustains or re-establishes social cohesion within the villages, as the foundations of reciprocity gradually fade away. In contrast to earlier periods, villagers now categorize individuals as Miskito even when they do not participate in the system of generalized reciprocity, or the redistribution of wealth. This is facilitated by an emphasis on defining an ethnic community that refers to an element common to both the elite and villagers, namely the shared experience of discrimination by major sections of Nicaraguan society. This discrimination has gained significance since the 1960s, due to the massive immigration of mestizo peasants from the Pacific and central parts of Nicaragua, and increased government efforts to control the natural resources of the Atlantic coast (Gabbert 1992: 302f.).

Conclusion

The discussion on indigeneity, autonomy, and the recognition of customary law shows that anthropological concepts such as culture and ethnicity play a central role both in other social sciences and in current political debates. However, political actors, and even some leading social scientists involved in the debate on multiculturalism, such as Will Kymlicka and Charles Taylor, still employ the term "culture" as being synonymous with a nation or a people, and in turn define these concepts as groups of individuals who pursue a collective end (e.g., Kymlicka 1995: 18; Taylor 1993: 20).[40] Similar ideas are widespread in the discourse and rulings of international institutions, NGOs, and national governments in relation to indigenous groups. Thus, the old model of the nation-state is applied to a new legal entity: the "indigenous peoples." In both cases, political rights are claimed for a community portrayed as organic and culturally homogeneous.

While Anaya explicitly rejects the equation of "people," "nation," and "state" for falsely generalizing a relatively modern concept of "mutually exclusive 'sovereign' territorial communities," he remains convinced that, while nation and state were quite specific forms of social organization, "peoplehood" was not. He defines "peoples" as "communities, each with its own social, cultural, and political attributes richly rooted in history" (Anaya 2004: 100f.).

The conceptualization of "peoples" as homogeneous cultural units runs the risk of fostering new forms of cultural homogenization, and of consolidating present relations of domination in indigenous groups. This can only be avoided by accepting the anthropological insight that the meanings of norms, culture, and community are almost always contested. Respect for cultural difference, therefore, not only means the recognition of the rights of certain collectives of people, but needs to ensure that decision-making processes within these groups meet fundamental democratic standards.

There can be no doubt that the social and economic situation of the majority of the indigenous populations in Latin America, and elsewhere, is critical, and that discrimination towards them is still widespread. Thus, independent organizations, in positions to articulate their legitimate demands, are of crucial importance. These organizations face immense challenges. They have the arduous task of establishing communication and relationships with the indigenous populations, many of which live dispersed throughout remote areas in Latin America. Furthermore, they frequently have to bridge existing conflicts and contradictions between indigenous populations (e.g., highland and lowland Amerindians in South America). However, acknowledging the need for indigenous organizations should not lead us to romanticize them. Neither indigenous people in their entirety, nor single language groups, or for that matter single communities, are always of the same opinion or share the same interests. Social and political relations among indigenous groups are neither more nor less harmonious than among other groups, and the notion that indigenous organizations always perfectly represent the interests of "their people" is a mere projection. If therefore we support an indigenous organization, we invariably decide to foster a specific political project, and not the "general will" of an indigenous people. Beyond this, the situation, strategies, and activities of indigenous actors can only be understood if we lend their different social positions, differentiated according to class, gender, and generation, their due weight.

Wolfgang Gabbert (Dr.phil., Berlin [Free University]) is a sociologist (PhD 1991) and an anthropologist (habilitation 2000). He is currently

Professor of Development Sociology and Cultural Anthropology at the Leibniz Universität Hannover. His main research areas are legal anthropology, the anthropology of conflict and violence, ethnicity and social inequality, migration, colonialism, and Christian missions in Latin America and Africa. He has authored the first book-length treatment of Nicaragua's African American Creoles (*Creoles: Afroamerikaner im karibischen Tiefland von Nicaragua* [Lit 1992]) and the first English-language study that examines the role of ethnicity and social inequality in the history of Yucatan, Mexico (*Becoming Maya: Ethnicity and Social Inequality in Yucatán since 1500* [University of Arizona Press 2004]). He has published widely on the history and cultural anthropology of the indigenous peoples of Mexico and Central America.

Notes

Earlier versions of parts of this chapter have been published in Gabbert (1999a) and Gabbert (2011).

1. Since scientific reasoning follows a different logic to that of political discourse, and should aim at the furthering of knowledge rather than the furthering of particular group interests (however legitimate they may be), to merge both fields of discourse is highly problematic.
2. Amerindian here refers to the numerous indigenous groups living in the Americas.
3. This led many Asian and African governments to adopt some version of the "saltwater theory" — limiting the concept of colonialism to the European variant and arguing that in their countries all citizens were "indigenous" (see, e.g., Baird 2011: 159f.).
4. See, for example, Fardon (1987: 177f., 181f.), Gomes (1988), Iliffe (1979: 318–41), King (1982: 27), Southall (1970), and Young (1985: 73–82).
5. This differentiating role of the state has also been highlighted by Barth (1994: 19), Hechter (1975), and Jackson (1995).
6. The *castas* in Latin America are not to be confused with the caste system in India.
7. Mestizo referred to people of mixed Amerindian and Iberian background; mulato was used to designate the offspring of Europeans and individuals of African descent.
8. See, for example, Chance (1978: 97, 100f., 128–42, 175f., 189f., 194–96), Lockhart (1984: 288, 316–18), and McAlister (1963: 355, 366–69).
9. To denounce this as an act of ethnocide, as many present-day observers suggest, seems problematic, since it projects current political ideas of multiculturalism on the past. "Indian" did not refer to an ethnic community, but was a colonial administrative category, and thus a symbol of exclusion and discrimination.

10. Several governments (e.g., Argentina) introduced extermination policies directed at indigenous minorities in the nineteenth century. Hunting and gathering groups that had not been integrated into the precolonial empires or states were the populations most affected.
11. Various governments in Latin America have been openly dictatorial, or controlled by a small group of elites for extended periods of time. Legal systems and the police are frequently experienced by members of the lower classes as oppressive, discriminatory, and corrupt (see, e.g., Méndez, O'Donnell, and Pinheiro 1999). These problems are further aggravated by many Amerindians' limited command of their countries' official languages (Spanish or Portuguese).
12. These modernization projects propagated the increased construction of infrastructure, such as railways and schools, the opening of economies to foreign investment, and further integration into the world economy with the introduction of new agrarian export products, such as coffee and bananas. The goals of the Liberal Reforms were the separation of church and state, and the generalization of capitalist forms of production and possession. Land owned by corporations, such as the church or indigenous and nonindigenous communities, was to be privatized.
13. See the overview in Coatsworth (1988), and Gabbert (2004b) for a Mexican example.
14. See, for example, Dilger (1985), Gabbert (1992: 256–65, 299–301), Muñoz Ramírez (2005), Schüren (1997: 48–61), Serrano (1990), and the recent two-volume set edited by Gutiérrez Chong (2013).
15. Guatemala 1985, Nicaragua 1986, Brazil 1988, Columbia 1991, Paraguay 1992, Mexico 1992 and 2001, Peru 1993, Argentine 1994, Bolivia 1994, Ecuador 1983 and 1998. See, for example, Assies (1999), Cabedo Mallol (2004: 143–280), and van Cott (2000b: 207f.). The real impact of such a significant change in the self-image of these nations, however, is somewhat restricted. Although many Latin American constitutions now recognize indigenous autonomy and legal practices in principle, the legislation required for implementation and conformity with other national laws is still lacking in many countries.
16. This, and all translations that follow, are my own.
17. See Pelican (2009) for a summary discussion of this issue, as well as a case study from Cameroon.
18. Cf., for example, Baird (2011), Lüdert (2013), Pelican (2009), Waldron (2002), and the contributions of Barnard, Guenther, Kenrick, Plaice, Thuen, Trond, Wolfe, and Zips in *Social Anthropology* 14, part 1 (2006): 1–32.
19. See, for example, Constitución … de Chiapas, Mexico (Art. 13). Brazil is an exception, defining as an Indian any individual of pre-Columbian ancestry identified as a member of an ethnic group which is culturally different from the national society (Art. 3 of the Estatuto do Indio-Lei nr. 6.001/1973 [see Semper 2003: 44]). Recently, self-definition has been adopted as a criterion for ethnic ascription in the censuses of some Latin American countries.
20. See, for example, Albó (1979: 481–83), Dennis (1987: 33), Dietz (1997: 165f.), Favre (1984: 135–45), Spores (1984: 208–25), Whitecotton (1977: 219, 246–53), and Zárate Hernández (1991: 119).

21. See, for example, Caso et al. (1954: 144–49), Collier (1976: 195f.), Farriss (1984: 148–51, 188, 357), and Favre (1984: 138f.). I therefore disagree with Nahmad Sitton (2001: 31), who urges us to acknowledge that the present-day indigenous peoples are geopolitical units, comparable to the Mixtec kingdom or the Aztec empire of pre-Columbian times.
22. There are some exceptions, such as the *resguardos* (reserves) in Columbia.
23. This does, however, not necessarily lead to separatist movements and the establishment of independent indigenous states.
24. See, for example, Anderson (1991, chapters 5 and 6), Hobsbawm (1990, chapters 2 and 3), and Hroch (2005: 62–70).
25. As I have shown in another publication (Gabbert 2011: 281–83), these formulas misconceive the character of the so-called indigenous customary law since the results of mediation, or the sanction applied for breaking a norm, depend on the social relations and the status of the litigants, and, in contrast to the state law, do not result from the application of an abstract rule.
26. See Gabbert (2011: 280f.) for the evidence.
27. See, for example, CNI (2001), Regino (2001), and several contributions in Morse and Woodman (1988). Cf. also Iturralde (1990: 51), Sierra (1995: 228), and Stavenhagen (1990: 33).
28. See, for example, Ardito (1997: 15f.), Esquit and García (1998: 15f.), Regino (2001), Sheleff (2000: 3, 13), Stavenhagen (1990: 29f.), and Yrigoyen Fajardo (1999: 356).
29. See Meillassoux (1983) for a succinct discussion of inequality and exploitation in the "domestic mode of production." Conflict dynamics in indigenous communities are discussed in Gabbert (1999b) for the case of the highlands of Chiapas.
30. The Barbados Group was founded during a conference on interethnic frictions in Latin America, on the island of the same name, in January 1971. The participants prepared a document that denounced the continuity of the colonial oppression that Amerindians were suffering. During a follow-up meeting, and with the participation of numerous indigenous activists, a second declaration was adopted in 1977 which identified elements necessary to achieve the "unity of the indigenous peoples."
31. See, for example, Bartolomé (1982: 51f.), Bonfíl Batalla (1982: 24, 29f.), and Varese (1982: 36–39). While Bonfíl was correct in stressing the colonial origin of the category *indio*, he and his colleagues ignored the importance of social and economic differences among the indigenous populations: think, for example, of the poor highland Amerindian colonists, on the eastern slopes of the Andes, who intrude into the hunting and cultivation grounds of lowland groups. In addition, they severely underrated the economic and political contradictions between Amerindian and non-Amerindian lower classes as well as the tenacity of racist attitudes, widespread in Latin America.
32. This is indicated, for example, by the rising numbers of indigenous teachers and health workers (see below). Social differentiation among indigenous agrarian producers has grown since the 1960s, as a consequence of the increasing monetization and export orientation of local economies, fostering more capital-intensive forms of production and land concentration

within their communities (e.g., Arias 1990; Collier 1994: 102–19; Fischer and Hendrickson 2003: 132–41).
33. See Gabbert (1999a, 2007) for a thorough treatment of these points.
34. Data are from Gobierno Federal (2002: 55), Münzel (1984: 79), and Ríos Morales (1993: 219). For Guatemala, see Adams and Bastos (2003: 140–42, 200–203).
35. This discrimination has its origins in the colonial period, but it could also be opportunistically employed in recruitment in the public sector to disadvantage educated Amerindians.
36. Rothschild (1981: 138–41) has made a similar point for ethnic leaders in general. Pelican (2009: 60, 62) hints at the importance of the educated elite for indigenous organizing in Cameroon. Hroch (1985: 12, 179–89) also stresses the importance of the educated elite in the nationalist movements of European "oppressed nationalities" and draws on similar processes of impeded social mobility to account for their participation.
37. See the theoretical considerations in Raschke (1988: 124–28, 146f., 159f.) and Rothschild (1981: 27–30).
38. More than half of the 1.5 million Mapuche living in Chile resided in the urban areas in the early 1990s. Over 500,000 members of this indigenous group lived in the capital of Santiago alone. The number of people (over the age of four) who speak an indigenous language and live in Mexico City rose from 350,000 in 1980 to 1.6 million in 1990 (Muñoz Ramírez 2005; Nolasco 1990: 3–5).
39. For the integration of outsiders into Miskito communities, see, for example, the description of the origins of Asang, a village on the Rio Coco, in Helms (1971: 57–59).
40. This comes very close to the "unholy trinity" of one language = one culture = one society (or people) which is, I would argue, an equally specific concept of Western origin, and ignores the post-Barthian discussion on ethnicity, which has shown, among other things, that ethnic communities are not simply the result of having a common culture (see, e.g., Gabbert 2001, 2006: 86–88, 91–93).

Bibliography

Laws and Decrees

CNI. 2001. "Declaración por el reconocimiento constitucional de nuestros derechos colectivos." In *3er Congreso Nacional Indígena*. Nurío, Michoacán. 2–4 march. Retrieved 24 July 2014 from http://www.ceacatl.laneta.apc.org/cni/3cni-dec.htm.
Constitución Política del Estado Libre y Soberano de Chiapas, Mexico, 9 October 1999.
Constitución Política de los Estados Unidos Mexicanos, 14 August 2001.
ECPI (Encuentro Continental de Pueblos Indios). 1990. "Declaración de Quito." *Alai* 130: 1–8.

Gobierno Federal. 2002. Programa Nacional para el Desarrollo de los Pueblos Indígenas, 2001–2006. Mexico City.
ILO (International Labour Organization). 1989. C169—Convention Concerning Indigenous and Tribal Peoples in Independent Countries. Retrieved 26 July 2014 from http://www.ilo.org/dyn/normlex/en/f?p=NORMLEXPUB: 12100:0::NO::P12100_ILO_CODE:C169.
League of Nations. 1919. The Covenant of the League of Nations. Retrieved 9 February 2014 from http://www.avalon.law.yale.edu/20th_century/leagcov.asp.
Ley de Derechos, Cultura y Organización de los Pueblos y Comunidades Indígenas del Estado de Campeche, 15 June 2000.
Ley de Derechos y Cultura Indígenas de Chiapas, 29 July 1999.
Ley de Derechos, Cultura y Organización Indígena del Estado de Quintana Roo, 30 July 1998.
Ley de Justicia Indígena del Estado de Quintana Roo, 14 August 1997.
Ley para la Protección de los Derechos de la Comunidad Maya en el Estado de Yucatán, 13 April 2011 [1 January 2012].
República de Bolivia. 2008. Nueva constitución política del Estado. Retrieved 26 July 2014 from http://www.patrianueva.bo/constitucion/.
UN (United Nations). 2007. United Nations Declaration on the Rights of Indigenous Peoples. Sixty-first session, Agenda item 68, Report of the Human Rights Council, A/61/L.67.

Books and Articles

Adams, Richard N. and Santiago Bastos. 2003. *Las relaciones étnicas en Guatemala, 1944–2000*. Antigua: CIRMA.
Aguirre Beltrán, Gonzalo. 1966. "Community Development." *América Indígena* 26(3): 219–28.
Albó, Xavier. 1979. "Khitipxtansa? Quienes somos? Identidad localista, étnica y clasista en los aymara de hoy." *América Indígena* 39(3): 477–528.
Anaya, S. James. 2004. *Indigenous Peoples in International Law*. 2nd ed. Oxford and New York: Oxford University Press.
Anderson, Benedict. 1991. *Imagined Communities: Reflections on the Origin and Spread of Nationalism*. Rev. ed. London and New York: Verso.
Ardito, Wilfredo. 1997. "The Right to Self-Regulation: Legal Pluralism and Human Rights in Peru." *Journal of Legal Pluralism* 29(39): 1–42.
Arias, Arturo. 1990. "Changing Indian Identity: Guatemala's Violent Transition to Modernity." In *Guatemalan Indians and the State: 1540 to 1988*, ed. Carol A. Smith, 230–57. Austin, TX: University of Texas Press.
Assies, Willem. 1999. "Pueblos indígenas y reforma del Estado en América Latina." In *El reto de la diversidad: Pueblos indígenas y reforma del Estado en América Latina*, ed. Willem Assies, Gemma van der Haar, and André Hoekema, 21–55. Zamora: El Colegio de Michoacán.
Baird, Ian. 2011. "The Construction of 'Indigenous Peoples' in Cambodia." In *Alterities in Asia: Reflections on Identity and Regionalism*, ed. Leong Yew, 155–76. London: Routledge.

Barth, Frederic. 1994. "Enduring and Emerging Issues in the Analysis of Ethnicity." In *The Anthropology of Ethnicity: Beyond "Ethnic Groups and Boundaries"*, ed. Cora Govers and Hans Vermeulen, 11–32. Amsterdam: Het Spinhuis.

Bartolomé, Miguel Alberto. 1982. "Ethnisches Bewußtsein und indianische Selbstbestimmung." In *Indianer in Lateinamerika. Neues Bewusstsein und Strategien der Befreiung: Dokumente der zweiten Tagung von Barbados*, 43–52. Wuppertal: Hammer.

Bonfíl Batalla, Guillermo, ed. 1981. *Utopía y revolución: El pensamiento político contemporáneo de los indios en América Latina*. Mexico, D.F.: Nueva Imagen.

———. 1982. "Die neuen indianischen Organisationen." In *Indianer in Lateinamerika. Neues Bewusstsein und Strategien der Befreiung: Dokumente der zweiten Tagung von Barbados*, 17–30. Wuppertal: Hammer.

Bourdieu, Pierre. [1979] 1987. *Die feinen Unterschiede: Kritik der gesellschaftlichen Urteilskraft*. Frankfurt: Suhrkamp.

Brass, Paul R. 1991. *Ethnicity and Nationalism*. New Delhi, Newbury and London: Sage.

Cabedo Mallol, Vicente. 2004. *Constitucionalismo y derecho indígena en América Latina*. Valencia: Editorial de la UPV.

Caso, Alfonso, et al. (eds). 1954. *La política indigenista en México: Métodos y Resultados*, Vol. I. Mexico, D.F.: INI/SEP.

Chance, John K. 1978. *Race and Class in Colonial Oaxaca*. Stanford, CA: Stanford University Press.

Coatsworth, John H. 1988. "Patterns of Rural Rebellion in Latin America: Mexico in Comparative Perspective." In *Riot, Rebellion, and Revolution: Rural Social Conflict in Mexico*, ed. Friedrich Katz, 21–62. Princeton, NJ: Princeton University Press.

Collier, George A. 1976. *Planos de interacción del mundo tzotzil: Bases ecológicas de la tradición en los Altos de Chiapas*. Mexico, D.F.: INI.

———. 1994. *Basta! Land and the Zapatista Rebellion in Chiapas*. Oakland, CA: Institute for Food and Development Policy.

Daes, Erica. 1996. *Standard-Setting Activities: Evolution of Standards Concerning the Rights of Indigenous People*. Working Paper on the Concept of "Indigenous People." United Nations, Commission on Human Rights, Sub-Commission on Prevention of Discrimination and Protection of Minorities, Working Group on Indigenous Populations. E/CN.4/Sub.2/AC.4/1996/2. Retrieved 8 February 2014 from http://www.unhchr.ch/Huridocda/Huridoca.nsf/(Symbol)/E.CN.4.Sub.2.AC.4.1996.2.En?Opendocument.

Davis, Shelton and William Partridge. 1994. "Promoting the Development of Indigenous Peoples in Latin America." *Finance and Development* 31(1): 38–40.

Deere, Carmen Diana and Magdalena León. 2001. *Empowering Women: Land and Property Rights in Latin America*. Pittsburgh, PA: Pittsburgh University Press.

Dennis, Philip A. 1987. *Intervillage Conflict in Oaxaca*. New Brunswick and London: Rutgers University Press.

Díaz-Couder, Ernesto. 1991. "Lengua y sociedad en el medio indígena de México." In *Nuevos enfoques para el estudio de las etnias indígenas en México*, ed. Arturo Argüeta and Arturo Warman, 143–92. Mexico, D.F.: CIIH/UNAM.

Dietz, Gunther. 1997. "Die Purhépecha in Michoacán: Das Erwachen der Comunidades." In *Das andere Mexiko: Indigene Völker von Chiapas bis Chihuahua*, ed. Ellen Schriek and Hans-Walter Schmuhl, 156–186. Gießen: Focus.

Dilger, Robert. 1985. "Die Kolonisation der karibischen Tiefländer Zentralamerikas." In *Ökozid 1*, ed. Peter Stüben, 82–101. Gießen: Focus.

Esquit, Edgar and Iván García. 1998. *El derecho consuetudinario, la reforma judicial y la implementación de los acuerdos de paz*. Guatemala: FLACSO.

Fardon, Richard. 1987. "'African Ethnogenesis': Limits to the Comparability of Ethnic Phenomena." In *Comparative Anthropology*, ed. Ladislav Holy, 168–88. Oxford: Blackwell.

Farriss, Nancy M. 1984. *Maya Society under Colonial Rule*. Princeton, NJ: Princeton University Press.

Favre, Henri. 1984. *Cambio y continuidad entre los mayas de México*. Mexico, D.F.: INI.

Fischer, Edward F. and Carol Hendrickson. 2003. *Tecpán Guatemala: A Modern Maya Town in Global and Local Context*. Boulder, CO: Westview.

Gabbert, Wolfgang. 1992. *Creoles: Afroamerikaner im karibischen Tiefland von Nicaragua*. Münster: Lit.

———. 1999a. "Cultura, autonomía y Estado: movimientos sociales indígenas en América Latina." In *Interculturalidad e identidad indígenas: Preguntas abiertas a la globalización*, eds. Andreas Koechert and Barbara Pfeiler, 13–25. Hannover: Verlag für Ethnologie.

———. 1999b. "Violence and Social Change in Highland Maya Communities, Chiapas, Mexico." *Iberoamerikanisches Archiv* 25(3/4): 351–74.

———. 2001. "On the Term Maya." In *Maya Survivalism*, ed. Ueli Hostettler and Matthew Restall, 25–34. Markt Schwaben: Anton Saurwein.

———. 2004a. *Becoming Maya: Ethnicity and Social Inequality in Yucatán since 1500*. Tucson, AZ: University of Arizona Press.

———. 2004b. "Of Friends and Foes: The Caste War and Ethnicity in Yucatán." *Journal of Latin American Anthropology* 9(1): 90–118.

———. 2006. "Concepts of Ethnicity." *Latin American and Caribbean Ethnic Studies* 1(1): 85–103.

———. 2007. "Ethnisierung von 'oben' und von 'unten': Staatliche Indianerpolitik und indigene Bewegungen im postrevolutionären Mexiko." In *Ethnisierung und De-Ethnisierung des Politischen*, ed. Christian Büschges and Joanna Pfaff-Czarnecka, 142–65. Frankfurt a.M.: Campus.

———. 2011. "Indigenous Law as State Law: Recent Trends in Latin American Legal Pluralism." In *The Governance of Legal Pluralism: Empirical Studies from Africa and Beyond*, ed. Werner Zips and Markus Weilenmann, 275–92. Münster: Lit.

Gomes, Alberto G. 1988. "The Semai: The Making of an Ethnic Group in Malaysia." In *Ethnic Diversity and the Control of Natural Resources in Southeast Asia*, ed. A. Terry Rambo, Kathleen Gillogly, and Karl L. Hutterer, 99–116. Ann Arbor, MI: University of Michigan.

Gómez, Magdalena. 1995. "Las cuentas pendientes de la diversidad jurídica: El caso de las expulsiones de indígenas por supuestos motivos religiosos en Chiapas, México." In *Pueblos indígenas ante el derecho*, ed. Victoria Chenaut and Maria Teresa Sierra, 193–218. Mexico, D.F.: CIESAS/CEMCA.

Gutiérrez Chong, Natividad (ed.). 2013. *Etnicidad y conflicto en las Américas.* 2 vols. Mexico, D.F.: UNAM, IIS.

Hamel, Rainer. 1990. "Lenguaje y conflicto interétnico en el derecho consuetudinario positivo." In *Entre la ley y la costumbre: El derecho consuetudinario indígena en América Latina,* eds. Rodolfo Stavenhagen and Diego Iturralde, 205–30. Mexico, D.F.: Instituto Indigenista Interamericano and Instituto Interamericano de Derechos Humanos.

Harris, La Donna and Jacqueline Wasilewski. 2004. "Indigeneity, an Alternative World View: Four R's (Relationship, Responsibility, Reciprocity, Redistribution) vs. Two P's (Power and Profit). Sharing the Journey Towards Conscious Evolution." *Systems Research and Behavioral Science* 21: 1–15.

Haviland, John. 2001. "La invención de la 'costumbre': El diálogo entre el derecho zinanteco y el ladino durante seis décadas." In *Costumbres, leyes y movimiento indio en Oaxaca y Chiapas,* ed. Lourdes de León Pasquel, 171–88. Mexico, D.F.: CIESAS.

Hechter, Michael. 1975. *Internal Colonialism: The Celtic Fringe in British National Development, 1536–1966.* London: Routledge and Kegan Paul.

Helms, Mary W. 1971. *Asang: Adaptations to Culture Contact in a Miskito Community.* Gainesville, FL: University of Florida Press.

Hobsbawm, Eric. 1990. *Nations and Nationalism since 1780.* Cambridge: Cambridge University Press.

Hroch, Miroslav. 1985. *Social Preconditions of National Revival in Europe: A Comparative Analysis of the Social Composition of Patriotic Groups among the Smaller European Nations.* Cambridge: Cambridge University Press.

———. 2005. *Das Europa der Nationen: Die moderne Nationsbildung im europäischen Vergleich.* Göttingen: Vandenhoeck and Ruprecht.

Hunt, Alan. 1976. "Law, State and Class Struggle." *Marxism Today* June: 178–87.

Iliffe, John. 1979. *A Modern History of Tanganyika.* Cambridge: Cambridge University Press.

Iturralde, Diego. 1990. "Movimiento indio, costumbre jurídica y usos de la ley." In *Entre la ley y la costumbre: El derecho consuetudinario indígena en América Latina,* ed. Rodolfo Stavenhagen and Diego Iturralde, 47–63. Mexico, D.F.: Instituto Indigenista Interamericano and Instituto Interamericano de Derechos Humanos.

Jackson, Jean E. 1995. "Culture, Genuine and Spurious: The Politics of Indianness in the Vaupés, Colombia." *American Ethnologist* 22(1): 3–27.

Karlsson, Bengt G. 2003. "Anthropology and the 'Indigenous Slot'." *Critique of Anthropology* 23(4): 403–23.

King, Victor T. 1982. "Ethnicity in Borneo: An Anthropological Problem." *Southeast Asian Journal of Social Science* 10(1): 23–43.

Köhler, Ulrich. 1975. *Cambio cultural dirigido en los altos de Chiapas.* Mexico, D.F.: INI.

Kuper, Adam. 2003. "The Return of the Native." *Current Anthropology* 44(3): 389–402.

Kymlicka, Will. 1995. *Multicultural Citizenship: A Liberal Theory of Minority Rights.* Oxford: Clarendon Press.

LASR (Latin American Special Report). 2003. *Indigenous Peoples and Power in Latin America (SR-03-04)*, ed. Eduardo Crawley. London: Latin American Newsletters.
Laughlin, Robert M. 1969. "The Tzotzil." In *Handbook of Middle American Indians*, ed. Evon Z. Vogt, 152–94. Austin, TX: University of Texas Press.
Lockhart, James. 1984. "Social Organization and Social Change in Colonial Spanish America." In *The Cambridge History of Latin America*, ed. Leslie Bethell, 265–319. Cambridge: Cambridge University Press.
Lüdert, Jan. 2013. "Latin American States and the International Labour Organization: Circumscribing Indigenous Peoples as Internal Outsiders." *Latin American and Caribbean Ethnic Studies* 8(3): 336–51.
McAlister, Lyle N. 1963. "Social Structure and Social Change in New Spain." *Hispanic American Historical Review* 43(3): 349–70.
Meillassoux, Claude. 1983. *Die wilden Früchte der Frau: Über häusliche Produktion und kapitalistische Wirtschaft*. Frankfurt a.M.: Suhrkamp.
Méndez, Juan E., Guillermo O'Donnell, and Paulo Sérgio Pinheiro (eds). 1999. *The (Un)Rule of Law and the Underprivileged in Latin America*. Notre Dame, IN: University of Notre Dame Press.
MISURASATA. 1982. "Vorschlag zum Landbesitz der indianischen und Creole-Dorfgemeinschaften an der Atlantikküste." In *Nationale Revolution und indianische Identität*, ed. Klaudine Ohland and Robin Schneider, 134–44. Wuppertal: Edition Nahua.
Morse, Bradford W. and Gordon R. Woodman (eds). 1988. *Indigenous Law and the State*. Dordrecht: Foris Publications.
Muñoz Ramírez, G. 2005. "Su lucha en vivo: El movimiento Mapuche en vivo." *Ojarasca* 100. Retrieved 20 June 2017 from http://www.jornada.unam.mx/2005/08/15/oja100-mapuche.html.
Münzel, Mark. 1984. "Neue Formen der Opposition bei Indianern." In *Lateinamerika vor der Entscheidung*, ed. Theo Ginsburg and Monika Ostheider, 67–84. Frankfurt a.M.: Fischer.
Nader, Laura. 1989. "The Crown, the Colonists, and the Course of Zapotec Village Law." In *History and Power in the Study of Law*, ed. June Starr and Jane F. Collier, 320–44 Ithaca, NY and London: Cornell University Press.
———. 2005. "The Americanization of International Law." In *Mobile People, Mobile Law: Expanding Legal Relations in a Contracting World*, ed. Franz von Benda-Beckmann, Kebeet von Benda-Beckmann, and Anne Griffiths, 199–213. Aldershot: Ashgate.
Nahmad Sitton, Salomón. 2001. "Autonomía indígena y la soberanía nacional: El caso de la ley indígena de Oaxaca." In *Costumbres, leyes y movimiento indio en Oaxaca y Chiapas*, ed. Lourdes de León Pasquel, 19–47. Mexico, D.F.: CIESAS.
Nolasco, Margarita. 1990. "Migración indígena y etnicidad." *Supplement to Antropología* 31: 2–12.
Otero, Gerardo. 2003. "The 'Indian Question' in Latin America: Class, State, and Ethnic Identity Construction." *Latin American Research Review* 38(1): 248–66.
Pelican, Michaela. 2009. "Complexities of Indigeneity and Autochthony: An African Example." *American Ethnologist* 36(1): 52–65.

Quintal, Ella, et al. 2003. "Solares, rumbos y pueblos: organización social de los mayas peninsulares." In *La comunidad sin límites: Estructura social y organización comunitaria en las regiones de México*, ed. Saúl Millán and Julieta Valle Vol. I, 291–382. Mexico, D.F.: INAH.
Raschke, Joachim. 1988. *Soziale Bewegungen: Ein historisch-systematischer Grundriß*. Frankfurt and New York: Campus.
Regino Montes, Adelfo. 2001. "Argumentos de un dirigente indio." *Masiosare*, 18 March.
Ríos Morales, Manuel. 1993. "La formación de profesionistas indígenas." In *Movimientos indígenas contemporáneos en México*, ed. Arturo Warman and Arturo Argueta, 199–223. Mexico, D.F.: CIIH/Miguel Angel Porrua.
———. 2001. "Usos, costumbres e identidad entre los zapotecos de la sierra norte de Oaxaca." In *Costumbres, leyes y movimiento indio en Oaxaca y Chiapas*, ed. Lourdes de León Pasquel, 71–90. Mexico, D.F.: CIESAS.
Rosenbaum, Brenda. 1993. *With Our Heads Bowed: The Dynamics of Gender in a Maya Community*. Albany, NY: Institute for Mesoamerican Studies.
Rothschild, Joseph. 1981. *Ethnopolitics: A Conceptual Framework*. New York: Columbia University Press.
Sanabria, Harry. 2006. *The Anthropology of Latin America and the Caribbean*. Columbus, OH: Allyn and Bacon.
Sanders, Douglas. 1977. *The Formation of the World Council of Indigenous Peoples*. IWGIA Document 29. Copenhagen.
Savigny, Friedrich Carl von. 1815. "Ueber den Zweck dieser Zeitschrift." *Zeitschrift für geschichtliche Rechtswissenschaft* 1(1): 1–17.
Schüren, Ute. 1997. "'Land ohne Freiheit': Mexikos langer Abschied von der Agrarreform." In *Lateinamerika—Analysen und Berichte. Band 21*, ed. Karin Gabbert et al., 33–65. Bad Honnef: Horlemann.
Schüren, Ute and Wolfgang Gabbert. 2013. "From Indio to Campesino and Back: Revolution, Agrarian Reform and Indigenism in Mexico." In *"Para quê serve o conhecimento se eu não posso dividilo?" "Was nützt alles Wissen, wenn man es nicht teilen kann?" Gedenkschrift für Erwin Heinrich Frank*, ed. Birgit Krekeler et al., 123–42. Berlin: Gebr. Mann Verlag.
Semper, Frank. 2003. *Die Rechte der indigenen Völker in Kolumbien*. Hamburg: SEBRA-Verlag.
Serrano, Fernando. 1990. "Modernization in the Ecuadorian Amazon: Indigenous People's Political Responses to State Modernization Policies." *The Latinamericanist* 26(1): 6–11.
Sheleff, Leon. 2000. *The Future of Tradition: Customary Law, Common Law and Legal Pluralism*. London and Portland, OR: Frank Cass.
Sierra, María Teresa. 1995. "Indian Rights and Customary Law in Mexico: A Study of the Nahuas in the Sierra de Puebla." *Law & Society Review* 29(2): 227–54.
Smailus, Ortwin. 1990. "Sprachen." In *Altamerikanistik: Eine Einführung in die Hochkulturen Mittel- und Südamerikas*, ed. Ulrich Köhler, 255–73. Berlin: Reimer.
Southall, Aidan W. 1970. "The Illusion of Tribe." *Journal of Asian and African Studies* 5(1–2): 28–50.

Spores, Ronald. 1984. *The Mixtecs in Ancient and Colonial Times*. Norman, OH: University of Oklahoma Press.
Starr, June and Jane Collier. 1989. "Introduction: Dialogues in Legal Anthropology." In *History and Power in the Study of Law: New Directions in Legal Anthropology*, ed. June Starr and Jane Collier, 1–28. Ithaca, NY: Cornell University Press.
Stavenhagen, Rodolfo. 1990. "Derecho consuetudinario en América Latina." In *Entre la ley y la costumbre: El derecho consuetudinario indígena en América Latina*, ed. Rodolfo Stavenhagen and Diego Iturralde, 27–46. Mexico, D.F.: Instituto Indigenista Interamericano and Instituto Interamericano de Derechos Humanos.
Tajfel, Henri. 1981. *Human Groups and Social Categories*. Cambridge: Cambridge University Press.
Taylor, Charles. 1993. "Politik der Anerkennung." In *Multikulturalismus und die Politik der Anerkennung*, ed. Charles Taylor, 13–78. Frankfurt a.M.: Fischer.
van Cott, Donna Lee. 2000a. *The Friendly Liquidation of the Past: The Politics of Diversity in Latin America*. Pittsburgh, PA: Pittsburgh University Press.
———. 2000b. "A Political Analysis of Legal Pluralism in Bolivia and Colombia." *Journal of Latin American Studies* 32(1): 207–34.
Varese, Stefano. 1982. "Ethnische Strategie oder Klassenstrategie." In *Indianer in Lateinamerika. Neues Bewusstsein und Strategien der Befreiung: Dokumente der zweiten Tagung von Barbados*. Wuppertal: Hammer, pp. 31–42.
Waldron, Jeremy. 2002. "Indigeneity? First Peoples and Last Occupancy." Quentin-Baxter Memorial Lecture, Victoria University of Wellington, Law School, 5 December.
Whitecotton, Joseph. 1977. *The Zapotecs: Princes, Priests, and Peasants*. Norman: University of Oklahoma Press.
Yashar, Deborah. 1996. "Indigenous Protest and Democracy in Latin America." In Jorge I. Domínguez and Abraham F. Lowenthal, 87–105. Baltimore, MD: The Johns Hopkins University Press.
Young, Crawford. 1985. "Ethnicity and the Colonial and Post-Colonial State in Africa." In *Ethnicity and the State*, ed. Paul Brass, 59–93. London and Sydney: Croom Helm.
Yrigoyen Fajardo, Raquel. 1999. "El reconocimiento constitucional del derecho indígena en los países andinos." In *El reto de la diversidad: Pueblos indígenas y reforma del Estado en América Latina*, ed. Willem Assies, Gemma van der Haar, and André Hoekema, 343–80. Zamora: El Colegio de Michoacán.
Zárate Hernández, José Eduardo. 1991. "Notas para la interpretación del movimiento étnico en Michoacán." In *El estudio de los movimientos sociales: teoría y método*, ed. Victor Gabriel Muro and Manuel Canto Chac, 111–29. Zamora: El Colegio de Michoacán.

11

FLUID INDIGENEITIES IN THE INDIAN OCEAN
A Small History of the State and Its Other
Philipp Zehmisch

Introduction

Throughout time and across empires, people nowadays labeled as "indigenous" have been depicted and named in various ways.[1] As a concomitant of colonial conquest, the multiple and dynamic discourses of savagery, cannibalism, tribalism, and aboriginality arose out of the contested relationship between the state and indigenous populations.[2] In contemporary national and transnational contexts, the term "indigenous" functions as the politically correct genealogical successor of older, more negatively connoted notions like "savage," "aboriginal," "native," and so on. It is still used as a means to establish and mark differences between groups in central and marginal positions of society. However, contrary to earlier conceptualizations, the construction of an indigenous voice or consciousness allows "indigenous peoples"[3] to participate in politics, and to articulate rights and privileged access to resources (cf. Tsing 2007: 38–39). As a consequence of this politicization, various identifications and modes of consciousness have become enmeshed in the dynamic notion of indigeneity. Its recent transformation, from a means of discursive Othering into a device of political articulation of Selves, proves that it is a ubiquitous term that can be vested with multiple meanings.

In this chapter, I examine the trajectory of such multiple notions of "indigenous-ness" in a particular ethnographic context, that is, of the Andaman Islands.[4] I propose that the Andamans' specific constitution, as a semantic site and as a space of imagination, is linked to the ascription of flexible and dynamic notions of indigeneity. Focusing on changing perceptions of both the indigenous islanders and indigenous migrants throughout different periods, I aim to throw light on how the very discourse of indigenous-ness is linked to the history of state institutionalization in the Andamans.

In what follows, I begin with a small biographical vignette from the Andamans, which serves to provide an overview of the context in which the research for this chapter has been conducted. Then I will elaborate on shifting notions of indigeneity in the islands throughout the last one and a half centuries. Going back to the nineteenth century, I will demonstrate that frontier colonization was accompanied by a discourse of "savagery" and "wilderness" that justified the "taming" and "civilizing" of the "primitive" Andaman Islanders.[5] This process of colonization was enacted by rehabilitated criminal convicts and "criminal tribes," and, in the twentieth century, by "aboriginal" migrant laborers from Central India, who were instrumental in clearing the forests to erect settlement infrastructure and support a timber-based export industry. As a next step, I highlight the impact of anthropological research on post-independence "tribal" policies, which aimed to both "protect" and "mainstream" the Andamanese through laws and regulations, as well as the creation of reserved tribal areas. Arriving in the present day, I explore how intersecting, transnational discourses of indigeneity and ecological conservation have had a crucial influence on both policies and politics concerning the indigenous islanders. Finally, I illustrate the way in which local political actors instrumentalize the contested notion of indigeneity in order to render their claims for recognition as Scheduled Tribes (ST), an Indian category of affirmative action, legitimate.

Setting the Context

The popular narration of indigenous pasts and presents is dominated by tales of loss, deprivation, and humiliation. After centuries of colonization, many of the approximately 370 million indigenous people around the globe have been displaced from their lands under the pretense of development (United Nations 2010). In the name of "progress" and "civilization," resourceful territories inhabited by indigenous peoples have been exploited by commercially ambitious governments and private enterprises. There are, however, always some exceptional stories to prove the rule: certain indigenous peoples have resisted, sometimes violently, against the forces of "civilization."

In 2001, during my first visit to the Andaman Islands, I came to be personally confronted with the devastating effects of territorial expansion, pacification, and assimilation policies. I had taken a bus ride on the Andaman Trunk Road (ATR), which connects the different islands of Great Andaman.[6] At Middle Strait, a creek between two of the islands, the bus and its passengers boarded a ferry. On the far side of the creek, the road continued through the reserve of the indigenous Jarawa.[7] The construction of the ATR in the 1970s increased interactions between Indian settlers and these hunter-gatherers, who number roughly four hundred individuals. When we landed, I saw two Jarawa boys, who were watching the arrival of the ferry. Being clad in loincloths and holding bows and arrows, they attracted the attention of the ferry passengers. The sight of Jarawa probably reminded most of the Indian settler population of a history littered with violent confrontations. In the past, many attempts by state officials to "befriend," pacify, and rule the Jarawa have failed. Because of that, the reserve has remained the largest stretch of primary forest in the islands, with a high level of biodiversity. Large parts of forest outside the reserve had been cleared for timber export or settlements.

Until recently, the Jarawa—and the Sentinel, who live on a separate, undisturbed island—have violently resisted outside interference in their lives. Since 1998, however, incidents of armed conflict and reprisal among the Jarawa and settlers have decreased (Sekhsaria and Pandya 2010: 8). Groups of predominantly young Jarawa have started to come to villages around the reserve of their own volition. As an extension of their gathering activities, and out of pure curiosity, they have entered into nonviolent relations with settlers (Chandi 2010a: 15). Because the Jarawa have now ceased to be violent, increasing numbers of outsiders illegally intrude into their reserve in order to poach game, fish, and remove valuable timber. This reduces the availability of resources necessary to maintain the Jarawas' hunting-gathering mode of livelihood. Reacting to this predicament, state agencies have increased their efforts to deliver welfare such as rations and medicine to them—despite the adverse effects of welfare policies in the last century and a half.[8] This has brought considerable changes to the Jarawas' patterns of consumption and social organization.

After my first visit to the islands, I started to study social and cultural anthropology in Munich. I was keen to get to know more about *The Andaman Islanders*, as they were called by Radcliffe-Brown in his structural-functionalist classic (1922).[9] Representations of the Andamanese, from medieval travel accounts to ethnographies or media reports, thrilled both metropolitan colonial as well as contemporary audiences. They contributed to popular imaginations of the islands as exotic places of "savagery." Studying this large variety of representations essentially taught me, however, more about colonization, statehood, and our "civilized" desires than about the Andamanese.

My studies of indigenous people–settler relations enabled the drawing of historical parallels to other frontier and settler colony settings around the world. Moreover, it led me to discover manifold other histories. As a colony of the British Empire and the ensuing Indian nation-state, the Andamans were a destination for various migrations from different parts of South and Southeast Asia. From 1858 onwards, a British penal colony was installed on the islands, to where subaltern convicts, soldiers, and contracted laborers were transported. After independence, refugees, repatriates, and landless mainland settlers contributed to shaping a multiethnic island society on formerly indigenous lands. These migrants were either settled by the government or encroached upon "free spaces" of forest land. As a result of migration processes, the population has grown to more than 400,000.

My subsequent academic work, including eighteen months of fieldwork, has focused on questions of migration, place-making, and the political relationships between the state and the population. The Andaman society has been described as a "Mini-India," because its migrant population belongs to a large variety of castes, as well as various linguistic and religious groups of the subcontinent (Zehmisch 2012). I, on the other hand, have never been able to entirely escape the topic of indigeneity: Mini-India has been defined as a space of "civilization" at a frontier with an indigenous space of "wilderness." The constitution of Mini-India is contingent on what it is not: the Other, who is out there, in the forests, beyond the boundaries of the settlements. The indigenous question has come to be enmeshed with negotiations of local belonging, and continues to haunt political debates. Thus, while doing fieldwork, I have had to consider the discourse of indigeneity as an implicit "subtext" of state-making and place-making processes.

Otherness and Savagery

The history of "civilization" or "culture" in many parts of the world is closely intertwined with the production of its own dichotomous counterpart: the "uncivilized" or "timeless Other" who lives close to "nature." Most prominent among numerous historical examples is the European conquest of the "New World," which needed to be legitimized by "the characterization of non-European societies as backward and primitive" (Anghie 2004: 4). Conceptualizations of "nature" applied not only to the natural environment, as the contemporary usage of the term implies, but also to humans, exemplified by the long-accepted Hobbesian notion of the "Natural Condition of Mankind" (Barnard 1999: 376). Within this discourse of mastery over colonized peoples, mobile hunter-gatherer groups served as the ultimate opposite to "modernity." The figure of the foraging "savage" became constitutive for the colonizers' own subjective position as technologically and morally superior.

Precolonial travel accounts, from Marco Polo among others, represented the Andamans as a wild, untamed Oriental space, inhabited by "savage cannibals" (Vaidik 2010: 17).[10] The Andamans' projection as a place of savagery intensified during the period of colonialism. Historian Satadru Sen pointed out that "[the] savage is not a uniform creature but a shifting and shifty reflection of evolving agendas that were contested between different groups of colonizers and natives" (Sen 2010: 1). Savagery was "a loose cluster of strategies and tactics" that opened up "a method and a rhetoric of control, resistance and liberation" (ibid.: 1). Modern man's savage encounter led to the creation not only of derogatory, but also of deeply fantastic, pleasurable, and often eroticized images of the savage.[11] In turn, encounters of indigenous people with the "civilized" enabled them to employ self-representations that were contingent upon "civilized" expectations and stereotypes (ibid.: 13).

In the Andamans, colonizers, colonized, and savages were enmeshed in enduring and momentous relationships after the mutiny/rebellion of 1857. Convicts from all over India and Burma were transported to the islands, where a penal colony was erected on indigenous lands. The successful and enduring institutionalization of the penal colony on the islands marked the beginning of an ambiguous relationship to the Andaman Islanders, in which savagery played a crucial role. From the very first days, the relationship of the colonizers to the Andaman Islanders was structured by domination, force, co-optation, and collaboration. After the Great Andamanese had been "pacified,"[12] some of them worked as trackers in the pursuit of runaway convicts, as well as participating in punitive expeditions against the Jarawa (Pandya 2010: 21).[13] The British and subsequent Indian colonizations of the islands have been closely aligned with the production of historical and administrative knowledge about the hostile, isolated Jarawa (Pandya 2009: 203). Since then, Jarawas, colonizers, settlers, and migrants have mutually signified their relationship and negotiated their "boundaries" through violent encounters (ibid.: 204).

The British did not conquer the whole Andamanese territory. Instead, they confined themselves to the twin processes of "civilizing" and medical interventions, which became metaphors for political control and governance (Sen 2010: 144). "Savage management" turned into one of the important elements of the colonial agenda within and outside the penal settlement (ibid.: 132). The civilizing mission of isolating and educating savages in so-called "Andaman Homes" resulted in mass infections with diseases like measles and syphilis, which were previously absent from the islands, and led to a rapid rise in mortality rates. While there were approximately 5,000 Great Andamanese in 1858, the 1901 Census registered a mere 625 individuals (Chandi 2010a: 17). The British believed that the Andamanese were a "dying race" that were becoming extinct as a result of outside contact (Sen 2010: 28). Thus, these savages came to be perceived as "living dead in a fossilized habitat," who needed to be protected from civilization (ibid.: 128). This, paradoxically, induced the administration to increase their medical interventions. Beyond that, surveillance and control of the diseases by the British served to bring the Andamanese under the authority of the colonial state (Sen 2000: 157).

The perceived threat of extinction led the British to gather all possible information about the surviving Andamanese (Sen 2010: 23). Anthropological journals published numerous detailed articles about them. These concerned not only their "primitive" way of life, but also their bodies. With an average height of 1.5 meters, dark skin color, and curly hair, they were a cause of curiosity among both laymen and professional anthropologists around the world. In 1927, the German anthropologist Egon von Eickstedt came to the islands and produced an anthropometric collection of the Andamanese (Icke-Schwalbe and Günther 1991: 10; Mukerjee 2003: 120).[14] From the early twentieth century onwards, Andamanese skulls and objects were sent around the world.[15] Their racial and linguistic differences to other South Asian populations, as well as their physical resemblance to the Semang in Malaysia and the Aeta in the Philippines, led researchers to classify them as "Negritos" (Icke-Schwalbe and Günther 1991: 11). Attempting to confirm the Out of Africa theory, researchers analyzed whether the Andamanese had a genetic affinity to the Congo Pygmies (Mukerjee 2003: 213). In spite of there being no established connection to Africa, some contemporaries continue to believe that the Andamanese are actually shipwrecked African slaves.

Moreover, satisfying the desires of colonial audiences with Oriental tales of exoticism, the figure of the Andaman Islander became a trope in British representations of Otherness, such as in Arthur Conan Doyle's Sherlock Holmes story "The Sign of Four" (Wintle 2013: 139–45): "Never have I seen features so deeply marked with all bestiality and cruelty. His small eyes glowed and burned with a sombre light, and his thick lips were writhed back from his teeth, which grinned and chattered at us with half animal fury" (Doyle, in Mukerjee 2003: 20). Such Othering can be regarded as an ideological mechanism of self-making that served to justify processes of exploration, conquest, and colonization. It functioned according to a binary logic, in which the "civilized" stabilized an inconsistent identity as superior in contrast to the archetypical "primitive" hunter-gatherer.

Criminals, Aboriginals, and the Conquest of Space

Apart from the desire to civilize the Andamanese, colonization can also be regarded as "ecological warfare" against jungles and their "savage" inhabitants; this "ecological warfare" was, especially, an element of Jarawa counter-insurgency measures (Sen 2010: 73–75). The task of developing infrastructure, clearing the forests, and drying the swamps was executed on the Andaman Islands by "criminal" convicts.[16] A rehabilitation scheme was set up allowing loyal convicts to settle with their families as free, self-supporting colonists at the end of their term (Sen 2000). This led to the locating of ex-convict settlers in specific ecological zones at the frontier, in geographical proximity to the indigenous islanders. These settlers and their descendants became the first non-indigenous permanent inhabitants of the islands. Furthermore, Moplah rebels from the Malabar Coast and members of the Bhantu community, a "criminal tribe" from North India, were settled on former indigenous lands in order to reform themselves through a sedentary and disciplined lifestyle (Coomar 1997: 23).[17] Additionally, the government aimed to further colonize the forests. It settled the Karen, a Burmese "hill tribe," in Middle Andaman as free migrants and pioneering cultivators.

The policy of populating and widening the frontier was combined with the expansion of commercial forestry. From 1918 onwards, specialized forest laborers, aboriginal migrants from the Chotanagpur region in Middle India, were contracted as "hill coolies" by the Catholic Labour Bureau in the city of Ranchi.[18] These laborers belonged to different aboriginal groups: most were Oraon, Munda, and Kharia. Referring to their place of recruitment, they were called "Ranchis" or "Ranchiwallahs" (Mukerji 1992: 113). In general, the British had classified "pure aborigines" from Chotanagpur as "first-class coolies," because they were assumed to be "docile," "hard-working," and "racially fit" to endure adverse climatic and ecological conditions (Ghosh 1999: 29–32). As a consequence, they assumed that the Ranchis, who were reputed peasants that hunted and gathered, would cope better with the harsh Andaman environment than most convicts (Raju 2010). The clearance of forests by Ranchi laborers thus turned into a decisive factor for the development of infrastructure, settlements, and the timber industry. Furthermore, I believe it is safe to assume that these aborigines were not accidentally sent to the forests, which were inhabited by the Andamanese. The Ranchis' labor served to enable the economic transformation of "unproductive," "wild," and "savage" jungle spaces into "ordered," "productive" settler colony spaces. Being considered by the colonizers as less "savage" than the Andaman Islanders, these aboriginal migrants became an integral part of the ecological warfare against jungles and savages. Consequently, the Indian administration of the Andamans, which in many ways emulated British colonial policy, continued to recruit thousands of Ranchis after independence.

Postcolonial Tribal Policies

During the age of colonialism, savages' or aboriginals' externality to the state functioned to stabilize the identity of the colonizers. In postcolonial nation-states, indigenous people became potential citizens and, therefore, targets of systems of patronage: education, welfare, development, and legal protectionism—these frameworks of recognition served to simultaneously co-opt and alienate. The term "tribe" was an important anthropological concept that gradually trickled into administrative language. It was originally used in African contexts and was then transferred to British India (Berger and Heidemann 2013: 6). In mainstream anthropology and among politicized indigenous peoples, the term is now regarded as derogatory due to its allusion to primitivism, racial inferiority, and backwardness. In postcolonial India, however, the usage of the term goes back to colonial administrative distinctions between "tribes" and "castes." Here, the term assumes a distinct meaning as an administrative category. For example, designated "Schedule Tribe" (ST) groups have been granted constitutional protection and privileges in a paternalist system of affirmative action (ibid: 6). STs have exclusive access to quotas of reserved government jobs and reserved seats in institutions of higher education. The system of quota reservation for STs has thus transformed into a means of social mobility for indigenous elites. As a result of growing political and cultural consciousness, tribal groups began to use the term "*adivasi*"[19] with considerable pride to express indigenous voice, identification, and belonging.

As an "exotic" legacy of colonialism, the now numerically reduced Andaman Islanders have assumed a special importance for the Indian nation-state (Pandya 2009: 264). Several prime ministers, among them Jawaharlal Nehru, Indira Gandhi, and Rajiv Gandhi, have pointed out that the Indian state is responsible for the survival of the "endangered" race of the Andamanese. Scientists have speculated that they are descendants of early *Homo sapiens*, who migrated from Southeast Asia to the islands during the last Ice Age. One physical anthropologist even claimed that they are descendants of the earliest race on earth (cf. Mani 2011). Even up until the present day, the Andamanese have been treated as humans on a lower evolutionary level. Many anthropologists, policy makers, and citizens have not yet realized that hunter-gatherers are not living remnants of "our" past or a "window" to evolutionary history, but contemporaries who just live differently.

Relegating the Andaman Islanders to the status of an "endangered" human species, researchers have continued to tackle the question of how these "unfortunate children of nature" can be protected from extinction. Here, the legacy of colonial theories of cultural and biological evolutionism and the deeply rooted "salvage paradigm" (cf. Pinney 1997, in Sen 2010: 182) have impacted ongoing public debates and policies. This led to the formulation of the Andaman Nicobar Protection of Aboriginal Tribes Regulation (ANPATR) in 1956, which aims to protect the remaining Andamanese groups. Additionally, several tribal reserves were created and, in recent years, a buffer zone of five kilometers around the Jarawa reserve was declared, and tourist and commercial activities within it were prohibited.

For many decades, an undisputed belief has existed that in order to survive, the Andamanese need to be "mainstreamed," i.e., integrated, assimilated, civilized, and educated (Pandya 2009: 264). Therefore, policies towards the Primitive Tribal Groups (PTGs)[20] of the Andamans have targeted the provision of welfare to the Great Andamanese and Onge, who have already been "pacified." During the 1970s, the resilient Jarawa and the Sentinelese became targets of "contact missions" that aimed to establish "friendly" relations (Chandi 2010a: 13–15). However, as interactions with the steadily growing migrant population have increased, the option to isolate them from the possible negative consequences of contact has found more support, in contrast with the paradigm of assimilation.

Two institutions have assumed crucial importance in negotiating the relationship to the Andamanese. The first is the Anthropological Survey of India (ASI), which established a center in Port Blair in 1951. The regional office produced 260 publications until 1994 (Singh 1994: xv), built up an ethnographic museum, has formed expert committees, and has advised the government on numerous occasions on how to deal with "its" STs.[21] The second institution is the Andaman Adim Janjati Vikas Samiti (AAJVS, Andaman Primitive Tribal Welfare Association), a body of the tribal welfare department of the Andaman administration. The AAJVS runs the everyday business of interacting with the Andamanese and delivering welfare. From personal conversations with employees of the AAJVS, I came to know that there are few qualified anthropologists and mostly low-paid, insufficiently trained social workers. Due to their low salary, some social workers use their monopoly of access to the Andamanese for exploitative ends. Another institution, the Andaman Nicobar Tribal Research and Training Institute (ANTRI), was founded in August 2013 in order to enhance research-driven tribal policy. Because it has been so recently created, its activities cannot yet be fully evaluated.

Since the beginning of the state's engagement with the Andamanese, their demography has been monitored like that of endangered animals: stabilized or increased population numbers among Great Andamanese, Onge, and Jarawas are regularly cited in order to show the success of state interventions.[22] The Great Andamanese have been the most intensive targets of welfare programs. After independence, the remaining twenty-three speakers of several Andamanese languages were transferred to tiny Strait Island, where they were subjected to government supervision (Chandi 2010a: 17). Their population has now risen to over fifty people. This happened, among other reasons, because some of their children have been fathered by tribal welfare employees. Some Great Andamanese have become government servants working in Port Blair. Recently, two boys passed their final secondary school exams, and another teenager successfully completed a year at an industrial training institute. All three were congratulated by the administration at an official function (*Andaman Chronicle* 2012).

The public highlighting of these boys' achievements involuntarily reveals the paradoxical agenda of postcolonial tribal management, which rests on the maintenance of difference. While their success in the education system officially disproves the widespread evolutionary assumption that "primitive" tribals cannot embrace "modern" life, they are still kept in the space of difference; now, they are positively discriminated against as "advanced" tribals. Kowal expressed this dilemma in the following way: "The tribesman must desire change to be eligible for development attention. To remain worthy of this attention, however, he must not change too much" (Kowal 2008: 338).

Presently, the Sentinelese are the only group that has not been submitted to any form of state domination. They live on North Sentinel, an island that is geographically separated from Great Andaman. Due to their hostility, they have never been studied face to face by anthropologists. After the tsunami in 2004, a defense helicopter landed on North Sentinel Island in order to look for survivors. The Sentinelese immediately fired arrows, so that no official could land on the island. In 2011, Census officials tried to count the "world's most isolated tribe," as the Sentinel have been labeled (Lahiri 2011). They did not land on the island, but rather rowed nearby. In an emulation of earlier gift-giving missions, they tossed coconuts and some other items into the water and waited for the Sentinelese to appear on the beach, a camera recording the whole scene. This ridiculous act, in which fewer than one hundred individuals were counted, illustrates another dilemma of postcolonial tribal management: it is caught between demands of omnipotent state power and an impotence of action because of a paternalistic responsibility to protect.

Indigeneity as Transnational Discourse

In the last few decades, the conservation of the environment has come to the forefront of transnational activist agendas. The paradigm of conservation, however, manifests itself not only in the protection of plants and animals, but also in advocacy for indigenous peoples and their environments. Gathering and hunting societies such as the Andamanese especially have been relentlessly romanticized as "natural" conservationists. Living in "harmony" with their environment, they symbolize the human hope of returning to a life in the Garden of Eden. This implies a specific antimodern criticism of the impending anthropogenic destruction of the global environment. Anthropologist Adam Kuper confirms this idea: "The image of the primitive is often constructed today to suit the Greens and the anti-globalization movement. Authentic natives represent a world to which we should, apparently, wish to be returned, a world in which culture does not challenge nature" (Kuper 2003: 395).

In the Andamans, too, transnational ideas about ecology and conservation have become enmeshed with the indigenous question. Academics and activists have placed the original island inhabitants within the global discourse of indigeneity (Pandya and Mazumdar 2012: 51). Construing the Andamanese as "ecologically noble savages" (Hames 2007), some activists have represented them, along with their "pristine" ecological environment, as a vulnerable part of "nature" that is threatened by civilization, modernity, development, and migration. As a consequence, many actors, such as news agencies and civil society organizations, have set the Andamanese's impending demise in relation to the fate of other indigenous peoples around the world. For example, hundreds of media organizations reported on the death of Boa Senior, the last speaker of the Great Andamanese Bo language.[23] In this transnational context, the extinction of an ethnic group and/or a language epitomizes the notion of the vulnerable, diseased, depressed, and often alcoholic "dying savage," who has been uprooted from her or his ancestral lands and "culture."

The Jarawa issue has also come to invoke images of the onslaught of "civilization" on vulnerable indigenous peoples and a unique ecosystem. The Jarawa's violence against the encroaching, poaching, intruding outsiders has served to protect the ecologically unique forests of the reserve. Since the Jarawa have turned "friendly," there has been continuous political conflict within Andaman civil society about how the administration should deal with the situation. The participants in this discourse can be divided into two factions. On the one hand, there are local entrepreneurs and politicians, who support settlers and migrants living close to the reserve. They regard the Jarawa "as an inconvenient annoyance standing in the way of the future development" (Chandi 2010a: 15). They are concerned that a numerically small group occupies such a large and commercially valuable territory as the Jarawa reserve. Criticizing current policies of isolation, they suggest that policy makers should remove development restrictions on the reserve, and enable the assimilation and "mainstreaming" of these "primitive tribes."

On the other hand, there are those "familiar with the fashionable rhetoric of 'environmental heritage'" (Pandya 2009: 226). These are transnational and national activists who have come to the fore and put pressure on the national Indian government and its administration to protect the indigenous population along with the vulnerable forest and marine environment. These activists proclaim the Jarawa as first and foremost protectors of the forests against the pressures of "civilization." For them, hunter-gatherers symbolize a longstanding balance of human–environment relations. In contrast, "opportunistic migrants," who have come from mainland India and Bangladesh, are relegated to the role of irresponsible destroyers of the Andamans' vulnerable ecosystem. As a consequence, Jarawa advocacy has become enmeshed with other political demands; arguments about conservation and indigenous rights are instrumentalized to support local claims and restrict migrations to the densely populated islands (Zehmisch 2012).

One of the most controversial issues in this debate is a Supreme Court order from 2002, which called for the closure of the part of the ATR that passes through the Jarawa reserve (cf. Sekhsaria 2007: 84–86). In utter contempt of the order, this section of road was not shut down by the local administration. As a result, tribal tourism has become established on the ATR. Travel agents have instrumentalized the "savage" branding of the Andamans, enhanced by stories about "cannibalism" of "stone age" islanders, and attract tourists with the prospect of seeing Jarawas along the road. Advertising induces tourists to book package tours, officially to visit some limestone caves and a mud volcano on Baratang Island. In order to get there, the packages include a drive on the ATR through the Jarawa reserve. Similar to wildlife safaris, tourists are keen to watch some members of the "most primitive tribes," as if they were in some sort of outdoor zoo. From their air-conditioned buses and cars, they wait like big-game hunters for their prey—the hope of spotting some "savages" along the road.

In turn, the Jarawa also come to the road and wait for the tourists. They even "dress up" for these "human safaris" by wearing "no clothes."[24] When vehicles illegally stop along the ATR in order to enable the tourists to photograph the "naked savages," the tourists and drivers provide the Jarawas with biscuits, bananas, or red cloth. It is common knowledge among the drivers and travel agents that most Jarawas like these items. In recent years, an international NGO has publicly highlighted the scandal of "human safaris." As a result, national and international media focused on the issue and sensitized large parts of Indian civil society. Public pressure led the Andaman administration to act promptly; some culprits were identified and charged, and some weak legal measures have been implemented to prevent this kind of tribal tourism. However, this random punishment of a few scapegoats has not effectively hindered the continuation of traffic and tourism on the road.

The Politics of Indigeneity: Diasporic *Adivasi*-ness and the ST Question

In a global context, the shifty notion of indigeneity appears in its contemporary "avatar" as a category of active political assertiveness. The notion of indigeneity is used by indigenous elites and activists to appeal to powerful actors within their hegemonic modes of speaking (Tsing 2007). The stereotype of the "ecologically noble savage" (Hames 2007), building on the duality of "nature" and "culture," provides indigenous actors with an idiom to articulate their voice in dominant Western frameworks. Hence, indigenous actors often represent themselves and their people in these terms, particularly when asserting political claims for legal rights and collective recognition (cf. Ingold 2000; Kuper 2003). For example, the image of Native Americans as "natural" conservationists has been taken up by groups in order to present arguments about property rights, sovereignty, cultural pride, and ethical superiority (Hames 2007: 182). Indigenous political leaders instrumentalize the notion of indigeneity as a political weapon; they use it to mobilize external political support, through (trans)national organizations, and within international frameworks such as the UN system (Merlan 2009).

In South Asia, the politicization of indigeneity has become closely intertwined with transnational struggles for the recognition of indigenous rights. Increasing identifications as *adivasi* (first people), *vanvasi* (forest dwellers), *janjati* (tribal), *dharati putr* (sons of the soil), *adi dravida* (original people or original Dravidians), and *pahari* (hill people) are linked to issues of social assertion and cultural recognition. The question of access to land, as well as to other symbolic and material resources, has turned into a central issue in *adivasi* assertions of identity against dominant groups (Carrin 2013: 109). *Adivasi* communities display the twin banners of custom and indigeneity, and project themselves as citizens (ibid.: 113).

Parallel to the transnational politicization of indigeneity, Andaman and Nicobar politics have become haunted by the Jarawa issue, which, as demonstrated above, has been transformed into a semantic site of multiple political negotiations. Media, government servants, and civil society members have dominated the discourse about the Andamanese, whose voices have gone largely unheard or unconsidered, while they instead remain "arrested" in the "jungle." This form of exclusion stands in stark opposition to the political articulations of other communities that consciously claim indigenous status: the Nicobar Islanders[25] and the Ranchis. For both communities, the ST category, which can be regarded as an avenue to social mobility, has turned into a contested means of self-assertion. While, however, the legitimacy of the Nicobar Islanders' claims for ST quota reservation has never been questioned,[26] the demands of the Ranchi community that they should also be recognized as ST have proven to be complicated. Ranchi leaders aim to fill vacant ST posts, reserved for recognized indigenous Andaman and Nicobar Islanders. Arguing that only a fraction of the Andamanese use these posts, they demand similar entitlements as a "migrated" ST group.

Before going into the details of why these politics have failed, I would like to elaborate on how the Ranchis appropriate preconceived notions of their ascribed aboriginality to express their "indigenous" belonging. As community politics are cast in the language of *"adivasi*-ness"—for example, in an interview, a Ranchi leader told me that they were "true *adivasis*" — most of the approximately 50,000 Ranchis represent themselves contextually as a united diasporic community based on their indigeneity; they emphasize their regional ancestry in Chotanagpur, their tribal way of life, their class affiliation as aboriginal migrant laborers, their political identification as *adivasi*, and their administrative recognition as STs on the mainland. To underline their political demands, they have organized several public demonstrations. In August 2010, for example, between 3,000 and 5,000 people participated in a rally to claim ST status (Raju 2010).

One reason for the Ranchis' lack of political success has been their social marginalization as aboriginal migrant laborers. Most Ranchis have remained invisible and silent in the public sphere. They have been cut off from the lines of social mobility. Instead, they have resorted to a life in the margins, largely illegally occupying encroached forest lands, where they continually live under the threat of eviction. Little has been done for their welfare. This neglect has been justified by their "tribalness," which rendered them, accordingly, "quite happy in the forest" (Saldhana 1989: 14). This representation is, of course, an indirectly official recognition of their very aboriginality; it is associated with cultural traits such as a particular kinship system, worldview, and human–environment relations.

Contrary to their common treatment as aboriginals, the recognition of Ranchis as ST is a complicated issue. Ranchi leaders refer to the fact that migrated *adivasis* from Chotanagpur have been recognized as STs in other states of the Indian union. Influential spokespersons of other communities, as well as government officials, argue that the indigenous Andamanese and Nicobarese deserve "special protection." If "more advanced" Ranchi elites were to compete with them for reserved posts and seats, the indigenous Andamanese and Nicobarese STs might lose their privileged access to the state system.

Another reason why the Ranchis' ST claim is not supported by many politicians is the opposition of the Nicobarese. With a population of approximately 30,000 (Ramanujam, Singh, and Vatn 2012: 4), the Nicobarese are known as a "vote bank" of the Congress Party. Political leaders fear losing these votes if Ranchis receive ST status.

This dispute vividly demonstrates that the notion of indigeneity has become a multifaceted political site through which communities actively negotiate their relationships to the state. If political and administrative stakeholders decide to give ST status to the Ranchis, the local political debate about indigenous entitlement might intensify and lead other migrant tribal groups on the islands—for example the Karen, or individual migrants coming from other *adivasi* backgrounds—to beget new claims for indigenous recognition. This may not necessarily be an "evil" or counterproductive development that stands in the way of the "protection" and "promotion" of the Andaman Islanders, but just a recognition of the fact that the notion of indigeneity continues to "travel" (Tsing 2007) and transform constantly.

Conclusion: Futures of Indigeneity

The most constant features of indigeneity are its flexibility, dynamism, and multiplicity. Definitions and understandings of the notion have changed and varied, across time and over different spaces and contexts. The discourse of indigeneity can be regarded as an entourage of the respective *Zeitgeist*; it became manifest as a concomitant of state institutionalization in different historical periods. This chapter has discussed the shifting notions of indigeneity throughout time by elaborating on state policies towards indigenous peoples. My specific focus has been on spatial arrangements and negotiations of contact: the colonization of indigenous lands was realized through population movement into primary forest spaces. In the course of this process, multiple terms and discourses of indigeneity were prevalent; colonial notions of savagery were indicative of indigenous warfare and co-optation at the frontier, and justified the "taming" and "civilizing" of primitives; spaces of wilderness were first colonized through the transportation of criminal tribes and the rehabilitation of criminals, some of whom were perceived as "evolutionary savages." Later, aboriginality was the main criterion for contracting the Ranchis, specialized *adivasi* forest laborers. After independence, anthropologically informed "tribal governance" led to protection acts, reserve zones, and welfare policies. At the same time, forestry, infrastructure developments, and migration pressure on resources contributed to the degradation of forests as an indigenous resource base and instigated further violent conflicts. Following the end of violent relations, transnational, national, and local civil society actors appropriated the notion of indigeneity for political purposes: conservationists and indigenous rights activists promoted their own "ecologically noble savage" agenda during the struggle for protection of the remaining Andaman Islanders and their habitat. In contrast, local politicians advocated the "mainstreaming" of "backward" *junglees*; additionally, claims for ST status by Ranchi *adivasi* elites demonstrated that the discourse of indigeneity had been transformed into a site of politics.

The trajectory of these conflicting and fluid characteristics of indigeneity can be regarded as an indicator for indigenous futures. By looking at past trajectories of indigeneity, one can understand the constant shifts of its meaning up until the present. This is liable to continue into the future. Indigeneity is contingent on definitions of Self and Other and, as such, it contributes to identification processes, and to political articulations of belonging. In the sphere of politics, indigeneity has become further and further detached from its negative connotations. Articulate indigenous elites might have gained some advantages from this redefinition, but I believe that such benefits will only increase the socioeconomic and cultural divide between indigenous elites and majorities. They will not solve larger problems. Stigmatization of indigenous peoples in their everyday interactions with non-indigenous people will surely not just vanish by recognizing single articulate indigenous members of civil society. The futures of indigenous peoples are, therefore, as uncertain as the impact of our scholarly discourse.

Philipp Zehmisch (Dr.phil., Munich) is Postdoctoral Research Fellow at the Center for Advanced Studies and the Department of Social and Cultural Anthropology, LMU Munich. His research interest lies at the intersection of postcolonial studies, political anthropology, and migration studies with a regional focus on South Asia. Philipp conducted twenty months of doctoral fieldwork in the Andamans between 2006 and 2012. His PhD thesis, "Mini-India: The Politics of Migration and Subalternity in the Andaman Islands," won the Dissertation Prize of the Faculty for the Study of Culture, LMU Munich, as well as the Frobenius Society's Research Award 2015 and was published in 2017 by Oxford University Press, Delhi. Along with Frank Heidemann, he has also coedited the volume *Manifestations of History: Time, Space, and Community in the Andaman Islands* with Primus (Delhi) in 2016. Philipp's postdoctoral research project, "Dichotomous Sovereignty: Cultures of Remembrance, Historiography and Nation-Building in South Asia," examines the contemporary reception of the partition of British India and its legacy from an ethnographic perspective.

Notes

1. I understand the term "indigenous" not as a signifier of any essential genetic or cultural properties, but as a contextual, relational, and politically

loaded term, which is consciously used by indigenous and non-indigenous actors alike, to claim protection, rights, and recognition from the state in the name of marginalized populations. Indigeneity can, therefore, be tentatively conceptualized as a dialectical process between essentialist ascriptions of identity and, in turn, processes of appropriation, reinterpretation, rearrangement, and camouflage of categories of indigenous-ness by those who are signified as Others.
2. Broadly generalizing, these discourses have been produced by states in order to create semantic boundaries between themselves and non-state populations. In turn, non-state or anarchic peoples have their own ways of dealing with states (Gibson and Silander 2011; Graeber 2008; Scott 2009); beyond the simplistic binary of collaboration and resistance, their strategies of maintaining spaces of cultural, social, economic, and political autonomy include practices of subversion, evasion, and deception that intersect with changing notions of belonging (cf. Scott 1985, 2009).
3. The term "indigenous peoples" is contested because it covers a wide range of populations living in different regional and national contexts, in which the "traveling models of indigeneity" assume ambiguous and often contradictory meanings (Tsing 2007: 38).
4. Together with the Nicobar Islands, the Andamans officially constitute the Indian Union Territory Andaman and Nicobar Islands. They are located in the Bay of Bengal, and altogether are comprised of 572 islands, reefs, and rocks (Sekhsaria 2009: 256). The islands are located in the geographical vicinity of Southeast Asia, more than 1,000 kilometers from the Indian mainland. Due to their strategic importance, this former British colony is now under the direct rule of the Indian central government in New Delhi.
5. I use the terms "Andaman Islanders" and "Andamanese" interchangeably, to refer to all groups of indigenous islanders.
6. The main land mass of the Andamans is called Great Andaman. It measures about 200 kilometers from north to south, with an average east–west breadth of 30 kilometers. Great Andaman can be regarded as one island, although narrow seawater creeks physically divide it into the islands of South Andaman, Baratang, Middle Andaman, and North Andaman (Lal 1976: 1).
7. The Jarawa Tribal Reserve was created in 1957 in order to protect the inhabitants under the Indian constitution, and to "ensure that members of the tribe get exclusive access to land, water and all the resources of the reserved territory" (Kumar et al. 2010: 59). The Jarawa were assigned a territory that today comprises approximately 1,000 square kilometers of forest land (Pandya 2010: 19).
8. British and subsequent Indian attempts to pacify and civilize the twelve Andamanese groups led either to their complete extinction or to a drastic demographic decline. Among the numerous monographs written about the relationship between the Andamanese and the state, I recommend Pandya (2009), Sen (2010), and Venkateswar (2004).
9. The colonial administration classified the Andaman Islanders into four tribes, and estimated their precolonial population at 6,500 in 1780 (Pan-

dya 2009: 74); the Great Andamanese with nine tribal subdivisions, distinguished by their dialects, numbered approximately 5,000 persons; the Jarawa around 600 persons; the Onge between 700 and 1,000 persons; and the Sentinelese between 50 and 100 persons. There was another group of Jarawa people, or "Jangils," on Rutland Island who died out before much was learned about them (Chandi 2010b: 32).

10. This belief in cannibalistic practices has survived, in part, to the present day. For example, passengers on an aircraft told me that when flying over North Sentinel Island, the captain announced that its indigenous people were the last remaining cannibals. Furthermore, I was repeatedly asked by tourists if the rumor that cannibals lived on the islands was true. In spite of the fact that the existence of cannibalism among the Andaman Islanders was disproved in the nineteenth century (Chib 1985: 45), popular belief in it persists. Such discrepancies between factual knowledge and the Orientalist myth are symptomatic of the postcolonial condition. Not only hearsay, but also literary representations of the islands, such as David Tomory's novel *Cannibal Isles: Time Travelling in the Andaman Islands* (2003), perpetually reify the trope of cannibalism. Paradoxically, the trope of cannibalism also existed among the Andamanese: in earlier times, the Great Andamanese regarded light-skinned, bearded seafarers who sailed by as *lau*: "spirits of the sea with a taste for human flesh" (Mukerjee 2003: 2; see also Mukerjee 2005).

11. Colonial fantasies of overseas exploration and conquest were heavily gendered and sexualized (Zantop 1997). For the discoverer, the Andaman Islands probably symbolized such discovery fantasies and the demarcation of "virgin" territory. Islands, as opposed to continents, stood for unboundedness and fluidity. They were associated with tropicality, moisture, heat, and fertility. Within this imaginary framework, the Andaman Islanders may have appeared as a human embodiment of tropicality and exoticism.

12. The memorial of the Battle of Aberdeen in the center of Port Blair town is reminiscent of this violent history. In 1859, Dudnath Tewari, a runaway convict who had lived among the Great Andamanese tribe of the Aka-Bea-Da for more than a year, had warned the British of a coordinated full-scale attack. What came to be known as the Battle of Aberdeen was in fact a massacre of around four hundred Great Andamanese by prepared British troops with firearms (Pandya 2009: 83).

13. Jarawa means "stranger" in Aka-Bea-Da, one of the nine Great Andamanese dialects. It indicates a longstanding, probably antagonistic relationship between the groups of islanders (Chandi 2010b: 32). The Jarawa refer to themselves as *Ang* (people/humans). The languages of the Jarawa and Onge belong to a separate language group from the Great Andamanese and differ in grammar, vocabulary, and sound systems (Abbi 2006).

14. Eickstedt's diaries have been evaluated by several researchers. Katja Müller (2016) wrote her dissertation about Eickstedt's research in South India. Dr Lydia Icke-Schwalbe from Dresden and Dr Carola Krebs from the Anthropological Museum in Leipzig are focusing on Eickstedt's journey to the Andamans.

15. The Anthropological Museum in Munich, for example, has recently published a compilation about its collection of Andamanese artifacts (Helbig 2012).
16. Interestingly, criminologists once conceptualized criminals as evolutionary "savages" who had been left behind as the rest of society evolved (cf. Anderson 2004: 182).
17. In 1871, the Criminal Tribes Act criminalized around 250 ethnic groups that lived autonomously from state structures and did not recognize the colonial state's authority, legitimacy, and sovereignty. As these often mobile peoples were difficult to control and govern, they were declared to be criminals and in need of reform (Sen 2000: 43).
18. The case of Chotanagpuri aboriginal laborers migrating to the Andamans must be regarded as embedded in historical processes of "coolie" migration. Large numbers of impoverished Chotanagpuris emigrated, as contracted or indentured laborers, to various parts of the Indian subcontinent and overseas (Bates 2000; Bates and Carter 1992; Ghosh 1999; Tinker 1993).
19. An equivalent of the word "aboriginal," derived from the Hindi word *adi*, "beginning" and *vasi*, "resident" (Carrin 2013: 107).
20. The terminology has recently shifted to Particularly Vulnerable Tribal Groups (PVTGs).
21. The ASI has a special status among anthropological research institutions. It is not part of a university or academic apparatus, but affiliated to and financed by a central government ministry. The ASI's main purpose is to research and inform government policies towards the huge tribal population of India, who altogether number more than ninety million people.
22. The public was regularly informed about cases of Onge births along with their actualized population numbers (111 persons) by the local newspapers *The Daily Telegrams* (cf. 18 February 2011; 11 May 2012; 20 August 2012; 10 October 2012; 24 January 2013), the *Andaman Chronicle* (cf. 21 August 2012; 2 September 2012; 13 February 2013), and *Andaman Sheeka* (11 April 2013).
23. Selected examples of media, provided by Survival International (in a mail to the Yahoo newsgroup andamanicobar on 16 February 2010) are: *The Hindu, Hindustan Times*, CNN, ABC News, *Times, Independent*, Bloomberg, Reuters, Agence France Presse, Al Jazeera, *The Guardian, Ottawa Citizen, Courier Mail, Straits Times*, USA Today, and *Gulf Times*.
24. According to Pandya, the wearing of clothes is a communicative practice and a measure of their changing relations to the settlers (Pandya 2009: 156). Many Jarawas wear clothes when going to Port Blair (ibid.: 179), or when meeting tribal welfare workers inside the jungle (ibid.: 190–91). However, along the road, Jarawas tactically remove their clothes (ibid.: 172).
25. The colonial project on the Nicobars was executed on a smaller scale compared with that on the Andamans, and its impact was therefore similarly smaller. The Nicobarese have, therefore, always remained the numerical majority in their islands. The term Nicobarese actually incorporates an internally diverse ensemble of four distinct cultural groups (Singh 2003).
26. The Nicobarese community has articulate leaders and government servants, who are able to publicly underline their claims as "indigenous" islanders, and hence to be entitled to ST quotas.

Bibliography

Abbi, Anvita. 2006. *Endangered Languages of the Andaman Islands*. Munich: Lincom Europa.
Andaman Chronicle. 2012. "Great Andamanese Boys Felicitated for Their Achievements," 4 June. Retrieved 21 June 2017 from https://in.groups.yahoo.com/neo/groups/andamanicobar/conversations/topics/8883.
Anderson, Clare. 2004. *Legible Bodies: Race, Criminality and Colonialism in South Asia*. Oxford and New York: Berg.
Anghie, Anthony. 2004. *Imperialism, Sovereignty and the Making of International Law*. New York: Cambridge University Press.
Barnard, Allan. 1999. "Images of Hunters and Gatherers in European Social Thought." In *The Cambridge Encyclopedia of Hunters and Gatherers*, ed. Richard Lee and Richard H. Daly, 375–383. Cambridge: Cambridge University Press.
Bates, Crispin 2000. "Coerced and Migrant Labourers in India: The Colonial Experience." *Edinburgh Papers in South Asian Studies* 13: 1–33.
Bates, Crispin and Marina Carter. 1992. "Tribal Migration in India and Beyond." In *The World of the Rural Labourer in Colonial India*, ed. Gyan Prakash, 205–247. Delhi: Oxford University Press.
Berger, Peter and Frank Heidemann. 2013. "Introduction: The Many Indias: The Whole and Its Parts." In *The Modern Anthropology of India: Ethnography, Themes and Theory*, ed. Peter Berger and Frank Heidemann, 1–11. London and New York: Routledge.
Carrin, Marine. 2013. "Jharkhand: Alternative Citizenship in an 'Adivasi State'." In *The Modern Anthropology of India: Ethnography, Themes and Theory*, ed. Peter Berger and Frank Heidemann, 106–20. London and New York: Routledge.
Chandi, Manish. 2010a. "Colonisation and Conflict Resolution: Learning from Reconstruction of Conflict between Indigenous and Non-Indigenous Islanders." In *The Jarawa Tribal Reserve Dossier: Cultural and Biological Diversities in the Andaman Islands*, eds. Pankaj Sekhsaria and Vishvajit Pandya, 12–17. Paris: UNESCO.
———. 2010b. "Territory and Landscape around the Jarawa Reserve." In *The Jarawa Tribal Reserve Dossier: Cultural and Biological Diversities in the Andaman Islands*, ed. Pankaj Sekhsaria and Vishvajit Pandya, 30–42. Paris: UNESCO.
Chib, Sukhdev Singh. 1985. *Caste, Tribes and Culture of India, Vol IX: Andaman and Nicobar*. New Delhi: Ess Ess Publications.
Coomar, Palash Chandra. 1997. *Migration and Social Change: A Study of the Bhantu of Andaman Islands*. Calcutta: Anthropological Survey of India.
Ghosh, Kaushik. 1999. "A Market for Aboriginality: Primitivism and Race Classification in the Indentured Labour Market of Colonial India." In *Subaltern Studies X: Writings on South Asian History and Society*, ed. Gautham Bhadra, Gyan Prakash, and Suzie Tharu, 8–48. Delhi: Oxford University Press.
Gibson, Thomas and Kenneth Silander. 2011. *Anarchic Solidarity: Autonomy, Equality, and Fellowship in Southeast Asia*. New Haven, CT: Yale University Southeast Asia Studies.
Graeber, David. 2008. *Frei von Herrschaft: Fragmente einer anarchistischen Anthropologie*. Wuppertal: Peter Hammer Verlag.

Hames, Raymond. 2007. "The Ecologically Noble Savage Debate." *Annual Review of Anthropology* 36: 177–90.
Helbig, Andrea. 2012. *It Was in the Days of the Ancestors: Die Andamanen-Sammlung des Staatlichen Museums für Völkerkunde München*. Munich: Verlag des Staatlichen Museums für Völkerkunde.
Icke-Schwalbe, Lydia and Michael Günther. 1991. *Andamanen und Nikobaren: ein Kulturbild der Inseln im Indischen Meer*. Dresden and Münster: Lit.
Ingold, Tim. 2000. *The Perception of the Environment: Essays on Livelihood, Dwelling and Skill*. London and New York: Routledge.
Kowal, Emma. 2008. "The Politics of the Gap: Indigenous Australians, Liberal Multiculturalism, and the End of the Self-Determination Era." *American Anthropologist* 10(3): 338–48.
Kumar, Umesh, et al. 2010. "The Jarawas and their Lands." In *The Jarawa Tribal Reserve Dossier: Cultural and Biological Diversities in the Andaman Islands*, ed. Pankaj Sekhsaria and Vishvajit Pandya, 58–63. Paris: UNESCO.
Kuper, Adam. 2003. "The Return of the Native." *Current Anthropology* 44(3): 389–402.
Lahiri, Tripti. 2011. "India's Most Elusive Address: The Remote and Hostile North Sentinel Island Is a Census Taker's Biggest Torment." Retrieved 11 December 2014 from http://online.wsj.com/article/SB10001424052748704076804576179751179017050.html.
Lal, Parmanand. 1976. *Andaman and Nicobar Islands: A Regional Geography*. Calcutta: Anthropological Survey of India.
Mani, Rajiv. 2011. "Humans Originated from Andamans?" *Times of India*, 23 May. Retrieved 11 December 2014 from http://timesofindia.indiatimes.com/india/Humans-originated-from-Andamans/articleshow/8532889.cms.
Merlan, Francesca. 2009. "Indigeneity: Global and Local." *Current Anthropology* 50(3): 303–33.
Mukerjee, Madhusree. 2003. *The Land of Naked People: Encounters with Stone Age Islanders*. New Delhi: Penguin Books.
———. 2005. "Lessons on Island Living." *South Asian Magazine for Action and Reflection (Samar)*19. Retrieved 30 December 2014 from http://samarmagazine.org/archive/articles/188.
Mukerji, Sarit Kumar. 1992. *Islands of India*, ed. Ministry of Information and Broadcasting, Government of India. New Delhi: Publication Division.
Müller, Katja. 2016. *Die Eickstedt-Sammlung aus Südindien: Differenzierte Wahrnehmungen kolonialer Fotografien und Objekte*. Frankfurt: Peter Lang.
Pandya, Vishvajit. 2009. *In the Forest: Visual and Material Worlds of Andamanese History (1858–2006)*. Lanham, MD and Plymouth: University Press of America.
———. 2010. "Hostile Borders on Historical Landscapes: The Placeless Place of Andamanese Culture." In *The Jarawa Tribal Reserve Dossier: Cultural and Biological Diversities in the Andaman Islands*, ed. Pankaj Sekhsaria and Vishvajit Pandya, 18–29. Paris: UNESCO.
Pandya, Vishvajit and Madhumita Mazumdar. 2012. "Making Sense of the Andaman Islanders: Reflections on a New Conjuncture." *Economic and Political Weekly* XLVII(44): 51–58.

Radcliffe-Brown, Alfred R. 1922. *The Andaman Islanders*. London: Weidenfeld and Nicholson.

Raju, Govinda. 2010. "Ranchiwallahs: The Pains of Dispossession." *The Light of Andamans* 35(2). Retrieved 21 June 2017 from https://in.groups.yahoo.com/neo/groups/andamanicobar/conversations/messages/6758

Ramanujam, Venkat, Simron Singh, and Arild Vatn. 2012. "From the Ashes into the Fire? Institutional Change in the Post-Tsunami Nicobar Islands, India." *Society and Natural Resources: An International Journal* 25(11): 1–15.

Saldhana, Cecil J. 1989. *Andaman, Nicobar and Lakshadweep: An Environmental Impact Assessment*. New Delhi: Oxford & IBH Publishing Company.

Scott, James C. 1985. *Weapons of the Weak: Everyday Forms of Peasant Resistance*. New Haven, CT and London: Yale University Press.

———. 2009. *The Art of Not Being Governed: An Anarchist History of Upland Southeast Asia*. New Haven, CT and London: Yale University Press.

Sekhsaria, Pankaj. 2007. *Troubled Islands: Writings on the Indigenous Peoples and Environment of the Andaman and Nicobar Islands*. Pune: Kalvapriksh and LEAD-India.

———. 2009. "When Chanos Chanos Became Tsunami Macchi: The Post-December 2004 Scenario in the Andaman and Nicobar Islands." *Journal of the Bombay Natural History Society* 106(3): 256–62.

Sekhsaria, Pankaj and Vishvajit Pandya (eds). 2010. *The Jarawa Tribal Reserve Dossier: Cultural and Biological Diversities in the Andaman Islands*. Paris. UNESCO.

Sen, Satadru. 2000. *Disciplining Punishment: Colonialism and Convict Society in the Andaman Islands*. New Delhi: Oxford University Press.

———. 2010. *Savagery and Colonialism in the Indian Ocean: Power, Pleasure and the Andaman Islanders*. New York: Routledge.

———. 2011. "On the Beach in the Andaman Islands: Post-mortem of a Failed Colony." *Economic and Political Weekly* XLVI(26/27): 177–86.

Singh, Kumar Suresh. 1994. *People of India: Andaman and Nicobar Islands, Volume XII*. New Delhi: Anthropological Survey of India.

Singh, Simron Jit. 2003. *In the Sea of Influence: A World System Perspective of the Nicobar Islands*. Lund: Lund University.

Tinker, Hugh. 1974. *A New System of Slavery: The Export of Indian Labour Overseas 1830–1920*. London: Oxford University Press.

Tomory, David. 2003. *Cannibal Isles: Time Travelling in the Andaman Islands*. London: Nthposition.

Tsing, Anna. 2007. "Indigenous Voice." In *Indigenous Experience Today*, ed. Marisol de la Cadena and Orin Starn, 33–67. Oxford and New York: Berg.

United Nations. 2010. "UN Report Paints Grim Picture of Conditions of World's Indigenous Peoples." Retrieved 11 December 2014 from http://www.un.org/apps/news/story.asp?NewsID=33484&Cr=indigenous&Cr1.

Vaidik, Aparna. 2010. *Imperial Andamans: Colonial Encounter and Island History*. Hampshire and New York: Palgrave Macmillan.

Venkateswar, Sita. 2004. *Development and Ethnocide: Colonial Practices in the Andaman Islands*. Copenhagen: Iwgia.

Wintle, Claire. 2013. *Colonial Collecting and Display: Encounters with Material Culture from the Andaman and Nicobar Islands*. New York: Berghahn Books.

Zantop, Susanne. 1997. *Colonial Fantasies: Conquest, Family and Nation in Precolonial Germany, 1770–1870*. Durham, NC and London: Duke University Press.

Zehmisch, Philipp. 2012. "A Xerox of India: Policies and Politics of Migration in the Andaman Islands." *Papers in Social and Cultural Anthropology* 2. Munich: Institut für Ethnologie. Retrieved 11 December 2014 from http://www.ethnologie.uni-muenchen.de/forschung/publikationen/studien/bd2_zehmisch_andamanen.pdf.

 Postscriptum

THE FUTURES OF INDIGENOUS MEDICINE
Networks, Contexts, Freedom
William S. Sax

The concept of "indigeneity" has become quite prominent, even fashionable, in recent decades. Terms like "indigenous knowledge" and "local knowledge" have become parts of international development discourse, and can even be found on the website of the World Bank, which praises "indigenous knowledge" in various contexts, such as agriculture, animal husbandry, ethnic veterinary medicine, use and management of natural resources, primary healthcare, preventive medicine, psychosocial care, saving and lending, community development, and poverty alleviation (World Bank n.d.). Acknowledging indigeneity seems like a good idea—and no doubt it is in many contexts—but it can also be problematic. In this postscriptum, I express some reservations about the concept of "indigeneity," especially with regard to what are called "indigenous medical systems." I argue that it relies on a problematic contrast between the global and the particular, and that ostensibly "global" knowledge is in fact "indigenous" because it is always applied in specific social and historical contexts, while some of the most prominent forms of "indigenous" knowledge are in fact global, because they have been heavily shaped by external influences.

Global Knowledge is "Indigenous"

Indigenous knowledge is characterized by Wikipedia as knowledge that is "embedded in the cultural traditions of regional, indigenous, or local communities," and is contrasted by Warren (1991) with "the international knowledge system generated by universities, research institutions and private firms." I think that this is a misleading contrast, because all knowledge is (or at least was, at some point in time) "indigenous," so that the idea of pure or enduringly indigenous knowledge is a fiction, like the idea of a "pure race." Just as human beings generally prefer to make love rather than war, thus guaranteeing that the gene pool is always mixed, so knowledge is always borrowed, copied, shared, or perhaps even stolen, but almost never purely "indigenous." The idea that some knowledge is indigenous while some is universal reminds me of the expression: "everyone has an accent but me."

Of course, one could argue—and many have—that certain knowledge systems began as forms of indigenous or local knowledge, but later transcended their origins to become universal. One candidate would be modern medicine, also known as *Schulmedizin* in Germany, Allopathy in India, biomedicine among medical anthropologists, and cosmopolitan medicine in some circles (Frankenberg 1980: 198). The latter term is meant to call attention to the fact that, despite its European origins, this form of medicine has become truly global.

So the claim is made that such knowledge systems have transcended their local origins—which one might call their "indigeneity"—and become global precisely because they have discovered certain universal and non-contextual truths that apply everywhere; truths that transcend (or are the foundations of) history and culture. This is scientific realism with a historical conscience, according to which the so-called "facts of nature" are more adequately described and understood by certain sciences than others. Or, to put it another way, the idea is that the modern sciences grasp such universal and natural facts more accurately than their historical predecessors, who have accordingly fallen by the wayside. Examples of the former would be chemistry, physics, and mathematics; of the latter, phrenology, mesmerism, and theories of demonic possession (cf. Daston 2000).

I reject this argument, too, because I believe that it misrepresents the nature of science in general, and knowledge in particular. I take my cues from historically minded philosophers like Bruno Latour, Annemarie Mol, and Ian Hacking. The idea of knowledge as an abstract and timeless system, divorced from its actual application, may have some heuristic value, but I would insist that "knowledge" is always *done*: it is acquired, owned, disputed, applied, and perhaps rejected, but without such "doings," a "knowledge system" has no independent status, no ontological "weight". Moreover, such doings are always historical and contextual.

Let us take the example of mathematics. It is often claimed that ancient Indian mathematicians made independent "discoveries" of universal facts, such as the Pythagorean theorem—that they invented the zero, and so on. But the context in which they did so was primarily a ritual one: mathematical activity in ancient India began as part of a "methodological reflection" on the sacred Vedas (Filliozat 2004); and mathematical calculations were used primarily to determine the correct time for performing the rites. It is said that the Indians discovered the Pythagorean theorem independently, but the sources make clear that this was a response to the practical problems of constructing fire altars. These forms of knowledge were practical forms of "doing."

One might even argue that the very words "mathematics" and "mathematician" are anachronistic misnomers when applied to the ancient Indians, if we intend to denote "pure science"; that is, science for its own sake. In any case, the problems to which these mathematical doings were applied were radically different in the two cultures. And because these "doings" were so various, the thing that was "done"—the mathematics—was various, too. It is not the same object, because theory has no existence outside of practice. Even if "practice" consists only of writing a theory down, or reading it in a book, or burning the book in which it is written, the abstract system has no independent existence outside of such human doings. The idea of theory without practice is incoherent, because a theory without a practice exists only in the moment of its postulation or representation, and in any case the act of representation is also a practice. To argue otherwise is mere reification. In short, knowledge is always local and historical; it always has a context. This is what the brilliant historian of science, Steven Shapin (2010), is seeking to convey by the title of one of his most recent books: *Never Pure: Historical Studies of Science as if It Was Produced by People with Bodies, Situated in Time, Space, Culture, and Society, and Struggling for Credibility and Authority.*

The case for such a contextual, historical, and cultural conception of science is much clearer when it comes to medicine, which is not really a science at all, but rather an art, assisted these days by some very sophisticated technology. We can begin with some basic categories of disease, the kind that are uncontroversially recognized by patients, doctors, and—most crucially these days—by the state and insurance companies, for purposes of reimbursement. But when we take a closer look at local contexts, it turns out that these categories are not quite so "uncontroversial" as they seem. This was shown by the medical anthropologist Lynn Payer ([1988] 1996) in her classic book *Medicine and Culture,* which pointed to—among other things—major differences between American, English, French, and German understandings of disease. At the time she wrote the book, French doctors tended to diagnose vague symptoms "as spasmophilia or something to do with the liver; German doctors as due to the heart or to low blood pressure; the British will see it as a mood disorder such as depression; and Americans are likely to search for a viral or allergic cause" (Payer [1988] 1996: xvii).

My point is that there is no single, naturalistic "medical system" that can adequately describe these diseases, particularly when we consider them as forms of human experience. They are the objects of indigenous, not universal, knowledge. They are not just physiological facts; they are cultural facts as well. Culture is part of their etiology: what they are depends on how you "do" the heart, how you "do" the stomach, and so on. When *Medicine and Culture* was published, West Germans attributed many more diseases to the heart than did the French or the English, and they used roughly six times the volume of heart drugs to treat them. An important German medical category, *Herzinsuffizienz,* could not be translated into English because it would not be considered a disease in England, France, or America. This all reminds me of an experience I often have while traveling on the suffocatingly heated public transport in Germany during the winter. I open a window and enjoy what is, to my mind, a very healthy draught of fresh air, until some German fellow passenger, convinced that I am endangering all the passengers' health by my irresponsible actions, marches to my window, slams it shut in my face, scowls at me, and says, "*Es zieht!*" (There's a draft!).

Context matters, and one of the most important contexts is the complex web of practice and signification that we call "culture." No doubt this goes some way to explaining why most of the eating disorders typical of young Euro-American women were hardly found in Asia until a few years ago, when the pervasive global media began promoting a European ideal of female beauty there. Nowadays, bulimia, anorexia, and so on are on the rise in these countries. In other words, women there are learning to "do" femaleness in new and unhealthy ways.

Menopause is another example of the importance of context for the understanding of disease, and one that, like eating disorders, is closely connected to ideas of femaleness. Earlier in Europe, the *climacteric* was a set of symptoms associated with aging generally. It affected men as well as women. But it was replaced by the notion of menopause, which affects only women and is associated with particular symptoms. In other words, female (but not male) aging was medicalized and pathologized, and this was seen as a promising area of research by the pharmaceutical companies, who developed estrogen-based drugs to "treat" this new disease. But the classical symptoms of menopause are hardly recognized by women in other parts of the world! Extensive research, particularly by the medical anthropologists Margaret Lock and Vinh-Kim

Nguyen (2010: 84–89), has shown that hot flashes, night sweats, and other symptoms thought to be characteristic of menopause are neither recognized nor experienced by women in Japan in the same way or to the same degree as by women in Europe and North America. This is one of the many facts that led Lock to develop her notion of "local biology," that is, the idea that different social and natural environments produce quite specific human adaptations; and thus that "biology" is not universal, but instead differs from place to place and from culture to culture (ibid.: 90–92). Again, context matters, and one of the most important of contexts is culture.

The term "nosology" means the classification of diseases, and the tension between those who defend a "scientific" and supposedly universal medical nosology on the one hand, and those who insist on local difference on the other, also informs the raging debate between advocates of evidence-based medicine and their critics, including clinical practitioners. Advocates of evidence-based medicine insist that in order to ensure the best possible healthcare, and to ensure the most efficient use of the health budget, medical professionals should use only those treatments whose efficacy has been demonstrated by the so-called "gold standard": triple-blind (formerly double-blind) randomized clinical trials. This has become the definitive standard for medical research, but it has also been subject to numerous critiques. It has been said that it is driven too much by the logic of cost cutting, rather than by what Mol (2006) calls "the logic of care." It has been said that it too strongly reflects the influence of the pharmaceutical companies, or that it neglects the personal experiences of patients. But here I wish to focus on another critique, which hinges on the distinction between clinical and epidemiological knowledge.

One of the sharpest debates in this field is that between clinicians and the advocates of evidence-based medicine. The efficacy of most therapies used by clinicians has not been proven by triple-blind randomized control trials. Thus, to use the rhetoric of the movement, most of the therapies your doctor employs are not "evidence-based." But this very rhetoric—that is, the way the term "evidence" is used—is a kind of *petitio principii* that inhibits discussion about what constitutes "evidence" by privileging only one kind of evidence: the triple-blind randomized control trial. By contrast, most clinicians insist that their experience has evidentiary value, even though, as Tonelli (1999) notes, the movement for evidence-based medicine explicitly attempts to supplant expert opinion, which is viewed as "the lowest form of medical evidence" (p. 1188). Tonelli goes on to argue that instead of being the lowest form, "expert opinion represents an alternative form of medical knowledge, one that may be complementary to empirical evidence" (p. 1187).

Proponents of evidence-based medicine tend to assume that medical nosologies are stable and universal; that is, that states of health and illness can be defined across a given population—say, the residents of Chittagong or Chicago—without considering the contextual variations within these populations: differences of culture, gender, class, and so on. And although it may be true that many epidemiologists welcome the opportunity to investigate how nosological categories are inflected by factors like ethnicity, class, age, gender, etc., still such studies are rarely done unless they are of likely benefit to the pharmaceutical companies; and, moreover, such contextual factors work in extremely complex ways, so that it is impossible to include a reasonable number of them in an epidemiological study and still obtain valid results. In short, the problem with contextual factors in health is not that they are too vague, but rather that they are too complex, and that our quantitative methodologies are insufficiently sophisticated to capture and analyze them, so that we must rely on other sources of knowledge: expert opinion, for example, which in this case shares several features with indigenous knowledge—in particular the fact that it derives from, and is located squarely within, local historical and local cultural contexts.

Before moving on to some specific cases of what are commonly thought of as "indigenous medicines," it is worthwhile noting one more aspect of biomedicine that is relevant to my argument, namely, the so-called "placebo effect." Placebo studies call many of the basic assumptions of conventional medicine into question, which is one reason they are so important and fascinating. But it is precisely for this reason that they are rarely undertaken: they don't represent a source of profit for pharmaceutical companies or manufacturers of medical equipment. On the contrary, they threaten such profits. It is important to point out that insofar as "placebo" denotes an inert substance with measurable effects, then the term itself is an oxymoron.

> If placebos are inert, they can't cause effects; if placebo effects occur, then placebos cannot be inert. Both cannot be true. And they are not. The conventional definition of placebo is not based on a rational assessment of empiric data. Rather, it reflects an [dualistic] understanding of the relationship between the mind and body, and an over-reliance on experimentally verifiable causal mechanisms. (Barrett et al. 2006: 179)

It is often assumed that mind and body work independently, and so the effects of the mind on the body—and vice versa—are ignored. But this is bad science; we have plenty of hard evidence to show that patients' states of mind affect therapeutic outcomes. Placebo research clearly shows that the words spoken by doctors, the attitude and demeanor of caregivers, the nature of the physical surroundings, and what Halliburton (2003) calls "a pleasant process of treatment" are all of great importance for successful outcomes, and yet these are precisely the kinds of things that conventional research typically ignores.

For example, the death of a spouse or another family member can influence morbidity and even mortality. Psychological traits like cynicism, optimism, sense of coherence, self-esteem, suspiciousness, and type A personality, along with states like anger and depression, are all associated with higher or lower rates of mortality. Acute and especially chronic stress are linked to important health outcomes. Gender and ethnicity may mediate the health effects of stress. Inequality and racism are especially unhealthy stressors. The number and quality of social relations is a strong predictor of important outcomes, including death. Specific attributes of interpersonal relations, such as hostility, emotional relationships, job control, religious observance, and social dominance have all been linked with major health outcomes.[1]

Most placebo research points in one direction, which is that if the patient believes and trusts in her therapist—and just as important, if the therapist believes and trusts in her own therapy—then patient and therapist are well on their way to a positive outcome. And the factors leading to this belief and trust are deeply historical and contextual; what leads a patient to trust a healer in one culture can lead to mistrust in another. Moreover, because the so-called "placebo effect" is built into most conventional medical studies, its size can be quite accurately measured. According to Moerman (2002), about 40 percent of the efficacy of all therapies, from psychiatric counseling to heart surgery, can be attributed to it.

Fortunately, cultural and contextual factors are increasingly recognized in medical research. Terms like "psycho-neuro-immunology," "neuro-psycho-pharmacology," and "psycho-neuro-endocrinology" are heard more and more frequently (see Barrett et al. 2006 for citations). Many scientists have concluded that *how* a patient is integrated into her society is of great importance for the outcome of her treatment, and that individual behavior and biology is strongly linked to local cultural contexts and values—an idea that resonates very strongly with Margaret Lock's concept of local biologies, mentioned earlier.

To summarize my argument so far: all knowledge, including medical knowledge, is indigenous; that is to say, it is local, particularly at the point of application. It is irreducibly, ontologically local, even when it claims to be universal. Why? Because knowledge does not exist apart from its "doing," even if that "doing" consists only of writing it down. And this "doing" always takes place in a particular historical and cultural context, which is why, as I now turn to what are popularly called "indigenous medical systems," it should be remembered that nearly everything I write applies to modern biomedicine as well.

"Indigenous" Knowledge is Global

Whether the object of our attention is biomedicine or traditional healing, it is important to be aware of what Bourdieu calls the "synoptic illusion"—that is, the fact that formal representations tend to engender a false notion of systematicity. When we see an anthropological kinship chart, we tend to think that the kinship system it represents is more systematic than it actually is, because the chart leaves out all of the exceptions. Similarly, when we read a modern medical textbook or a conservative historiography of medicine, we tend to think that modern medical science is systematic, internally coherent, and contextually independent—a kind of therapeutic "mirror of nature," whereas, in reality, it is a hodgepodge of practices, theories, and assumptions that are not always mutually compatible—a kind of Rube Goldberg machine that sometimes gets the job done, but usually in a rather haphazard and indirect fashion.[2]

To reiterate, when we compare what are called "indigenous medicines" with modern biomedicine, we are *not* comparing local, context-bound systems with a universal, context-free system, because there *are* no forms of knowledge that are free of context. Rather, we are dealing with networks of different sizes. I use the term "network" here in a simplified way, to indicate circulation in general: circulation of people, practices, and knowledge in global networks. For biomedicine, the forms of circulation include such things as medical schools, scientific publications, and experiments; for indigenous medical systems, they include techniques that are often religious in nature, like yoga and meditation, but they may also include word-of-mouth information, cassettes and CDs, popular books, even the jinn that are imported without a license by Asian ritual specialists passing through Heathrow airport.

Such forms of circulation involve what Hacking calls "looping" (1995a, 1995b, 1998, 1999; cf. Brinkmann 2005; Kirmayer 2012), a process of social, textual, and epistemological iteration that, depending on its speed and volume, contributes to the stability and identity of transcultural objects, in effect "thickening" them with every iteration. So, for example, when the World Health Organization (WHO) identifies mental health as a leading global priority, Indian psychiatrists begin producing statistics that emphasize the burden of mental illness in their country, and those statistics are used in turn to support the priorities of the WHO. Such forms of circulation flow in all directions: psychiatry is exported from north to south, while yoga and acupuncture are exported from east to west. This results in what Kirmayer (2006) calls the "ironies of globalization"—which means that even though forms of knowledge are being exchanged and transformed faster than ever before, nevertheless many people insist on cultural difference and boundary demarcation at the same time; so, for example, Hindu nationalists claim that Indians have intellectual property rights for yoga.

Let us slow down and take these cases one at a time, starting with Ayurveda. It is quite true that Ayurvedic medicine is based on a textual tradition going back more than two thousand years. That is what justifies all of the rhetoric about the ancient wisdom that it supposedly embodies. But the fact is, we know hardly anything about the relationship between these texts and the actual practice of Ayurveda in precolonial times. Unlike Chinese medicine, for which there exist detailed records of patients' symptoms and therapeutic interventions from a very early period, for Ayurveda we have virtually no historical evidence regarding how it was practiced. It is likely that there were major differences in how Ayurveda was practiced in different regions of South Asia, not only because these practices were passed along hereditary lines, but also because the physical environments in India are so diverse, each with its associated diseases and available herbal remedies. But this is only a hunch, and there is simply no evidence to prove it, one way or another.

What we do know is that the colonial authorities not only failed to support Ayurveda, but in some cases actively campaigned against it. With the rise of Indian nationalism came a growing pride in this form of "indigenous knowledge," which was seen as equal, or even superior to, imported Western biomedicine. Thus emerged a movement for the revitalization of Ayurveda, and this movement eventually split into two broad factions: the reformers, who wished to adopt some of the more useful Western ideas and practices, like anatomy (which was quite undeveloped in classical Ayurveda), and the purists, who opposed any changes in the system. To make a very long story very short, the reformers won.[3] Not only were significant elements of biomedicine incorporated into Ayurveda, but the entire structure of Ayurvedic education was modeled directly on European medical schools. No longer does one serve a long apprenticeship at a guru's side; instead, the curriculum is divided into pharmacology, forensic medicine, toxicology, and so on. Even the examination questions are split between an English term—for example, "heart"—and a corresponding Sanskrit term like *hrdaya*, with separate answers expected for each. At the end of the day, such schools produce those oxymoronic creatures that my colleague Harish Naraindas calls "modern doctors of traditional medicine," and indeed, it is now illegal in India to practice traditional Ayurveda, grow your own herbs, make your own medicines, and so on, unless you have graduated from one of these government schools.

Traditionally, Ayurvedic doctors would use various techniques to test the quality and potency of their medications. One of the most reliable of these was taste: it is amazing what fine distinctions can be made by the tongue. But these days, Ayurvedic medications are evaluated almost exclusively by laboratory techniques, and they are subjected to clinical trials, which have no roots in traditional Ayurveda. Of course, this is being done in order to provide evidence of these medications' efficacy, with the hope that, eventually, they can be legally prescribed and purchased by national health systems outside of India. They are being pharmacologized.

Ayurvedic tourism has also come to be a very big business, with tens of thousands of foreigners—mostly Germans—going to India to receive Ayurvedic therapy which, they imagine, resembles that deeply German institution, the *Kur*. This has resulted in two major changes in how Ayurveda is practiced. First of all, Ayurvedic doctors in India quickly realized that many or most of the Germans arriving for therapy complain of "stress," a term with no parallel in Ayurvedic theory. It wasn't long, however, before they reconciled this new complaint with their medical practice, and nowadays there are dozens of Ayurvedic clinics in South India specializing in stress relief. Similarly, if you are familiar with modern Ayurveda, or its representation in tourist advertisements, then you will know that massage plays a central role in it. However, this is a recent invention: massage plays a relatively minor role in traditional Ayurveda, except as an occasional method for introducing medications through the skin, which is classified as an organ. Contemporary Ayurvedic massage, which is so central to how it is practiced in Europe, and so important for health tourists in India, has been created as a response to European fantasies and desires.[4]

Traditional Chinese medicine (TCM) was also created as the result of transnational and transcultural processes. In the 1910s and 1920s, it seemed that biomedicine would eliminate TCM altogether; however, indigenous practitioners banded together to defend and adapt their practices, in a manner reminiscent of Ayurvedic doctors' response to colonial antipathy in India. Later, under Mao, a proletarianized version of TCM was exported to the countries of the so-called "Third World," especially Africa. Even later, in the 1980s and continuing into the twenty-first century, there was an increasing orientation towards trans-Pacific connections, and TCM was strongly promoted among white, middle-class people, especially in the USA. During this period, it began to focus on conditions that biomedicine was unable to cure, and it acquired a "hip" and middle-class sensibility.[5]

In other words, "traditional Chinese medicine" is neither traditional, nor particularly Chinese. This is beautifully illustrated by Mei Zhan's 2009 book, *Other-Worldly: Making Chinese Medicine through Transnational Frames*, which nicely illustrates how context determines the way that TCM is understood. For example, because TCM is still marginalized in relation to biomedicine, its practitioners are compelled to use the language of "medical miracles" to account for its power. Zhan argues that if TCM were more mainstream, such language would give way to the language of clinical efficacy and evidence-based medicine. She also shows how different agents in China and the USA variously emphasize the "traditional," "Chinese," and "medical" aspects of TCM. For some, the "traditional" is to be overcome on the road to modernity; for others, the "traditional" proves elusive but remains the source of TCM's power and efficacy, hence the language of "miracles" and the continuing orientalization of China by TCM consumers.

In her book, Zhan attempts to apply Latour's actor-network theory to illustrate the role of various human actors in a TCM network that extends beyond China to the USA and Africa. However, she gives less attention than I would have liked to the nonhuman actors—acupuncture needles, herbs and other substances used in TCM tinctures, meridian charts, jars used for cupping, authoritative medical texts, and case studies. Such nonhuman "actants" may be even more important than human ones, because the efficacy of TCM relies on efficacious materials as much as it does on "authentic" practitioners. One of Zhan's interlocutors discusses how the needles used in acupuncture make Americans nervous, requiring the use of smaller-gauge needles than are used in China. How does this transform the practice of acupuncture, and what effects does it have on its efficacy? What are the supply chains and collection practices of TCM practitioners in the USA and Africa in the composition of tincture recipes? Not all of the ingredients are available everywhere, and local conditions surely influence the materials that are distilled into medical substances.

This brief summary of the recent histories of Ayurveda and TCM clearly shows that they are not forms of pure indigenous knowledge with some kind of eternal, context-free validity. On the contrary, they are to a large extent recent innovations, responding to contemporary needs and contexts. Over time, their "indigeneity" has become less a matter of regional contexts, and more a matter of global ones; less a matter of local knowledge, and more a matter of entangled, hybrid knowledge. The driving forces are all peculiarly modern: nationalism, mass tourism, the discourse of heritage, and market capitalism.

Other examples abound: neo-shamanism, for example. One could debate endlessly about how "shamanism" should be defined: from a very strict definition limiting the phenomenon to the Tungus shamans, from where the word comes, to the much more expansive, popular definitions where shamanism seems to include almost any kind of trance-based healing. One could also debate the origins of neo-shamanism around the world: Eliade's famous—but deeply misleading—study of shamanism (1964) did not directly contribute to the movement, even though it is now often cited as a source text. The books of Carlos Castañeda no doubt had much to do with the emergence of neo-shamanism, even though they have been largely discredited. But perhaps more than anyone else, it was Michael Harner (1980), with his impressive academic pedigree in anthropology and his gift for popular writing, who managed to capture the imagination of a great many people, and transform shamanism from an esoteric religious technique to a multi-million dollar international industry, appealing to a certain kind of consumer: liberal, educated, and interested in esoteric experiences. As Jizek (1971) pointed out years ago, the Western fantasy of shamanism has undergone many twists and turns over the course of time, and the shaman has been represented, in turn, as spiritual guru, hopeless psychotic, cultural rebel, ecstatic religious visionary, and, most recently, auxiliary psychotherapist. It is this latter fantasy that has had the most to do with the astounding popularity in Europe and North America of neo-shamanism, which is viewed as one among many options for self-cultivation. But what is of greatest relevance to my argument here is the fact that indigenous peoples themselves, particularly in Nepal and South America, have begun to seize on this fundamentally European understanding of shamanism and to transform their own beliefs and practices accordingly. They have begun to internalize and transform a category from the anthropology of religion, identifying it as an essential aspect of their own cultural heritage and identity, and using international forums, tourist advertising, and especially the internet to develop new forms of pilgrimage, ritual, education, and therapy, so that they too can participate in this lucrative global market, while at the same time asserting pride in their cultural and ethnic heritage. Not only can they be modern, hip, and indigenous—all at the same time—but they can make money by doing so. None of this was even thinkable just thirty years ago.

Perhaps the most thoroughly researched and discussed example of the globalization of "indigenous" knowledge is yoga. Most readers grew up thinking of yoga as an ancient Indian form of self-cultivation involving meditation, and the holding of certain bodily postures that are thought to promote flexibility, strength, and the integration of mind and body. And yet, as quite a number of scholars have conclusively shown in a series of books and articles over the past ten years, this form of what is now called "postural yoga" is a very recent invention, hardly dating beyond the beginning of the twentieth century. In an impressive example of international cooperation, Indian gurus collaborated with Western spiritual seekers and scientists to produce a body of knowledge and practice that quickly spread around the world (Alter 2004; Singleton 2010).

Scholarly revelations about this invented tradition continue. For example, David White (2009) has shown that in medieval times the yogi was not thought of as a peaceful, meditative seeker of spiritual truth, but rather as a dark and dangerous magician who, like a vampire, periodically took over the bodies of the dead and exploited them for his own purposes. White claims (2012) that even the most fundamental text of the tradition, the *Yogasutra* of Patanjali, was hardly known until quite recent times.

Yoga has become ubiquitous in the West, with a burgeoning number of styles and approaches, many of which no longer have any particular connection to India; it is now quite possible to be a successful yoga teacher without having had any contact with India or Indians. Yoga is taught in prisons, schools, hospitals, and private firms for purposes of health and self-cultivation, and has been transformed from a spiritual practice into a purely health-related one. Perhaps most importantly for my argument, it has been re-exported in its Westernized form to India, the land of its purported origin, where it is celebrated and promoted as a form of ancient Indian wisdom. This is a particularly good example of what Agehananda Bharati called the "pizza effect," where a cultural item is exported to an unfamiliar context, radically transformed, and then returns to its land of origin where it is reclaimed as something "indigenous."[6]

My research on Muslim healing in the UK also illustrates the degree to which "indigenous" or exclusive traditions rapidly become globalized in the contemporary world. I had originally planned to investigate ritual healing among members of the South Asian diaspora in Europe, especially the UK. This led me eventually to what its promoters call "prophetic medicine"—healing practices that are grounded in the Holy Koran and the life of the Prophet. In particular, I am interested in what is called *hijama*, basically an Islamic form of wet cupping, where an incision is made on the skin, a vacuum is created, and blood withdrawn from the body for therapeutic purposes. This practice is spreading very quickly among young, educated Muslims in the UK, and this rapidity has to do with questions of ethnic identity. To put it rather simply, young Muslims seem to be looking for "their own" forms of indigenous knowledge, and *hijama* is a popular candidate. Meanwhile, the technology of *hijama* borrows heavily from similar Chinese traditions of cupping, so that the suction cups are often imported from China; and the actual practice of *hijama*—which is usually combined with Islamic exorcism or *ruqiya*—makes extensive use of twenty-first-century technologies.

I was able to observe this myself one evening when I was visiting an exorcist and practitioner of *hijama* in the north of England. As we drove along the motorway in his car, he took several calls on his cell phone from clients with various problems. One call came from a woman in the USA whose mother was afflicted by jinn. He instructed the woman to hold her phone next to her mother's ear. He then asked me to hold the cell phone so that he could keep both hands on the wheel, and began reciting from the Koran, occasionally directing me to speak with the daughter and ask how her mother was reacting to the treatment. In this way, I experienced the reality of twenty-first-century Islamic healing as we hurtled down the expressway from Bradford to London.

My remarks are meant to be neither cynical nor negative. If scientific tests show that modern postural yoga can relieve stress, lower one's chances of coronary disease, and contribute to general well-being, then why not teach it? If people feel that they are expanding their intellectual and spiritual horizons by joining a shamanic men's group, why not do so? If clients in Texas find spiritual relief from a healer in the UK via telephone, why not? My point is simply that it is not very useful or accurate to think of yoga, shamanism, TCM, Ayurveda, and *hijama* in their current forms as kinds of indigenous medicine. Rather, these forms of healing have developed under particular historical conditions, out of the interactions between healers, patients, nationalists, scientists, politicians, academics, and entrepreneurs from various cultural backgrounds. They are fundamentally historical and contextual, and they have become utterly global as well—just like modern medicine.

To say that biomedicine, Ayurveda, or TCM are "global" means that they are employed in an increasingly diverse array of contexts, and that their meanings, along with the material and personnel that they use, are correspondingly diverse. It does not imply that they have become standardized. Ayurveda is practiced very differently, depending on whether the context is a North Indian Ayurvedic surgery, a South Indian Ayurvedic resort, or an Ayurvedic clinic in Europe. TCM is practiced very differently in China, the USA, and Africa. Biomedicine may have the most extensive networks of any healing system, and it may strive to normalize and standardize its procedures around the globe, but I would nevertheless insist that a vasectomy in the USA is not equivalent to a vasectomy in India or in China, because in each context, the meanings of the operation (and the way it is conducted) vary so greatly. In other words, and to repeat, healing is, like all forms of knowledge, always contextual at the point of application. Systems of knowledge may strive for global uniformity and even, in some cases, achieve a remarkable degree of standardization (think of ISO standards, or the calibration of clocks, or exchanges on the stock market), but when these forms of knowledge are actually applied, their contextuality becomes apparent.

Medicine, Modernity, Freedom

Classical modernization theory failed to see this. With its naïve optimism about human progress, and its arrogant assumption that the path to such progress was contained within itself, it failed spectacularly in one of its central and explicit claims: to predict the course of world history. It had, for example, predicted that as soon as biomedicine was well established, traditional forms of healing would wither away. This was to be part of a long-term and irreversible trend, away from ritual and tradition, and towards modern, scientific rationality. But this has not come to pass. In fact, the use of complementary and alternative medicines (CAMs) has been growing at a steadily increasing pace. A US government website says that 40 percent of the American public uses them, although other estimates put the figure much higher. Similar estimates for the so-called "developing countries" are as high as 80 percent.

Why is it that these forms of healing are so wildly popular? What accounts for their spectacular growth in recent decades? I would argue that the answer has to do, once again, with the issue of context; specifically, that the rapid growth of CAMs in recent decades results from a widespread dissatisfaction with medicine's attempt to break free of context. What does this mean?

As I noted above, there is a widespread ideology associated with natural science in general, and modern medicine in particular. According to this ideology, there are certain truths that exist outside of history and culture, and these can be "discovered" using the techniques of modern science. Modern science appears to be in the possession of certain techniques for producing facts with universal, or near-universal, validity. Many results are fully replicable in multiple environments, so long as the correct procedures are followed, and certain regularities—for example, physical constants like the speed of light in a vacuum, the gravitational constant, and Planck's constant—appear to be invariant.

But in the realm of medicine, most of these ostensibly universal facts are actually probabilistic values within a given range. And the modern edifice of randomized double-blind clinical trials is not built upon invariant and context-free universal facts, as is commonly believed, but rather upon probabilistic values established within a range defined as "normal"—all of which was brilliantly shown by Foucault's guru, Georges Canguilhem (1978). However, a norm defined in terms of variation within a range is a slippery and shifting entity that changes over time and according to context. In this way, medical "facts" are not so much discovered as they are produced; I refer not only to the decisive role of technology, as extensively discussed by Latour and his acolytes, but also to the establishment of norms, which is always historically and culturally mediated. In the end, these modern practices lead to a view of health, illness, and medicine that takes the human being out of his or her particular historical and cultural context and breaks their body down into its constituent units, which can then be treated. It supports a fragmentation of the human body, and a fragmentation of scientific disciplines into ever more limited specialties.

In a practical sense, this scientific fragmentation of the human body is related to the increasing specialization of medicine itself. There are medical specialists for eyes, ears, and teeth; for the heart, the liver, and the womb. There are bone specialists, skin specialists, and brain specialists. They have done wonderful things, they have increased our knowledge a thousand-fold, they have developed therapies that no one dreamed of even twenty years ago. But this knowledge has come at a price, and the price is that hardly anyone specializes in human beings any more, but only in parts of human beings.[7]

This kind of therapy is very effective, but it is also limited and narrow. Indeed, it is effective *because* it is narrow. It has freed itself from the historical and cultural context of the person, which it regards as being of limited interest, and achieved the cold utopia of context freedom. But survey after survey has shown that one of the greatest causes of dissatisfaction among patients of conventional medicine is their feeling that they are depersonalized; that doctors are not interested in them as individuals; that they are treated without awareness or concern for their personal histories and contexts; that doctors are not interested in their stories, and so on. This is the Brave New World of universal, context-free medicine, and it is precisely this that many people reject, turning instead to CAMs.

But as I have argued, the notion of a non-historical and non-contextual medicine can be supported neither philosophically nor practically, a truth that was clearly recognized by the great pathologist, activist, and founding member of the German Anthropological Association, Rudolf Virchow. Virchow criticized the fragmented definition of illness as a context-free *thing*—what he called the "ontological conception"—and proposed his own contextual definition of health and illness, as follows:

> If disease is nothing other than life under changed conditions, then "healing" means, in general, the [re]creation of the usual, normal conditions of life, or of its processes. To eliminate the ontological conception of disease is at the same time to eliminate ontological therapy, the school of the specialists. The object of therapy is not diseases, but rather conditions; it has everywhere to do with only changing the conditions of life. (Virchow [1849] 1856: 30–36, my translation)[8]

In the end, I believe that a form of medicine that recognizes the historicity and context dependency not only of health, illness, and healing, but also of its own knowledge, will result in an improved (though no doubt much more complex) medical science. It will understand that all forms of medicine are indigenous, including itself. And this will lead to better science, clearer understanding, and healthier people.

William S. ("Bo") Sax (PhD, Chicago) studied at Banaras Hindu University, the University of Wisconsin, the University of Washington (Seattle), and the University of Chicago, where he earned his PhD in anthropology in 1987. From 1987 to 1989 he was Lecturer in Anthropology at Harvard University, and post-doctoral fellow in the Harvard Academy. After that he taught Hinduism in the Department of Philosophy and Religious Studies at the University of Canterbury in Christchurch, New Zealand, for eleven years. In 2000, he took up the Chair of Anthropology at the South Asia Institute in Heidelberg. He has published extensively on pilgrimage, gender, theater, aesthetics, ritual healing, and medical anthropology. His major works (all published by Oxford University Press) include *Mountain Goddess: Gender and Politics in a Central Himalayan Pilgrimage* (1991); *The Gods at Play: Lila in South*

Asia (1995); *Dancing the Self: Personhood and Performance in the Pandav Lila of Garhwal* (2002); *God of Justice: Ritual Healing and Social Justice in the Central Himalayas* (2008); *The Problem of Ritual Efficacy* (2010, with Johannes Quack and Jan Weinhold); and *The Law of Possession: Ritual, Healing, and the Secular State* (2015, with Heléne Basu). He is currently working on a book about archaic polities in the Western Himalayas, tentatively entitled *In the Valley of the Kauravas: From Subject to Citizen in the Western Himalayas*. His 1991 book *Mountain Goddess* has been translated into Hindi under the title *Himalaya ki Nanda Devi* (published by Wimsar).

Notes

1. This paragraph is adapted from Barrett et al. (2006); see the online version for extensive citations.
2. An excellent example is provided by Bowker and Star (2000), whose cultural historical analysis of the contents of the American Psychiatric Association's *Diagnostic and Statistical Manual* quite clearly shows the contingency of many of the nosological categories therein.
3. See Leslie (1976) for the standard account of these developments.
4. For a clear and lively discussion of contemporary Ayurvedic health tourism, see Cyranski (n.d.).
5. The previous paragraph draws heavily from the review of Zhan (2009) in *Social History of Medicine* (Luesink 2011), and the following paragraph draws from Matthew Wolf-Meyer's (2010) online review of the same book.
6. The term refers to the fact that pizza was originally a rather modest dish, but was transformed by Italian immigrants in the USA into a rich pie with numerous ingredients, quite different from the original. When this Americanized pizza was exported back to Italy it became quite popular there, so that now, when one orders pizza even in the most remote Italian villages, one gets the American version. This is the story of shamanism and yoga as well, practices that were radically transformed overseas—typically in Europe and America—and then re-exported back to their lands of origin, where they are celebrated as forms of "ancient indigenous knowledge."
7. Some time ago, I was having foot problems, so I went to see a foot specialist, and I do not think he ever looked at me above my knee.
8. Original text in German: "Wenn die Krankheit weiter nichts, als Leben unter veränderten Bedingungen ist, so bedeutet Heilen im Allgemeinen das Herstellen der gewöhnlichen, normalen Bedingungen des Lebens oder Herstellen der gewöhnlichen, normalen Vorgänge desselben. Die Vernichtung der ontologischen Auffassung der Krankheiten ist auch eine Vernichtung der ontologischen Therapie, der Schule der Specifiker. Der Gegenstand der Therapie sind nicht Krankheiten, sondern Bedingungen; überall handelt es sich nur um das Wechseln der Lebensbedingungen" (Virchow 1849: 21).

Bibliography

Alter, Joseph. 2004. *Yoga in Modern India: The Body between Science and Philosophy.* Princeton, NJ and Oxford: Princeton University Press.
Barrett, Bruce, et al. 2006. "Placebo, Meaning, and Health." *Perspectives in Biology and Medicine* 49(2): 178–98.
Bowker, Geoffrey C. and Susan Leigh Star. 2000. *Sorting Things Out: Classification and Its Consequences.* Cambridge, MA and London: MIT Press.
Brinkmann, Svend. 2005. "Human Kinds and Looping Effects in Psychology: Foucauldian and Hermeneutic Perspectives." *Theory and Psychology* 15(6): 769–91.
Canguilhem, Georges. 1978. *On the Normal and the Pathological.* Dordrecht: D. Reidel Publishing Company.
Castañeda, Carlos. 1968. *The Teachings of Don Juan: A Yaqui Way of Knowledge.* Berkeley, CA: University of California Press
———. 1971. *A Separate Reality.* New York: Pocket Books.
———. 1972. *Journey to Ixtlan.* New York: Simon & Schuster.
Cyranski, Christoph. N.d. "Oil Massages, Purges and Beach Holidays: Ayurvedic Health Tourism in Kerala, South India," unpublished PhD dissertation. Heidelberg University.
Daston, Lorraine. 2000. "Preternatural Philosophy." In *Biographies of Scientific Objects*, ed. Lorraine Daston, 15–41. Chicago, IL: University of Chicago Press.
Eliade, Mircea. 1964. *Shamanism: Archaic Techniques of Ecstasy.* Princeton, NJ: Princeton University Press.
Filliozat, Pierre-Sylvain. 2004. "Ancient Sanskrit Mathematics: An Oral Tradition and a Written Literature." In *History of Science, History of Text*, ed. Karine Chemla et al, 137–157, 360–375. Dordrecht: Springer Netherlands.
Frankenberg, Ronald. 1980. "Medical Anthropology and Development: A Theoretical Perspective." *Social Science and Medicine* 14B: 197–207.
Hacking, Ian. 1995a. *Rewriting the Soul.* Princeton, NJ: Princeton University Press.
———. 1995b. "The Looping Effect of Human Kinds." In *Causal Cognition: A Multidisciplinary Debate*, ed. D. Sperber, D. Premack and A.J. Premack, 351–383. Oxford: Oxford University Press.
———. 1998. *Mad Travelers: Reflections on the Reality of Transient Mental Illnesses.* Charlottesville, VA: University Press of Virginia.
———. 1999. *The Social Construction of What?* Cambridge, MA: Harvard University Press.
Halliburton, Murphy. 2003. "The Importance of a Pleasant Process of Treatment: Lessons on Healing from South India." *Culture, Medicine and Psychiatry* 27(2): 161–86.
Harner, Michael. 1980. *The Way of the Shaman*, 3rd ed. San Francisco: Harper & Row.
Jizek, W.G. 1971. "From Crazy Witch Doctor to Auxiliary Psychotherapist: The Changing Image of the Medicine Man." *Psychiatria Clinica* 4: 200–220.
Kirmayer, Laurence. 2006. "Beyond the '*New Cross-Cultural Psychiatry*': Cultural Biology, Discursive Psychology and the Ironies of Globalization." *Transcultural Psychiatry* 43(1): 126–44.

———. 2012. "The Future of Critical Neuroscience." In *Critical Neuroscience*, ed. S. Choudhury and J. Slaby. Oxford: Wiley-Blackwell.

Leslie, Charles. 1976. "The Ambiguities of Medical Revivalism in Modern India." In *Asian Medical Systems: A Comparative Analysis*, ed. Charles Leslie, 356–367. Berkeley, CA, Los Angeles, and London: University of California Press.

Lock, Margaret and Vinh-Kim Nguyen. 2010. *An Anthropology of Biomedicine*. Oxford: Wiley-Blackwell.

Luesink, David. 2011. "Review of *Other-Worldly: Making Chinese Medicine through Transnational Frames*." *Social History of Medicine* 23(1): 202–3.

Moerman, Daniel. 2002. *Meaning, Medicine, and the "Placebo Effect"*. Cambridge: Cambridge University Press.

Mol, Annemarie. 2006. *The Logic of Care: Health and the Problem of Patient Choice*. Oxon and New York: Routledge.

Payer, Lynn. [1988] 1996. *Medicine and Culture*. New York: Henry Holt.

Shapin, Steven. 2010. *Never Pure: Historical Studies of Science as if It Was Produced by People with Bodies, Situated in Time, Space, Culture, and Society, and Struggling for Credibility and Authority*. Baltimore, MD: Johns Hopkins University Press.

Singleton, Mark. 2010. *Yoga Body: The Origins of Modern Posture Practice*. New York: Oxford University Press.

Tonelli, M.R. 1999. "In Defense of Expert Opinion." *Academic Medicine* 74(11): 1,187–92.

Virchow, Rudolf. 1849. *Einheitsbestrebungen in der wissenschaftlichen Medizin*. Berlin: G. Reimer.

Warren, D.M. 1991. "The Role of Indigenous Knowledge in Facilitating the Agricultural Extension Process." Paper presented at the *International Workshop on Agricultural Knowledge Systems and the Role of Extension*, Bad Boll, 21–24 May.

White, David. 2009. *Sinister Yogis*. Chicago, IL: University of Chicago Press.

———. 2012. *The Yoga Sutras of Patanjali: A Biography*. Princeton, NJ: Princeton University Press.

Wolf-Meyer, Matthew. 2010. "Review of *Other-Worldly: Making Chinese Medicine through Transnational Frames*." Retrieved 30 October 2014 from http://somatosphere.net/2010/04/mei-zhans-other-worldly-making-chinese.html.

World Bank (ed.) N.d. *What is Indigenous Knowledge?* Retrieved 16 October 2014 from http://www.worldbank.org/afr/ik/basic.htm.

Zhan, Mei. 2009. *Other-Worldly: Making Chinese Medicine through Transnational Frames*. Durham, NC and London: Duke University Press.

❋ Index

aboriginal, 18, 173, 270–71, 276–78, 283–85, 289nn18–19
activism, viii, 20–21, 32, 92–99, 101, 104, 106–7, 111–12, 120, 131–33, 144
 indigenous activism, 2, 4, 6–7, 10, 12–14, 20, 32, 93, 95, 97–98, 101, 107, 120, 131, 133, 144, 222
 political activism, 21, 112, 147–49, 158, 162–63
 transnational activism, 7, 93–94
 See also discrimination; movement
activist, 2–9, 13, 18, 30–34, 37, 44–46
 activists engagement, 96
 activists movement, 5, 13, 92–94, 107–8, 110
 activists realm, 108
 activists researcher, 93
 See also movement
Adivasi, 221–23, 225–26, 230, 233, 284
Africa, ix, 5, 14–15, 96, 101, 143–48, 150, 152, 156–59, 161, 166–67, 174, 228, 240–41, 247, 256, 259, 275, 277, 304, 308
Afro-American population, 175
agricultural production, 42, 95
agriculture, 11, 42–43, 45, 52–53, 56, 101, 179, 180, 194n1, 243, 252
Aka-Bea-Da, India, 288
Akha, Southeast Asia, 57–58, 64
Alaska, x
Amazonia, 12, 30, 184–85, 191, 193
American governments, 184, 244, 254
Andaman, India, 18, 270–76, 279–82, 286, 287n4–6, 288n14, 289n18
 Andaman Islands, 18, 270–71, 276, 286, 288n10–11
 Andaman society, 18, 270–86, 287nn4–5, 287n14, 289n18, 289n25

Andaman Trunk Road (ATR), 272, 281–82
 South Andaman, 287n6
Andamanese, 271–281, 283–84, 287–89nn5–15
Andean highlands, 172, 175–76, 178, 180–81
anthropology, x, xi, 15, 17, 20–21, 45, 87–88, 112, 136, 143, 166, 234, 259, 260n18, 272, 277, 286, 305, 310
Asia, xi, 5, 11–12, 13–15, 20–21, 33, 37–38, 49–51, 55–56, 60–64, 64n5, 93, 95, 98, 101, 112, 126, 130, 136, 137n6, 143–44, 166–67, 223, 234, 240–41, 259n3, 273, 275, 278, 283, 286, 287n4, 297, 301, 306, 310–11
 South Asia, xiii, 14, 21, 33, 95, 112, 126, 130, 136, 223, 234, 273, 275, 283, 302, 306
 Southeast Asia, 5, 11–12, 38, 50–51, 55–56, 63–64, 101, 130, 137n6, 234, 273, 278, 287n4
Asia Indigenous Peoples Pact (AIPP), 56, 61, 132
Asian Development Bank (ADB), 61–62
attachment, 120. *See also* belonging
Australia, 12, 30, 49, 98, 101, 109, 145, 247
authenticity, 3, 31, 109, 222, 246, 280, 304
autonomous, 40, 83, 208, 248
autonomy, 8, 15, 108, 129, 174, 180, 182, 184, 186, 189, 203–4, 241, 244–45, 248–49, 251, 255, 257, 260n15, 287n2
awareness, 95, 113–114n16, 128, 134, 161, 204–5, 227, 248, 310

Ayurveda, 302–4, 307–8. *See also* medicine

Backwardness, 1, 4, 16, 18, 95–96, 100, 105–6, 114n22, 126, 150, 154, 173, 200, 224, 243, 254, 273, 277, 285
Bangladesh, 13–14, 20–21, 92–93, 95–109, 111–12, 113nn3–5, 113n7, 113n14, 113n16, 113n21, 119–25, 127–29, 131–36, 137n2, 137n4, 224, 281
  Bangladeshi activists, 93, 97–98, 106
Barbados Group, 252, 261n30
barbarism, 192, 243
belonging, 3, 11, 13–14, 16, 20, 34, 40, 44, 64, 71, 75, 83, 93–94, 97, 101, 106–7, 109–12, 120–21, 125, 129, 136, 161, 167, 210, 213, 222, 242, 248, 273, 277, 283, 286, 287n2. *See also* attachment
Bengali, 13, 14, 46n6, 92, 95–97, 100–1, 103–6, 108, 110–11, 113n9, 119–20, 122–29, 131, 136, 137n4
  culture, 96
  -dominated, 13, 110
  majority, 14, 110
Bolivia, 5, 172, 177–78, 180–81, 183–87, 188–91, 193, 194n1, 194n3, 194–195n7–8, 213, 247–248, 260n15,
border, 33, 50, 73, 77, 93–94, 101, 107, 109, 111, 123, 157, 224, 231
boundary, 13, 53, 119, 125, 225, 302
  closure, 109, 302
  enlargement, 95, 107
Brazil, 12–13, 73, 77, 86, 88n5–6, 186, 190, 260n15, 260n19
Buen vivir, 5, 189–93, 194n7

Cambodia, 11–12, 49, 51–55, 61, 63–64, 64n10, 137n6
Cameroon, 15, 143, 146–56, 161–63, 165–66, 167n1, 167n7, 168n10, 260n17, 262n36
Campeche, Mexico, 247, 249–50, 263
Canada, 145, 247
Casta, 242, 259n6
Chakma, India/Bangladesh, 93, 96–97, 100, 113n10, 123, 125

Chiapas, Tzotzil, 247, 252, 260n19, 261n29
China, 50, 64n10, 137n6, 224, 227, 247, 304, 307–8
Chittagong Hill Tracts (CHT), 113n6
Chotanagpur/Chotanagpuri, 276, 284, 289n18
Christianity, 36, 40, 42–44
citizenship, 17, 21, 49, 55–56, 136, 175–76, 178–81, 185, 190–92, 215n5, 241, 253
civil society, xiii, 7–8, 10, 18, 60, 93, 98, 104–5, 108, 128, 132–33, 147, 159, 161, 179, 233, 280–83, 285–86
  organizations, ix, 3, 6–7, 10, 16, 34, 51, 55–56, 60–61, 92, 97–99, 102–4, 106, 108–9, 113n4, 114n21, 124, 126–27, 129–30, 132–34, 136, 146–47, 150, 152–54, 158–60, 163–65, 175–79, 180–84, 191, 211–14, 241, 244–46, 248, 253–56, 258, 281, 283
class, ix, 15, 18, 32, 46n4, 50, 53, 75, 94, 110–11, 149, 151, 154, 175–76, 178–80
Clientelist networks, 201, 204, 211–212
climate change, 8, 61
colonization, ix, 1, 4–6, 8–9, 11–12, 14–15, 18, 21, 30, 32–33, 41, 46n6, 49–50, 55, 63, 95–96, 102, 105–6, 114n22, 120–21, 123–29, 131, 135–36, 146, 148–49, 151, 157, 161, 167, 173–76, 181–82, 190, 194n1, 194n4, 221–28, 230, 234, 240, 242–44, 246–49, 256, 259n2, 259n9, 261nn30–31, 262n35, 271–78, 285, 287n4, 287n9, 288n11, 289n17, 289n25, 302–3
  colonial times, 15, 40, 102, 106, 175–76, 194n1, 194n3, 216n11, 302
  colonialism, 1, 5, 9, 21, 30, 49, 95, 136, 146, 174, 176, 224, 242, 246, 259, 259n3, 274, 277
  coloniality, 15, 174–175, 181–182, 190, 194
  colonized, ix, 8, 30, 41, 49–50, 63, 120–21, 124, 131, 135, 148, 244, 274, 285
  colonizer, 120, 173, 175, 240, 244, 274, 277
communal land title(s), 52–53

community, xiii, 10, 17, 29–32, 34, 36–37, 40, 42–44, 52–54, 56–57, 59, 72–73, 77–78, 81, 84, 120, 127, 136, 144, 147, 152–56, 160–61, 163, 176, 186, 201–6, 208, 210–11, 214, 216n5, 229, 232–33, 246, 248, 250–52, 254, 257–58, 259n9, 276, 283–84, 286, 289n26, 294
    development, 154–155, 254, 294
    leaders, 52, 77, 127, 129–30, 152–55, 159, 178, 187, 192, 200, 206–207, 210–11, 226–27, 262n36, 283–284, 289n26
    members, ix, 13, 16, 30, 39, 50, 52, 64n2, 77, 81, 94, 100, 108–9, 113n4, 113–114n16, 125–26, 144, 148, 153–54, 160–67, 200–4, 208–12, 214, 244, 246–48, 250, 252, 254, 256–57, 260n11, 262n38, 276, 282–83, 286, 287n7, 306
    projects, 2, 43, 61–63, 165, 166, 179, 182, 187–88, 192–93, 200, 202, 205–6, 208–10, 216n8, 243, 254, 259n9, 260n12
Comunidad, 78, 181, 201–5, 207, 209, 214–15
conflict, 199
connectedness, 20, 30, 42
constellations of belonging, 13, 92–95, 99, 106–9, 111–12, 173
constitution, 17, 41, 52, 59, 78–79, 97, 101, 114n21, 133–35, 137n4, 145, 151, 167n4, 178, 186, 188–93, 195nn7–8, 223, 227, 232, 240–41, 244–45, 247, 260n15, 270, 273, 277, 287
constitutional recognition, 5, 7, 97, 100, 129, 133, 134
context, 4–5, 8, 10, 18–19,
convict, 18, 121, 271, 273–74, 276, 277, 288n1
coolie, 276, 289n18
cosmology, 43, 86–87
cosmovision, 189, 194–195n7
credibility, xi, 30–31, 150, 156, 183, 296
Criminal Tribes Act, 289n17
cross-ethnic alliances, 108
culture, ix, 3, 5, 9, 10–11, 13, 17, 19, 30–32, 34, 58–59, 76, 78, 82, 92, 96, 97, 100, 103–4, 106, 129, 131, 144, 157, 162, 182, 188–90, 193, 213, 230, 240, 243, 246–47, 249–50, 253–58, 262n40, 273, 280–82, 286, 295–300, 309
cultural change, 72, 82
cultural promoters, 254
cultural show, 105
cultural survival, 7, 158, 173
Customary law, 18, 225–26, 233, 241, 250–51, 257
customs, ix, 8, 32, 130, 202, 225–27, 246–47, 249–51
cycle of cultivation, 38–39

Declaration on the Rights of Indigenous People, 6, 15, 51, 97–98, 100, 134, 137n7, 143, 145–46, 152, 167n4, 172, 174, 189, 245. *See also* rights
demography, 253, 279
dependency, 20, 208–9, 310
deterritorialized, 20
development, 2, 5, 7, 13, 15, 18, 54, 57–58, 60–63, 82, 85, 93, 96, 98–99, 101–6, 109, 113n4, 113n11, 114n16, 143–44, 146–47, 150, 152, 154–56, 158, 160–65, 167n8, 168nn9–10, 173, 175, 215, 216n8, 240, 243, 311n3
    developmental hierarchies, 221, 229, 279, 285
    developmental knowledge, 102, 104, 187, 244, 294
    development assistance, 102, 179
    development cooperation, 98, 102–4, 113n11, 187
    development policy, 199–200, 244, 254, 277, 281
    development program, 5, 15, 60, 98, 101, 143, 155, 204
    development strategies, 103
    translocalization of development, 104
Dhaka, 20, 92, 111, 136
diaspora, 3, 113n4, 306
dignity, 3, 7, 10–11, 20, 62, 135, 155–56, 245
disadvantaged, ix, x, 63, 102, 253
discourse, xiii, xi, 1, 2, 4–6, 8–10, 12–16, 18, 76, 95, 99–100, 103,

110, 114n20, 120, 122, 124–25, 127, 128, 130–31, 143–44, 146–47, 151–52, 154, 156, 163–66, 190, 199–200, 210, 212–13, 221–22, 241, 245–46, 249, 253, 256–57, 259n1, 270–71, 273–74, 280–81, 283, 285–86, 287n2, 294, 305
discrimination, ix, x, 32–33, 59–60, 93, 97, 108, 121, 132, 174–76, 212, 244–45, 255–58, 259n9, 262n35. *See also* disadvantaged; inequality; racism; women's rights
distinctiveness, 103, 143, 145. *See also* hierarchy
diversity, xi, 10, 13, 22n3, 59–60, 92, 129, 182, 189, 244, 253. *See also* heterogeneity; homogeneity; Mestizaje
domination, 15, 18, 110, 135, 241–42, 251, 256, 258, 274. *See also* hierarchy; inequality

ecology, 18, 31, 81, 149, 162, 173, 183, 186, 271, 276–77, 280–82, 285
  ecological justice, 186
  ecological knowledge, 31
economy, 41, 103, 157–58, 162, 190, 223, 254, 260n10
economic conditions, 162, 246
education, 7, 9, 72, 76, 78, 82, 102, 133, 135, 150, 157, 160, 164, 178–79, 180, 185, 188, 192, 203, 205, 207, 209, 211, 222, 226, 243, 254–55, 277, 279, 302, 305
elite, 18, 108, 111, 133, 149, 153–54, 157, 163, 189–90, 193, 226, 232, 242–43, 248, 253, 255–57, 260n11, 262n36, 277, 282, 284–86
environment, 5, 7–8, 20, 29–31, 34–37, 42, 44–45, 59, 61, 99, 103–4, 183, 195n9, 273, 277, 280–81, 284, 298, 302, 309
  Environmental Defense Fund, 7
  environmentalism, 5, 8, 29
  environmentally friendly, 103
epistemological, 15, 19, 301
essentialism, 9, 221, 227
ethnicity, 3, 21, 30, 49, 53, 58–59, 62–64, 94, 106, 112, 146, 149, 154, 166–67, 232, 241, 253, 257, 259, 262n40, 299–300
  ethnic boundaries, 107
  ethnic category, 107, 148, 172
  ethnic minorities, 14, 49, 52, 55–56, 100, 154, 161, 183
ethnogenesis, 182, 241, 248
ethnography, xi, 4–5, 8, 17–18, 31, 35, 38, 72, 81, 87, 93, 113, 121, 137n1, 200, 246, 270, 272, 278, 286
ethno-nationalist, 33, 44, 46n6
Europe, ix, 12, 19, 21, 49–50, 55–57, 93, 109, 114n21, 166–67, 248, 297–98, 303, 305–6, 308, 311n6
European Commission, 98, 113n13, 132
exclusion, 5, 13, 17, 37, 40–41, 44, 94–96, 110, 135, 188, 189, 259n9, 283
exotic, 12, 105–6, 109, 121, 124, 126, 135, 272, 277
exoticization, 105
exploitation, 1, 44, 102, 110, 175–76, 180, 190–93, 244, 252, 256, 261n29

farmer, 41, 95, 103
forced displacement, 96
foreign development organizations, 106
forest, 1, 7, 10–11, 17–18, 30, 37–39, 53–54, 56–57, 59, 61, 71, 73, 75–76, 192, 223, 226, 229, 233, 271–73, 276–77, 281, 283–85, 287n7
  deforestation, 22n3, 56, 62
  forest laborers, 18, 276, 285
  forest laws, 17
  People's Movement, 7
  rainforest, 7, 71–73
  See also Vanvasi
Fragmentation, 18, 173, 189, 241, 248, 309
Free Prior and Informed Consent (FPIC), 62
freedom, 1, 6–7, 137n7, 149, 153, 184, 229, 294, 308–9
frontier, 18, 86, 107, 144, 224, 271, 273, 276, 285

Garo, India/Bangladesh, 11, 33–45, 45–46n2, 46n4–6, 131

gender, 88n7, 94, 108, 110, 152, 154, 156, 159, 163, 205, 211, 215, 223, 228, 232–33, 250, 252, 258, 288n11, 299–30. *See also* discrimination; women's rights
geography, 20, 64
global, xi, xiii, 1–7, 10–15, 18, 20, 22, 30, 35, 43, 45, 50–51, 61, 63, 77, 82, 93–95, 97–100, 102, 106, 108, 111–12, 120, 124, 132, 143–48, 150, 154, 156, 158, 161, 163–65, 167n8, 173–74, 189, 221–23, 249, 280, 282, 294–95, 297, 301–2, 305–8
  global discourse, xi, 2, 6, 99–100, 147, 165, 249, 280
  global ethnoscape, 7, 120
  global ideas, 45, 99
  global knowledge, 294
  global level, 10, 97–98
globalization, 2, 6, 12, 280, 302, 306
government, viii, 3, 5–6, 12, 15, 18, 30, 49–53, 55–63, 64n2, 64n4, 75, 77–78, 96, 98, 100–1, 105, 109, 113n4, 113n14, 114n21, 122, 124, 126, 128, 131, 133–34, 143, 145–47, 149–56, 158–66, 167n8, 168n10, 176, 179–81, 185–91, 193, 195n9, 209, 215n2, 224–26, 228, 232, 234, 242–45, 247–48, 250, 254, 257, 259n3, 260n10–11, 271, 273, 276–79, 281, 283–84, 287n4, 289n21, 289n26, 303, 308
  government assistance, 209
Great Andaman/Great Andamanese, 272, 274–75, 278–79, 281, 287n6, 288nn9–10, 288nn12–13. *See also* activism; environmentalism
groupism, 94
guerrilla war, 17

healing, 19–20, 301, 305–8, 310
healthcare, 89n9, 157, 160, 164, 226, 294, 298
heterogeneity, 18, 107, 111, 211, 241, 249. *See also* diversity
Hill People, 95, 113n8, 124, 129, 135, 283
Hindu, 29, 96, 125, 229, 302
history, 3, 12, 20–21, 30, 41, 56, 58, 73, 86, 95–96, 101, 144, 146, 148, 150, 155, 162, 173, 215n4, 227, 249, 256, 258–59, 271–73, 278, 288n12, 295, 308–9
Hmong, Southeast Asia, 50, 58, 64
homogeneity, cultural, 6, 96, 250. *See also* exclusion
human rights, 6–7, 10, 62, 93, 98–100, 104, 108–9, 112n3, 113n4, 113n16, 119, 128, 131–33, 150, 152–54, 156, 163, 173, 245
hunter-gatherer, iii, ix, 73, 146–147, 151, 155, 159, 272, 274, 276, 278, 281
hybridity, 3

identity, ix, 2–5, 7–10, 12–14, 16–17, 20–21, 31–32, 59, 62, 83, 94–95, 98, 105, 107–8, 119–21, 124–36, 144, 149, 152, 164–66, 178, 181, 191, 194, 201, 205, 212, 245–47, 252–53, 257, 276–77, 283, 286–287n1, 301, 305, 307
  identity politics, xiii, 2–5, 8–10, 14, 21, 64, 95, 98, 105, 108, 120, 127, 131, 136, 152, 165–67, 173–74, 181, 194
imaginaries, 13, 16, 206, 211, 223
immigrants, 311n6
imperialism, 174, 183, 186. *See also* colonialism
inclusion, x, 13, 17, 32, 40, 94, 97, 99–100, 107–108, 111, 123, 133–34, 186, 188
India, viii, ix, 11, 15, 17–18, 29–30, 32–33, 40–41, 45, 46n3, 93, 95, 101, 104–5, 110, 113n5, 113n7, 114n19, 125, 132, 137n6, 180, 182, 184, 185, 188, 221–25, 227–28, 230–34, 247, 259n6, 271, 273–74, 276–78, 281–82, 287n4, 288n14, 289n18, 289n21, 295–96, 302–3, 306, 308
  Mini–India, 273, 286
Indian(s), America, 12, 22n3, 101, 172, 174, 177, 240–44, 248–49, 252–58, 259n2, 259n7, 259n9, 260n11, 260n19, 261nn30–31, 262n35
Indian(s), South Asia, 32, 272, 296, 302, 306
indigeneity, xi, xiii, 1–21, 32, 45, 49–64, 71–73, 93–95, 98, 101, 104,

320 • Index

106–8, 111–12, 119–21, 124–25, 131–36, 143–47, 150, 152, 154, 159, 161, 164–66, 167n3, 172–79, 181–82, 190, 192, 200–01, 206, 210–11, 214–15, 216n11, 221–23, 240–41, 246–48, 250, 270–73, 286, 287n1, 287n3, 294–95, 305
   in global notion, xi, xiii, 1, 6, 14, 18, 120–21, 125, 135, 174, 221, 234, 271, 282–86
   in global representations, 2–10, 13–14, 17–18, 189
indigenous
   activists, 2, 5, 7–8, 13, 18, 30–31, 33–34, 37, 46n6, 58–59, 94, 100–4, 112n3, 114n21, 134, 176, 250, 261n30
   "biologically" indigenous, 181–83, 190, 192, 195n9, 200, 226, 229, 232, 242, 244, 251–53, 258, 260n11, 261n31, 276, 284, 299, 304
   indigenous claims, 5, 45, 105, 109
   indigenous community, 29, 52–54, 78, 210
   indigenous cosmopolitanism, 4
   indigenous customary law, 18, 241, 250, 261n25
   indigenous groups, 16, 18, 58, 94, 96, 100, 108, 120, 124, 129–32, 154, 182, 189, 200, 202, 207, 208, 210, 211, 214, 243, 248, 249–59, 259n2
   indigenous ideals, 99
   indigenous knowledge, 19, 61, 294–95, 299, 301–2, 304, 306–7, 311n6
   indigenous medicine, 19, 294, 299, 301, 307
   indigenous movement, ix, 5, 10, 31, 56–57, 61–62, 64n5, 94, 99, 106–8, 110–11, 130, 172–74, 183–87, 191–92, 194n7, 241, 245–46, 248, 252–56
   indigenous peasant movement, 176
   indigenous people, viii, xi, 1–19, 30–32, 42–45, 49–63, 64n2, 64n5, 64n9, 72, 77, 83–84, 87, 88n2, 92–108, 113n6, 119–20, 124, 128, 131–35, 137n7, 143–59, 167n4, 172–93, 200–1, 206–7, 211, 216n8, 216n11, 221, 240, 245–53, 256–59, 261n21, 261n30, 270–74, 277, 280–81, 285–86, 287n3, 288n10, 305
   indigenous population, x, 7, 18, 82, 96–97, 100–4, 110–2, 113n8, 131, 137n7, 151, 158, 174–76, 179, 188–90, 195n9, 200, 207, 212, 243–44, 250–51, 254–55, 258, 261n31, 270, 281
   indigenous psychology, 9, 21
   indigenous rights, xi, 2, 13, 15, 56, 93, 97, 125, 131, 143–66, 193, 222, 240–41, 247, 281, 283, 285
   indigenous rights movement, xi, 15, 131, 143–48, 150, 156, 158, 161, 163–66, 240
   indigenous slot, 31, 120
individual, xiii, 5, 20, 42, 55, 88n6, 94, 103, 105, 107, 109–111, 113n4, 114n21, 127, 133, 147, 149, 154–57, 160, 163–65, 191–92, 242, 248, 255, 257, 259n7, 260n19, 272, 275, 280, 285, 300, 310
industrialization, 2
inequality, 97, 241, 259, 261n29, 300. *See also* domination; hierarchy
institutionalization, 7, 94, 97–98, 177, 271, 274, 285
Inter-American relations, 177
international
   international community, 10, 144, 147, 160, 163
   international consensus, 174
   International Day of the World's Indigenous Peoples, 10, 92, 99–100, 105, 133–34
   International Labour Organization (ILO), ix, 6–7, 50, 62, 97, 100–1, 124, 126, 137n7, 144, 151, 174, 179, 183, 244, 246–47
   International Labor Organization (ILO) Convention, 169 7, 62, 100, 137n7, 174, 183, 186, 245–47
   international visibility, 159–160
   International Work Group on Indigenous Affairs (IWGIA), 51, 59–61, 109, 114n16, 147, 150, 167n8, 173
   International Year of the World's Indigenous People (IYWIP), 7, 174
Islam, 96, 150, 307

Japan, 12, 51, 298
Jarawa, 272, 274, 276, 278–79, 281–83, 287n7, 288n9, 288n13, 289n24
Jatee, 127–128, 131
Jharkhand, 17, 30, 104, 110, 223–33
Jhum, 102–3, 114n20, 128–30, 136, 137n3
JSS, 126, 129–133, 135
Jumma, 14, 95, 108, 113n6, 119–20, 129–31, 135
jungle, 35, 37–38, 75–76, 78, 231, 276–77, 283

Karen, 18, 56, 58, 276, 284
Kheyang, 123
Khumi, 14, 119–28, 130–36, 137n1, 137nn3–4
knowledge, 13, 19–20, 31, 72, 78, 86–87, 89n14, 93, 99, 102, 124–25, 130, 134, 136, 173, 208, 210, 259n1, 274, 282, 288, 294–95, 311n6
knowledge repertoires, 103
knowledge systems, 19, 99, 294–95
local knowledge, 19, 94, 103, 294, 305

labor migration, 208
land
  land grabbing, 61, 96
  land struggles, xi
  land tenure, 168n9, 254
language, ix, 3, 5, 30, 34, 51, 59, 64n8, 73, 95, 100–1, 111, 121–22, 124, 126–30, 136, 147, 156, 159–60, 173–74, 181, 189, 222, 227, 233, 242, 247–48, 250, 254–59, 260n11, 262n38, 262n40, 277, 279, 281, 283, 288n13, 304
Laos, 11, 49–53, 55, 59–64, 64n10, 137n6
Latin America, 15, 17, 167, 172, 176–77, 179, 181–82, 186–88, 194, 194nn2–3, 234, 240–41
law, ix, 17, 18, 51–54, 59–60, 64, 78, 123, 128, 161, 180, 182–83, 190–91, 193, 202, 225–27, 233–34, 241–43, 246–52, 257, 260n15, 261n25, 271
legal system, 17, 230, 240, 243, 245, 250–251, 260n11

lifestyle, 1, 3, 34, 53, 58, 71–72, 75–77, 84–85, 105, 110–11, 128, 149, 276
linguistic autonomy, 8
livelihood, 30, 56, 58, 62, 101–2, 130, 147, 158–60, 162–64, 192–93, 228, 272
local, ix, xi, xiii, 1–7, 10–19, 22n3, 34, 46n2, 50, 53–54, 58–61, 71–72, 76–79, 81–83, 94, 96, 99–104, 108, 110–11, 113n5, 119–25, 130–33, 135, 137n3, 147, 149–52, 156, 161, 163–66, 173, 176–78, 180, 182, 185, 189–90, 193, 199–15, 215n5, 216n6, 222, 224–25, 227, 229–33, 241–42, 245, 248–49, 251–55, 261n31, 271, 273, 281–82, 284–85, 289n22, 294–96, 298–301, 304–5
local actors, 111

Maasai, 15, 144, 146–147, 156–164, 166, 167n8
majority, 2, 12, 14, 17–18, 30, 36, 43, 54, 92, 95–96, 100, 106, 110, 120, 124–28, 130, 132, 151, 154, 161, 165, 211, 228, 247, 252, 255, 258, 289n25
Maoists, 17, 228–231
Maori, ix, x
marginalization, 5, 7, 15, 93, 95–96, 121, 143, 145–46, 151, 159, 162, 165, 244, 252–53, 284
marginalized, ix, 2, 16, 40, 108, 131, 150–152, 159, 165, 200, 206–207, 286–287n1, 304
market, 32, 40–42, 106, 123, 125, 133, 195n9, 305, 308
  market-oriented, 42
  market economy, 157, 162
Marma, 119, 123, 125, 131. See also medicine
Masai, 157
Mbororo, 15, 143, 146–56, 161–66, 167n1, 168nn9–10
means of livelihood, 130
medicine, 19, 272, 294–99, 301–4, 307–10, 311n5
  biomedicine, 19, 295, 299, 301–4, 307–8
  Chinese medicine (TCM), 302–4

membership, ix, 95, 109, 111, 247, 256–57
Mestizaje, 176, 194n2, 253. *See also* diversity; heterogeneity
methodology, 21
Mexico, 16, 176–77, 179, 187, 199–201, 204, 211–15, 215nn2–4, 216n10, 243, 248, 250, 252, 254, 259, 260n15, 260n19, 262n38
migrant, 18, 50, 57, 100, 209, 212–14, 229, 271, 273–74, 276–78, 281, 284–85, 311n6,
minorities, x, 2, 6, 14, 49, 52, 55– 56, 60, 96–98, 100, 133, 146, 151, 154, 161, 183, 186, 244–245, 260n10
Miskito, 249, 256–57, 262n39
missionary, 257
mobilization, 15–16, 178–89, 203, 208, 252–53, 255. *See also* activism; movement
modernity, 1, 13, 72–73, 81–82, 84–87, 126, 200, 221, 225, 274, 280, 304, 308
modernization, 1–2, 6, 11, 42, 71–72, 82, 86, 179–81, 191–93, 194n4, 207, 223–24, 254, 260n12, 308
movement, viii–ix, xi, 5, 7–10, 12–13, 15, 31, 55–57, 59, 61–63, 64n5, 85, 92–95, 97, 99, 105–12, 119, 127, 130–33, 143–50, 156, 158, 161–66, 167n8, 172–93, 194n7, 200, 204, 225–26, 228–31, 240–41, 244–46, 248, 252–56, 261n23, 262n36, 280, 285, 298, 302, 305
  Green Movement, 8
  movement's legitimacy, 108
  See also activism; indigenous movement; mobilization
Mru, Bangladesh, 119, 131
multicultural, 17, 60, 174, 186–87, 190, 193, 240, 244–45, 257, 259n9
  multiculturalism, 186–187, 190, 257, 259n9
multiethnic, 13, 94, 107, 112, 148, 172, 186, 273
Munda, India, 30, 224–26, 228, 230–33, 276
Muslims, 92, 307. *See also* Islam

nation, 2–7, 10, 12–20, 30, 40, 46nn2–3, 50, 61, 77–78, 93, 96–112, 119–21, 124–31, 135–36, 137n6, 146–53, 156–66, 173, 175–76, 178–79, 182, 188–90, 192, 194n1, 200, 240–41, 244, 247, 257–58, 277–78, 286
nationalism, 5, 14, 97, 108, 121, 127–28, 181, 302, 305
nationalist ideals, 6
national movement, 97
nation-building, 4–5, 10, 96, 286
  See also state
nature, xi, 1, 7, 9, 11, 29–33, 34–37, 42, 44, 53, 57, 106, 134, 144, 182, 191, 225, 232, 256, 273, 278, 280, 282, 295, 300–1
natural resources, 2, 8, 10, 12, 22n3, 31, 51–52, 54, 57–59, 64, 145, 149–50, 157, 162, 190, 192, 195n9, 243–44, 254, 257, 294
negotiation, 5, 7, 16, 39, 44, 99, 104, 145, 200–1, 203–6, 208, 223, 225, 227, 232–33, 273, 283, 285
neo-indigenismo, 186
neoliberalism, 2, 147, 183, 188, 193
  neoliberal policies, 163, 255
networks, 1, 7, 14, 16, 19–20, 93, 103, 108–9, 111, 119–20, 132–33, 160, 165, 174, 201, 204, 211–12, 294, 301, 308
New Zealand, 12, 49, 145, 247, 310
NGOs, x, xi, 51–53, 56, 60–62, 64, 88n6, 102–3, 108, 126, 130, 133, 136, 154–55, 158–59, 164–65, 173, 229, 248, 253, 257
Nicaragua, 215, 249, 256–57, 259, 260n15
Nicobar, 278–79, 283–84, 287n4, 289nn24–26
noble savage, 18, 30, 105–6, 280, 282, 285
Non-Government Organization (NGO), x–xi, 51–53, 56, 60–62, 64, 88n6, 102–4, 108, 123, 126, 130–31, 133, 136, 137n3, 147, 154–55, 158–59, 164–65, 173–74, 229, 248, 253, 257, 282
norms, 174, 185, 210, 250–51, 258, 309

Ocamo (river), Venezuela, 74–76, 78, 80–81, 89n9
Onge, India, 278–279, 288n9, 288n13, 289n22

Oraon, India, 229, 276
Orinoco River, 71–72, 79, 86
otherness, 14, 87, 221, 273, 275
outsider, 33, 44, 78, 167–168n8, 208, 211, 256, 262n39, 272, 281
ownership, 11, 30, 35, 40–41, 43–45, 145, 225

Pahari, Bangladesh, 14, 95, 113n6, 113n9, 119–20, 123–35, 137n4, 283
Pakistan, 14, 113n7, 121, 123, 125–26, 128, 137n2
participant observation, 105
pastoralist, 15, 143–44, 146–51, 156–65, 167n1, 167n8
patron-client relationships, 108
Philippines, 12, 51, 64n10, 93, 215, 275
philosophy of science, 10
physical landscape, 86
pluri-national, 15, 189–91
politics
  political participation, 158, 176, 179, 185, 190, 241
  political party, 110, 184, 211–13
  political pressure, 174
  political resource, 5, 11, 14, 16, 107, 167, 206, 210–11, 214, 216n11
  political science, 20, 234
  political self-representation, 165
  politics of representation, 8, 16
  political strategies, 161–62, 233
  political struggle, 32, 147, 149, 159
  political system, 16, 128, 175, 179, 199, 201, 203, 214
  politicization, 15, 88n6, 179, 182–83, 193, 270, 283
population, ix–x, 1–2, 14–15, 39, 46n6, 53–55, 59, 71, 73, 82, 92, 96, 100–6, 110–2, 113n8, 120, 122–123, 137n3, 143, 147–51, 154, 156, 161–62, 165, 175–76, 179–80, 189–90, 194, 200–3, 207, 212, 241, 243, 246, 248–50, 253–55, 272–73, 278–79, 281–84, 285, 287n9, 289nn21–22, 299
postcolonialism, 9, 21, 136
poverty, x, 103, 113n9, 131, 154, 159–60, 164, 188, 195n9, 200, 216n10, 227, 233, 244, 253, 256, 261n31, 294

power, iii, 1–3, 7, 9, 11, 15–16, 18, 21, 33, 49, 77, 86, 88nn6–7, 113n8, 127, 133, 135–36, 151, 160, 172–75, 181–82, 192, 204, 207, 210, 212, 223–24, 227, 232–33, 240–41, 244, 250–51, 255, 280, 304
  power hierarchies, 210
  power relations, 16, 18, 174, 180, 241, 251
  See also hierarchy
primitive, viii, xi, 18, 35, 54, 96, 105, 124, 126, 129, 135, 222, 224, 271, 273, 275–76, 278–82
primordial, 44
privatization, 11, 43, 45, 157, 164, 183, 189, 244. See also neoliberalism
progress, 1, 82, 160, 180, 223, 243, 271, 308
psychology, 9, 20, 255
public, 12–13, 16, 29–30, 34, 62, 88n7, 92, 105, 112
public space, 13, 104, 182, 221, 224, 248, 250, 252, 255, 262n35, 284, 289n22, 308

Quintana Roo, Mexico, 249–50

race, 4, 50, 121–22, 146, 194n2, 275, 278, 295
racism, 175, 183, 186, 243, 300. See also discrimination; nationalism
radical revisionism, 17
Rainforest Action Network, 7
Ranchi, India, 18, 224, 227, 230, 276–77, 283–85
recognition, 1–2, 5, 7, 10, 13, 17–18, 51, 54, 58, 63, 92, 97–100, 104, 106, 129, 131–35, 148, 150, 152, 158, 164–65, 173, 175, 178, 180–81, 186–89, 191, 193, 241, 250–51, 257–58, 271, 277, 283–85, 286–287n1
REDD, 62
religion, 34, 36–37, 40, 42–44, 78, 124, 173, 232, 242, 305
  religious belonging, 97, 125
representation, 8, 12–13, 16, 18, 20, 76, 83, 85, 93, 95, 99, 104–6, 111–12, 149–50, 165, 175, 185, 201–2, 205–6, 211, 214, 222, 233, 241,

249, 272, 274–75, 284, 288n10, 296, 301, 303
representation of indigenous demands, 104
representation of activist, 95
research, qualitative, 93
resistance, 52, 61, 223, 227, 232–33, 274, 287n2. *See also* activism; mobilization; movement
resources, 2–3, 5, 8, 10–12, 16, 18, 22n3, 30–31, 33, 37, 41, 51, 54, 57–59, 64, 102, 108, 145, 149–51, 157, 159, 162, 167n3, 178, 181, 190–92, 195n9, 203, 206–8, 210, 241, 243, 246, 254, 257, 270, 272, 283, 285, 287n7, 294
rhetoric, globalized, 94
rights
  ancestral rights, 3
  collective rights, 6, 97, 145, 191–92, 247
  individual rights, 191–92, 202, 245
  land rights, 31, 56–57, 64n5, 101, 113–114n16, 167n8, 233, 243, 252, 255
  minority rights, 4, 97, 99, 107, 113n8, 155, 166, 168n10
  property rights, 35, 283, 302
  social rights, 186
  women's rights, 108
ritual, 30, 36, 39–40, 45, 77, 86–87, 89n10, 105, 122, 124, 129, 229, 232, 256, 296, 301, 305–308, 310
romanticism, viii, 202

savage, 1, 30, 105–6, 124, 126, 135, 222, 233, 274–77, 281–82
savagery, 18, 270–274, 285
Scheduled Tribes (STs), 32, 114n19, 221, 271
school, 71–72, 76–84, 86–87, 88n1, 88n6, 88n8, 119, 130–31, 136, 160, 202, 207, 225, 250, 260n12, 279, 301–303, 306, 310
self–
  self-administration, 33
  self-determination, 50, 98, 101, 129, 145, 163, 183, 245, 247, 249
  self-organization, 180, 185, 187, 201–2, 204–5, 215n5

  self-representation, 16, 85, 150, 165, 201, 274
Sentinelese, 278–80, 287–288n9
shamanic, 13, 72, 80, 83, 86–87, 307
social cohesion, 6, 16, 205, 210, 257
social structure, 18, 37, 188, 241–42
sociology, 9, 20–21
sovereignty, 4, 163, 183, 283, 286, 289n17
space, xiii, 3, 5–7, 10, 13, 18, 20, 86, 95, 98–99, 101, 104, 111–12, 119–20, 127, 129–31, 136, 152, 154–55, 158, 163, 180–82, 194n4, 203, 205, 208, 211, 221, 229, 270, 273, 274, 276–77, 279, 285, 287n2
spatiality, xiii, 52, 64, 94, 167
spatial orderings, 95
state, ix, xi, 1–7, 10–11, 14–18, 20–21, 29–35, 40–41, 45, 46n3, 50, 52, 54, 56, 59, 73, 75–78, 80, 84–85, 89n9, 89n11, 96–98, 109–10, 113n7, 119, 121, 124–30, 132–33, 135–36, 145–46, 149–50, 154–63, 165, 172–73, 175–78, 180–82, 185–93, 194n1, 199–204, 206–14, 221–28, 230–34, 240–47, 249–52, 257–58, 259n5, 260n10, 260n12, 261n23, 261n25, 270–73, 275, 277–80, 284–85, 286–287n1, 287n2, 287n8, 289n17, 296
state agents, 203–4
state formation, 5, 10, 96
state policy, 96, 125
stereotype, viii, 206, 208, 274, 282
subaltern, 15, 176, 183, 186, 200, 221–23, 227, 233–34, 273
subsistence, 42, 75, 77, 103, 194n1
Survival International, 7, 29, 45n1, 109, 173, 289n23
sustainable, 19, 31, 57, 59, 159, 183
  sustainable development, 173
swidden cultivation, 34–35, 37–38, 40–42, 44–45, 120, 129

Taiwan, 12, 51
Tanzania, 15, 143–44, 146–47, 156–66, 167n8
teachers, 78, 80–82, 207, 210, 216n11, 254–55, 261n32
technocratization, 104

Index • 325

territoriality, 3
Thailand, 11, 49–51, 55
timber, 271–272, 277
time, ix, 3, 14, 15, 17, 18–19, 38, 40, 60, 75, 83, 86, 102, 106, 114n19, 119, 121, 123, 126, 128, 162, 175–76, 194n1, 194n3, 216n11, 224, 246–47, 249, 261n21, 273, 296, 306
top-down approach, 102
trade union movement, 178, 180, 184
tradition(s), ix, 10, 17, 32, 59, 78, 84–86, 104, 106, 122, 130, 173, 194n2, 213, 228, 241, 246, 247–48, 250–51, 256, 294, 302, 306–8
traditional, ix, xi, 13, 19–20, 31, 33–35, 42–44, 46n4, 52, 54, 56, 71–73, 75, 77, 81–82, 84–87, 88n2, 100, 103–6, 111, 113n10, 133, 172, 180, 185, 187, 190–91, 195n9, 206, 210, 213, 224–25, 227–31, 233, 250–51, 301, 303–4, 308
  traditional indigenous culture, 106
  traditionalism, 200
  traditionalist, 84–85, 103–104
  traditionalist ideology, 202
transformation, 11, 16, 18, 34, 45, 75, 85, 89n10, 103, 105, 113n9, 119, 168n9, 181, 189, 200–1, 206, 208–9, 211, 214–15, 216n9, 270, 277
translocal, 4, 13, 16–17, 50, 95, 99, 101, 104, 108, 111–12, 119–20, 135, 200, 208
  translocal activism, 99
  translocalization, 92, 104
transnational, 4, 6–7, 13–14, 16, 18, 93–94, 99, 106, 108–9, 111–12, 119–21, 125, 130–31, 134, 136, 173–74, 176, 186, 189, 191, 203, 212, 216n9, 270–71, 280–81, 283, 285, 303–4
  transnationalization, 208, 210, 212, 215
  transnational space, 13
tribe, 14, 17–18, 29–30, 32, 34, 45, 55–57, 76, 95, 114n19, 119, 125–29, 221, 223, 227–29, 233–234, 241, 271, 276–82, 285, 287n7, 287n9, 288n12, 289n17
  tribal, 17–19, 29–30, 32–34, 40, 56–57, 95–96, 105–6, 120, 125–27, 130, 135, 221, 222–23, 225–26, 228–29, 233, 244–46, 270–71, 277–80, 282–85, 287n7, 287–288n9, 289n20
  tribal costumes, 105
  See also Upajatee
Tripura, India, 124–125, 131

United Nations (UN), viii, x, 6, 31, 50–52, 55, 57, 61–62, 64n2, 92–93, 98, 100, 124, 131, 134, 143, 145, 148, 150, 152, 156, 158, 167n4, 173–74, 241, 244–45, 247, 271
  UN Decade of the World's Indigenous People, 97
  UN Human Rights Council, 7, 153
  UN Permanent Forum, x, 164
  UN Special Rapporteur on the Rights and Fundamental Freedoms of Indigenous People, 7, 137n7
  UN Declaration on the Rights of Indigenous Peoples (UNDRIP), 98, 137n7, 172, 174, 189, 245
  General Assembly, 7, 97, 134, 137n7, 145
United States, 49–50, 109, 145, 153, 212–13, 240
universalist claims, 1, 6
Upajatee, 14, 119–20, 125, 127–29, 135
urban, 31, 33–35, 45, 125–26, 133, 154–55, 181, 183, 194n1, 200, 202, 226, 243, 262n38

Valle de Mezquital, 199–202, 204, 208–9, 211–215, 215n3, 216nn9–11
Vanvasi (forest dwellers), 221, 283
Venezuela, 12–13, 71–73, 75, 77–78, 80, 82, 86–87, 88n2, 88nn5–6, 89n11, 186
vernacularization, 99
villagers, 11, 34–35, 40–43, 45, 119, 124, 126, 130, 133, 135, 201, 202–5, 209–10, 213, 215–216n5, 224–26, 229, 256–57
violence, 6, 18, 106, 225, 230, 243, 259, 281
vision, 2, 5, 17, 31, 72, 97–98, 104, 158, 163, 167n7, 182, 188, 203, 221, 232–33, 246

Washington Consensus, 188
West Singhbhum, India, 17, 230–31
window of opportunity, 100, 102. See also discrimination; movement
Working Group on Indigenous Populations (WGIP), 7, 97, 137n7, 158, 174, 189
World Bank, 6, 61, 82, 187, 241, 294
worldview, 8, 13, 30, 83, 247, 250, 256, 284

Yanomami, 12–13, 71, 73–78, 81–87, 88n2, 88nn5–6, 89nn9–10, 89nn12–13, 89n15
Yoga, 301–2, 306–7, 311n6
youth, 17, 34–36, 119, 130, 133, 135, 153, 155, 228–30, 232–33
Yucatán, 249–50, 259

www.ingramcontent.com/pod-product-compliance
Lightning Source LLC
Chambersburg PA
CBHW070906030426
42336CB00014BA/2311